SIMON WESTON

THE COMPLETE STORY

TED SMART

This edition Ted Smart 1994

The moral right of the author has been asserted

Walking Tall first published 1989
Copyright © by Simon Weston 1989

Going Back (Simon Weston with John Man) first published 1992
Copyright © 1992 by Simon Weston, Malcolm Brinkworth and Geoffrey Hamilton-Fairley

Picture sources
David Thorpe/*News of the World*: pages 1, 2, 3, 4. *bottom*, 5 *bottom*, 6, 7, 8. Press Association: page 5 *top*. The maps on pages 44 and 94 are by Neil Hyslop.

John Man is the author of *The Survival of Jan Little* and *The Waorani: Jungle Nomads of Ecuador* and co-author, with Pin Yathay, of *Stay Alive, My Son*

Simon Weston: The Complete Story first published 1994
ISBN 0 7475 1739 8

Printed in Britain by Clays Ltd, St Ives plc

WALKING TALL

AN AUTOBIOGRAPHY

Simon Weston

To Mam and Gran

Without you I would be nothing
You both mean so much and I love you both

CONTENTS

Preface   1

1 Early Days   6
2 A Brush with the Law   20
3 Joining Up   27
4 Berlin   40
5 Northern Ireland   51
6 Kenya   68
7 Sailing South   80
8 Going Ashore   88
9 The Fire   105
10 Evacuation   111
11 Aboard the *Uganda*   119
12 Coming Back   125
13 Home   131
14 Out of Hospital   143
15 Tenerife   154
16 Down Under   157
17 Weston Spirit   165
18 Flying   168
19 Looking Back   175
20 Looking On   178

Postscript   185

ACKNOWLEDGEMENTS

There are many who deserve to be thanked and given a mention — unfortunately, far too many to put down on paper. However, I must say a big thank-you to the people of my village, Nelson, for all the support they have given me and my family. A few who must be mentioned for their loyalty and friendship are Carl Dicks, my best friend, Nigel Saunders, Bobby Brain and Keith Cullen. Another I must acknowledge, although he'll never read this as he left us far too young, is Ken Bolton, a special friend to my family and me for as long as I can remember. He will never be forgotten in our hearts. I am also grateful to Ron and Eileen Chapman, who helped Mam no end, and to Captain Graham Taylor of the Welsh Guards, who was always on the end of a phone for Mam and always willing to help if it was in his or the regiment's power.

A special mention of thanks must be given to Martyn Forrester, who worked so hard to convert my many hours of tapes into coherent prose. I wish Martyn and his family all the best for the future.

Last, but not least, I want to mention someone who over the last seven years has become my confidant, adviser, comforter and closest friend, who made the documentaries and also did so much work on the book, Malcolm Brinkworth, who I can't thank enough and who I love like the big brother I never had and now feel I've got.

Thank you all; you'll always be very special to me, as will the many who aren't mentioned here but who have helped me so much in so many different ways.

PREFACE

It was about ten o'clock on a bright, August Saturday morning when Liz, my instructor, got out of the plane. We had already been up once that morning in Yankee Whisky, the little yellow-coloured Piper Cherokee that had become my friend over the last month.

'You're going to do the next circuit on your own, Simon,' she said. 'I shall be in the control tower. If there are any problems, don't forget, we can talk on the radio. If you're in doubt when you're coming in, or you're too high, or too fast, or the wind is too strong, then call the tower, "Yankee Whisky – going round," and make another circuit.' She closed the door and began walking away from the plane. After just a step or two she turned and smiled. 'Oh – and good luck.'

I paused for a while to collect myself. This was it – I was going 'solo'. I was nervous, but quietly confident. I had been preparing for today in my mind for weeks. 'Come on then, Wes,' I said to myself, 'you can do it. Let's go.'

I ran through a series of checks on the aircraft before radioing the tower and requesting permission to taxi to the runway.

'Golf Yankee Whisky, taxi to runway two-one,' came the reply.

I was off. There were a few planes ahead of me, which meant that I had to wait my turn for clearance. God, that was an awful time. The longer I had to wait, the more nervous I felt. I kept myself busy, checking this, checking that. Just in case, I checked it all again. I must have gone through every drill at least three times before I asked, and received, permission from the tower to take off. By now my stomach felt as if it could fill a Tristar's hangar with butterflies.

'Go for broke, big boy,' I said to myself. I applied the power, and the little yellow Cherokee buzzed into motion. A few seconds later we were racing down the runway, and my mind was working

1

overtime on what I had to do next. Watch the revs, watch the speed, keep it straight, where's the wind, increase to full throttle, seventy knots – here we go – pull back on the stick. Airborne.'

I climbed steadily to twelve hundred feet, and the airfield at Kidlington suddenly seemed so small. But at least the rest of Oxfordshire had plenty of fields for me to land in.

I was now heading back on the downwind leg of my circuit, and had about a minute or so before I would have to prepare myself to land. It was a magical minute. Corny as it sounds, I began to sing to myself. Cornier still, the song was the theme from the old Nimble bread commercial: 'She flies like a bird . . .' The sun was out, the sky was blue and there wasn't a cloud to spoil my view . . . except that I still had to land this little technological wonder. I couldn't stay up here all day.

I eased off the power slowly and gradually lost height. After two good pulls on the trimming wheel, I turned into the final leg. Seven hundred feet. I cut the revs a bit more, but kept the nose up slightly to maintain my speed.

Two stages of flap: one on the plane, one inside me.

'Yankee Whisky to tower, finals to land.'

'Yankee Whisky, clear to land.'

Here we go, I thought. Don't make a fool of yourself here, Weston, you'll never live it down.

I had managed to keep my head up so far, and the theory is that if you do a good circuit, with everything steady and under control, you'll do a good landing. Well, that's the theory, anyway.

I was down to sixty-five knots. I lined the plane up with the centre line and applied the final stages of flap to slow me right down. There was little wind, thank God, and I began my own internal chit-chat again. Keep the nose up, pull back, watch the height . . . nose up, no . . . no . . . OK, easy now Wes.

At that moment, I cut the power and Yankee Whisky plopped on to the runway with only a slight hint of bounce. It wasn't quite the copybook landing I'd wanted to make, but we were down. And that was all that mattered.

By the time I'd parked the plane on the grass in front of the clubhouse, I was sweating. When I climbed down from the aircraft, it felt like the hottest day of my life. The sweat was pouring off me. That solo flight had put the fear of hell into me, but I had done it.

PREFACE

I could see everyone waiting in the clubhouse, ready to start the celebrations, but I needed a moment alone.

'Simon Weston,' I said to myself, 'soldier, player of rugby, digger of dirt, you've come a long way.'

It was almost six years to the day since the troopship *Sir Galahad*, on which I was an unsuspecting passenger, had been hit by a 2,000-pound Argentinian bomb during the Falklands war. It was a sad anniversary – six years since forty-six of my comrades had perished in the carnage; six years since that blazing inferno had changed my own life for ever.

By all known laws of medical science I should have died within seconds of the Argentinian Skyhawk's bombing the *Sir Galahad* as it lay at anchor off Fitzroy settlement on Thursday 8 June 1982.

Horribly burned over half my body, I had hung on to life against all the odds because I was determined to see my family again. Doctors had given me a minimal chance of survival. Yet thanks to their exceptional skill, I had returned to Britain alive and had later taken part in *Simon's War*, the first of three BBC television documentaries.

Over the last few years, numerous people have urged me to write a fuller, more detailed account of my experiences. I have always replied, rather sheepishly, that I was sure no one would ever want to read it. The suggestion both flattered and appalled me.

My first objection was that although I am often accused of having verbal diarrhoea, putting it all down on paper is a different thing entirely.

My second thought was that I didn't want to seem to be capitalizing on the Falklands aftermath or to be selling my story for the sake of a few pieces of silver.

My third reservation was that most autobiographies are written by people with years of experience and a fund of well-tuned stories. Where did I fit in?

The more I thought about it, the more objections I raised. But friends kept on at me, and I began to see a way of being able to give something more important than a list of anecdotes, of being able to tell what happened to me, and a host of others, to generations who have already forgotten the Falklands war – and a generation who weren't even aware of it.

This book is not intended to open up old wounds or to hurt

3

anyone. There will be episodes that will, for whatever reason, arouse strong emotion in some individuals. But – and it is a vitally important 'but' – I am not bitter. I am not writing in anger. I am a man at peace with what has become of me.

The object of telling my story is to offer what I have been through, and what I have learned as a result, to others in the hope that they will benefit. A central point of course lies in the explanation of what actually happened on the *Sir Galahad*. It is a story I have never told before, and it is a deep and private one. It is a story that has haunted me, that has lived on in nightmares on the faces of those I saw burn to death, and on every occasion when I see a soldier in uniform.

In the Army there is a tradition of turning everything into humour and not horror: you may share a tragedy with your colleagues and perhaps with your family, but it goes no further. In writing this book I am breaking with that tradition, but I'm sure that most of my army friends and former colleagues will understand why I have done so. I apologize to the families of those who died on the ship if they are upset by anything they read. I hope that they, too, will understand that writing this is something I have had to do for my own peace of mind.

Speaking out is not easy. I am not prompted by a deep psychological desire to bury ghosts: I shall not feel any lighter for having written the book and told the truth about how so many men met their deaths. So why bring it out into the open? I want people to realize that war is not always about victories or glorious moments. It is about friends, husbands, brothers and fathers, and the reality of their lives and deaths.

What follows is not a military history of events in the South Atlantic in 1982. It will certainly not become a textbook for historians who want to fathom the innermost depths of the minds of the strategists and the decision-makers – I simply do not know enough of what went on elsewhere to attempt that. This is not to say that after my recovery I didn't feel the need to find out a bit more about what had happened on that fateful day, and what it meant, if anything. I researched, I dug around, I spoke to people. But I have not set out to point the finger or to catalogue the political and military mistakes that changed the lives of so many people who were aboard the *Sir Galahad* that day.

Some things have become clearer as time has passed, and my

perspective has changed. But I have tried my best not to relate the story as I see it now, but as I saw it then.

Under conditions of extreme stress, the human memory can be unreliable, to say the least. What is more, no two people's memories are ever the same. But I have not taken any conscious liberties with the truth; some things I have simply chosen to leave unsaid. I have not written every line I might have written describing my desperation and pain after the bomb. If I had done, the book would have been twice as long as it is, and even the most sympathetic reader bored rigid.

So this book is unashamedly about Simon Weston – or rather, about the two Simon Westons: the proud, swaggering young lad who left the small village of Nelson in Wales to join the Army and eventually go to a war that we all thought could never happen; and the rather more caring and thoughtful Simon Weston who came home. As my sister, Helen, says, 'My little brother never did come back.'

I have changed in many ways. I notice things now that I would not have noticed before, like a small item on an inside page of the newspaper, a report on a woman whose face has been badly burned in a fire. I'm startled now by how regularly such accounts appear. Ahead of her will lie many agonizing months of operations and skin grafts and rehabilitation. And if this book achieves nothing other than to help her and others like her, then it will have been worth the effort.

1
EARLY DAYS

In the summer of 1961, Pauline Weston and her two-year-old daughter, Helen, travelled home to her native Nelson in Mid Glamorgan from the RAF married quarters where she lived in Wegberg, West Germany. On 8 August, at Caerphilly Miners' Hospital, she gave birth to what she reckoned was the ugliest baby she had ever seen.

She announced to my grandmother that she was going to call me Robert – in her view, 'a nice bland name'.

'The hell you will,' said Granny. 'You'll call him Simon like you always said you would.'

And so Mam did. In my family, as I would soon find out, you don't cross swords with Nora.

I'm told I had jowls like a bloodhound's. 'You were revolting,' my mother says, 'but as I said to the doctor, "I don't care if he's a dog. I'll keep him anyway." ' The doctor didn't speak to her after that.

I gather it was a short labour but hard work. After my birth I cried non-stop, and there was a suspicion that I might have contracted an infection. My grandmother lifted me quietly into her arms one day and, without telling my mother why, wandered off down the corridor to the piano room. She wanted to perform a few unofficial tests to assure herself that I wasn't blind or deaf. Happily, I passed.

We stayed with my grandparents in their two-up, four-down in Commercial Street, an old terraced cottage with winding stone stairs. Besides the adults there were also my aunties, Pamela and Penny – eleven-year-old twins – and Judy, aged nine, and my uncle, Jeremy, just ten weeks old. Granny was a bit embarrassed about Jeremy, because of her age. The moment Granny had come out of hospital with her new little son, my mother had gone in and had hers.

I adored my mother. She has always had the most marvellous qualities of stillness and strength. To this day her warm, brown-eyed smile soothes even my most tortured, helpless moments. As a child, I would not let her out of my sight. Once, she was busy somewhere and I couldn't see her, and I fretted so much that she tied a cotton sheet around herself, papoose-fashion, and said to Gran, 'Right, put the little bugger in there.' They never heard another peep.

From the minute I first opened my eyes I was hungry. By the time I was a month old I was wolfing down boiled eggs, together with all Jeremy's leftovers and any other scraps in sight. I just swallowed the food whole, I didn't even chew. I was also drinking several full bottles of milk a night. Perhaps I turned to food as a comfort in the face of the confusion I had been born into: when Jeremy and I began to talk, I could never understand why I called my grandmother 'Granny', while Jeremy had to call her 'Mammy'. That my mother was Jeremy's sister was like a concept from another planet. As far as Jeremy and I were concerned, we were brothers.

The two of us slept together with about two dozen furry toys of every description. Some belonged to my sister, Helen, who was not much more than a toddler herself. She used to try to reclaim some of them, and the result would be mayhem – especially when at the age of nine months I started walking, and could carry the battle to her. But most times I'd just let the dust settle, then sneak them back when Helen was not around. These clashes over toys were the first of many bust-ups I was to have with my sister, but at least in those early days we didn't throw knives or red-hot pokers at each other.

My father completed his tour of duty in Germany and was posted to Nocton Hall in Lincolnshire. It was a lovely place in the country, pleasant, flat and clean, with a village shop that opened twice a week.

Dad was a Scot from Edinburgh called David Weston. He was a serving member of the RAF, working as an operating-theatre technician. My mother had left home when she was seventeen, intending to go into the police force. But when she was told that she was too young, she joined the RAF instead, as a cook. My parents met and fell in love in the RAF canteen that my mother was running. I'm not surprised, with her cooking. She was nineteen then. My sister, Helen, was born in Ely, Cambridgeshire, in 1959, and then came the posting to Germany, where I was conceived.

Nourished by Mam's meals, I soon grew into a strapping young tearaway, and from the start I seemed to be involved in every scrap of mischief going. I remember when I had chicken-pox. I wasn't allowed out, but I somehow sneaked out of the gate and was found on top of the dustbin with my mother's best bread knife, cutting up chunks of jelly to give to my friends.

Once I set a fire-hose off in a Nissen hut. Another time, the station commander even called in the civilian police because he'd caught us trying to get the goldfish out of his pond. Helen was just five and a half and I was three and a half, but I suppose he wanted to give us a shock.

'You were inquisitive and easily led, rather than mischievous,' Mam says charitably. 'And you had no sense of danger.'

I must admit, Helen used to put me up to a lot. There were three of us in our gang: Helen, myself and a big Old English sheepdog from somewhere in the officers' quarters. He spent more time with us than with his real owners.

I missed Jeremy a lot when we moved to Nocton, but at least we went down to Wales at holiday times. In exchange, Pamela, Penny and Judy would go up to stay with my parents in Lincolnshire. Once, when my grandmother came up with Jeremy, I stood in the corner for the whole week, while Jeremy thumped the hell out of me. I didn't retaliate; I never did. Because of my size, everyone thought I was aggressive, but I wasn't. It would take a lot to get me steaming. The day the boys next door came and stood on my cars and broke them, I stood on their heads in return. I liked all my things to be perfect; I hated them being damaged.

I was obsessed with climbing, which nearly always ended with me collecting a cut and a bruise or two. Once, I scaled a wall and got on to the roof of the garage, and started throwing bottles down in between the garage and the wall. Unfortunately, I forgot to let go of the last bottle.

Another time, my sister and I clambered on to a large, solid wood packing-case and began jumping up and down trying to catch the washing-line. For some reason, my sister shoved me off. I went right over and broke my wrist. I was rushed off to hospital with the broken limb supported in a magazine. My sister was given a hiding. 'And this,' my father said, as he treated me to a liberal helping of the same a few days later, 'is for giving your sister the opportunity to push you off in the first place.' I believe it was what you call a no-win situation.

Two years later, my father was posted to Singapore. Helen and I went to stay in Nelson for two months while my parents arranged for the storage of our furniture and effects and the handing over of their quarters. My poor grandparents had their hands full, but Granny devised a plan. She allocated Helen and Jeremy to the older girls, who were by this time fifteen, and me to Judy, who was thirteen. The girls became our 'nannies'.

At breakfast, each girl had to make sure that her charge ate properly and made as little mess as possible. Then they all washed and dressed their own child, and saw him or her safely off to nursery school before going to school themselves. At night, they would shower themselves first, and then, in their nighties, they would oversee the showering and feeding of us young ones. They took nightly turns at reading us a bedtime story.

A friendly rivalry sprang up between them as to who was the best 'mam'. My grandmother says that this helped to shape the characters of all of us, the older girls as well as us youngsters.

We lived in a secure little world, and from an early age our minders instilled into us their own ideas and notions of discipline. Gran, of course, was always an influence. She impressed upon us that we must always be true to ourselves; then we could never let ourselves down. 'Never try to be what you are not,' she used to say, and the idea stuck.

Commercial Street was a very happy home, although money was short. Mam and Gran used to go without to make sure we were well fed. We were warmly clothed, mostly because Gran's and Mam's main hobbies were sewing and knitting. My grandfather's contribution to cost-cutting was to build absolutely everything himself. To Grandad, a foil pie-dish was a lampshade, and a pile of old sheets of corrugated iron and some spare piping became a natty outdoor shower unit.

We had what was supposed to be a wire-haired terrier, but he was really more of a Heinz 57. He was all white. My grandparents had had him since Jeremy was born, and he was our constant companion. Wherever we went, Yogi went too. Often when Gran called us we would hide, but Yogi could never resist sticking his nose out from behind cover. He would have made a useless infantryman.

Then, disaster: it was time to go to Singapore. Gran had a party for me on my fourth birthday, the day before we were due to leave. It was not a very cheerful one for the adults, but I enjoyed it. Gran and Mam did their best to put on a brave face.

'When we said goodbye to you at Cardiff station we were devastated,' says Gran. 'You were going so far away. It took us months to get over it, and we never did get used to the emptiness your going left.'

I went to Singapore as one of the 'service brats,' as they are affectionately known by servicemen who dislike children. My sister seemed to take the same view of me. She used to lock me in my room and then wouldn't let me out. On the few times she did, I would spend my hours of liberty catching grasshoppers and putting them in jamjars.

My mother hated the place. It was humid, the sanitation in our hotel was awful and my father was on duty a lot. Mam didn't like being so close to the ocean, with no other noises besides the crashing of surf. But I loved it. I played with the fishermen and watched, fascinated, as the locals observed their custom of burying their dead at sea. Sometimes I'd go to the pool and jump into the deep end. It was a pity I couldn't swim.

I missed Jeremy, but apart from that the only drawback with the Far East was that my fair skin couldn't take the heat. I got terribly burned, even though there was no direct sunlight, and I ended up in hospital with huge green blisters on my shoulders and down my back as far as my waist. I had to spend a lot of time sitting in the bath, or lying face down on my bed.

Gran wrote every day, sending us tapes they had recorded. The girls were in a choir at school and they sent us one tape they had put together of Welsh songs. That made my mother more homesick than ever.

When we moved out of the hotel, we rented a bungalow from some people who had moved out of their home and lived in the chicken-sheds at the back. It seemed so wrong to Mam. What was more, white people were not allowed to work out there, and she wanted to. She couldn't even do the laundry. She didn't want servants, but she had to have them. She missed the fun of working in the RAF stations, and the stimulus of the company. Most of all, she missed home and the rest of the family. Before long it was decided that, for everyone's sake, we ought to go back to Nelson and leave my father out there to finish his tour.

We arrived at Heathrow just before Christmas in 1965. I couldn't get to Nelson fast enough. Throughout the journey I kept asking, 'Are we nearly there? I want to see Jeremy.'

'There was never such a reunion between two little boys,' says Gran. 'The two halves were complete again, and you gathered all your toys together and went into your bedroom once again, in your own little world.'

At last, I was home.

It had always been my parents' intention to settle in Nelson when Dad left the RAF, and our names had been on the council waiting-list for years. Within days of our arrival, we were allocated a house. Needless to say, Grandad painted it at once.

'What a wonderful Christmas we spent that year,' Gran recalls, 'the family complete again, except for your father.'

Our house was on the prefab estate, built just after the war as a short-term housing measure. It wasn't pulled down until twenty years later. The estate was one of the greatest housing complexes ever, a marvellous place to be brought up in. You could run through anyone's back garden; there were plenty of places to play. There was a real sense of community.

Having said that, I must admit I spent very little time in our new home, mostly because I wanted to get away from Helen. I would take a few clothes to go and spend the weekend at Gran's; then between nine and twelve months later I would go home for a couple of days, have another row with my sister and make a tactical withdrawal back to 36 Commercial Street.

In those days the central part of Nelson had more of a flavour than it will probably ever have again. It was superb; everyone seemed to be alive, and the women still used to sit on the doorsteps and talk, sometimes shouting across the street to each other. When they pulled those houses down in 1973 they demolished more than just bricks and mortar.

Nelson is like a crossroads, where three major roads meet. It used to have a railway station, but now that's closed and there's just a bus station. It has always been a fairly busy place, with a cattle market and a little horse-trading. Within my memory, there was still a blacksmith's. You drive into the village up valleys and through forestry plantations. After passing the odd slag heap, you're greeted by rows of typically Welsh Victorian terraced houses, with no front gardens, and with slate-coloured roofs. There is a church on the hillside – very grey, very squarely built, very wonderful if you're Welsh.

A lot of people were employed by the collieries in our area, but not actually down the pits. There have been no mines in our village for over seventy years. Nelson is still a centre for the colliers, but that's changing because of the industrial revolution of the eighties. Now people work all over – Cardiff, Pontypridd, Caerphilly, Bridgend. It's like a commuter belt, the equivalent of what Surrey is to London. The population now must be about 5,500, and the houses a mixture of Victorian and modern. There are six estates, none of them rough, built between the late sixties and the early eighties.

In 1968 we moved into a new house, which was part of an estate built by Laing's. It was a sandy beige colour, with a diagonal-shaped roof. The estate wasn't the most attractive; from the outside, the houses looked like rejects from the architect's pad. The insides were fine enough though, and some people made an effort to make the surroundings look attractive.

One building that still stands is Llanafabon, my old infants' school. I hated it. Helen and I had both picked up a strong English accent while we were overseas and, children being children, we were given a hard time for it. We were picked on by other kids for being dressed too poshly as well. Mam remembers that I was often chased home with the taunt of 'Snob' ringing in my ears.

My first week was horrific. I cried like a baby for two days, and then they couldn't keep me awake in class. I'd go to sleep all the time, I just wasn't interested. They had to get my sister to come and sit with me in class. For some reason that seemed to keep my eyes open. But I know Helen resented it: she was being held back, she needed to be in a higher class.

Things didn't improve much when I moved up to Nelson Junior School. I remember its little canteen and tiny chairs, and the desks, each with its individual inkwell. It was built of sombre grey stone, with red tile-brick outlining the windows and corners, and inside it always seemed hollow and empty, with its big thick walls and cabinets full of musty books, and quarry tiles on the floor.

The school was just at the back of Gran's house, and at playtimes she would sneak us out a few snacks. Jeremy's dog, Yogi, would wait outside the school gate until playtime, then join us. The teachers made no objection; he was almost one of the class.

'You are the most disgusting little boy I have come across in twenty years of teaching,' the headmaster said to me on one memorable occasion. All I'd done was peep over the top of the wall of the girls' toilets. Some of the other boys had actually been jumping over the wall and running through. I had just been looking, sizing up my opportunity – and I was the only one who got caught. As a public punishment for my shocking crime I was made to stand in the corner of the big hall while every child in the school filed past. I was only a little lad of seven, but the embarrassment and humiliation have stayed with me from that day to this.

My basic problem was that all the time when I was sitting in a classroom, I really wanted to be down at the Wern. This was the place we used to go to at weekends, an old disused quarry that had been filled in with coal and everything else. We'd play in the trees or pretend we were on a desert island fighting off prehistoric monsters. It's been bulldozed away now for a new sports complex.

The Wern played an important part in our Guy Fawkes preparations each year. Every 5 November, we had a bonfire and fireworks party on Granny's piece of wasteground. All the neighbours and children from the immediate area would bring their fireworks and we would burn the Guy. Gran's house was the canteen. She and Mam made soup and hot dogs for everyone, and the kids got sugar mice, too. The kitchen looked like a disaster area when it was all over. The next morning, I couldn't wait to go out and look for dead fireworks, which I collected in a bucket.

We always used to go to the Wern and chop up dead trees for the bonfire. We'd spend hours dragging them back down to Gran's and then weeks amassing them and building them into a huge pyre.

'And now you can pull it all down again,' said our local bobby one year. 'Your next-door neighbour has complained that it's right underneath her telephone wire.'

No matter. The telephone wire got burned down anyway.

In my mother's opinion I was never a nasty or evil child. 'What you are,' she'd say, 'is wicked.' I think that was because I never committed the same crime twice. Not because I'd learned my lesson, but because I was always on the look-out for a new way of causing mayhem.

There was a fruiterer who used to park his wagon on a piece of ground my grandmother owned. Everyone parked their cars there – and left the doors unlocked; those were the days before joy-riding and car theft. My gang used to climb into the back of this fruiterer's wagon when he'd parked it. We'd have a bit of a scout around and maybe we'd find half a crown or something that had been dropped. If he came back unexpectedly, we'd climb into the top shelves and hope and pray he wouldn't see us. He drove off once with us all inside. We went the entire rounds of Nelson without his ever finding out he had six extra lemons in the back.

I used to love going down to Gran's; so did everyone else in the street. They'd always go to her with their problems. She was a tough old girl, a real disciplinarian. She still is – although she's mellower now than she used to be. I've got a little wooden bird that hangs from the rear-view mirror of my car. Gran bought it for me for fifty pence. I call it Nora, because its mouth is constantly open.

My grandmother always seems to be talking – except when she's either eating or smoking a cigarette, or when she's asleep! But to this day, the first thing I do when I go home is visit Gran.

'Hello Gran, put the kettle on – a man could die of thirst in this house!' If we didn't have some of that kind of banter, she'd think something was up, she'd wonder what she'd done wrong. There's a very strong bond between the whole family and my grandmother.

Nelson was a very close-knit community, and Commercial Street in particular. Everyone helped everyone else; it was a cocoon that enveloped adults and children alike. Every house was open to anyone who wandered in, and if someone was in trouble the others would rally round.

Gran's house was always full of kids. Once a week we were allowed to visit Aunty Lizzy, who lived next door. This was a real treat, as she was a wonderful, dear old lady. There'd always be a plate on the table, and on that plate would be some Riley's Toffee Rolls and a couple of pennies each. With a penny you could buy quite a lot in those days – four Black Jacks, two Flying Saucers or a three-foot liquorice shoelace.

I moved to live at Gran's; I spent more time there than at home, so it seemed to make sense. Mam still washed and ironed my clothes, though, and every few months I'd go back home for a spell. I didn't miss Mam; she visited Gran every single day anyway. I could go home any time I wanted; my bedroom was still there. So, unfortunately, was Helen. I remember that on one of my short stays back at home I got sunburned, and to get out of the sun I was having a rest indoors on her bed. She came in and swung me off, right into the baseboard, and I fractured my nose. On another occasion she slammed the door on my foot, taking the toe-nails off my toes. She also pulled great lumps of hair out of my head one night during an argument: she put her feet on my shoulders, grabbed hold of my hair and – rip! I really went through it with my sister.

It wasn't Buckingham Palace at Gran's, but it was full of love. We bathed in an old tin bath in front of the fire, and slept upstairs, sharing the beds. We had a rather special *en suite* lavatory, too: the dawn chorus for me was the sound of water pounding into a tin bucket, and the sight of my aunties' feet sticking out from behind the wardrobe door.

After a while the bath routine was promoted into taking a shower out the back. The only problem was that when the shower was in use we had to go out of the front door and walk around the back lane into the garden to use the outside toilet. And even then we would have to wait until the shower was finished before we could refill the cistern, as they both were fed by the same hosepipe.

Every time I went back to Gran's, Grandad had changed something. If you give him a hammer and a piece of wood, he was happy. One of Aunty Pamela's and Aunty Penny's hobbies was making models and hanging them from the front-room ceiling. The front room was the best room in the house. One night Jeremy and I went in there with a tennis racket and slapped them all down. Like my mother said, not nasty or evil – just wicked.

On Fridays, Gran, Grandad and the girls used to go shopping. We'd hope and pray that they wouldn't get back before the end of *Top of the Pops*. Then we'd all watch *It's a Knockout* together, while tucking into our treats. There was always a bar of chocolate, a packet of crisps and a tin of Coke for each of us. I used to love Friday nights. They were special.

Staying at Gran's was all about flannelette pyjamas, sitting in front of the fire, watching the Marx brothers, and my grandfather bringing us each a small pie and chips on his way home from work. There was always the strength and the security of that, and to me that's what life is all about, what families are all about, what love is all about – being able to share.

By now, Dad had left the RAF, but work was scarce and Mam had it very hard. She got a job scrubbing pub floors to pay for her driving lessons, and then, at the age of twenty-eight, she started training to be a psychiatric nurse. Dad used to work all the hours that God sent. He worked at the pit for a time, and at a chemical works with my grandfather, making up bath salts and vitamin capsules with gelatin. On one occasion Grandad fell into a vat of caustic soda, but he managed to stand on a pile of hides and lift himself out. He was lucky; the vat was twenty feet deep. The other workers hosed him down and put him under the shower, but he lost a lot of skin.

Money continued to be tight, but somehow we managed. I don't think we were unique in that. I do know that we didn't suffer. Mam and Gran saw to that; they used to go without food so we could have it.

As a result, holidays were rather special. We'd set off – usually for Porthcawl in west Wales – in Mam's little sky-blue Morris 1100, with nine of us aboard: Mam in the driver's seat; Gran with us two boys in the front; and Grandad in the back with my three aunties and my sister.

We'd have day trips to the beach, with the crack in your bum getting wider and wider because you were sitting on someone's knee. On birthdays, the big treat was a visit to the pictures. We couldn't afford all the trimmings; when Mam lost her lighter and a packet of cigarettes in a café it was a total tragedy. We went back to look for them, but they'd gone. Because we couldn't afford sweets, Mam and Gran would make sandwiches for us to take when we went to see *Herbie Rides Again* or *Bedknobs and Broomsticks*.

I was always accident-prone. I was bumped by cars, and I fell through roofs. Once I jumped on to the asbestos roof at the rugby club and fell straight through. I landed, unconscious, astride a rocking horse, and came to with blood pouring from my ear. Poor Mam nearly fainted when she heard the news. She had to pay for the new roof.

After school one day, Jeremy and I went to play in a field with a friend. We didn't realize, until it was too late, that there was a ram in this field. The ram charged us, and Jeremy and the other lad scarpered. I thought I'd do my John Wayne bit and protect them, and ended up gripping the brute by its horns.

'Get a stick!' I yelled to Jeremy. But my faithful mate Jeremy was already legging it rapidly down the lane, laughing his head off.

Luckily for me, a neighbour of ours asked the two of them what they were laughing at. Realizing that I was in danger, this kind man ran all the way to the field and rescued me. I then ran all the way home, ready to break Jeremy's neck.

'Where's Jeremy?' I asked Gran. 'I'm going to kill him. He deserted me when I needed him.'

Poor Gran, she didn't know what was going on. Then the neighbour explained, and she came upstairs to find me. I'd already packed my things. I had been betrayed, and I was going home to my mother.

My grandmother was always there for any one of us. Whenever we had a problem, she was always willing to listen and help. She still is. That's why she's not just a granny, she's our best friend. We all complain about her, but only because we love her.

I cut my wrist open once, playing on the school railings. It was pretty bad, and I ran round to Gran's, blood dripping everywhere, just as she was getting into the shower my grandfather had rigged up in a tin hut in the back garden. I banged frantically on the door.

'What the hell do you want?'

I banged some more. She flung the door open and played holy hell with me, until she saw the blood pouring from my arm.

'Oh my God,' she said, shutting the door in my face. I stood outside, my life-blood ebbing from me, while she went off to get dressed.

She told me to keep my arm up in the air and keep pressing on it. I was dragged crying like a stuck pig up to our house in the prefabs, a ten-minute jog away. The doctor came along and I watched him put the fish-hook through my wrist. I've hated stitches ever since.

There's no denying it, Gran was the head honcho. Her first husband, my mother's real father, was killed in the war. He was on his motor bike, overtaking another vehicle. An army truck with a roll of barbed wire on it was coming down the road towards him, and everyone aboard was too busy eyeing up a group of bathing beauties to notice him. He saw them, but a bit too late; he couldn't stop, and went under. He lived for a couple of hours and then died. Gran was seven months pregnant with my mother. I've seen pictures of him, and, as I'll explain later, his spirit has watched over me in more ways than one.

Gran was known as a staunch disciplinarian throughout Commercial Street as well as at home. When she lived in the centre of the village, the Queen of Hearts club opposite her used to have some really vicious hit-men on the door. One of them attacked my Aunty Pamela as she walked past the club one day, and Nora was out just like Supergran. She let fly at him with her bunched fists and it was left, right, good night.

Another time, one of the bouncers decided to shunt my mother's car backwards with a Bedford van. He obviously didn't know my grandmother very well, or he wouldn't have left his little side-window open like he did. The gap was just big enough for her to stretch herself back, peel one right off her lap and land it smack on his chin.

People coming out of the club were often drunk, and would use bad language. Nora hated this. One night she asked a reveller to keep his voice down because there were children within earshot. When he continued to eff and blind, Gran pulled on her dressing-gown and stormed out to confront him. The man was silly enough to laugh at her, and she took a swing. He ducked – and the punch landed in his wife's face instead.

Gran looked at the collapsed heap on the ground for a moment or two. 'Coward of a husband you've got there,' she said, then turned on her heel and walked away. I never saw those two around the club again.

We had trouble from other club-goers as well. They used to park their cars on Granny's piece of wasteground, even though she'd spoken to the manager and warned any customers she could get her hands on not to. When they persisted, she went down to the Co-op and bought half a pound of sugar, and then waited patiently for Saturday night. When the unofficial car-park filled up as usual, Gran crept out and put spoonloads of sugar into each petrol tank. It took the AA a whole day to tow all the stranded vehicles away – and it was the last we heard of illegal parking.

Nora's an incredible lady. If she says she's going to do something, she does it. My mother's the same.

The thing with my family was, if we hadn't done anything wrong, they'd stand up for us; but if we had, then they were the first people to give us a hiding. They were very law-abiding people, but if they ever said, 'Don't worry, everything will be all right,' then we knew we could trust them. When you've got that, you've got security. They loved us totally; there was almost more love than any kid could handle.

And that makes it all the more difficult to understand why the fourteen-year-old pride of the Weston family now took it into his head to go off the rails in such spectacular style that he ended up in police custody just twelve months later.

2

A BRUSH WITH
THE LAW

I was a big boy now, so I moved up to the secondary modern school, called the Graddfa, a bus-ride away in the next village.

Appearances were terribly important in my family, and if everything wasn't polished or just so, I'd hear about it from either Gran or my mother. I was a very tidy and reasonably placid lad, but at the Graddfa Jeremy and I were continually pestered and bullied by one of our fellow pupils. Someone must have noticed this and told my family. So, one day, my grandmother accosted this lad in the street and warned him that he could push me too far.

'Simon is a very even-tempered lad,' she said, 'and left alone, he'll not go looking for any aggravation. If you carry on bullying him, don't bring your parents back to us complaining that he's taught you a lesson.'

The boy took no notice, and that day eventually came.

We were getting off the bus in Nelson after enduring the usual torture session all the way home. He said something – I can't remember what – and I felt myself just floating over the edge. I flew at him. Nobody intervened; I was doing what everyone else was too frightened to do. He was in a very sorry state when I'd finished with him, and his days of giving people a hard time were over. But if he thought he had problems, they were nothing compared with mine. I had to go home and face Nelson's answer to the Godfather: Gran.

I still had one other tormentor in my life though: my sister. Mam was working in Cardiff now, and used to put our food in the oven for us. One night I somehow knocked a few of my sister's chips off her plate, and in retaliation she flung everything off mine. She ran off upstairs and I launched my chicken-and-mushroom pie up the stairs after her. Splat! – all over the wall. My mother wasn't too pleased.

At other times, we'd get the poker red-hot in the fire and chase each other round the house. I even threw the carving knife at her once after she'd had a go at me, but she closed the door just in time. I was going off her in a big way. I thought I'd found the solution one day during a school visit to Windsor Safari Park. I bought a six-foot spear from the souvenir shop and, despite my teacher's fury and protests, lugged the thing all the way home. Mam took one look at it and knew at once what I had in mind.

'Chain it to the wall,' she said to my father, and he did.

Thanks to her intervention, Helen never did get the impaling I had planned.

There was another problem at home. My father was not particularly involved with either of us kids. Dad just wasn't a real dad to us, the sort who'd come to watch me play rugby or Helen play hockey or netball. There was no encouragement at all from him, and he never showed us his true feelings. He was just the man who sat in that chair over there and ate his tea on his lap, or who was out working all hours. He wasn't a man you could talk to. I missed that. My grandad was more of a father to us. He used to regale us with his old war stories, and was always a soft touch when it came to begging for a day off school. My dad just didn't want to know. It was as if he was sitting watching us on television. And when it came to discipline or taking an interest, he switched off. He just wasn't a member of the family.

Mam and Dad's relationship was also under strain. There were several instances when Gran had to come up and put the old man in his place, because of the way he was acting. To see a man you've known all your young life start doing totally irrational things really hurts.

People just fall out of love, I suppose. I never asked my mother what happened; I never thought I had the right to. All I knew was that I felt the atmosphere – although it probably affected my sister more than me, because despite everything she was a daddy's girl. I took my usual defensive action and moved back to Gran's.

School continued to be a pain, in spite of my efforts to liven things up. One day the art master had to leave the room for some reason, and while he was gone I painted on myself, with black paint, a pair of spectacles, a huge curly moustache and a goatee beard. It was a major contribution, I felt, to everyone's art education. Unfortunately the master didn't see it that way. Out came the cane, and the Laughing Cavalier was soon laughing on the other side of his face.

Our religious-instruction master, a man with a head that looked as though it had been shoved in a pencil-sharpener, had always faithfully preached the maxim 'turn the other cheek' until he and I had a little run-in one day. The poor man broke a lifetime's rule when I rubbed him up the wrong way: he grabbed me by the lapels of my blazer and slammed me up against a cupboard. Heaven knows what I'd said to offend him, but his teaching lacked conviction for a while after.

Parents' Day arrived, and my mother and grandmother went along to speak to the teachers about my and Jeremy's academic prowess and scholastic achievements. They were pretty soon disillusioned. Everyone said that we both lacked concentration and must do better; one teacher told Gran that Jeremy was always clowning around. When they got to the metalwork teacher, he said that Jeremy was not interested in the subject, but he was ecstatic about me. He said he had given me ninety per cent in my exam.

'Thank goodness he's good at something,' my mother said. 'When I said the name Simon Weston to the other teachers, they all wanted to throw up!'

In the car on the way home Gran gave us both a good dressing down. 'You will end up driving an ash-cart,' she said, glowering at me, 'and Jeremy a court jester dancing behind it.'

Jeremy and I were in pleats laughing.

On the home front, Mam and Dad were now very close to breaking-point. Judy was ill and having a baby. Helen was about to do her O levels. The focus certainly wasn't on me. I wasn't getting the strict discipline I needed. I was a big, strong boy for my age. I didn't communicate, I was sullen and, like any other fourteen-year-old, I found it difficult to talk about my emotions.

I was suddenly in trouble everywhere, mostly for fighting. I was wagging off school quite often now; Helen had a lot of free-study time and she'd always find me in the village, smoking. She always snitched on me. If she was in the Mafia, she'd be holding up a flyover by now. One day I was bunking off school and Helen grassed me up to Gran, who dragged me home and thrashed me with a stick. She wanted to make me aware that I was still subject to the strict discipline I had been brought up with. I'm afraid it didn't do much good. The atmosphere on the streets was one of aggression and inter-village gang fights. Like most other lads of my age I got involved. Dad couldn't have cared less; he had other things on his mind.

I never knew my father well. I knew he had been in the RAF, and that he was one of three brothers. My Uncle James was the only one of the three not to go into the services. He ran a garage in Edinburgh and loved nothing more in life than taking his dogs out shooting. Uncle John was in the Queen's Colour Squadron. On the Weston side of the family there was probably quite a big clan up in Scotland, but I didn't meet many of them. I met my grandmum and my grandad in Scotland before they died, but never many of the rest.

Dad left home the week before Helen sat her first O level. I packed up my things at Gran's and moved back to look after Mam. My father had taken everything with him, but all I cared about was that he'd gone. It was such a relief. Helen had a harder time. She wrote to him, which upset Mam especially; but she was sixteen, and felt she was adult enough to run her own life. He was still her father; the fact that he'd left home didn't change that.

After a particularly fierce row one day between my mother and my sister, I cornered Helen outside her school.

'I heard you were looking for me,' she said.

Words were exchanged, and she took a swing at me. I reciprocated. It took two of my mates to drag me off. For both of us, a lifetime of tension and dislike had finally come to a head. I couldn't believe how angry we were with each other. Our true feelings were out in the open now, and the damage was done. Helen left home very shortly afterwards to live with her boyfriend's family.

I was a big lad for my age, and I was confused. My family had just split up and I had lost any real aim or constructive direction in life. My family were strong and loving, but I needed the authority of a man I respected. With my father gone, I was beginning to lose my sense of values.

I don't honestly think I was any worse than any of the other kids. I smoked, I got the occasional flagon from the off-licence, and I went into pubs – with platform shoes being all the rage, I had the height. My problem was that I just wouldn't listen to reason. I was easily led, but you can't blame others for your moments of weakness.

One Saturday night, to celebrate Manchester United's beating Liverpool 2–1 in the FA Cup, I got so drunk that I was sick all over my clothes and bedding. First thing on Monday morning, while I was still nursing my throbbing head, Mam was off down to the Army Careers office in Pontypridd to collect leaflets.

Mam had begun to assume the dominant role in our set-up, shouldering the burden of being a father as well as a mother to me. She was in charge, and she was going to sort me out. In my heart of hearts I knew she was right. I needed the sort of discipline that the Army would give me, and I went along willingly to do the preliminary selection tests.

My performance was just above average, which wasn't very difficult considering all the tests were about as easy as Pin the Tail on the Donkey – without the blindfold. I had an interview, and felt slightly stupid having my mother in tow. It didn't seem very military to me somehow. I was forever being embarrassed by having my mother on my arm. She was always there; the family used to think that besides making the decisions they actually had to be there with you to give moral support.

Afterwards, as we pulled out of the car-park, Mam drove straight into a government-property lamppost. 'That's a great start to my career,' I thought.

Things were fine for a few days afer that, but if Mam thought I had finished with letting her down she was in for a nasty shock. There were eight of us involved in stealing cars the night I got arrested. At fifteen, I was the youngest. The oldest was twenty-eight and had already been inside. On the scale of criminal offences, pinching cars probably isn't that terrible – except to the people whose cars they are. But my only defence is that I was drunk. We'd been to the pub and had held a drinking race. Egged on by the others, I'd got more and more ratted. I had no particular interest in stealing cars; I couldn't even drive. But when one of the lads explained that you could open a car with a pair of nail scissors, I thought we were being dead clever.

We finished our drinks and stumbled out into the night. It had been raining. As we chose our first target, a Vauxhall Viva in a badly lit car-park, I started to shiver.

'Scared, Wes?' the boy next to me said.

'Just cold,' I replied, grinning foolishly. I pulled up the collar of my coat and my shoes crunched over some broken glass as I walked, less willingly now, after the others. I suddenly realized that these guys were actually going to do it.

They were in the car and we were off in no time at all.

We got as far as Cardiff before we stalled at some traffic-lights right next to a police car and were arrested. I was sobering up fast. Given the choice, I decided, I'd prefer to have Helen break my nose again to what was about to happen.

We were bundled out of the Black Maria and into the harsh, neon-lit interview room at the police station.

Soon afterwards, I learned later, the police were knocking at my mother's door to tell her where I was. Mam listened to the officer but didn't understand at first what he was talking about. She'd thought I was down at Gran's. Then she went as white as a sheet, and the policeman had to put out an arm to steady her. He went into the kitchen and made her a cup of tea. I could not be seen, he said, until midday.

Mam got dressed and drove straight to the police station. 'I've got diabetics to attend to,' she told the desk sergeant, 'I've got to go back now – please don't do this to me, I've got to see him.'

They brought me out. Mam was beside herself, her face an ugly red and streaked with tears. I'd never seen her like that before. The thought that I was responsible for her condition made me cry, too. I put my arms around her and said, between sobs, 'Mammy, please, don't cry like this, I'll never do it again.'

But Mam pushed me away and looked at me with undisguised hatred. 'How *dare* you, Simon?' she shouted. 'The shame of it! Did you even stop and think for a moment that you were invading someone else's privacy, someone else's hard-earned property?'

'Can't you see what you've done to your mother?' one of the policemen said. 'Your mother is the only one who's come here.'

They took me away for fingerprinting and to take a statement. Even from the interview room I could hear the noise, so alien to my image of her, that my mother was making – like a mourner at the graveside, grieving a loss.

She didn't let me off the hook for ages after that. 'Whose car are you going to steal tonight?' she would ask every time I went out. When I came in – I had to be home by 7.00 – she'd say, 'Seen any good cars?'

She never gave me the chance to explain, and she never looked me in the eye. She didn't have to. I could feel the vibrations of shame and disappointment. It was only much later that I discovered that half of her emotions were directed at herself. She felt a deep sense of guilt that my father wasn't there, that she had tried to play two roles and had failed.

But she was still my mam. She found me a solicitor, and he arranged it with the magistrate so that I'd only be punished with a £30 fine. That way I wouldn't have a prison record, and I would be allowed to go ahead with joining the Army.

Mam instructed me never to breathe a word to Gran about what had happened; the upset, she felt, would be too much for her. I obeyed. That I did so at once and without question marked a major turning-point in my life. At last, it seemed I had found not only the mother I could love, but also a figure I could respect. From that moment, my allegiance was transferred from Gran to her — and I felt secure.

3

JOINING UP

Having crossed the first recruitment hurdle, I now had to go to the selection centre at Deepcut in Surrey for more tests and interviews. I was terrified that the Army might find out about my past. There were rumours going around that if they found out you'd been in trouble with the law they wouldn't let you join. I never thought about what my mother's reaction would have been if I'd been turned down because of the car incident. I don't think I could have lived with the shame. I don't think I'd have been allowed to, either.

Deepcut, it turned out, was little more than an old country house near Blackdown. It wasn't my idea of Butlins, with terrible, horrible, lousy, stinking food. It was more like Butlitz. I suppose the idea was to get us used to army cooking. The cooks' course in the Army has got to be the hardest in the world. Not one of them has passed it yet. It's amazing how they can take the best raw materials available and turn them into tasteless mush with the wave of a magic wooden spoon. It's a real art.

The tests at Deepcut were more demanding than the ones I'd taken in Wales. This time you would be confronted with two round shapes and a square one, and have to say which was the odd one out. Or you'd have to say, from the following series of dominoes, what would be the next in the sequence: double one, double two, double three. Unbelievably, people actually failed. If brains were made of chocolate, the people who fail the infantry test wouldn't fill a Smartie with theirs.

The stamina and fitness tests weren't quite of SAS selection standard, either. Three heave-ups to the beam, three dips on the parallel bars, seven sit-ups, and Bob's your uncle. Then came my interview. After the other tests, it surprised me that the Army put itself out quite so much when it came to delving into the individual's feelings, wishes, aspirations and qualities. I was asked my choice of regiment, and whether I was still happy to join. Were

27

my parents worried about my joining up? (Worried? I thought. They'd throw a party when I finally left home.) What subjects interested me at school? (None, I thought, but I said, 'Geography.') Did I have any hobbies? (Yes, rugby and Manchester United. 'Metalwork, sir.') Did I drink? (Is the Pope a Catholic? 'Occasionally, sir.') Did I know anybody who took drugs? Did I have a criminal record? Oh dear. They believed my story about being easily led, and for all I know it probably improved my chances of getting into the infantry.

I don't remember very much else about Deepcut, except the look of vague panic on everyone's face; that in the evening we had a little shop open for chocolate and cigarettes; that there was no beer and no TV; and that I shared a room with a Teddy boy from Putney. The rest is lost in a blur of dominoes and indigestion.

While I was still at school, I had worked on and off for a local firm of metal-fabricators as a basic labourer. The money was good – £10 a day. It knocked spots off schoolwork. When I left school, in July 1977, I worked for them full time; then, in December, I signed up with the Army. By the time I came to join the Army officially, on 10 January 1978, I already felt it was going to be a good move. I wanted and needed discipline. I was already starting to grow out of the phase that had got me into trouble. I knew I couldn't carry on like that. I needed to be a somebody, I needed to have something to identify with. Just growing up and living in Nelson wasn't going to give me that. I needed a sense of adventure, excitement.

I had actually wanted to join the Royal Regiment of Wales, a South Wales regiment, but my court appearance had coincided with their joining-up time. My next choice was the Military Police, but I was told they had no vacancies. On the telephone, I was offered the Welsh Guards. I hadn't heard of them – or any other Guards. But since the only other option was to wait six months more, I took what I was given. Or rather, I took what my mother was given. I was out when they phoned, and she very kindly accepted the appointment on my behalf.

When I heard that I'd got through, I suddenly felt worried. It was going to be the first time I'd left the home, the nest, and I thought about being away from the family. It frightened me.

I got a great send-off from the lads. They carried me home from the social club, deposited me on the doorstep, rang the doorbell and ran off. The next thing I knew, I was at the station with all my suitcases, my toothbrush all packed up with a nice little bow on it, and Mam beside me, weeping. 'My little boy's off to join the Army,' she cried as the train pulled out of the station. But not just yet. I'd got on the wrong train.

I didn't realize my mistake until it failed to stop at Reading. That meant that I couldn't catch the connection at Brookwood, and that there would be no one to pick me up and take me to the depot. I had a nasty feeling in my stomach and my throat began to tighten. I phoned the camp from Paddington and they very patiently gave me instructions to Brookwood, via Waterloo and Woking. Panic was setting in fast: I'd never been to London before, let alone used the Underground.

I was just sixteen, and still very sheltered, coming from the valleys. I asked thousands of people if I was on the right train. I worried about everyone; they were weird-looking people. I was terrified.

'He must be a drug addict,' I thought to myself, 'and he must be a criminal. That one over there must be a rapist, and she's a lunatic.' Everyone had a label on them. Everyone frightened me. This was the big macho lad who was about to join the finest army in the world. I had a skinhead haircut, check shirt, denim jacket, baggy denim jeans and cowboy boots. I thought I was the kiddy. I must have looked bloody ridiculous.

On the platform at Waterloo I met a group of scouses who were joining the Irish Guards. The rest of the journey to Brookwood didn't seem to exist. I was on cloud nine, I'd broken the ice; we realized we were probably all going to join the same platoon. A minibus met us at the station. We were delivered to a reception centre where they took all our details, put us into groups, formed us up into three ranks, got us to swing our arms and were ever so sweet to us. They didn't want us to run away just yet. God, if we could only have seen ourselves two weeks later! It was murder. The instructors, who were all Guardsmen, didn't give us a minute's rest. The names will be etched into my memory for ever: L/Sgt Morcombe, L/Sgt McGowan, L/Sgt Lavery, Sgt Walker, L/Sgt Jenkins, Sgt McCudden, Sgt McNally, Training Soldier Evans, Lt Trehan, Lt W. de B. Pritchett-Barrett. Some 100 of us started on that cold, January day. After twelve months, only twenty-four would be left.

We were put in large dormitories. Fourteen of us in my room were originally destined for the Welsh Guards. That number was eventually whittled down to four. Some were rejected by the Army on medical grounds, others rejected themselves. We had one lad whose dad was a teacher in Hong Kong. He went out there on his first leave and just never came back. His problem was that we were marched everywhere, and this poor bugger just couldn't march. This meant that he got singled out for a really hard time – and that's like capital H, capital T.

The first few weeks were a terrible shock to the system. However tough or fit you think you are when you arrive, you soon discover that you are not army fit. I absolutely hated it. Everything was so hard. Sometimes the instructors would poke us about a bit. If you did things wrong, you'd cop a right-hander. It must have been frustrating for the instructors. We underwent assessments every seven weeks, and if too many of us failed or were back-squadded, it reflected on them personally. They had to train us to move instantly and instinctively when the order came; one day our lives, and those of others, might depend on it.

We were issued with our kit. This consisted of someone saying, 'Size?' and running a tape measure around your head if you were in any doubt. Then they'd just pull something off a pile and throw it at you. Besides our clothing we also each ended up with a prepacked suitcase of military whatnots. We were lumbered, we could hardly move. A gas-mask round our necks, a pile of webbing over our shoulders, a big army mac draped around us, and a whole sausage-bag full of equipment to drag. Then it was back to our rooms to learn how to lay out the large, wardrobe-like lockers beside our beds.

In our rooms, the blue lino tiles were sparkling clean and the whole place smelled faintly of polish. Everything, absolutely everything, was neat, straight and lined up. Even to a person as tidy as myself, it all looked rather ominous. But even I hadn't yet appreciated that there were two versions of clean, straight and tidy. There was clean and there was Guards clean – and by God, was I to learn the difference.

Our next lessons were in how to square off our bed-blocks and how to remove the pimples from the leather of our boots with a hot iron and beeswax them. We were shown how to wash and press clothes Guards-style, and how to look after all the rest of our equipment. We cleaned and polished the floors, practised the bed-pack yet again, and did a bit more ironing. Anything that was visible had to be pressed, starched and immaculate. If it didn't shine, it was dirty. We even had 'shining parades', peppered with questions on regimental history.

Many things seemed unbelievably, mind-blowingly pointless. A prime example was the bed-block – a squared-off stack of blankets and sheets, worked to obsessive accuracy, all parallel lines and right angles, everything absolutely, mathematically bloody perfect. Someone asked why, and the answer was an educational blow to the head. An important lesson was taken on board: never, under any circumstances, question the logic that underpins even the simplest of orders.

There was no time to be homesick. Too much was happening, too much information was coming in. Life was a blur of lectures on rank recognition, on who to salute and when, on when to speak (when we were spoken to), when to stand to attention, when to clean our teeth and when to wash our feet. And every day, it seemed, there were a few more dotted lines to sign, and more bloody needles stuck in us than made sense. We all reckoned the army doctors were sadists. ·

Official getting-up time was 6.30, but we were so useless we had to drag our bruised, stiff and protesting bodies out of bed at 5.30. We constructed bed-blocks together, we sprang to attention together. The atmosphere was one of we're-all-in-the-same-boat, plus a nasty air of expectancy about the horrors yet to come. You find that you pull together when you're put up against it – at least to start with. The first couple of days you try helping others, then you realize you've got to look after yourself or you're going to run out of time.

Some of our time at the Guards depot at Pirbright was fun; most of it was sheer hell. If the instructors were in a good mood when they came in, fine, you knew you were in for a good day. But if they weren't, then God help us all.

Inspections were ruthless. The only thing that didn't get shined or polished was the inside of the tea-bucket. They picked up on stray threads, specks of dust, every unshaven whisker, every dodgy bit of ironing. It was uncanny how they managed to home straight in, and, however trivial the sin, it was treated with disbelief, fury and outrage, in rapid succession and with maximum decibels. If one took it into his head, your kit would go out of the window. And when you're in a first-floor room that means your boots will smash on the concrete below and your highly polished toe-caps will turn into crazy paving. The instructors' favourite trick was to pull all your kit out on to the floor and give you fifteen minutes to sort it all out. Perhaps they hadn't reckoned on the spirit of comradeship, however, because all the lads would rally round to help the victim meet his deadline. Perhaps that was the whole point of it all: to try and make us work together as a team, to instil in us a sense of discipline and of pride in ourselves and our appearance as Guardsmen. Although it was hard, there was a point. Competition was encouraged, and winning the weekly room inspection made all the effort seem worthwhile. The winning room was allowed the colour telly for the week – and the chance to watch the sport on Saturday afternoon and *Top of the Pops* on Thursday.

Being in the Army was new, it was exciting. Well, that's how I felt for the first day or two, anyway. It soon changed. My first letter home to Mam read: 'Dear Mam, Starving, send me a food parcel. Love Simon.' The food was terrible. It cost my poor mother a fortune to keep me in the Army, what with all the Scotch eggs and tins of corned beef and pasties she had to post me.

After a while you become so accustomed to it all that you just know that anything afterwards is going to be very, very easy. Nothing in your entire life will ever be worse than going to bed exhausted at 2.00 a.m., only to get up again at 4.00 because some NCO with a sadistic streak wants you to run around the parade ground in your underpants and slippers, or because some sergeant thinks he's being funny by putting you on 'shining parade', which entails being up all night shining your boots and the toilets.

There's that old cliché that in the Army the floors have to be so clean you could eat off them. Well, I can vouch for the truth of that one. You could see your face in them – usually a haggard, exhausted, bleary-eyed face. Boots, lockers, hallways, stairs, company offices, platoon offices, outside areas, the whole damned lot had to be pristine. You had to iron your counterpane and your mattress cover, you had to iron everything. Your suitcase had to be immaculate. Often just the nerves of an impending inspection would kill you. I'd do so much and then I'd say, 'That's it, lads, I need my sleep, I'm going to bed.' Somehow, I always got away with it.

You could never go on the 'runway' – a strip of road outside the main offices affectionately known as the M4 – without marching. God help you if you were caught just walking. You'd be 'rifted' – marched up and down very quickly. I did my fair share of rifting, and I can tell you, it's hard.

Everything we did seemed to be designed to demoralize us. I was crying to my mother after six weeks, 'Get me out, buy me out. Please Mam, I don't want to play any more, I want out, I've had enough.' I was sick and tired of people shouting at me, telling me what to do, how to live. I wasn't depressed or anything, it was just getting on my nerves. I'd simply decided that Simon Weston didn't want to do it any more. It was hard work, no rest, we were constantly on the go, and I never had a good night's sleep.

I cried like a baby to Mam. She told me to stick it out. 'Give it a day or two,' she said. 'If you still feel the same I'll sign your papers.' I think a day or two in my mother's mind meant two or three months.

The strictness and severity had to be maintained as a way of getting people to say, 'OK, I want out,' because the Army has to have a good reason to throw someone out. It's much easier if they can get the undesirables to go voluntarily. In those circumstances, a certain amount of harshness and ill-treatment is necessary, as part of the weeding-out process. The system has to be hard to get the best out of people. I was glad I stuck it out. I know it got the best out of me.

As time goes on, it doesn't become any easier, but it seems to, because in the end you simply get used to it. Unless, like one of the other Welsh lads, you're driven to punching the wall and busting your hand up completely in order to swing yourself a medical discharge.

For the first seven weeks, I had to exist on the princely pay of £3 a week. We had to buy all our own polish and rags, and after that all I could afford was a packet of cigarettes at the weekend, a finger roll with egg in it, a pint of milk and twenty plays of 'Montego Bay' on the juke-box. If I wanted more, I had to scrounge 'shrapnel' – loose change – off the rest of the lads.

I went home on leave after eight weeks, and realized suddenly that though there was plenty for me to do in Nelson, there were just no challenges. Going home was like going on holiday. But as one feels on most holidays in the end, I needed to go back to work. The Army was where I felt I belonged. I looked in my bedroom mirror one morning and realized how well I felt. I'd lost a lot of weight, and I was fit. The Army had given me that. I found I was just as glad to be going back to the depot as I had been to leave it. I decided I would stay in.

I told Mam all the stories. About the first run we went on in drill boots. They were new, they were hard, and they were murder. We ran up a muddy canal, and you were glad if a friend fell down in front of you so you could at least get some grip by running over the top of him. I told her about the first time we had to make a bed, when Clive Sergeant just couldn't get the hang of hospital corners. They tried explaining it to him for half an hour, then gave up. I ended up making it for him.

Clive was a lovely fellow, from Doncaster. We called him Donkey. He was always singing about Doncaster Rovers. He was big, tall — six foot six — and as gentle as they come. That was his problem. He was too nice to be in the Army. He just couldn't cut it in the end.

Then there was the first time I tried saluting. I made a total pig's ear of it, lifting my hand the short way up like I'd seen John Wayne do it, and shouting, 'Surrr!' just like in the movies. The officer bent up laughing, but at least I'd had a go.

Mam listened with disbelief when I told her about locker inspections, and how I often had my stuff turfed out of the window if something had a crease in it. They'd throw your boots against a wall, too. There was nothing you could do but feel suicidal and do it again. Some lads sat up all night doing them.

'Is that how you got that lump on the back of your head?' Mam asked. 'From a flying boot?'

'No, Mam, that was from last week's practice with the GPMG.'

'GP what?'

'General-purpose machine gun. I just couldn't get the hang of it. In the end the instructor hit me straight on the top of the head with the working parts of it. I was in agony. Sergeant Maxi McDonald, his name was, Mam — write that down in evidence.'

We both laughed.

Looking back, I suppose I must have enjoyed a lot of it. I loathed march-and-shoots, which started with a four-and-a-half-mile run with all your equipment, GPMG and belts of ammo, personal weapon and spare magazines, and full belt order, then continued with a trip over the assault course, an inspection and then a run to the live firing range. We did those at least once a fortnight. To ring the changes, we'd do twelve-mile runs with all the section equipment – radios, a 'Charlie G' (Carl Gustav anti-tank weapon) – the full Monty. The worst thing about these runs was that at the end, when we were feeling absolutely knackered and sweating like pigs, Sgt Ray Walker, one of our instructors, would still be looking fresh and as if he was ready to start on another twelve miles. We hated him for that.

Another thing I hated doing was compound guard on my own. There were a lot of foxes around, and they had a mating call that sounded like someone being raped. At the age of sixteen, hearing that, I'd run to get up into the tower and turn on the searchlight.

A typical day at the depot was organized along the lines of a school timetable. We got up at 5.30 or 6.00, cleaned the room, went for breakfast and fell in for muster parade. Then we marched off to our first lesson or two, after which we'd have a couple of hours of drill. We might have weapon training in the afternoon, followed by range work, practice at signals, then battle swimming or general fitness. We ran every day.

I always felt stupid doing certain things, such as skirmishing. Getting up, running forward, getting down, I always felt someone was about to laugh at me. But most of the time I was proud, bordering on arrogant. Some people would say arrogant, bordering on bloody arrogant. But I wasn't the worst.

On Sunday mornings there was a voluntary church parade. But you could safely bet a pound to a pinch of salt that the instructors would be in hounding us as usual at 8.00 a.m. Their definition of voluntary didn't seem to square up with the one in the dictionary.

With the IRA becoming increasingly active, we had our fair share of bomb scares, and they were the biggest pain in the bum. Except, that is, when a company of WRAC girls moved into the camp. When the alarm sounded at 2.00 a.m. they had to turn out at once like all the rest of us – only they were in their nighties. It would warm the heart of any frozen red-blooded boy soldier.

Then – at long last – the big day arrived. I'd just turned seventeen and a half and I was going to pass out of the Guards depot.

By the time of that passing-out parade, we could pile out of transports, laden with full fighting-order combat equipment, carrying large packs stuffed with our sleeping-bags and bivouac capes and extra clothes, our rear pouches crammed with equipment and ammunition, then run several miles, go round an assault course and at the end of it put half a dozen bullets in a one-inch group in a target 100 metres away. Well, at least try.

We were allowed to get up really late on passing-out day – 6.30. The extra lie-in was very welcome: the night before, we'd held our 'platoon smoker', when we went to the NAAFI and all our training NCOs and sergeants joined us in a boat race with pints of beer. For the first time, we saw NCOs out of uniform, in their true colours as human beings. Those hysterical, overbearing men with no compassion whatsoever suddenly turned into wonderfully nice people who laugh and smile and tell jokes. There were twenty-four of us out of the original 100 or so at our platoon smoker. We clubbed together and presented our platoon sergeant with a pace-stick. Not much to my surprise, nobody told him where he could put it.

The training had been hard – the same programme, the same regime as for Paras or Marines. The only difference between the regiments is that in war, Marines invade from the sea and establish a beachhead, and never move inland further than five or ten miles. The Paras – well, parachutes are just another form of infantry transport. If you want to know who does all the hard fighting up the sharp end, ask a Guardsman. Every infantry regiment has specific skills. Ours was to walk – and to clean and shine everything in sight. As the saying goes, 'Join the Army and see the world. Join the Guards and sweep it.'

Although every soldier swears an oath of allegiance to the Crown when he signs up, traditionally it is his regiment that he fights – and, if necessary, dies – for. The Welsh Guards might be the most junior regiment in the Household Division, but we've got a proud history. I was certainly chuffed to be one of them.

Just a week or two after mounting their first King's Guard on St David's Day 1915, the Welsh Guards were fighting in France as part of the Guards Division. Ceremonial duties in London followed between the wars, but the regiment also saw service in the Middle East.

In 1939 the 1st battalion (1 Bn) was in Gibraltar. Early the next year they were back in France, as part of the British Expeditionary Force (BEF). German tanks were advancing fast towards Dunkirk, and 1 Bn soon found themselves pitched against Rommel's 7th Panzer Division. The 2nd battalion, with 2 Bn Irish Guards, held the perimeter at Boulogne until overwhelmed. It was in the course of these defensive actions, which bought enough time for the BEF to be lifted from the beaches, that a Welsh Guardsman won the regiment its first VC.

In July 1944, as part of the Guards Armoured Division, 1 Bn landed in Normandy. 2 Bn, meanwhile, had been formed into the divisional reconnaisance regiment. After a fierce battle around Bayeux, the break-out was achieved, but the division still had to overcome bitter hand-to-hand fighting with the retreating Germans. In August, the Welsh Guards were reconstituted within 32 Guards Brigade, 1 Bn as mechanized infantry and 2 Bn in Cromwell tanks. The drive on Brussels began on 3 September, with the Welsh Guards on the right of the seventy-five-mile axis of advance, and the Grenadier, Coldstream and Irish Guards on the left. With their throttles on maximum welly, the Welshmen were the first to reach the centre of the liberated capital. After many months more of hard fighting, the division finally reached the Elbe on 5 May 1945.

The regiment later saw action in Palestine, Aden and Cyprus. And new Guardsman Simon Weston, 24469434, was about to join its ranks.

We got into our full dress uniforms and received our final inspection as recruits. I was terrified. If I made a cock-up on this one . . . It was my only chance to show the family. Mam, my stepdad Loft, Gran, Grandsha – they all were there. This was my glory, this was my finest hour.

We had crammed one heck of a lot of rehearsing into the last week. We had drilled, had our photographs taken, drilled, had a final kit muster, rehearsed our regimental cap-badge presentation, drilled and then drilled just a bit more to make sure. Then it was the big day, Friday, the last day of our last week as recruits at Pirbright.

The cars began to arrive, and the families and friends – dressed up to the nines for the occasion – began to file through on to the tiers of wooden grandstands facing the drill square.

Our kit was in immaculate order. My uniform fitted like a glove, my boots were gleaming. The sun shone down brightly as everyone formed up in their own platoon and companies. We were 'lead platoon', the passing-out platoon. We had a frontage of eight men, and I hoped to be among them. I was certainly tall enough.

But Sgt Ray Walker had other ideas. 'Weston, it's not that your kit's scruffy – it's not – or that you can't march – you can – but you're just such a bloody odd shape . . . into the middle rank with you.'

Never mind. All I wanted was for the day to be over, so I could go home on leave.

The mixed band of the Guards depot marched on to the square, followed by the rest of us, resplendent in our immaculate no. 2 dress. We crashed to a perfect halt, opened order and dressed off. The platoon commander, ceremonial sword in hand, stood us at ease to await the inspecting officer who was to take the salute.

'Platoon – platoon, 'shun!'

On the order we shouldered arms, and the inspecting officer and the commandment of the depot solemnly mounted the podium.

'Platoon, general salute, present arms!'

Our platoon commander informed the visiting colonel that we were ready for inspection. We stood to attention like ramrods as the senior officer passed along the ranks. The only comments were compliments or pleasantries; our turn-out was beyond reproach.

After inspection we went into the drill routine we had so lovingly rehearsed. We marched in review order, in quick time, in slow time, with eyes right, paying the salute to the officer taking the parade. Not a single mistake was made as we worked to the beat of the drum.

In front of the podium we dressed off. The Colonel made his speech, something about the Guards being like a family. He praised all the hard work that we had obviously put in so far. 'But remember,' he said, 'this is only the end of the beginning.'

'Alamein Platoon, right turn – quick march!'

We followed the band off the sunny square, leaving the podium and the stands behind. There would be drinks, and lunch, and then a spell at home on leave. But for the moment, all I was conscious of was that I was now a Welsh Guard.

We marched off the parade ground and were halted, and we whooped as we threw our caps in the air. From now on we were going to be treated as men, not as numbers. It was the great achievement of my life – not because I was about to become a proper soldier, but because I had made my mam proud. Since getting into trouble with the law I had really wanted to make it up to her and to wipe out an unpleasant memory of a hard lesson well learned.

'I left Nelson at six in the morning with Gran, Loft and Grandsha to make sure we got to Brookwood on time,' Mam said. 'It was a very proud moment, and I wasn't going to miss it. When I saw you out there on the parade ground I was so pleased – you had lost weight, and there was an air of determination about you. You were no longer a child.'

Her reaction was worth a great deal to me. I knew that a bad phase in my life was now over – but I also knew that it would never be totally forgiven or forgotten by one very special person.

I made some marvellous, lifelong friends in the depot. We were always under pressure to be the best at everything we did, and to be aggressive. They took innocent sixteen-year-olds and turned them into homicidal maniacs. But then again, you can't have innocent youngsters going to war, or on to the streets of Northern Ireland; you've got to have people who can be nice when they want to be, but bone-crunchers when they need to be. The depot taught me that, along with independence and self-discipline. But most of all it taught me how to respect myself. That's what made me hold my head up high on the parade ground when the moment came; that's what gave me the stance that made my mother so proud.

Training was over. Now came the easy bit. The day stayed gloriously sunny, without a hint of a breeze. There was an open marquee for a buffet lunch on paper plates, and I remember Mam meeting my instructors, and them saying nice things about me. Mam wanted to go to Windsor afterwards, but all I wanted to do was sleep. I stayed in the car, with my toes sticking out of the window and my feet going wah-dum, wah-dum from all the marching. It was 10 December 1978, and in just four weeks' time I was to take up my very first appointment as defender of Her Majesty the Queen, in the far-flung outpost of West Berlin.

4

BERLIN

'Our job,' the CO announced to his assembled troops with much gravity, 'is to delay the Russian advance through Berlin.'

Fair enough, I thought. I can hack that, I'll do my bit. But there did seem to me to be one tiny flaw in Whitehall's master-plan. Berlin, as I could dimly remember from the one geography lesson at the Graddfa when I had my ears open, is 100 miles inside Eastern Bloc territory. And as the CO now went on to explain, there were, within twenty miles of the city, some 90,000 troops of the Warsaw Pact – as well as close to 8,000 tanks. That was almost three tanks for every British soldier in Berlin. Spanking fresh from the depot, I was as keen as the next man to have a go. But despite my enthusiasm, I still wondered for just how long I'd be able to hold out against my personal quota of three marauding T-72s.

The worst thing about Berlin was getting there. We had to travel from Pirbright – via London – to Luton Airport by public transport, carrying with us virtually every item of a Guardsman's equipment bar our rifles – roughly the equivalent of three airport-trolley loads per man.

Five of us set off from the depot together. With hindsight, it might have been easier if we'd clubbed together and chartered a freight train, but instead our plan was to claim whichever carriage happened to be opposite our mountain of luggage when the train pulled in at the platform. There was certainly no way we could have walked up and down the train looking for vacant seats.

The train arrived, but the carriage that stopped opposite us already had someone in it. No problem, we staggered aboard anyway, piled what luggage we could into the overhead racks, and arranged the rest in a neat ceiling-high stack in what had previously been the leg-room between the seats. We felt we deserved a smoke and lit up with gusto.

'Excuse me,' said a voice from the other side of the wall of baggage. 'I think your luggage is on fire.'

'No,' said the boys, 'but our cigarettes are!'

'Well put them out,' said the voice. 'This is a non-smoker. And in any case, I'm a jolly good friend of your colonel.'

I looked at the No Smoking sign on the carriage window. 'Well,' one of the boys piped up, 'I'm a jolly good friend of his too. Perhaps we can all have dinner in Berlin.'

The lecture about social responsibility that followed lasted all the way to the stop before Luton. There the owner of the voice got up, still hidden behind the pile of luggage, and disembarked. We never did get to see what he looked like.

Berlin was covered in snow. It was freezing. Breathing in was like inhaling broken glass. There before us, at last, was the gleaming, modern city we'd come to defend, the former German capital, home of the Brandenburg Gate and Checkpoint Charlie, steeped in centuries of history and romance. 'Jesus,' I muttered, 'I'm glad I brought my duffel coat.'

A four-ton truck was there to pick us up and we were soon on our way. I was both excited and nervous. At last, I was joining the battalion.

Meeting Muppet for the first time was an incredible experience. All three of us were put in the same room as this character, whose real name was Blethyn. He had a bright shock of ginger hair, was as fat as mud, and hardly ever slept in camp. He spent every night with his girlfriend instead.

Every morning at dawn, Muppet would creep into our room and crash out on the settee rather than have the bother of remaking his bed later on. At reveille, it would take the strength of four men to wake him. His sleep was the sort of deep unconsciousness I hadn't seen since Gran laid out that bouncer in Commercial Street with her prize haymaker. Muppet finally copped it in Northern Ireland. He fell asleep at a machine-gun post when he was supposed to be guarding an explosives convoy going into Newton Hamilton, and was caught.

Though Muppet could sleep anywhere, not even he could rival the feat of another notable Welsh Guardsman. 'You know, Wes, it's incredible,' said Jimmy Salmon, 'but you are the only person

I've ever met who can fall asleep for one minute.' It was true. I could fall asleep on the edge of a chicken's lip.

We started two weeks of draft training the next day. This came as a bit of a shock to us all, because we had rather been under the impression that we knew it all. But we soon discovered that the rifle drill and foot drill we had so painfully learned in the depot had in fact been taught to us in slow motion, to help us get the timing right. Now we had to get them up to battalion speed. We also met the commanding officer, the RSM and, inevitably – because at some time or other during our stay we were going to have a run in with him – the regimental police sergeant.

The rest of the company make it very clear to you that you're 'new draft', a 'crow', a rookie. Crows are given all the worst jobs to do, and crows are what you remain until another new draft arrives from England. Luckily for us wasters, that was just two months later.

Apart from drill, the rest of draft training consisted mainly of familiarization with the camp and immediate area, and a lot of runs. It was also the start of learning to become a proper soldier by getting properly drunk.

After ten days, we were assigned to particular companies. There is no magic formula about this selection process in the Welsh Guards; it has nothing to do with intelligence or aptitude or anything like that. It's simply a question of height. If you're short you go to 3 Company, if you're middle-sized you go to 2 Company, and if you're very, very tall you go to Prince of Wales Company. At five foot ten, I was assigned to 3 Company. They were known as 'the little iron men' – mostly 'drama merchants'. In the Army you never cause trouble, you just cause drama. We called Prince of Wales Company the Jam Boys, because they were so jammy at getting the best jobs with the best perks and the most time off. And because to them we were so small, they called us the Munchkins.

After draft training, you get presented with your Berlin flash – a black patch with a red circle in which are the letters BERLIN. You wear it on the shoulder of your right sleeve. As for your beret, the camp tailor takes off the shiny Stay-Brite training badge and sews on a cloth cap badge. It doesn't shine, and that means that you're ready to go into the field. To me it was a symbol that I'd actually joined the regulars, the professionals. I was now a soldier.

Usually your first duties as a crow were in the kitchen, but I somehow managed to dodge that. However, one thing even I couldn't get out of was guard duty. It was freezing work, trudging around in the snow, swinging a pickaxe handle – or 'pick-helve', as they were known. Mounting our very first guard, Jimmy Salmon and I were well ready to do our bit for Queen and country. We had the cap badges and the pick-helves and we were the men, swinging our sticks, patrolling the perimeter so that our comrades could sleep soundly in their beds. Unfortunately, we got chased by two great drunken members of Prince of Wales Company. We had the weapons, and they were legless, but we still kept running away. It wasn't the most glorious start, especially as Jimmy dropped his stick and had to go back and plead for it. I provided covering fire from the corner of a building 100 metres away.

Berlin was divided up between the four Allied nations at the end of the Second World War and has been frozen like that ever since. The British are scattered outside the city centre, in barracks at Spandau and other suburban points, and they tend to come into the centre itself only for the occasional binge or to show their visiting relations the Berlin Wall – four feet thick, and built in a half-moon shape around the Brandenburg Gate by the Russians. There are lights focused on the gate itself, showing up the white-painted East German observation post, which patiently watches and photographs all visitors who mount the viewing platforms on the western side. These platforms are to the right of the old Reichstag building. East Berlin itself is dimly lit behind the glare of the Brandenburg Gate. The atmosphere, at what used to be the centre of rip-roaring Berlin, is rather like that of a military cemetery.

I did Spandau guard a couple of times, and actually saw Rudolf Hess. He was allowed out for two hours a day for physical exercise, but because he was so old he tended to do all his exercise in the garden, working out with a pair of secateurs. He was a waster, Hess. There was only one path within the perimeter walls of the prison, and regulations stated that you couldn't walk past him, couldn't have any contact with him at all. So when the reliefs were posted, he often used to walk out from behind the bushes on to the path in front of you, just to send you round the other way. Then he'd have a good laugh and get back to his roses. I felt desperately sorry for him – it was at the stage where he could do no harm to anybody. I don't know why there had to be such a massive guard on him. He was hardly going to have another go at hijacking a Messerschmidt and flying to England, was he?

I never actually heard it myself, but people said he screamed at night. I can still remember how eerie it was at the back of Number Three post. From all the other posts you could talk to each other. But Number Three was isolated, and very, very dark. There was a story that an American had hanged himself there, and that Rudolf Hess had once taken a rifle off a young soldier. Stories like that keep you alert when you've only just turned seventeen.

I only did the duty four or five times. By and large, I enjoyed it, despite the hours. The usual system was two hours on, four hours off. But if your first stag ended at 2.00 a.m., it was often 2.30 by the time you were relieved. After tea and an egg sandwich, and getting undressed, it would be 3.15 before you actually got your head down. Then you were woken up again with tea at 5.45, fifteen minutes before your next stag. This rota could last for up to seventy-two hours. One time when I was on main-gate duty by the guardroom, they phoned all the posts in an attempt to keep everyone awake and to break the monotony. If my memory serves me right, out of eight guards, only two were awake. It's the same in England when you mount the Queen's guard. You count yourself lucky if you get four hours' sleep.

Guard duty was also hard because of sheer boredom. Your mind goes numb, you start counting spots or dots or bricks in the wall or blades of grass, or try to identify noises, or try to sneak out of your tower and knock on somebody else's door and run away. There was even a telephone quiz among the sentries on the 'death watch' – which was between 2.00 a.m. and 4.00 a.m. – just to keep us on our toes. Nobody took Spandau duty seriously except the Russians. They had one married and one single guard on the towers. The married man was supposed to keep an eye on the other; the idea was that with a family back in Russia, he could be trusted not to run away. I felt sad for them.

My fondest memory of Spandau is of when we marched in through the main gates one day to take over from the French. We formed up in three ranks, and watched patiently while the special French drill squad marched on to parade. There was one little chap who was the spitting image of Jou-Jou in the Inspector Clouseau cartoons. He wore a pill-box hat like all the others, but I think he must have put on the wrong one by mistake. As he marched, his hat started to drop further and further down his head with each step, until only his moustache was visible. Not just any moustache, either, but one of the biggest, squarest moustaches any of us had ever seen. The Frenchmen halted and snapped to attention facing us. Right in the front row, little Jou-Jou with his hat down over his eyes stood only feet away from a platoon of hardened, irrepressible Welsh Guards. He must have seen the first suppressed laugh, because we saw his moustache twitch. Then, as more and more of us noticed him, it became harder and harder not to giggle and risk facing a charge for bringing the Welsh Guards into disrepute. Soon his moustache had taken on a life of its own and was twitching all over the place. A major international incident was averted only by our doing ourselves serious medical damage by stifling our laughter. By the time we eventually marched off parade, our throats were hurting like hell. Sadly, when we went back to try the take-over once more, little Jou-Jou and his dancing moustache were nowhere to be seen.

When we weren't drinking we went on boat trips or for walks along the Havel river. West Berlin is a wonderful and rich city, but it can be very claustrophobic. It's 110 miles from the nearest point in West Germany and only fifty miles from Poland. The Russians encircle it completely, leaving the three air corridors and the main road and rail routes to Helmstedt as the only available lines of physical communication, for the Allies, with the West. This made getting away for the weekend rather difficult.

I didn't play much rugby in Berlin. The team was settled and very strong, though I did have a few trials with them. I was prop forward. A decidedly average prop forward. Quite quick, but otherwise nothing special. It was only when I got back to England that I played for the regiment regularly, as well as playing one or two games for the army under-21s and the Household Division. The only game I played in for the regiment in Berlin was the French Army cup, which we won — but we didn't get any medals. I played in the first half, then CSM Evans wanted to come on; because I was the newest and youngest member of the team I was taken off. The French gave us the trophy, but not medals, on the grounds that their opponents hadn't been French. Mysteriously, that trophy later got lost while in Welsh Guards hands, and that was the last the French ever saw of it.

We also won the Berlin Field Force tug-of-war, mainly because the best team, British Field Hospital, didn't enter. I was anchor man. It was a job that called for a lot of brute strength and not very much intelligence. It was made for me. I was immensely proud of the team, who were competing against tough opposition. All the different corps used to draft in specialist sportsmen. Top rugby players found themselves in 21 Engineer; good tug-of-war players were sent to the missile regiments or the Field Hospital. They trained indoors, outdoors, all the time. Luckily for us, they weren't in Berlin to play against us. Tug-of-war is a good cheering sport when you've got a few bevvies inside you, and it doesn't take much thought to watch. We always had a good turn-out of support.

I was getting to know most of the company by now, and as a result of one good day's shooting I was picked for the shooting team. I quickly earned the nickname Hydraulics, because when I was going down to take aim I was fairly slow. It didn't occur to me that you had to be quick. I never really fitted in with the shooting scene, but my mate Jimmy Salmon went on to win Bisley three times as a major force in the Welsh Guards team.

I spent a lot of time making excuses to get out of work. I was the most work-shy person ever to join the Guards. If there was a bluff going, I was bluffing it. I didn't spend a single Christmas on duty in my whole career, and that takes some doing.

I got a little tipsy one night with a few of the lads. At 4.00 a.m., behind the big cookhouse, two of them decided to have a willy fight. They were waving their weapons around to see whose was bigger when we suddenly heard a loud blast on a whistle. The camp guard had been turned out, and there were six Guardsmen with pick-helves ready to deal with us. I got up in the morning with no memory at all of having been charged. One of the lads was sent to get me from the shower, and took me to parade in front of the duty drill sergeant. I did so in a T-shirt, jeans and flip-flops, still drunk and giddy from the night before. We weren't the only criminals being charged that morning. Guardsman Lonnegan had been apprehended while standing in a tree, peeing on people when they went past. The cookhouse contingent marched in first.

'What were you doing round the back of the cookhouse?' the drill sergeant asked.

'Having a willy fight, sir,' said Steve Matthews.

'A what?'

'A willy fight, sir.'

The drill sergeant's face betrayed no emotion as he tore us off a strip, reminding us of our responsibilities as defenders of the Crown and things like that. Then he told us to dismiss. We did a right turn and were just about to march away, when he called out, 'Just one question, boys.'

'Sir?'

'Who won?'

Even drill sergeants can handle the occasional joke.

It was just as well. We were called out on emergency exercise one night at 2.00 a.m., when Steve Steele (we called him Tommy to start with, then Tommy Tit when we discovered that one of his nipples was really small, and one really big) and I were slumped comfortably in a bar. We got back to the barracks and I began trying to throw together my kit. I stuffed a pillow in my backpack to make it look good, but everything I did, Steve undid. Then he decided to play the drums on my mess tins and he was on the floor, like Hiawatha, banging them with his hands. We were late on parade, but somehow we weren't charged. The trouble was, we were still drunk the next day. We had to do house-clearing, and the Parachute Regiment were playing the enemy. We were now high on adrenalin as we were fighting in a built-up area. We dragged one poor Para out of the window, leapt on top of him, ripped his jacket open and confiscated his map. We were chuffed with our intelligence coup, but the umpires went berserk. A major strode up to us quoting the Geneva Convention and God knows what else. It was a brilliant exercise.

Berlin was probably the best time of my army career. It was a gentle introduction into the battalion. The food was excellent. So were the people. There were plenty of days off, filled with swimming, soccer (which we watched at the Olympic stadium), skiing, tobogganing and going to the cinema. If you wanted to play a sport for the Guards, it was an honour that was encouraged. Sadly, I'm told that the battalion's whole attitude to sport has changed. Different commanding officers have different priorities.

There were some rough times in Berlin, fights and such, but that is only to be expected. You're away from home, nobody knows you, you have that sort of wild-boy attitude and lots of money to spend, lots of cheap beer to drink. Also there were a lot of hard men there, boxers and all sorts – psychopaths, some of them. There was always somebody getting beaten up. Soldiers are soldiers. I got duffed up when I first joined, by a gang of lads from the Welsh Guards. It was no big deal. We were fighting men.

We have to keep a presence in West Berlin, we were told, because Britain has a right, under the terms of Germany's surrender, to military occupation of its own sector. If we weren't there, the East Germans might be tempted to steam in to exploit the weakness. One strange custom that has arisen is that both sides have daily 'flag tours' of each other's sector. We were told that in the unlikely event that any of us was involved in a driving mishap in East Berlin, we must not deal with the East German police, because that would imply that the British recognized East Berlin as a separate city, which we do not. Instead, you would have to ask for an officer of the Russian Army – whose presence in East Berlin we do recognize – and deal only with him.

East Berlin was like a black-and-white film, in slow motion. We went there on a day trip once, and it lacked the hustle and bustle and fun of Western cities. On the way back on the bus, East Germans come aboard and search for stowaways. Everything there is dirt cheap by our standards, though expensive to the inhabitants. When we threw away some pfennigs on the ground, an old woman saw us and went crazy. We'd bought some hot dogs, and had just thrown away the change. The coins were worthless to us. We couldn't exchange them when we got back, and there seemed no point in keeping what amounted to just a few pence. The old lady reacted immediately, poking and pushing us and reproaching us in German, no doubt telling us we were reckless capitalists with no understanding of the value of money. Then she went and picked them all up.

We gave another pile of East German pfennigs to an old tramp in a beer garden. He had a week's growth of stubble and watery eyes and was wearing an old military greatcoat. He told us he'd been at El Alamein. We gave him some friendly banter about Monty's victory. He was laughing when we left him, but he wasn't when the plain-clothes policemen set about him. We thought they were going to kill him.

Driving back on the bus through all the checkpoints made me think about the plight of all those people who try to escape. There is a museum at Checkpoint Charlie that commemorates various daring escape bids. One family lived in a toilet for three days until they got the opportunity to fire a crossbow bolt across to an accomplice, then hoisted themselves over on a pulley. Another woman broke her legs so that she could fold herself into two suitcases glued together. After seeing the secret police in action on that poor old tramp, I could understand their desperation. The police probably thought he'd spend our money on a ticket to the West. I would have done. What had been harmless chat had turned into something far more sinister.

My stay in Berlin often seemed like one long exercise after another – 'rocking horses' they were called by the German population, and we always knew when one was about to happen just by picking up a local newspaper. They always printed a picture of a rocking horse to warn people what was coming. Why a rocking horse, I never found out. But I do know that during the first full-scale invasion exercise, with Allied forces playing the Russians, some people threw themelves out of windows and hanged themselves because they thought the Soviet troops really were on their way.

We practised mobilizing for underground warfare – fighting in the woods, in subway stations, in built-up areas. By the end, it all became totally instinctive.

We used to train in American Huey helicopters. The American pilots, I decided, were absolute maniacs – but superb aviators. They'd pick us up on tiny little beaches on the Havel, with trees on all sides. How they didn't smash their rotors I'll never know. They also liked to hover over snowdrifts and play little games with us.

But the best day of my whole stay in Berlin was, without a doubt, the Allied Forces Day parade. It was brilliant. We came on to the city streets, marched down three or four of them in the shape of a circle, took the salute and fell out. My easiest day's work ever.

We came back to Britain in July 1979. Coming through customs, I got stopped. I hadn't even bought any duty-frees because I didn't have any German cash. What I did have was a microphone that somebody had given me, a set of headphones that somebody else had thrown away, and some LPs and cassettes I'd bought in anticipation of buying a stereo in England. To the customs officers, all this evidence could add up to only one thing:

that somewhere amongst this Guardsman's kit there lurked an illicit stereo. They unpacked every last bag, down to the last handkerchief – with no success. I almost felt sorry for them. Until I realized that it's not part of a customs officer's duty to do the repacking.

I'd saved up £1,000 in Berlin. I was stinking rich. I came back from Germany thinking I was God's chocolate. Back at Pirbright I rushed around, did a few things and collected my money, and then I went home to Mam. For once in my life, I didn't phone to ask to be collected from the station. Instead, along with another Nelson lad, Aidie Williams, I took a train to Cardiff, the bus to Pontypridd and then a taxi to the old home town. Finally, at about 1.00 a.m., I got to our house. I opened the front door and walked in, and my mother came rushing downstairs.

'He's home! He's home!' she shouted.

We hadn't seen each other for eight months, the longest we hadn't seen each other in my whole life. We had a cup of tea and I gave her the little Berlin bears I'd bought her in East Germany. When I went to bed, I felt like a king.

5

NORTHERN IRELAND

I woke at 6.00 and jumped out of bed, ready for another day of delaying the Russian advance through Berlin. Then I remembered I was a gentleman of leisure for the next month, and I jumped back in again. I resurfaced at a more civilian hour, and there then followed four weeks of eating, drinking and merriment.

My old room was untouched. There was still a skeleton hanging outside the door, and a sign in Dymotape that read: 'Simon Weston's Room. Helen Weston Keep Out.'

I spent a lot of the first couple of days just unwinding, telling all the stories to my mam, getting back into the Nelson swing of things. With a friend from Berlin, a cook called Michael Jones – whose nickname was Cardboard – and Aidie Williams, I went to Blackpool for a holiday. With so much cash in my pocket after Berlin, no expense was spared when it came to choosing our accommodation. We stayed at a little old guest house in a terraced street, sharing two double beds between the four of us. It was delightfully located in the shadow of the local gasworks. The food was awful and we had to pay ten pence for a cold shower. We had a great time, but you can give me Porthcawl and one of Mam's cheese sandwiches in the Odeon any day.

Then – and it felt as if my leave had been only a twenty-four-hour pass – it was back to Elizabeth Barracks at Pirbright, and the start of our Northern Ireland training: eight weeks of intensive preparation for our first real soldiering, at Salisbury Plain, Hythe and Lydd in Kent, and Thetford in Norfolk.

The course covered everything from checkpoints and vehicle searches to procedures for arrest and house-clearing. We learned the 101 places inside a car where bullets and detonators can be concealed – in door panels, ashtrays, cigarette-lighters; anywhere in fact where you could put your finger, including under hubcaps and wheel trims and inside the lining of the roof. There were practical demonstrations of how and where to search the human body – in hair, beards, wigs, crooks of elbows and bellybuttons, and between the toes, fingers and even buttocks. We were shown how to use 'Stop or Shoot' cards, how to cover ourselves against sniper fire, how to do vehicle-plate checks, how to just talk to people.

It was all basically a joke to us at the time, even though we knew we were practising for a serious job. We stripped cars, quelled riots on the parade ground, and hid in covert observation posts on Salisbury Plain. And every single slip, error, blunder and cock-up was videoed for our enjoyment by NITAT – the Northern Ireland Training Advisory Team. After each session we watched the action replays of incompetent Guardsmen falling over, banging their heads, tripping up on paving stones. We cringed with embarrassment, but the technique must have worked, because by the end we had learned to do it properly – or so we all hoped.

Several more weeks were spent learning how to patrol, and simply soaking up all the laws and regulations. Then came the final assessment, which entailed running from one 'stall' to another around the hills overlooking Imber village. At each stall were different sets of examiners, who would test you rigorously on their particular subject. You don't know what you're running to, whether it's a casualty to be treated or a plate check to be done, a vehicle to be searched or a full P check (person check) to be carried out – politely but thoroughly.

On the calm summer morning of 27 August 1979, the Provisional IRA murdered Lord Louis Mountbatten and two members of his family at Mullaghmore, County Sligo. Just a few hours later, eighteen members of the 2nd Parachute Regiment died in an IRA ambush along the border at Warrenpoint in the southern hills of County Down. It was not only the single worst disaster to date suffered by the security forces in Northern Ireland, but the worst set of casualties the Paras had suffered since Arnhem.

We were at Salisbury Plain when we heard the news. To a man we were revolted and upset. If the IRA were hoping by these outrages to shock us into leaving the North, then they certainly had another think coming. We were angry. The incident changed the tone of our training from then on. Suddenly, we knew that there really were bullets and bombs out there, and that we were the targets.

We moved on to Hythe and Lydd in Kent for range work, using electric targets. You sit in an attic with your rifle and you've got to shoot at targets of different combinations of blue and yellow — blue tops and yellow bottoms for civilians, yellow tops and blue bottoms for the IRA. Ninety-five per cent of the Guardsmen shot the civilians to start with. Lucky we all improved.

We moved on to the 'muff range', where a rifle goes off and you have to identify whether it was high or low velocity, and what direction it was fired from — which window in which building, or which alleyway or car. Then we graduated to live firing with .22 bullets. When the shooting starts, a door might open, and in pops a person. It might be a terrorist, it might just be a man with a cup of tea. Lucky for many of the innocent people with cups of tea, they were just plywood figures.

The next stage of training concentrated on how to shoot from moving vehicles, using night-sights, and generally move through an area while under attack from bricks and bottles and with explosions happening all over the place — under paving slabs, in milk bottles, behind bricks. Once again, and whatever we did, there was no escape from the cameras of NITAT. By the end though, if we walked into an ambush in a built-up area, any one of us was totally capable of returning fire almost instantaneously, alerting the rest of the patrol as to where the shots had come from, signalling whether we thought we'd scored a hit in return, and then carrying out the appropriate mopping-up procedures.

Not everything about Hythe and Lydd was sweetness and light. We never seemed to stop training and we lived in sleeping-bags for the duration. We only saw the NAAFI once in three weeks. We also had to queue endlessly outside the little cookhouse, for food that was foul to start with, and even fouler the longer you waited.

We had some fun waiting to go on the ranges though. Impromptu concert parties would spring up, with people getting on tables and entertaining the others like something out of *It Ain't Half Hot Mum*. My favourite was a pop group with the impressive line-up of lead and bass shovel, cupped-hands trumpeter and a vocalist who sang into an entrenching-tool microphone.

There were occasions, however, when things weren't quite so amusing. I missed one day's training because of other duties, and the next day we all had to go and jog up and down in a chamber full of CS gas. On our tour of duty in Northern Ireland we might have to use the stuff to control a riot, so we had to practise soldiering within the confines of the S6 respirator.

We stood around outside the ominous-looking building, waiting for our turn to go in, nervously fiddling with our masks. Mine was a new respirator, and the sick thought dawned on me that I had never checked it. Going into the gas chamber, I wished I had. A dozen at a time, we were summoned inside. The door closed behind us, and there was the instructor, a match already held to a gas pellet. The room filled with white, noxious fumes faster than you can say 'Jack Flash', and we started to breathe hard inside our respirators.

The first sensation I noticed was a slight tingling of the exposed skin, then a burning as the gas reacted with the moisture on it. The instructor made us jump up and down to make sure we breathed even harder and appreciated the full efficiency of the respirators, and it was then that I noticed that my eyes, too, were burning. This wasn't right. My eyes were inside the respirator. They shouldn't have been burning. Tears started to cascade down my face, and my throat felt so tight I thought it was going to explode. I had a leaking mask. I made a dash for the door, my throat blazing and contracting, and a powerful urge growing inside me to recycle my cornflakes.

'Where do you think you're off to, lad?' asked the officer who was standing guard by the door.

Without answering him, I reached for the handle.

So did he. 'You're not going anywhere, boy,' he said.

'I am, sir,' I finally gasped, 'you just watch me.'

I'd always hated being cooped up, not being able to breathe. I collapsed on to the grass outside and ripped off the mask, sucking in fresh, cool air, coughing and spluttering, my eyes still on fire. I was convulsed with dry heaves, and my saliva glands went into overdrive, pouring liquid down my tortured throat. Amazingly, the cornflakes stayed where they were. Soothed by the clean air, my eyes stopped streaming and my breathing became almost normal again. Nothing, I thought, could ever be as bad. Dear God, I thought, never put me through anything like that again.

The main training village was an old army quarters, with the local population played by another company from the battalion. Many WRACs were invited along to add realism to the pub scenes, and some played the part of wives and girlfriends so well that they even chipped in for the carry-outs, and came home with us for the party. The company that was playing the civilian population then played the part of the Army on patrol with the RUC. Sometimes a patrol was intentionally uneventful; at other times it was packed full of incident. After two and a half days of this we watched the videos courtesy of NITAT. Of the two roles, I have to say I preferred playing the civilian – climbing on roofs, throwing down tin cans, generally giving Prince of Wales Company a hard time. There were two pubs in the training village – The Green Dragon and The Three Stars – and also the Republican Club. We could order as much beer as we wanted, although in line with true army benevolence we had to pay for it. We were usually quite merry by the time the snatch squads came in, and we gave them hell. They repaid the compliment.

It was at about this stage of training that I was called into the office at Hythe and Lydd and told to phone home because my grandmother had died. I was devastated. I thought the world had come to an end. The phone was engaged the first few times I tried, and my desperation grew. By the time I got through I was close to tears. Strangely enough, Mam didn't sound as upset as I'd thought she would be. It turned out that it wasn't my grandmother who had died, but my great-grandmother. I hadn't even known her that well. All I knew was that she'd had a hard life and a good innings, but it hit Grandsha very hard. I accepted the week's compassionate leave that was offered to me.

When I returned from Wales, I'd arranged to meet a couple of the lads in a pub near Thetford railway station. I was having a quiet pint when they arrived, accompanied by a driver. They were all dressed in civvies. It was a standing order that all personnel who were training to be drivers in Northern Ireland had to carry pistols with them at all times, to practise for the months ahead when they could be ambushed at any moment. There were a lot of IRA road-blocks, and the only way you were going to get out of one of those alive was to get them before they got you. You certainly didn't wear your seat-belt.

'Going through the windscreen is the least of your worries,' one of the drivers told me once. 'If the car is stopped, you have to get out quick and engage the enemy. If you're trapped, that's you well and truly stuffed.'

For the same reason, they ware trained to drive at breakneck speed. 'The faster you go, the less time you stay in the blast area of a bomb that may have been planted by the roadside or in a culvert . . .'

Anyway, this driver who came to the pub had a Browning .9-mm automatic pistol tucked down his trouser belt, and hidden under his sweater – until he sat down. The locals were horrified, and it was case of drink up quick before someone called the police.

Most of the time in Norfolk passed comparatively peacefully. I only managed to get to the NAAFI for a drop of Norfolk cider once. I found out that it's very strong and does funny things to your system if you're not used to it. I certainly wasn't. That same night we went out on patrol and I was drunk. I know we started off in the back of a four-tonner, but from then on I can only remember snatches. I survived by walking behind my partner. He was carrying the radio, and there was a loose cap on it which clicked as he walked, like a blind man's stick. It was just as well. Everything else in front of me was a complete blur. I fell over at one point, lost the barrel of my gun in the dirt, found it again, staggered on and finally fell asleep in a hedge. The other lads had to come back and fetch me.

At last we got into a defensive position for the night and I could go back to sleep. I was awoken when it as my turn to go on duty. I took up sentry position, was sick, and promptly fell asleep again. I woke to find that it was mid-morning and I'd let everyone sleep five hours longer than they should have. To make matters even worse, I couldn't find the light machine gun that I'd been carrying. Platoon Sergeant Larry John read me the riot act, but I wasn't charged. This was not only because Larry was a good bloke, but also because everyone at our observation post had been sleeping so soundly that the 'enemy' had apparently been unaware of our presence, and the sergeant had been congratulated on our skills.

We were allowed home for a spot of leave before the start of our tour, and I celebrated by having a night out with a few mates at the Double Diamond Club in Caerphilly. It was a magical evening. The ceiling was covered with chicken-wire and lots of little lights. After a while they started to spin, and very soon afterwards I thought someone had stolen the roof, because all I could see was stars.

I was nervous about going to Northern Ireland – but then, as an eighteen-year-old soldier on his first tour there, who wouldn't be? But at least I was trained and I knew how to react in a professional way. It was more difficult for my family. I hate goodbyes anyway, and when it was time to leave, I simply stood in the doorway, said, 'So long,' and left.

The whole battalion marched down to the railway station and boarded the train for Liverpool. There, we went by coach to the docks, and boarded the transport ship that was to take us to Northern Ireland. She was an LSL (landing ship logistic). Weighing 5,674 tonnes and carrying 68 crew of the Royal Fleet Auxiliary – most of them Chinese – she could do 17 knots, carried two 40-mm guns, had a facility for helicopter operations and could accommodate 340 troops for an extended period, or 534 for a short time. Like other LSLs, this one was not graced with the most beautiful of lines. She had a high stern with a ramp, bows that could open sideways and a flat bottom that made her roll like an elephant on wet grass. Also, like other LSLs, this one was named after one of the knights of Arthurian legend. Her name was *Sir Galahad*.

There was a force 8 gale blowing in the Irish Sea, and we worked out that the letters LSL certainly don't stand for Luxury Service Liner. It was so rough I saw men literally turn green. They give us special plates and places to put our cups, because otherwise the whole lot would have gone flying. God, it was an awful journey. Men weren't allowed on deck in case they were washed overboard.

The troops we were to relieve, one of the Highland regiments, were waiting at the docks when we arrived. For probably the first time in history, a Welsh regiment wished their Scottish comrades good luck. They wished us good luck in return. We staggered on to coaches and proceeded to South Armagh. Sick as we felt, we still worried about the fact that the coaches were not armour-plated. We arrived at our destination and 3 Company were told to de-bus. 2 Company were going on to Newry, and Support Company and Prince of Wales Company were to be flown out to Newton Hamilton and Crossmaglen.

Battalion HQ and 3 Company were based at Bessbrook, South Armagh, just outside Newry and to the north of the Crossmaglen salient, which sticks down into the Republic. Our patch was therefore surrounded on three sides by some forty miles of twisting border. It is a beautiful area to look at, with rolling hills and acres of bogland and small fields marked by tall hedges of hawthorn and wild rose, and a wide sweep of hills on the horizon. But appearances are deceptive. The Army call it bandit country, because, just twenty miles from the Irish Republic, it is the single most dangerous strip of land for the soldier and the civilian in the whole of Northern Ireland.

The area is known to be one of IRA activity since there are several possible escape routes across the border – main roads, minor roads and dirt tracks. The IRA could detonate bombs by remote control and slip away across the border long before their firing position was discovered. They could set up mortar-firing tubes on lorries near our bases, set the automatic firing mechanism for maybe five or ten minutes' time, and be back across the border again before the mortar bombs were even on their way. At the time of my arrival, one in six of all soldiers killed in the whole of Northern Ireland had been killed in Crossmaglen. There had been only one outfit in the last twelve posted there who had not had a man killed. Sadly, Prince of Wales Company were also to suffer one fatality: Paul Anthony Fryer, who was murdered at Silverbridge at the age of eighteen.

No wonder that the first thing we new arrivals at Bessbrook could sense was the distinct atmosphere of unease. The bad vibes weren't felt just by soldiers. Near the border the majority of people are Catholics and, though they may not always be ardent Republicans, they know that they can be taken away and tortured, perhaps to death, if they give so much as a friendly wave to the security forces, let alone concrete assistance.

The barracks were in half of an Irish linen mill, behind twenty-foot-high panels of corrugated iron, designed to block the vision of any attacker and to give us some slight protection against the casual lobbing of grenades. Immediately behind the corrugated sheets was a row of cages, each one housing a sniffer dog.

We used the top floor, which had a sangar – a protected observation post – on top of it, reached via a fire-escape. The sangar's armour consisted of breeze blocks, the theory being that if IRA snipers couldn't see you, they wouldn't know where to shoot. And to my increasingly sensitive eye, the only place offering any real protection against the mortar bombs the IRA were now employing with growing frequency seemed to be under a concrete staircase, where 200 of us would have had to huddle in a space that might have comfortably taken a platoon.

Inside this decrepit old building, with no visibility to the outside world, lived all 200, including the Royal Engineer search teams trained to clear roads and houses of bombs. The roof leaked, and big puddles would appear upstairs when it rained. The drying machine either didn't work, or kept you awake if it did. I should know, our room was right next to it – in fact, between it and the telephone box. My main entertainment came from listening to some of the funny phone calls the boys made home to their wives.

There were three others in the room besides me, and it was so messy you could hardly move. Eventually we got rid of two of them and smartened the place up. Everywhere was flimsy hardboard partitioning, and the rooms were cold and horrible. Our whole company was on this one floor. The only social area was the TV room. The best room was earmarked for the signallers – it was warm, with single beds, and provoked a rash of transfer applications from those less fortunate. The sergeants lived in the TV room, and therefore felt entitled to dictate what we watched.

Then there was the 'Choggy Shop', and that was really something else. A bit like an Indian take-away, but without the nice Indian food to take away. It was run by a guy whose culinary repertoire extended to just two items: Choggy burgers, with or without cheese – but always with grease and indigestion. These items of kit were not fit for man or beast.

Below us lived the Close Observation Platoon, weird men who used to hide in bushes and take pictures of sneaky-beaky things. Then there were were the intelligence rooms, where you got briefed up, the company offices and, right downstairs, the gymnasium, together with a big canteen (where the food was remarkably good) and a larger version of the Choggy, with Space Invader machines. In the cookhouse, you could make an 'egg banjo' – an egg sandwich – at any time of day or night. Outside was the guardroom, the heliport and, near the gate, the huts housing the QRF (quick reaction force) and ARF (airmobile reaction force), who manned the PVCP (permanent vehicle checkpoint) which stopped car bombs being driven right into the barracks itself.

We were the heliborne company when we came back from

Berlin, fully experienced in all aspects of helicopter operations. Naturally, this meant that the Army put us on foot patrol for most of our tour. Our routine included 'mill clearance' – patrolling designated areas, up to three miles out, that had to be monitored and checked. We walked, talked to the general public and kept our eyes and ears open. It was just like being a policeman on his beat. To start with, people would come up to us and say, 'Welcome to Northern Ireland, lads.' It had nothing to do with them recognizing fresh faces, but more with the fact that we hadn't yet learned not to dress in full battle order, with all kinds of things hanging from our belts, and our faces completely cammed up. Soon we stopped going out as if we were looking for war, and started wearing just sweat-shirts under our jackets, because they were easier to wash than the horrible regular army-issue shirts. I wouldn't put one of those on a dog.

'Right, lads,' said the sergeant. The barrack gate swung open and he stepped smartly out into the street, his rifle ready in the firing position.

I stepped out behind him when he was the regulation distance ahead. 'Remember now, keep against the wall, and don't make a silhouette of yourself. Take advantage of whatever cover you can find.' His words echoed in my head.

Keep five to ten metres behind him, Weston, not any closer. Then, if one of us in the brick is taken out by a bomb, the rest may escape. And for Christ's sake, remember what else you were taught: if you are fired on, don't fall flat at once – it's much easier for a gunman to hit a stationary target. Look for the nearest cover and get to it, running crooked if you can.

I had been in Northern Ireland for only a short while. But in those few days I had made the mental adjustment that is necessary if you are to stand any sort of chance against an unseen enemy. We were stalked by murderers who can justify any atrocity to themselves, even the killing and maiming of young children and the totally innocent. I knew from Warrenpoint that there were Armalites out there, and that they were looking for soldiers. I could only listen to and follow – for probably the first time in my life – every word of advice my platoon sergeant passed on to me. And start thinking for myself. When it comes down to it, you have only yourself to rely on against an unseen, unknown enemy.

The regulation patrol is in the form of what is called a 'brick'. It consists of a rectangle, at the corners of which are four men. In practice, the formation is almost diamond-shaped, so that no man walks directly in line with, or behind, another. One bullet might kill them both if they did. The brick could fire through a complete 360 degrees, if there was trouble.

We moved along the street, the two soldiers on the right and left at the front swinging their automatic rifles from side to side. You know that a moment's carelessness may cost you your life. Your eyes scan the broken windows, the roof-tops, the boarded doorways, each corner ahead. The two at the rear do the same, turning around constantly as they go.

Our brick commander was Larry, and we were the first out. Our brief was to get to know the area, get used to looking at the map and familiarize ourselves with the reference points, the houses and, most of all, the alleyways.

Alleyways – and ditches and gates and culverts – take on a quite different appearance in your mind's eye when you remember that soldiers have been blown to pieces by bombs placed in or near all of them. Often these bombs have been placed months before the IRA decide to trigger them.

You keep checking. Is the door of that derelict house open when before it was closed? Bombs in derelict houses are one of the worst dangers. Some devices have been set to go off when the front door is opened, others when it is closed again. Some are designed to explode when a floorboard is stepped on, others when the pressure on the board is released. Some are even fixed so they can be detonated by a remote-control device in the nearby hills.

Even to cross an open space, any space, entails a certain risk. You have to concentrate all the time. It is dangerous to think about anything except the matter in hand. Is there something suspicious about the car ahead? Is there a movement behind the curtains of any of the surrounding houses that might indicate the presence of a sniper?

If your patrol suspects a bomb, you seal off the area and call for the experts – the dog-handlers or the engineers, perhaps with a 'wheelbarrow', an electronically controlled, wheeled device that can inspect a bomb, explode it, or even take it to pieces while everyone stays a safe distance away.

We had to gather information for the intelligence boys, too. Was a familiar face missing from its usual haunts, and if so, what was it up to? If a car was parked in a street where it hadn't been an hour before, who did it belong to? Why was it there? If a street-lamp was broken, had it been smashed deliberately to make a dark area when night fell?

On and on you go, picking your way watchfully, almost holding your breath, hoping that the last man in the brick is close enough behind to cover your back. You are always tense and always nervous, until you learn to relax into it. Your eyes are constantly flicking over every window, every door, every dustbin, every alleyway. Always, the alleyways. And always the thought that against instant death there is no possible precaution, except crossing your fingers and praying. It took quite a while to learn to relax.

I was always worried about what might happen if I was careless. I wore an air of arrogance, because I had the weapon, but there was always the feeling that it only took one coward from behind a bush or a rock half a mile away to press a button or pull a trigger and you could be killed.

The thoughts churned around inside my head. If a bomb went off near you, would you feel terrible pain, or would your brain not have time to register as your body was mashed to pulp? The only thing I was sure of was that everyone else burned up just as much nervous energy as I did in concealing their own fear from others. Even good friendships felt strained in the first few weeks. Most of us were not even twenty years old.

After the first patrol, you have to forget the terror and just get on with it. We weren't trained in anything fancy like interrogation or intelligence. But we knew how to use our rifles, a machine gun, a radio and our feet. We knew never to kneel down by a car without people in it, and we knew always to be suspicious of a car with two aerials or with loose wires. Anything unusual was to be treated with great caution and deep suspicion.

The relief when the well-oiled gate at Bessbrook was closed behind us was always immense and immediate. We'd begin to laugh and joke again, after we had removed the ammunition from our rifles, keeping the barrel carefully pointed at the mound of sandbags set up near the entrance for just this purpose. Northern Ireland makes life suddenly seem incredibly worth living. It would be tragic for a soldier, having survived a patrol, to die from a spare round left in a friend's rifle. I was in the guardroom once when a

Marine's GPMG had a negligent discharge. He must have fired half a dozen rounds into the mill wall before controlling the weapon. The bootneck's reward was a hefty fine – and worse, our derision.

Mill clearance and patrols of the 'cuds' – the area around the village – tended to last maybe only three or four hours, starting and ending at variously staggered times to confuse would-be attackers. You could be unlucky and draw a ten- or twelve-hour patrol, or even one lasting almost a week. You could wade through waterlogged or frozen ground and then stay holed up in it for four or five days. You could lose all feeling in your feet for up to a fortnight afterwards. And sometimes not just your feet.

We also did sangar duty in the breeze-block pill-box by the front gate and on the helipad. This got boring – and that was when it was dangerous. You're staring through binoculars all the time, checking the number plates of passing vehicles to see if they've been stolen. You're supposed to keep the list of numbers in a notepad, but your mind goes numb. Most of the time you're just thinking about the fact that nine-inch breeze-block walls are no protection if a gunman opens up with an Armalite on the off-chance of hitting an invisible target. And as for a machine-gunner raking the pill-box, well, that keeps you alert. Sangar duty lasted two hours. Then you'd try to grab a bit of sleep before you were back on stag again for another two.

Other times we'd go out and set up a VCP (vehicle checkpoint) by walking in front of every car that turned the corner and asking to see identification. We'd question the driver and passengers closely – and with great courtesy – about where they had come from, where they were going, and when they were likely to be coming back. NITAT would have been proud of us.

In general, the company's job was to watch everything. Time off was virtually non-existent, until one day I said to our platoon sergeant, Bryn Samuels, 'Is there any chance I could have half an hour to myself?'

'OK,' said the sergeant, much to my surprise, and gave me a day off.

It bought me a few precious hours on my own, while everyone else went off to man the security cordon for some explosives that were going into the quarry at Newton Hamilton. I rested, and pressed my kit. It felt like the first time I had slept since I got there.

You were always too busy during the day, and at other times you had to contend with patrols trooping back in and people crashing around. Nobody had a set hour. Multiple bricks (patrols three or four times larger than normal) might come in at 2.00 in the morning or the afternoon.

We were never allowed out of the compound when we were off duty, and I can only recall wearing civilian clothes once, when I went on a mail run up to Belfast. There was never much time off anyway. You always seemed to be either briefing or debriefing, washing your kit or cleaning your weapons and checking the ammunition for water, rust and grit, to prevent a dreaded jam if you were in a firefight.

In our few hours off, we would kick a football around or go to the gymnasium. Videos had just come out then, and there was a big campaign back home to buy them for 'our boys in Northern Ireland'. Our machine was set up in the TV room, and woe betide anyone except the storeman who tried to touch it. At other times the lads played cards or, having saved up their beer ration, drank six or seven cans in one go, slept it off, and then went back on duty. For the first time in my army career, I never touched a drop all the time I was in Northern Ireland. I had learned from my training in Norfolk.

Moments of light relief were few and far between. Our hearts went out to one poor bloke who earned himself a hard time after falling down a quarry. He was taken in for a check-up, and the Para major who saw him said he was all right and pronounced him fit for service. He continued to make the odd reference to the pain in his damaged elbows, so the sergeants made him shine the floors using a 'bumper' – a big pole with a heavy piece of metal on one end and a wooden board bolted across it, with a broom. It's a tough process at the best of times, so we almost sympathized when he still continued to complain, now a little more vehemently. Eventually, to humour him, a sergeant took him off for an X-ray. It was discovered that the bones in both his elbows had been chipped in the fall.

I couldn't believe my luck when I was given four days' R and R at Christmas time, and allowed to spend it in Wales – although I nearly didn't get there, because the driver taking us to the airport got 'stuck' at a Christmas party and we had to find a replacement.

It felt very strange leaving Northern Ireland without my

weapon, and even stranger walking the streets at home unarmed. When I went out to do my Christmas shopping, I couldn't stop myself looking everywhere, scanning the roof-tops, avoiding parked cars with multiple aerials and slowing every time I approached an alleyway.

I had the feeling for the first time that I was something that other people weren't. Not in any sense superior; quite the opposite, in fact. I was vulnerable. Soldiers got blown up in their home towns as well.

My good luck continued, because when it came to going back I was delayed by a day, because an engine came off the wing of our aircraft and scattered itself all over the runway. (Thank God I wasn't on the plane. This thrill I was to experience later.) A few hours out of Northern Ireland felt like a lifetime. My only regret about being away then was that I missed the sight of one of the finest traditions of the British Army, the officers serving us men our Christmas dinner in our own dining-room, and pouring us our drinks.

In the year before my arrival in Northern Ireland there had been several major incidents, apart from Warrenpoint, involving the deaths of British soldiers. Looking back, we were lucky not to suffer any major disaster during our tour of duty. Our Company only ever encountered minor riots, whereas 2 Company in Newry were fire-bombed, and other units were sniped at. However, we were involved in a number of situations that did raise my pulse rate a beat or two.

One day a bomb went off in our area, on the main Belfast–Newry road. It was teeming with rain. A flat-bed lorry with hay bales on the back had been sighted parked at the roadside, but no one had taken any notice. One lad had even run his hand along the side of it. Unbeknown to the patrol, a 350-pound bomb was hidden in the hay. Luckily for them, the IRA's target was not the soldiers on patrol, but two four-ton lorries. Perhaps they hoped that they would be full of squaddies. Instead, they were full of our rations. Never has a load of meat pies been so valuable. When the last of the lorries went past, the bomb was detonated. The driver, Pete Oldfield, lost an eye, but the soldier in the back, snuggled down amongst the rations, was – amazingly – unscathed. Except that he was covered from head to foot in gravy.

The blast was big enough to shake the foundations of the

heliport where I was. My bottom was blowing bubbles; I was terrified. Then adrenalin took over and we were in the helicopters and up and gone. We jumped out at the site of the explosion, hit the deck, and the medical team went forward. The rest of us fanned out and formed a protective cordon.

We never caught the cowards who placed the bomb.

Another pulse-enhancer was when about 150 young lads began throwing bricks and petrol bombs at us. We were patrolling in the freezing snow with a couple of RUC men, when we heard all these youngsters starting to whistle. One of the RUC chaps turned around and said to me, 'Trouble.'

Next thing we knew, over came the stones and bottles. The kids ran tauntingly close to us because they knew we couldn't shoot them. Our hands were tied, and they knew it.

Lots of men have been severely hurt by stone-throwers, and your first reaction is fear. Certainly my trousers were only a hair's breadth away from a visit to the cleaners. How do you defend yourself? You can't shoot, you can't throw stones back.

Then a surge of adrenalin comes to your rescue. The knowledge that there is no other way out but to fight tends to focus the mind wonderfully. You get angry as the adrenalin pumps round, because you know this could be more than just a few kids running around giving you a hard time, it could be a mask for a shooting, the classic smokescreen for a sniper attack. There were occasions in Northern Ireland when I cocked my weapon – and would have used it – and this was one of them.

The kids ran into the community centre and we ran after them. But when we got to the door, the manager wouldn't let us in.

'No way,' he said. 'No one's in here.' I didn't know whether he was terrified or stupid.

We barged in anyway, threw ourselves at the door, took it off its hinges. Hot pursuit, it's called. We found ourselves in this huge hall where hundreds of people were playing bingo. There were kids in there, sixteen or seventeen years old, and the adults swore blind they'd been in there for the last six hours – even the ones with wet hair and snow on their jackets. The police could only arrest those without adults to lie for them. We went into the Gents: nothing. Then, along with the police, we checked the Ladies. We peered under each cubicle door, but all we could see were rows of women's legs, two per cubicle, and all facing forwards in the regulation position. The police sergeant asked the women to open the doors. One of them refused.

'Kick the door in,' shouted the sergeant.

Any embarrassment we might have felt at carrying out this order soon disappeared when we found the kids we were looking for – standing off the floor, feet astride the toilet bowl.

It's a wicked situation over there, but it's not a wicked place. The country is beautiful; there are lots of good people, lots of frightened people – and, in the shape of the IRA, a tiny minority of very evil people.

The IRA never care who they hit, or how many, as long as they hit the headlines. That's all a soldier or a bullet or a bomb is to them, a part of their publicity machine. But the British Army is only there because they've been ordered there. It's always governments that do the starting and the finishing of things, it's never the British soldier; he just does what he's told.

The farmers of South Armagh are the salt of the earth. It's not us they're terrified of, we don't tar and feather them or shoot away their kneecaps. It'll never end now, because they've indoctrinated the youngsters, and, once formed, you can't change these opinions. It's just a pity that we soldiers are the ones left in the middle.

6

KENYA

We went back to Pirbright, and in a disco in Guildford one night I met Sue. A whole crowd of us had gone there to let our hair down a bit after Northern Ireland. I was drunk and looking up her friend's skirt, lying flat on my back, pretending to be a film cameraman. She thought I was disgusting. Some of the boys wanted to nickname me Slug at the time, which didn't impress me, but she thought it was appropriate.

Brian Shanklin was there – nicknamed Big Bird because of his nose – and Gary Williams 45 – known as Geldof, because he thought he was dead cool – and Phil Hicks – called Omar, because the RMP girl he was with once said he looked like Omar Sharif. (We wanted to call him Captain Ahab, the one who shot Moby Dick, because she looked like a great white whale, but we restrained ourselves.)

The four of us somehow got fighting with double figures of REME (the Royal Electrical and Mechanical Engineers). Gary Williams dragged Sue out, as if she was with him, and he got away with it. Shanklin grabbed her friend, Omar grabbed any girl – and I got arrested. The police shouted at me, and told me to get out of Guildford as fast as I could. I did.

That was the first time I saw Sue. The next time was when I asked her out, and she said yes. I met her again months later, when I was a lot slimmer, and that was it. She fell in love with me, and I with her.

I saw Sue as ofen as I could then. If I wasn't with the lads, I'd be with her. She worked for the Earl of Onslow as a groom, and I'd often make my way over to his estate at the end of the day. One night I proposed, and she accepted. Her dad had been in the RAF for many years, so she knew I would be away quite a bit. It didn't seem to worry her. It was in a dark corner of the same disco where I had first met her – a real seedy dive – that I popped the question.

She was a lovely lass, she was a cracker, a wonderful person. Best of all, she loved having a laugh. I enjoyed her company so much, felt so good with her, there was nothing to do but ask her to marry me.

I was only nineteen. Her family thought it was highly amusing. Almost as funny as me making myself a chip butty in their house. I phoned Mam, who said, 'Congratulations.' What could she say? I'm sure she thought, 'You're a fool, you're too young.' I *was* too young to make that sort of commitment – but at the time, you can't be told.

I didn't have much time to consider what I'd done. The Army had obviously had its eye on me, and had singled me out for a very special mission.

What do you do with a soldier who's completed his first tour of duty in Northern Ireland and has just come back to barracks after his leave? Well if you're the Army, you now put him in charge of preparing an area for the camels at the Royal Tournament at Earls Court. Then you let him go home for the weekend, taking his overalls with him for his mam to wash, and the result is the evacuation of half of Nelson.

Luckily I wasn't confined to camel duty for too long. The options were: security duty, work party, or fatigue party. I was lucky, I was put into the work party. Apart from other jobs, my personal responsibility was keeping the red carpet in a fit state for royalty and VIPs to walk on.

This is not as easy or cushy as it sounds. Moments before an important arrival, I would just be adding the finishing touches to my immaculate carpet when across it would walk some grotty member of the public, leaving sawdust footprints everywhere. And everyone else seemed to meet the royalty, everyone except me. I'd always be doing something else.

In our off-duty moments we used to ride around on pallet trolleys, which we jacked up and rode as scooters, with two people aboard for double leg-power. You had to rely on the person in front to steer properly, and the result was many an unscheduled 'parking', and much skin off our elbows. One pair drove straight through a partition wall.

My finest moment came when the drill sergeant was showing round three new members of 3 Company. Several of us had been detailed to paint the walls of the quarters where the Kenyan Army band were going to sleep. Among those present were Geldof, Big Bird and young Omar.

We started the job well enough, but then one or two tiny flecks of paint failed to connect with the wall and landed on one or two of the boys instead, and one thing soon led to another. It was *shlop*! on the face, and *whack*! on the overalls. Within minutes we were brushing all over other people's backs, duelling and jousting with twelve-inch paintbrushes. Unfortunately, the drill sergeant chose this moment to arrive with the newcomers.

'Weston! Come here!' He looked at me, he looked at the impressionable new recruits, and he looked back at me. 'Look at him,' he said at length. 'Now, boys, what I'm going to say to you should have a bearing on the whole of the rest of your lives. This,' he went on, pointing his swagger-stick at my chest, 'is a Guardsman from 3 Company. Try, with all your might, never to emulate him.'

There was a trail of sticky paint footprints as I marched smartly away.

In the Army, when confronted with a job you'd rather not do, either you can bluff your way out of it or you can go to the NAAFI. Nine times out of ten no one is hurt by this; there are always enough people around for the job to get done. And soldiers get paid pretty poorly when you consider they're on duty twenty-four hours a day, seven days a week, fifty-two weeks a year.

After Earls Court, I was lucky enough, and large enough, to find a universal get-out for most duties: tug-of-war. I played most of the summer for the battalion, then went straight into the rugby squad. I only had to do proper duties for four months of the year, and played rugby for the rest. It was a sportsman's dream.

I'd played for the Guards depot senior side when I was a junior, as a hooker. I was only sixteen then, and I used to run like hell with the ball because I was scared stiff of them. I got punched during one game by a sergeant.

'You're boring through,' he snarled.

'No I'm not,' I said meekly, rubbing my jaw. 'It's just that your side isn't binding properly.'

'Is that right?' he said, drawing back his fist again. 'Well bind this . . .' The punch landed, and my memory of the rest of the game is a bit clouded.

The Army Cup was a great occasion when I was in the Guards.

KENYA

There was a wonderful atmosphere at our semi-final, with plenty of soldiers from the regiment turning out to watch. Half the battalion must have been there that day, some 600 men. Even though I was reserve, I can remember the tense warm-up, the smell of the changing-rooms, of liniment, and the sight of everyone going through his own little quirks: Para Pete, mad as a hatchet, swallowing Vaseline to coat his throat and stop himself feeling thirsty; me just dabbing it behind my ears as protection if we came down too tight, and applying thick tubular bandages to my feet because the studs used to come up through my boots.

We'd trained very hard for this opportunity, much of the time on a huge manmade sandhill.

'Look at Squeaky go up there,' I can remember Bill 'Sledge' Evans laughing. 'Remember at the beginning of the season, he couldn't even run a bath!'

Every game was a big game if you were playing for the regiment. I took it very seriously. Some didn't – they were so talented they didn't need to. When everyone in the team hit form, we played some remarkable rugby. We'd played strong teams of the day, like Maesteg Celtic and Southampton University, and won.

Against Maesteg Celtic I played the best game of my rugby career. I made a thirty-yard rush after taking the ball from the front of the line. They'd taken it cleanly but I managed to steal in, robbed it, peeled off and went blind down the wing. I bulldozed a winger out of the way, the full-back came over and tried to tackle me but ended up dislocating his shoulder after half taking me round the neck.

'Play for yourself,' Sergeant Cliff Elley had said to us before the game. 'But when you need to play as a team, play as a team.'

When you make a break like that, it's up to the rest of the team to catch up with you.

I transferred round about this time to support company, mortar platoon, because they had been so depleted by people leaving. I found myself among vagabonds and rebels. God, the instructors had their work cut out getting us into shape. They bounced us from morning to night, inspecting this, inspecting that. But at the end of eight weeks of solid training we knew our jobs and we were functioning as a team. Now we could go out to Kenya and practise our new-found skills.

We flew out from Brize Norton in October 1981. We landed at

Nairobi, loaded ourselves into wagons, and I rode shotgun in the secure Land Rover that was carrying our small-arms ammunition. One of the Kenyans we drove past looked a bit strange to the unsophisticated Welsh eye. This chap, clearly a businessman, was dressed in a well-cut suit that looked really dapper – until you checked him out below knee-level, and saw that the bottoms of his trouser legs were missing, and the gaps covered by a pair of Wellington boots.

Except for the insects and the dust, Kenya was a marvellous place. As ever, I couldn't handle the sun, and developed a sore and itchy prickly-heat rash. We went to our holding post, transferred into jungle fatigues, and then it was on to Nanooki at the base of Mount Kenya for two days, the start of eight superb weeks of training. Some people didn't enjoy it at all. I loved the newness, the wildness, the openness, the freeness; there appeared to be no law out there in the bush.

In Kenya we had five firing areas, way up in the north, away from people and wildlife. Transport could be a bit different: the anti-tanks had to be mule-packed in. There was so much open space, we could even live-fire our mortars on charge 8, the highest allowable, and use Milans with high-explosive warheads. Some of the more experienced mortarmen had a crack at shooting down a tree on an escarpment miles away. It took them just seven rounds, without sights. Impressive stuff.

Cold mornings, cool nights, sand, insects, boiling-hot days: these are my enduring memories of Kenya; plus little tiny bags of horrible Kenyan crisps, and Tusker and White Cap beer. I remember the lack of water when we went to a place called Archer's Post; and the baboons at Mpala Farm, a solid building used as the armoury and quarters for the officers and NCOs. If you wanted to go to the toilet at night, you needed an armed guard. The baboons loved the latrines, which made performing your bodily functions not exactly the pleasurable pastime it used to be. They would go for you, and they can kill. I went down once, opened the door – and there one was. I ran like hell. I peed against the back of the officers' quarters after that.

At Archer's Post, a chap called Gee from Manchester – Fred, we called him, after Fred Gee of *Coronation Street* – went off to the thunderbox one day and a snake reared its head and hissed at him. All we could hear were screams of 'Boys, boys, help!'

Poor Fred, he was about two stone lighter by the time we got to him. We threw rocks and the snake slithered off into the bush.

We were visited too by massive scorpions. One lad stuck his machete down a scorpion's hole, and we heard the chink of its sting on the metal. Another lad, Norman Jones, decided to wear a face-veil one night. 'Nothing'll get to me in this kit,' he said. When he woke up in the morning there was a scorpion tangled up in the veil, no more than a quarter of an inch from his face. Norman froze – and he was still frozen when we went to find him an hour later because he hadn't turned up for breakfast.

At night we played charades – and a highly original game called 'bomber run'. This involved picking up big beetles in the beam of your torch as they lumbered overhead in the darkness; then more and more 'searchlights' would lock on to the unfortunate beast – and finally, so too would a heavy salvo of boots. It was lucky for us that all the boots were marked, because each twenty-man marquee sent up its own wall of flak, and the pile of spent ammunition to be sorted through in the morning was mountainous.

We pitched our bivvies one night near a magnificent safari house, specially designed for American tourists who liked their Africa comfortable. The owners gave us an enormous meal and we fell asleep by the open fire because we weren't used to the warmth. I drank Bacardi and Coke because it was the most sophisticated thing I could think of. Some of the lads slipped off for a quiet midnight dip in the swimming-pool. The owners rushed out when they heard what was happening, shouting that at night the pool was taken over by snakes and nasty insects. The boys came out of the water like submarine-launched Polaris missiles.

Ants were everywhere, all the time. Once, staying on a game reserve, we had to move the kitchen about six times because they kept finding it. Then we moved it a seventh time and they found my tent. I slept the rest of the night standing up against a tree.

The mortars played football against the Kenyan Army and got stuffed 10–1. Then we played the staff of the safari house that had given us the meal, and we lost 5–1. The rugby team won all their matches, though, including the one against the President's XV.

I remember steak sandwiches in Nanooki that cost next to nothing. An elephant scratching himself against the side of our four-tonner and making it rock so much that it nearly tipped over.

The day I trod on a thorn about six inches long, which went straight through my shoe and my foot – one of the chaps had to pull it out with his teeth. And the night a few of us got merry and tried to jump higher than the natives during a tribal dance. It was the greatest fun I had had since Berlin, and as far as I was concerned, army life was going from strength to strength.

We went back to Pirbright in December 1981. The rugby team had to do some public duties at weekends, but not much. We worked hard enough during the week: we won every cup we went in for, we delivered the goods. Our final tournament, though, the army seven-a-sides, was cut dramatically short.

Thousands of miles away, on 19 March 1982, a group of scrap-metal workers had stepped ashore at Leith Harbour in a place called South Georgia, in defiance of all British customs and immigration requirements. When the authorities at the tiny settlement at Grytviken demanded that they either obtain a visa or leave, the demolition gang suddenly decided that their visit was one of international importance. Two weeks later, despite fierce opposition from a small contingent of Royal Marines, Argentinian troops successfully invaded the Falkland Islands.

'Let the world be under no illusion,' I heard John Nott say on the radio while I was at home in Wales on leave. 'These people are British. We mean to defend them. We are in earnest and no one should doubt our resolve.'

It certainly put the kibosh on the 1982 army seven-a-side tournament.

In the following hectic weeks of preparation, the Task Force was put together. If you were involved, this was the moment you had been training for. But being left behind, as we were, was awful. We knew that as soldiers we were as good as anyone else in the British Army, and we felt we had been cheated of the chance to prove it.

The Welsh Guards had just come off a six-week period as spearhead battalion for the UK, which meant that we had been on twenty-four-hour standby for anywhere we might be needed. When the Falklands conflict flared up, we suddenly found ourselves part of 5 Infantry Brigade. The brigade was officially designated Britain's 'out of area' force, earmarked for operations outside north-west Europe, and comprised 2 Para, 3 Para and 1st/ 7th Duke of Edinburgh's Own Gurkha Rifles. But on 2 April the

Paras were transferred to 3 Commando Brigade, and in their place came us Welsh Guardsmen, together with 2 Bn Scots Guards. Things were looking up. We began training in earnest.

On 22 April we went to Sennybridge in the Brecon Beacons for Exercise Welsh Falcon: two weeks of battalion attacks, intensive live firing, helicopter movements with Pumas, and practice amphibious assaults. To a humble Guardsman used to government cut-backs and tight-fisted quartermasters, Welsh Falcon was unbelievable. It suddenly seemed that we could have any stores we wanted, and any facilities. We practised with our mortars on ranges that normally we would never have been able to get on to, with ammunition that we would never have been able to procure. I'd never seen so many helicopters in all my life. It was like something out of Vietnam. I can still remember the constant 'wop-wop' sound as they swooped and hovered over the Welsh hills, and the hot, eye-watering blast of Avtur aviation fuel exhaust that hit you every time you jumped on or off.

It's tough sometimes as a soldier to convince yourself that you're training for something that is really going to happen. Berlin was like that – it was very hard to get into a state of mind that made you think the Russians were going to stream across the border the next morning. Now the training felt as if it was for real, but we still had no particular thoughts about going to war. We weren't. War didn't exist. It only really came home to us when we said goodbye to Jed, the farmer's son from west Wales who had become a great army mate.

I have such a vivid memory of that parting on the parade ground, just before we stepped on to the coaches that were to take us to Southampton.

I'd spent that last evening with Sue. We'd been given strict orders to be back in camp by 11.00 p.m., because the battalion would be leaving by midnight. I got a taxi from Clandon, the Earl of Onslow's estate, and arrived back to find tension hanging over the barracks. Everyone felt it. People kept getting on other people's nerves. My best friend, Yorkie, came close to assaulting one of the NCOs.

I finished packing and went down to get on parade. Jed was there, but he wasn't in uniform. He was leaving the Army on a compassionate discharge; his dad hadn't been well for a long time, and the family needed him to keep the farm going. Jed's discharge had been granted only days before the whole Falklands business started.

We delayed boarding the coaches for as long as we could. Jed was upset; we were all upset. Big rough-tough soldiers that we were, he and I got hold of each other and shared a hug.

'So long, Jed, be lucky. See you when we get back,' I said.

His shoulders were hunched and there were tears in his eyes. 'Look after yourself, Wes,' he said simply.

It was one of the saddest moments of my army career. We all knew how much he wanted to come with us. He had an obligation to his kith and kin, but we felt that we were a special family too. And now the family was breaking up.

It was then, for the first time, that I felt that something was not going to be right when we came back. I can't explain it, but I know the feeling was the same for the rest of the gang.

We drove south through the night. There was plenty of cheek and banter, with many of my fellow Guardsmen acting rough-tough and warry-tory. Nobody wanted to be on that bus, but it was what we were paid to do; it was our job. There was no particular emotion at the forefront of my mind as I dozed; I was so used to the Army saying do this, do that, it was almost a day like any other. I certainly wasn't thinking about war – probably because I didn't want to think about it. Like most of the others, I was too aware of what the terrible reality might be. It wouldn't be John Wayne.

The mood on the bus was very mixed: some people were gambling, others just wanted to be left alone with their thoughts or to go to sleep.

I woke up as we neared Southampton and it was just getting light. It was a dirty old morning, drizzly and foggy, but by about 9.00 it had brightened up.

All the kit had been laid out on the dockside; you had to find yours and put it with the rest of your platoon's. Then, in true army fashion, there followed a good few hours of 'Hurry up and wait.'

We queued up inside a huge hangar, waiting for the order to get on the ship. We were in platoons, baggage piled up around us in all the luggage-bays, everyone with their arms full of gear. Everyone was fed up with the waiting; we just wanted to get aboard, unpack, and get back on deck and wave at people. But I suppose you can't mobilize 3,000 men without hitches. Eventually, we shuffled outside and dragged our mountains of equipment up the gangplank.

The press and media people almost outnumbered the Task Force. They tried to snatch interviews as we moved. One lad – and there is a record of this on film – said, 'I'm proud to be going to do for my country what I should be doing.' What he omitted to tell the reporter was that he'd gone AWOL, and it was only three days ago that the military police had finally caught up with him.

We were allocated berths and then called together to be given our briefings – told what we could and couldn't do, where we could and couldn't go. Needless to say, nobody really took much notice. The majority of our heavy equipment was to be stowed inside a big bay in the middle of the ship, and we needed a guide to show us the way. You would soon have got lost without one. The QE2 was just like an enormous floating hotel – stripped of all its trimmings and trappings: even the carpets were hidden beneath layers of cardboard to protect them from the barbarians.

There was almost a carnival atmosphere below decks. You'd have thought everyone had just been de-mobbed, not mobilized for war. As far as we were concerned, we were just going for a trip on the QE2, the most luxurious ocean liner in the world. Ahead, we hoped, lay many weeks of magnificent food and drink and relaxation. That was enough for most of us for the time being.

The sun came out and I went up on deck to see if I could see Sue. I was hoping desperately that she might have managed to get the day off to come and see her soldier off to war.

The scenes below the ship were amazing. The dockside was thick with people – thousands of them, it looked like, possibly tens of thousands. Everywhere I looked there were Union Jacks and gigantic handwritten signs saying 'Good Luck Dave' and 'Gary We Love You.' Red, white and blue streamers were being waved by the hundred, and enormous net-loads of multicoloured balloons were released. But Sue's face was nowhere to be seen.

Men said goodbye to their wives and children, their mums and dads and loved ones. Families had travelled miles – in some cases hundreds of miles – just to watch the ship pull out. Tough sergeants were surprised to find tears in their eyes, but not ashamed.

In amongst the sadness of the farewells there were some lighter moments, scenes that are now probably familiar to everybody in the country because of the coverage on television. A kissagram girl cavorted about in fish-net stockings, getting a fair bit of attention from the boys on board. Then someone's wife peeled off her bra, and the dockers put it on a crane-hook and winched it over. But mostly, people just waved or cried, or both.

I was at the top of the ship, sitting on a lifeboat winch, still scanning the upturned faces below me for Sue, when I spotted Mam. My grandfather was there too, and my stepdad, Loft. Gran hadn't made it; later, I found out that the emotion had been just too much for her. I waved my cap until Mam saw me. She cupped her hands to her mouth to make herself heard, but it was no good. She had to use signs and mouth the words to ask me if I had my St Christopher on, the medal she had bought to keep me safe in Northern Ireland. I nodded and she looked relieved. I didn't tell her, but I didn't actually have it on, it was sitting in my pocket.

Then she signed, 'I love you,' and I suddenly felt more guilt and remorse than I'd ever felt in my life. I realized that this might be the last time I ever saw the three of them, and there had been times when I'd treated them so badly.

I knew in that moment that I'd never forgive myself for not having given Mam the one or two moments of decent farewell that she would have loved and remembered for the rest of her life. It suddenly seemed I had behaved disgracefully to her and to others who loved me, and it was too late to make amends.

I had gone back early off my leave, and had spent my last few hours with Sue rather than with my family. To Gran I had simply said, 'So long' – no more – as if I was going down the road for a bag of chips. My only excuse was that I thought it would be over well before we got there; it never really occurred to me at the time that anything serious could happen. It wasn't part of my master-plan.

I felt I had short-changed that smashing little group down there on the dockside. I didn't think I had given them the time or the respect they deserved. And if I died, it would be without having told them that I loved them.

I could see that my mam was crying, and that my grandsha had a cold again; he always has one when he's emotional. Then I think there must have been a bit of a breeze straight into my face, because my eyes started to water and I had to turn away. I can't remember anything else that we said to each other. What can you say to a son who's going to war? 'Come back safe.' 'Keep your head down.' What advice can you give?

Sue never came. But Mam was there.

Tugs and pleasure-boats sounded their sirens. Songs were tried from the quayside as well as the decks; some died the death, some were taken up. 'You'll Never Walk Alone.' 'Rule Britannia.' And, naturally, 'Land of Hope and Glory'. It was all unbelievably moving.

I felt an enormous lump in my throat, and waved even more frantically. Then the band started playing 'Auld Lang Syne', and the first thing I thought was, God, I hate this tune. It means that some of us won't be coming back.

To the strangely haunting sound of 'Sailing', the ropes were slipped and the QE2 edged slowly away from the quayside. We lined the rails shoulder to shoulder, catching our last glimpses of the people we loved, the families, the wives holding up small children for a final farewell wave. Tugs and small private boats buzzed around us like flies as we moved out into Southampton Water. Fire-tugs sent plumes of spray high into the air until we nosed carefully down the channel past the river-mouth at Beaulieu and the old army mental hospital at Netley. Soon after the accompanying flotilla had turned back, we all went down below, and the distant cheering from the jetties and small boats had already become a special memory. We all had work to do, and none of our officers wanted us to wallow in the sadness.

None of us really accepted what was happening. It was unreal. We didn't see it in the context of Northern Ireland or any other conflict. None of us had actually been in a full-scale war.

I just thought briefly about where we were going and what we were going to do and what might happen, but with no thoughts of horror or carnage or pain or suffering. I was a soldier. There was a wrong to be righted. Then, for some odd reason, I remembered the pictures that had been broadcast on television of the crowds in the main square in Buenos Aires. It occurred to me that except for the banners and the red, white and blue streamers I'd seen on the dockside, it was almost impossible to distinguish between our lot and theirs.

7

SAILING SOUTH

At the docks in Southampton, one of the Welsh Guards, Chris Duggan, had put up a banner that read: 'Mrs Thatcher, thank you for our holiday cruise.' We all thought the war would be over by the time we got there.

'Bet you a penny to a pound we'll end up as the brass-collecting team,' Yorkie said gloomily. 'Picking up all the spent cartridges, putting them in sacks and weighing them.'

'How much does the Army get back on the empties, then?' I asked our sergeant, Cliff Elley.

'About enough to buy breakfast and a haircut, Squeaky.'

'Or feed the rest of the battalion for the whole campaign,' Yorkie grinned.

It seems extraordinary now, but we celebrated every time we heard that an Argentinian plane had been blown up. It meant that something was still happening, it would still be there for us when we arrived.

On 25 April South Georgia had been retaken by elements of the Royal Marines, in conjunction with the Special Boat Squadron and the SAS. I wondered at the time if Buenos Aires would see the light and pull out, but on the day after the Total Exclusion Zone came into being on 30 April, the airfield at Port Stanley was bombed by the first Vulcan raid. Then the Sea Harriers from the carrier group went into action.

News had filtered through that the Argentinian cruiser *General Belgrano* had been sunk by a British submarine. I was shocked. The extensive loss of life was not known straightaway, but when it was gradually learned that between 300 and 400 sailors had been killed when the warship went down, we all felt sad for the families of those men. The British quarrel was with a junta in Buenos Aires, not with people like that. There was another sobering thought: what a British submarine could do to an Argentinian cruiser, an

Argentinian submarine could do to a British ship. Two days later HMS *Sheffield* was hit by an Exocet missile. She was mortally damaged and abandoned to sink. Twenty-one men lost their lives. Many others were appallingly burned or injured.

The loss of the *Sheffield* to a solitary air-launched missile — against which she was purpose-built to defend herself — rang warning bells in my head. I suddenly felt less confident about the eventual outcome of the war, more conscious of my own mortality. Amongst the lads there was less talk now of giving them a good hiding. The Argentinian air force, at least, had proved that it had teeth. And it was to the air force, I felt sure, that the surface ships would prove most vulnerable.

We still felt in limbo. War hadn't even been declared; the 'conflict' had sprung from a military dictator's time-honoured attempt to take his people's minds off the political and financial problems he had created for them at home. Me, I went down to the Falklands to stop a regime telling people that they couldn't be British.

Like a lot of the lads, I never had gung-ho expectations of the Falklands war. We were correcting a wrong. If a diplomatic solution had been found, then wonderful, I don't think anyone would have complained one jot. But as things stood, we felt we had to step in, tell the playground bully to pick on someone his own size. And that attitude, really, marked the extent of our political view. The squaddies of the Welsh Guards weren't really into the Whitehall dance routine. We were just good soldiers — well, as good as any other regiment.

We slept three men to a cabin — two in single beds, the other on a camp-bed. The singles were arranged along the seaward wall, and to one side was a counter with a wash-basin, dressing-table and mirror. I hate to criticize Cunard, but that cabin was not as spacious as it might have been when it came to three lusty soldiers trying to clean their kit at the same time, or stow it in their bergens. Those jobs were best done out in the hallway, even if it did mean bringing all other traffic to a standstill.

The first night was all banter and madness, and we were allowed two tins of drink apiece. It was a laugh, but early next morning the Captain's voice came over the tannoy: 'Gentlemen, the crewmen's bar is now out of bounds.' The crew were friendly enough; I think they were just worried that their stocks might be exhausted before we even got outside British territorial waters. The main off-duty activity switched to buying crates of lager and getting drunk in your bunk. Nobody seemed to mind that – least of all, I suspect, the manager of the *QE2*'s off-licence. Personally, I didn't touch a drop. I didn't drink beer at that time, only cider, and they didn't sell it. For me, as the trip went on, the highlight of cabin life became the crate of Coca-Cola that we always kept in the bottom drawer, and the ice-making machine that we had working flat out. Believe me, after a hard day's preparing for war, a pint or two of Coke and ice really is the real thing.

Life on board soon settled down to a steady routine of training and recreation. Everyone was out for themselves as usual – and besides 1 Bn Welsh Guards, that included 2 Bn Scots Guards, 1st/7th Duke of Edinburgh's Own Gurkha Rifles, 97 Battery Royal Artillery, HQ 4 Field Regiment, 656 Squadron Army Air Corps, 10 Field Workshop REME, 16 Field Ambulance, 81 Ordnance Company and a Forward Air Control Party.

The units were separated by floors. The Gurkhas were right at the bottom, crammed into what looked like ten-man bunks, but they seemed to like roughing it. They were unbelievably amiable. Our officers had the top berths, the best accommodation as usual. The various units would get together in the evenings to play darts in the main hall and discuss the relative merits of their regiments.

The cinemas were good, and whoever had chosen the films had gauged their audience well. We had *The Exterminator* almost on continuous loop. Other entertainment was more homemade. Lads were already falling in love with the cleaning ladies and washroom attendants. Some of them had affairs with the boys – or so the story goes.

We had fitness training all the way south, lap after lap of pristine Cunard deck. It wasn't long before the Captain's voice came over the tannoy: 'Gentleman, would you please wear pumps, the vibration of your boots is damaging my decks.' We all trained together, and support company had more than seventy men in the mortar platoon alone. Then there was the anti-tank platoon, recce platoon, and echelon – about another 120 in all.

Four laps of the *QE2*'s upper deck were equivalent to one mile, so we'd start a PT session with a dozen laps. Then we'd run up and down all the stairwells, right from the bottom of the ship to the top, and back to the bottom. I counted twenty steps per flight, and between twelve and eighteen flights. Running up and down with combat boots on was damned hard; you'd feel sick and dizzy at the top, and then you'd have to run all the way down again. And up, and down, until you'd done ten 'circuits'. People fell down the stairs all the time, but that didn't particularly matter: squaddies are the most shock-proof pieces of equipment ever designed. The lack of fresh air hit me hardest. Even if the exercise finished right at the bottom of the ship, I'd drag myself back up on to the deck to fill my lungs with the stuff.

Our company commander was Major Bonus – a great guy, well liked by all the lads. He stuck with us, and he knew his job. Captain 'Daisy' Dimmock was in charge of the mortars, and he too was a man who knew what he was about. Some of the other officers were tidy enough guys. Others weren't, but you get one or two dough-balls everywhere.

As ever, the real control was in the hands of the sergeants. Our section sergeant was Clifford Elley – a fine soldier and a bloody fine rugby player. His second-in-command was Mark Pemberton, who was in charge of my detachment. In the field, these two NCOs were to be our control post operator (CPO) and assistant CPO.

The mortars were the largest platoon in the battalion, being not far off company strength. Most of the lads had had their run-ins with authority at one time or another. It was all very much 'head west on a fresh horse' in the mortars. But at least nobody stood in awe of anyone else.

There were four sections of fourteen men (including NCOs) to a platoon, with two mortars to a section. In theory that gave us a total of eight 'tubes', but we'd had to lend two to the Scots Guards because they'd forgotten to pack their base-plates. Much later on, I discovered that these were the only Welsh Guards mortars to be fired in anger – on Mount Tumbledown.

My section consisted of me, Yorkie, Colin Parsons, 11 Hughes, Boring Oris (Hugh Trigg), Paul Green, 58 Hughes (Gareth) and seven others. Yorkie was my best friend at the time; I'm godfather to his boy, Andrew Johnston Walker.

My particular detachment comprised 58 Hughes, Colin, 11 Hughes, Yorkie and myself. I'd been in mortars for ten months. I'd already become much closer to those lads than the duty company

I'd previously been with, even though I'd spent less time with them. We lived in each others' rooms. Yorkie was closest, because he and I had played rugby together so much. He had also come to stay once or twice at our house in Wales.

All the way down to the Falklands we seemed to have lessons on every topic from what type of rockflows are hard to walk over and what ground not to put your mortars on (because they'd bounce or you'd lose them) to first-aid skills and Spanish. The basic phrases we were taught would have been pretty useless in combat. Orders like 'You are a prisoner', 'Hands up', 'Put down your weapons' and 'I am a British soldier and you are my prisoner of war' aren't really much help in the heat of battle. The only one I can remember now is 'Manos arriba'.

We were briefed on the state of the Argentinian forces on the ground in the Falklands. A lot was already known about the defences around Port Stanley, the heavy mining of the beaches, and the ridges running into the capital from the west, like Sapper Hill. We could expect to meet the 105-mm howitzer certainly, and perhaps the 155, which out-ranged anything the amphibious force had brought with it. They were also armed with 75-mm, 90-mm and 105-mm RCLs (recoilless rifles), the 105 being a high-explosive anti-tank weapon whose shell could penetrate 400 millimetres of armour. Then there were Bantam and Cobra ATGWs (anti-tank guided weapons). The principal infantry small arms were the Belgian FN – the same calibre and virtually the same weapon as the British SLR – and the FMK 39-mm sub-machine-gun – similar to the Israeli Uzi. In the air, there were Super Etendards and the Pucará, the latter a turbo-prop aircraft basically used by the Argentinians for counter-insurgency. We were told we would have to be particularly wary of the Pucará. Anyone caught out in the open could expect to make his wife a widow. Nobody mentioned the A-4 Skyhawk.

There were lectures too on survival, and on how and when to use morphine and how to treat burns. We also dusted off our standard infantry skills, practising weapon-handling until we were blue in the face, and firing weapons off the front of the ship just to keep our eye in. We had a go at handling mortars with our great big thick arctic gloves on, which seemed like an odd thing to do when the sun is so strong you should be wearing bathing-suits.

The weather got better and better, until all our off-duty moments were spent either sun-bathing – 'bronzing' or 'bronzying' as various other units called it – or playing crab football, a lunatic game with four teams and four goals, played in the QE2's suntrap with its high windows. On some occasions, upwards of 100 men would be playing at the same time, all chasing after the same ball. If anyone had fallen over, it would have meant much more than an early bath – at the very least, a helicopter ride to the hospital ship, or more likely, a burial at sea.

Then, at 6.00 in the evening, everything would stop for dinner. It was so civilized, and so unreal. I found it very hard at such times to convince myself that 5 Brigade were going to war.

By the time we reached Freetown in Sierra Leone we were having a lot of fun. Some of the boys took it a little too far, hanging over the rails and making coins red-hot with their cigarette-lighters before throwing them down for the locals to catch. We sailed into the harbour past the wrecks of other ships, and a swarm of bum-boats clustered around the hull within minutes of us docking. Because of the danger of infection and disease, trading with the native pedlars was banned. That was a pity, because they were offering us not only fresh fruit and coconuts, but also a natty line in native spears, and even monkeys. Instead of haggling, some of the troops amused themselves with the coin trick, or by tossing down hexamine blocks from their personal cooking stoves, covered in camouflage cream, and watching the recipients take a bite. I walked away and went down to my bunk. The powers that be had kept us fit, but they hadn't kept us particularly entertained. The men's aggression was growing; it needed an outlet, and this wasn't it.

We weren't allowed ashore, either. A lot of the lads were disgruntled, but I wasn't. The air was hot and wet, and Freetown looked to me to be no more than a shanty town, thinning out in the distance where the hills were thick with tropical vegetation.

There was an Argentinian ship in the harbour, and a Russian trawler. I'd never realized until then that a simple fishing vessel needed quite so many aerials. Nor, until they trailed us all the way down to South Georgia, that fishing grounds could be quite so far-ranging.

The mood changed after Freetown. The sigh of 'We'll never get there' became the alarmed 'Jesus, we're going all the way.'

Everyone tuned in to the World Service news for a fair and honest account of the war. Apart from the radio, all there was in the way of aural entertainment was the officers' idea of rock music – 'Roll Over Beethoven' with string quartet and lead soprano. The lads wanted to hear something else – anything that wasn't some cheap cover version of what was originally a good song – but the officers said no. The piped music became a kind of torture.

'I hope it *is* all over before we get there,' I seem to remember thinking as we sailed further south, 'but I hope we're *not* picking up all the spent cartridges.'

Until two years before, I'd never thought much about anything before doing it. Now, some of the implications of what I'd embarked on were slowy sinking in, and I felt a long way from home.

We arrived at Ascension Island, where Major General Jeremy Moore and his staff came abroad to join us for the rest of the trip. I don't think he was informed that I was on board; he certainly didn't pop down to my cabin to discuss strategy over a glass or two of Coke.

We sailed on southwards, through wonderfully calm seas. One day I went up on deck for a breath of fresh air and found myself under a clear and very, very pale blue sky, moving through dark, dark water, with no waves, only slight ripples. Mirrored in the sea were a hundred white-blue icebergs. They looked incredible. It was cold, but not freezing, and everyone on the deck just walked and thought, in silence. To a man, I know we were deeply moved by what we saw, and the beauty and size and sheer brooding menace of these great white tower-blocks somehow brought home to us what we were involved in, and what we were about to do. Nobody spoke. After a while, when the cold began to get to us, we all went back inside. In a strange way, it was as if we all now knew what had to be done; the decision had been made, and we had to get on with it. There was no room for discussion, and no need for comment.

We continued to hang on World Service bulletins in the wake of the San Carlos landings. The news from further south was good. The boys had gone ashore and encountered only minimal resistance, which they'd quickly sorted out. They'd dug in, consolidated, moved on. Patrols went on pushing further and further, until the Paras reached Goose Green. Then, suddenly, it looked as though the Argentinians weren't going to cave in after all. Goose Green wasn't taken straightaway; it looked as though the planners were holding back until we got very close. They were waiting for us. Going into action was no longer such a distant prospect. The war was becoming a reality.

We were issued with will forms, and the whole atmosphere on the ship became more purposeful. Nobody was talking about zapping Argies any more; we were too busy looking at the big boards that were positioned at the head of the main staircases, checking how many Pucarás and Skyhawks and Super Etendards had been destroyed. We knew that the Exocet was their major weapon; the ship buzz had also started to carry stories of napalm. But what we wanted to work out was what they really had left, what firepower capability remained.

The ship plunged deeper into the South Atlantic, and the weather got worse. It grew colder, the days began to draw in, and with each mile it seemed more obvious to us that we were going to get deployed. It finally dawned on us that this could be our last journey. 5 Brigade was actually going to war.

We'd sailed from Southampton on 12 May. On 28 May we steamed into Grytviken in South Georgia for cross-decking to the *Canberra* for our final passage. This was as far as Mrs Thatcher and the War Cabinet – or was it the insurance underwriters – were willing to risk the *QE2*. In other words, we were in dangerous waters, and vulnerable at any moment to Argentinian attack.

8

GOING ASHORE

I was in the cinema when we got the call. *An American Werewolf in London* was on the screen, and it had got as far as the spooky scene on the moorlands. I never saw what happened next.

'Support company, 1 Bn Welsh Guards,' the tannoy barked, 'report at once to your company lines.'

'You must be joking,' I groaned to my mates. 'They must mean the Scots Guards. Surely it'll be the Scots Guards. Check the paperwork.'

But there was no joke, and we all grumbled and moaned as we climbed over hundreds of legs in the darkness and made our way back to our cabins. We collected the kit that we'd packed and repacked a hundred times in readiness for the 'off'. I felt almost sad as I looked around the poky cabin for the last time. It wasn't much, but it had been home.

Up on deck, we found that the *QE2* was moored some way off the coast of South Georgia, away from the attentions of Argentinian bombers. 'We will be cross-decking as soon as possible to the *Canberra*,' the tannoy announced. This wasn't welcome news. We certainly didn't take kindly to being shunted down market. But there was worse to come. The transfer, they said, was to be effected by fishing trawler. I felt a nasty, familiar feeling begin to stir in the pit of my stomach and rise towards my throat. I was such a brilliant sailor, I'd even felt seasick anchored in the dock at Southampton. We left through open doors, jumping on to the trawler after handing over our kit. Suddenly, seasickness was the least of my problems.

There was an unexpectedly emotional farewell from the staff and stewards of the Cunard liner. I expect they were only cheering because they were glad to get rid of us, but I'd like to kid myself that there was a bit of sadness there, too. We'd got to know each other well during the two-week trip south. They threw us down carton after carton of cigarettes, and one woman called out, 'Good luck lads, keep your heads down.'

'Keep my head down?' I said. 'I'll sink so low I'll crawl under a snake's belly with a top-hat on.'

The gift of tailor-mades was very welcome. Like most squaddies, I had only my usual rolling tobacco – and trying to make a decent roll-up in a force 10 gale can be a right headache. I tried it only once, and my tobacco ended up all over the Falklands. If the weather had been hotter down there they'd have been knee-deep in tobacco fields by the end of the year.

The waves were only six or ten feet high, but from on board the trawler they looked as big as houses. As we made our way out to the Canberra, spray cascaded over the superstructure.

Cross-decking was nearly the end of me. We were roped to the Canberra, but to get aboard you had to jump from the rails of the fishing boat and in through a door in the side of the liner. The relative motion of the two vessels meant that if you timed your jump wrong, the rails and doorway would become the two slicing blades of a food-mixer.

When it was my turn, I somehow got a rope caught around my backpack. I jumped, and was half inside the Canberra, but my feet didn't connect with the floor. The rope had checked my leap in mid-air, just as the fishing boat started to rise on a wave and go higher than the top of the door-frame. My body was just a split second away from being cut in half. Thank God for the Marines. A big burly one saw what was happening, grabbed my pack and hauled me back on to the fishing boat – just as the top of the door-frame crashed down past my eyes.

Aboard the Canberra we stowed our kit, went to the eating area, received our instructions – and started whingeing. It was late at night. I was wet. My quarters were right at the bottom of the ship, near the engine-room. There were four of us in a tiny space, and there was nothing to do but play Scrabble. What made things worse was that none of us could spell.

We listened to the World Service all the way to San Carlos – a week's journey. The Scots Guards were also on board. The Gurkhas had left us at South Georgia.

In the cold dawn we saw our first evidence of war: the wreckage of a helicopter that had been shot down; the holed Argentinian submarine Santa Fe; and some of the injured being transferred from the *Canberra* to the *QE2*. There were Argentinians among them, and they looked so pitiful, so young. I tried to talk to them, but they were too terrified to respond. They'd heard tales about us being cannibals. I felt sorry for them. They were just kids.

The rest of the trip was spent moving mortar ammunition from the hold up on to the decks. This was a tedious job, because mortar bombs are heavy, and there were a hell of a lot of them. On the entertainment front there was a brilliant concert by the Royal Marines band, some of whose members were to be stretcher-bearers when we went ashore. Various lads did their party pieces. One was a magnificent formation wheelchair display – only without the wheels – complete with pilots in flying-helmets and scarves. The rest was left to our imagination.

Soldiers from any war will tell you how important mail is for morale. When you're part of the Army twenty-four hours a day, letters from home are the only truly private 'space' you have – the only proof, sometimes, that you have any existence other than as a cog in the machine. It could be depressing not to hear a line or two from your loved ones, but at least you could always rely on your mates to let you have a read of theirs, even if they were from a wife or girlfriend. Minus the sports pages, of course.

The *Canberra* looked a bit readier for war than the *QE2*, but not much. GPMGs were sited around her decks as defence against air attack, but they can only have been there for cosmetic reasons. Perhaps it was the Mickey Mouse quality of these defences that made us continue to feel that the war itself was not a reality. Still we believed that we were somehow there just to make up the numbers.

Then, close to San Carlos, the most awesome sight: we were suddenly sailing through ship upon ship upon ship of the assembled Task Force. Battleships, aircraft-carriers, tankers, supply ships and cross-Channel ferries with the British Rail sign on their funnels. It took my breath away. This was it. We were going into action.

Others, too, were moved by the scale and majesty of it all into discourse of the most profound and philosophical nature.

'This is bleedin' unbelievable.'

'Flippin' 'eck, ain't it good to be British?'

'Christ it's cold.'

I doubt that any Briton had really felt like that since the Second

World War. I knew that back at home the Task Force had in some small way rekindled the street-party spirit of forty years ago. I had the sudden, naïve thought, why can't it always be like this? Why can't Britain just become the sort of place it was, with everyone pulling together and mucking in? Why can't people be more concerned with living their lives than wishing they were someone else, wanting what others have, not accepting and enjoying what they've got themselves?

The next night I was up on deck, enjoying a smoke, thinking about everyone back in Nelson, wondering what was happening around the dartboard in the social club. It was a beautiful night. The sea was flat and dark as a Welsh slate roof, and the Southern Cross glittered overhead. I felt such a small part of this enormous universe. I turned and went back inside, and as I did so a shooting star flickered across the darkness like tracer, drawing my eyes to that blank space in the sky above the South Pole which is so dark by comparison. Something about the emptiness and blackness of that spot brought home to me the fact that war was just around the corner.

The next morning, 31 May, we were mustered in the library as the *Canberra* steamed towards the round shoulders of the hills on either side of Falkland Sound. I pocketed a couple of books I hadn't finished reading, and then watched through a window as Fanning Head came up on the port side. Beyond it I could see the entrance to San Carlos Water. I'd had a butcher's at the map, but instead of rearing straight up out of the water as the contour lines had suggested, the hills around San Carlos Water seemed to slope gently down into the sea. In such terrain we were not going to present enemy aircraft with a difficult target. I had an instant and overpowering urge to get ashore.

Predictably, nothing much happened for the next hour or two. We were allowed up on deck, and stood there as the day wore on, stamping our feet, having a natter, drinking tea, and staring at this strange country we were about to purge of its invaders. It was unbelievably cold, and the air was very clear. You could see for miles. It was ideal flying weather, for Harriers and Pucarás alike. East Falkland looked green and pleasant – a ringer, I thought, for Pembrokeshire, with its little clusters of whitewashed, red-roofed houses beside the shore.

To relieve the boredom we tried selling one lad to the cooks. A real gay boy, he was all for the deal. Then all at once the skies started buzzing with helicopters, nine or ten of them hovering above the ships at any one time, before hauling away across the sky like flying tractors, bulging cargo-nets swaying beneath them. Come in, number 24469434, your time is up.

We were told to get ready to disembark. We went down through the kitchens and passed our kit down to the waiting landing-craft through a door in the side. Then we jumped down ourselves. It was the first time most of us had ever been on a landing-craft. We crouched in the 'rubbish-skip' bucketing towards the beaches, with spray drenching us and our weapons. I didn't feel scared; everything seemed too organized, too programmed, for there to be any scope for individual fear. But I was full of nervous anticipation.

When we went ashore, the Marines made fun of the fact that some Welsh Guardsmen had worn plastic bags over their boots – only a few, but enough to warrant a slagging. The Marines said it was to keep them nice and shiny. In fact, it was to keep our feet dry. To them and all our other detractors I'd just say this: any bootneck can get his feet wet; it takes the ingenuity of a Guardsman to keep them dry.

It was Saturday 29 May, the day after the surrender at Goose Green. There was lots of activity on the jetty. We staggered up towards a building at the end of the jetty, past hundreds and hundreds of dismantled tents. That was an encouraging sight. Perhaps we wouldn't have to bivvy in trenches after all. There seemed to be plenty of helicopters, too, but they were shifting containers, not troops. That wasn't so good. We went on past soldiers who were resting and patrols who were coming back in. We eventually reached a little gully in the foothills some distance away and were ordered to dig in. That night you could see little camp-fires twinkling all over the hillside. It wasn't lax security; in thick, low cloud, visibility was down to just a few metres.

The military operate an 'oppo' system, whereby each soldier has a best friend on whom he can rely and who will look after him when necessary. My oppo, with whom I was going to share my trench, was Colin Parsons. When we tabbed to our first position, I had to carry his bergen, my bergen and my own equipment, because he had to stay behind with all the large equipment. I laid my back against the load, pushed my arms through the shoulder-straps, sat up to my knees and stood up slowly and painfully under the weight of double equipment. The pack gouged my lower back and the weight already hurt my shoulders. I walked four miles, dug a four-foot-deep trench which filled up half-way with water, set up the bivvy, walked all the way back, picked up Colin and the rest of the equipment, and then walked up to the top of the hills again. All on the first day. I was knackered. As his share of the workload, Colin brewed me a nice cup of tea.

The original plan for the southern advance was for the Guards to be helicoptered to Darwin, and then move overland towards Bluff Cove and Port Stanley. What helicopters? We were ordered to set out on foot over the Sussex Mountains, loaded down with bergens weighing over a hundredweight.

The reason we had so much kit was that stories were circulating of weather casualties in other battalions. It was decided that we couldn't risk leaving any of our equipment behind; but whoever it was who made the decision obviously didn't have to carry it. And the bergens weren't actually designed to carry such heavy loads, so they started to break apart.

It was a long drawn-out process. We didn't have any tracked vehicles at our disposal; the best we got was a wheezing old tractor, which instantly got bogged down in the mud. For some odd reason we weren't allowed to have any of the Sno-Cat all-terrain vehicles, even though at least two dozen empty ones surged past us on the way up the mountain.

This was the chess game viewed by the pawns, and the moves that made sense to the grandmasters controlling the play seemed to me at times to be unintelligible, or worse. Probably it was all just a matter of bad planning. When it comes down to it, some officers are like lighthouses in the desert – brilliant, but totally useless. Anyway, we tabbed for three hours before the move broke down; when we got to the top of the mountains we were called back to our first positions. Someone must have had second thoughts and decided after all that it wouldn't be too clever to exhaust the entire battalion merely in getting them to Bluff Cove.

We now stayed dug in in our old positions for the best part of a week, with me being scared out of my wits by cows and horses on the bridge next to us during the long hours of darkness. On the slopes the earth was soft and the trenches quickly filled with water

WALKING TALL

up to boot height. The deeper we dug, the greater the seepage. Some guys tried putting stones at the bottom of the trenches, but the water always found a way through. In between digging, hexy stoves were lit and 'wets' brewed, and ration-packs opened.

There was no point in attempting to sleep in the trench: it was an unequal struggle against the water seepage. I tried perching on the edge, inside my sleeping-bag, with my knees up, using my bergen as a back-rest. It was numbingly cold, even in layer upon layer of clothing and with my boots on. My feet were freezing, and I knew from bitter experience in the Brecons and on Salisbury Plain that it is almost impossible to sleep with cold feet. So Colin and I slept in the bivvy.

The nights were long, fourteen hours of darkness in which there was nothing to do but sleep, or brood about the desolation of the place. There was nothing there. The Falklands are a god-forsaken place. The islands are empty, bleak, desolate, inhospitable. I never saw a single tree. I never saw one of the famous sheep, and only ever spotted one or two of the locals. And no birds sing there. All I heard was the constant 'wop-wop' of helicopters. All I smelt was the powdery tang of chopper fumes and the parafinny smell of hexamine fuel blocks.

Two days later we were ordered back to San Carlos Bay. We had to dig in all over again. It was still freezing. Again, I shared my accommodation with Colin Parsons. It was so cold that I tried snuggling up against him during the night, but I think he got me all wrong because he moved away. A little later I tried again, and he moved even further. I gave it one more go – and poor Colin ended up outside the bivvy altogether. Then we both froze.

The food was not going to inspire Floyd on the Falklands, but I heard few complaints. Everyone was too hungry and too tired. I'd never thought the day would come when I would pray for the appearance of the cabbage mechanics and slop jockeys of the catering corps, but now I did. Our last meal on the islands, however, was the best I'd ever had. I should know, I cooked it. It was an all-in-one meat-and-vegetable stew. Here's the recipe: take three tins of baked beans and anything else you can find in your ration-packs and throw it all into a big pot. There must have been enough food for six people, and Colin and I ate the lot. We washed it down with water from the brook treated with Puritabs and boiled up with a couple of sachets of Nescafé.

Disposing of such meals after nature had taken its course was no easy task for a shy young Welsh mortarman. The latrines consisted of what the Army call a 'long drop' – a long ladder dangling over a pit, supported at either end on crates. Privacy was non-existent. I turned up one night for my constitutional to find six bottoms already *in situ* on the rungs. I joined them and sat there for a while, whistling, but nothing happened. I was constipated by modesty. In the end I had to wander off into the shadows on a private shovel recce, hoping against hope that I didn't end up squatting on an Argentinian sniper.

On the evening of Friday 4 June, B Company of 2 Para took the settlements at Fitzroy and Bluff Cove. Now, to keep the offensive on the roll, it was imperative that the 1,200 Welsh and Scots Guardsmen got to Bluff Cove immediately. The only snag was, how? All the troop-carrying Chinooks had gone down on the *Atlantic Conveyor*. And to march for several days would cost the momentum of the whole campaign. It was decided to take the risk of bringing us around by ship.

The assault ship HMS *Intrepid* would take the Scots Guards that night to Lively Island, near the mouth of Choiseul Sound, but no further. It was known that the Argentinians had land-based Exocets on the coastline south of Stanley; the Navy was licking its wounds after the loss of several capital ships already, and didn't want to risk losing another. From Lively Island, Major Ewen Southby-Tailyour, the Marines' amphibious-operations expert who only two years before had charted every inch of Falklands coastline, was to take the Scots Guards on to Bluff Cove in four landing-craft. We were due to make an identical voyage aboard HMS *Fearless* on the night of 6 June – the anniversary of the D-Day landings in Normandy.

The Scots had a nightmare journey to Bluff Cove in the open landing-craft in rapidly deteriorating weather. The wind was gusting to seventy knots, and Guardsmen were drenched in freezing sea-spray. The journey lasted seven hours. They eventually staggered ashore at Bluff Cove to find that four of their number were suffering from advanced hypothermia.

To save us a similar ordeal, the captain of the *Fearless* agreed to take a risk: he would carry us beyond Lively Island to Direction Island, much nearer to our destination. As he had done with the Scots Guards, Major Southby-Tailyour would then rendezvous with the *Fearless* with his landing-craft and carry us into Bluff Cove.

We walked back down to San Carlos and stood in the torrential rain for two and a half hours, waiting to embark on the landing-craft that would take us out to the *Fearless*. Some of us took the opportunity to have a quick scout around, appraising the overall military situation and seeing if there was anything worth scrounging – we were as hungry as hell. I decided to recce a stores-hut I had spotted a little way up the shoreline, and was casually sauntering towards it when I heard a shout. 'Air raid! Get down!'

I ran towards the nearest trench I could see, leaping over an enormous puddle on the way. Wee Scouse Farrall, a medic, also took a run-up at the water – but landed right in the middle. It was about four feet deep. Scouse just stood there, a look of quiet resignation on his face, which was just about all of him that protruded above the surface.

I hesitated on the lip of the trench and asked the big Marine inside it, 'Do you mind if I join you?'

He looked at me as if I was stupid. Then he shrugged and said, 'Be my guest . . .' Before I knew what was happening, my feet had left the ground and I was falling towards him, blasted forwards by the force of the six other Welsh Guardsmen who had also earmarked this particular trench as their shelter. We lay at the bottom of the waterlogged trench for several moments like a collapsed scrum. Then, from somewhere in the mud beneath me, I heard a muffled voice say, '. . . why not bring a few friends?'

That afternoon, we were to embark on HMS *Fearless*. We weren't lucky like the Marines and the Paras, with all their elaborate all-weather gear; we had to make do with inadequate little spray-proof capes. The craft were dipping into the waves, and we were getting deluged. Everyone was trying to find the best spec on the landing-craft, and the Marines crew were constantly shouting, 'Get back on this side! Keep the balance!' – and the boys gave as good as they got, cussing the bootnecks out. The smokers amongst us were clagging for a snout. But there was no way anyone could light a cigarette, everything was too wet. Everyone huddled together for warmth. We arrived at the *Fearless* after about fifteen minutes. It was raining hard, waves were coming in over the side, and I was cold and soaked. A typical trip by landing-craft, basically, and the longest, coldest, wettest quarter of an hour of my life.

The *Fearless* was an LPD (landing platform dock) with a large flight-deck on the stern and a rear-entry internal dock which took four large LCUs (landing-craft utilities) – large steel landing-craft each capable of carrying up to 100 men.

We docked through the stern, and there was a welcome clattering of metal as the landing-craft ramps went down. We unloaded the mortar ammunition first – hundreds of bombs which, as any weary infantryman will testify, are pretty heavy to lug around. Every man carries mortar bombs in the field, because the mortars are everyone's support. The order came to move upwards into the ship and find a spot to settle down in for a couple of hours. There was a predictable scramble for warm pipes and, up in the canteen, a stampede for chips. I don't think the poor naval chefs knew what they were taking on, the best part of a battalion of Welshmen, all hungry for chips. We also robbed as many freshly baked bread rolls as we could, and shovelled them into our faces until the butter was running down our chins. Then everybody headed for the showers.

For all fifty or so of us, it was the first chance we'd had to wash after more than eight days in arduous conditions. Heaven knows how the plumbing took the onslaught. We changed our underwear and washed our socks, and then tried to find warm pipes to dry them on. To some people the struggle apparently didn't seem worthwhile: I saw several pairs of underpants being flung overboard. After eight days on their owners, they were stiff enough to fly away like frisbees.

I settled down to write a letter. I had things I wanted to tell Sue, and it wasn't easy in the madding crowd of cussing soldiers. Eventually I managed to find myself a tiny space at the bottom of a flight of stairs. A naval guy passed me and said, 'Come with me, mate. I know a place where you can write a letter in peace and quiet.' He led me through a little hatch underneath some pipes, and it opened up into a tiny room with a desk, lit by an orange light.

It was just the lift I needed. My morale was ready for a boost: the ship was pitching around like a cork in a jacuzzi, and I was starting to feel ever so slightly queasy. The weather deteriorated so much that Major Southby-Tailyour couldn't get his landing-craft out of Bluff Cove. Even so, the *Fearless* dispatched two of her own LCUs into the stormy darkness, laden with two companies of very depressed Guardsmen. 'You'll get sick!' we shouted and jeered. 'You'll freeze!' We gave it loads. I thanked the Lord I wasn't among them – but we did wish them luck.

A group of SAS boys had also left earlier on. At first glance, you would have sworn they were civilians togged up for a walk on the fells, even down to the woollen, knee-length walking-breeches and socks. But there the resemblance ended. They had knives strapped to their legs and they carried shotguns and stupendous amounts of other kit and firepower. They wore bobble-hats and their hair was long – not in line with the army rule of 'What's under the cap is yours and everything else is the Army's.' I wouldn't have tackled one of them on a rugby field, let alone a battlefield.

Some 250 Welsh Guards went ashore that night at Bluff Cove – 2 Company, the anti-tanks, a machine-gun platoon and HQ staff. Wet and miserable, they set up position slightly forward of the Scots Guards. The remaining 300 men of the battalion – Prince of Wales Company and 3 Company, including us mortars – together with 16 Field Ambulance and the field engineer crew, were left aboard for the return journey to San Carlos, eating toast and drinking tea. I had never counted myself so lucky in all my life.

The *Fearless* returned to San Carlos Water, where the decision was taken that she could not be risked again. Instead, the remaining Guardsmen would be taken to Bluff Cove aboard an LSL. So, at lunch-time that Monday, the 'rubbish-skips' came into the back of the ship, and men, heavily-laden and in groups of 100, lined up for transhipping.

Two Canberra bombers from the Argentinian air force chose this moment to fly overhead. The *Fearless* responded with a pair of Seadart missiles. One blew up the leading bomber, and the wreckage in turn blew up one of the Seadarts. The second Canberra turned tail pretty smartly and headed for home. Men had died, but it didn't register with me. It was as if I was back on the *QE2*, watching a movie.

It was a very calm day as we chugged over to the LSL, which was the *Sir Galahad*. I'd been aboard it once before, *en route* for Northern Ireland. The platform was lowered at the rear, just like on a back-to-front cross-Channel ferry. We hopped off the landing-craft and on to this ramp, the continuation of which inside

THE BOMB HITS THE SIR GALAHAD

TANK DECK

TANK DECK

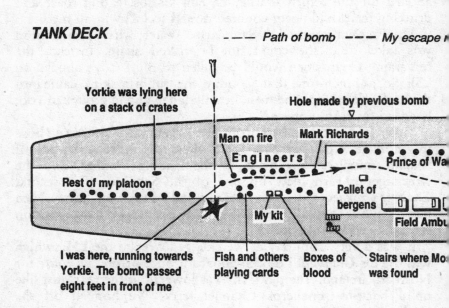

— — — Path of bomb — — — My escape r

Yorkie was lying here
on a stack of crates

Hole made by previous bomb

Man on fire

Mark Richards

Engineers

Prince of Wa

Rest of my platoon

Pallet of
bergens

Field Ambu

My kit

I was here, running towards
Yorkie. The bomb passed
eight feet in front of me

Fish and others
playing cards

Boxes of
blood

Stairs where Mo
was found

the ship was called the 'roadway'. This was narrow to start with –
no more than twenty feet or so across – but then opened out into a
much larger cargo area. Again just like on a ferry, there was a
corridor outside the 'car deck' area with sleeping accommodation,
and stairways leading up. I sat about fifteen yards from the ramp,
on the right-hand side of the roadway. Opposite me, against the
other side, were pallets of blood. Behind me, behind the steel
bulkheads, was one of the two engine-rooms, and thousands of
gallons of diesel fuel.

We had been greeted aboard the *Sir Galahad* by the smiling
faces of her largely Chinese crew. Our only let-down was the
discovery that the spare cabins we had been hoping for had been
wrecked by a bomb – which fortunately didn't explode – on the
morning of the San Carlos landings. The big consolation was the
news that we could stay aboard all the way to Bluff Cove.

The mortar platoon joined me in my prime position at the end
of the roadway and pitched camp. It was a good spot, out of the
way, far from the prying eyes of anyone organizing a work party.
The rest of the battalion were scattered along the side of ship. We
enjoyed a hot cup of tea and the sensation of just generally drying
out. We were happy.

There were no naval escorts for us as we steamed towards Bluff
Cove, and therefore no protection against air attack. I presumed
the theory was that we would be ashore under cover of darkness
long before the Argentinians could send in their air force. But the
Sir Galahad had sailed late, because at the last moment 16 Field
Ambulance had been ordered to join us. By the time the medical
teams had got themselves aboard, our departure was four hours
behind schedule. Then it was discovered that the direct channel to
Bluff Cove was too shallow for the *Sir Galahad*, so we headed
instead up Port Pleasant towards Fitzroy settlement. At 7.00 a.m.
the *Sir Galahad* rounded the point and dropped anchor in the bay,
not far from her sister ship, the *Sir Tristram*.

Some of the gear started going ashore, but the beaches at Fitzroy
were far from perfect as landing-sites, because not only were they
very narrow, but also they led immediately to steep banks. At high
tide and a couple of hours either side of it, getting kit of any size
ashore was just about impossible, so unloading the *Galahad* was
taking much longer than it should have done.

On the map, Fitzroy and Bluff Cove are less than four miles

apart, but they are separated by a deep inlet. The bridge that crossed it had been blown up by the enemy; if we went ashore at Fitzroy, only a couple of hundred yards from where we were anchored, we would face a march of perhaps twelve miles.

I learned much later that Major Southby-Tailyour arrived towards lunch-time. He was horrified by the spectacle of the LSLs lying unprotected in the bay. Crammed full of troops, in broad daylight, they were in grave danger of being subjected to Argentinian air attack. He commandeered the landing-craft – half-loaded with ammunition from the *Sir Tristram* – and motored across the water to the *Sir Galahad*.

With a major of the Royal Corps of Transport, he urged our officers to put as many of us as possible aboard the landing-craft. He wanted us moved off the ship to the safety of the shore, just 200 yards away – an operation, he argued, that would take only twenty minutes. I was told that our senior officer, Major G. N. R. 'Gunner' Sayle, declined: it is a military regulation that men and ammunition do not travel in the same boat. Our officers had been aboard the *QE2* during the first week of air attacks that had earned San Carlos Water the name Bomb Alley; they, like us squaddies, had not witnessed what the Argentinian air force could do. After a long and heated dialogue, Southby-Tailyour stormed off, refusing to be held responsible for the disaster that he felt was imminent.

'Gunner' Sayle was determined that we should not be mucked about any more after all the shenanigans of the previous few days; he wanted landing-craft brought out in which we could be sailed direct to Bluff Cove.

But Southby-Tailyour didn't want the matter to rest there. He headed straight to shore to seek out staff of 5 Brigade. The first staff officer he came across didn't believe there were any men left aboard the LSLs. 'They've all got off,' he said. He thought we'd all left from the *Fearless*, the night before.

As soon as the Marine had put him right, the staff officer set off at a hot lick to organize the unloading of the Rapier launchers that were intended to provide Fitzroy's defence against air attack. Someone else sent a landing-craft to the *Galahad* to bring off the troops. Meanwhile we stayed moping around the ship, some watching videos, some gathering their equipment. Some boys went up on deck to look at the desolate little bay, and beyond it the mountains rising into the distance. I stayed below, happy as Larry with my tea and sticky buns. It made a lovely change being able to be a greedy squaddie again.

We dozed, played cards, talked about home. One of my few excursions from my snug spot in the roadway was to the toilets. The *Galahad* had been hit by a bombing raid on 24 May, taking an unexploded bomb through her side. The bomb had come in through the wall of a toilet cubicle, and the gaping hole was still there. If you'd been sitting there reading a newspaper, the bomb would probably have ripped it – and it would certainly have cured your constipation.

Looking out, I could see that it was a beautiful day. There was no wind, and the sea was steel-blue and calm. I took several lungfuls of the clean, sweet air. It was quiet, too, now that the *Galahad*'s engines had stopped. The sun, pale and cold, was high over the mountains. Then came the order to muster on the tank deck, to assemble our weapons and equipment. It would not be long now before we started to offload our ammunition and begin the last leg of our journey to Bluff Cove.

Prince of Wales Company were to disembark first, together with some mortarmen. Then it would be 3 Company's turn. The landing-craft approached, and docked against the stern ramp of the *Galahad*. The big men of Prince of Wales Company kitted up ready to move, and we in the mortars started stacking our mortar bombs. Then there was a hitch. The front loading ramp of the loading-craft failed to operate. Running repairs failed, and there were no spare parts. The landing-craft had to change position and tie up alongside; we'd have to get aboard down scramble nets, whilst all our heavy equipment, including the deadly bergens, were loaded into nets, winched up through the opened tank deck and lowered over the side using the ship's cranes. Everyone was still on board, and eager to go.

It was 2.10 p.m. when those on shore saw a Skyhawk appear at the mouth of Port Pleasant, as if from nowhere, no more than fifty feet above the glassy sea. Then came a second Skyhawk, and a third, and a fourth, streaking across the water. Even if there had been time, the *Sir Galahad* and the *Sir Tristram* were too far away for anyone to shout a warning.

9

THE FIRE

'If anything goes wrong now, at least they'll have some blood to slap into us,' I joked to Byron Cordey as I sat down with my back against some boxes of plasma.

I'd played rugby with Byron. He was one of the big lads in Prince of Wales Company who were disembarking just ahead of us. Our platoon had been called to load bergens on to a pallet for winching out, and it was great to meet up with my fellow rugby player again. There was a definite buzz in the air as we got ready to go ashore and do some fighting. There wasn't much time for a chat though: my name was called, and I had to take forward my bergen.

'So long, Byron,' I said. 'Your round when we get to Stanley.'

He grinned. 'Sure. Take care of yourself.'

I lifted my pack and started to move away from the roadway towards the pallet, which was now piled high with bulging bergens. Above me was the open deck. Further ahead of me were the field-ambulance Land Rovers and big stacks of jerry-cans, each of which contained several gallons of spare petrol.

'Get us a cup of tea, Squeaky,' said Corporal Pemberton. His tone told me it wasn't an order, more a friendly request.

'Ah, come on Pem, ask someone else, will you? I'm doing things.'

Pem shrugged his shoulders and called over another Guardsman, who duly set off towards the kitchens via a hatchway and the corridor that ran between the tank deck and the hull itself. Thinking myself lucky to have got off this particular chore, I decided to jog back to the part of the roadway where I knew Yorkie was. Against regulations, I had left my webbing and sub-machine-gun by the blood bank, together with my spare small-arms ammunition.

I spotted Yorkie stretched out on top of a stack of packing-cases, his hands behind his head, his beret tilted over his face in a way that was peculiarly his. His snores indicated that he was involved in a deeply serious session of Egyptian PT. I wondered what would be a good way of waking him up. I know, I thought, I'll shout 'Air raid!' down his ear.

But someone else did it for me. At that precise moment, a voice echoed, loud and urgent, down the whole length of the tank deck: 'Air-raid warning green! Air-raid warning green!' There were Argentinian planes in the vicinity and we should be prepared for a strike.

The trouble was, we hadn't been briefed in air-raid drill. We just looked at each other a bit quizzically, unsure of what to do next. Then there was another shout: 'Air-raid warning red! Get down! Get down! Get down!' and all around me people sprang into action. True to my old shooting-team nickname of Hydraulics, I seemed slower than everyone else in responding. Facing the stern, I managed to get myself into a sort of semi-crouch, then decided to look up through the open deck above me in the hope of catching a glimpse of an enemy plane.

The bomb came through the port side of the ship and across in front of me, a great grey streak flying from right to left. It had sliced through the port engine-room and flew across the roadway towards the starboard engine-room, against whose bulkheads I had dumped my kit. The image cannot have lasted more than a split second. I heard jet engines screaming from above as the planes went over, then there was a brilliant flash from the engine-room, and the beginning of my personal Hiroshima.

The flash was yellow and orange, like an oil-rig flare. A moment later there was the warmth of summer in the air, only there was no breeze, nothing moving at all.

Nobody did anything. Nobody said anything.

A cloud bellied outwards and upwards and we just watched it engulf us. It was all so quiet. The lad next to me was standing as still and rigid as a statue.

Suddenly everybody sprang back to life, but now men were shadows, silhouettes with brilliant, whole-body haloes of the most beautiful colours I had ever seen – a sunburst that I could touch and yet couldn't touch: it was touching me, I couldn't touch back. I felt the air sucked from my lungs and then a surge of hot air washed over me. No sensation yet of the cruel, excruciating, unrelenting heat: in that first blinding flash all my exposed nerve-endings had been scorched away.

The bomb, a 2,000-pounder, had landed right in the middle of what seconds before had been a circle of happy, smiling faces. I can't have been more than twenty feet away from it when it exploded.

I stood up straight with my fists clenched in front of me. 'Bastards! Bastards!' I yelled over and over at the unseen enemy. I thought they had napalmed the ship. We'd all heard the rumour that they were going to use the stuff. Pain drew my eyes to the backs of my hands and I watched, transfixed by horror, as they fried and melted, the skin bubbling and flaking away from the bone like the leaves of a paperback burning on a bonfire before being carried away by the wind.

I looked around me for help. Other people were in desperate trouble. I saw somebody I recognized on the floor, a mate from depot days, and I tried to help him to his feet. His uniform was blazing and the flames ate into my palms as I lifted against the weight. It was useless. My hands were strangely slippery, as if they had wet soap on them and I was trying to grip an aluminium pole. My friend slid time and again from my grasp and I finally staggered back defeated. It was then that I saw, on the front of his burning combat jacket, the layers and layers of skin that had flaked off my palms. My hands were raw.

Bodies were everywhere on the floor, on fire, or smouldering, and so still that they frightened me, but the colours, the vivid colours that the bomb had created were still magnificent. It was like watching the northern lights, but from only a few feet away, and against a sky that was profoundly, impenetrably black. A kaleidoscope of colours – reds, browns, yellows, golds – unbelievably intense, more beautiful than anything I had ever seen, dancing around my friends and then enveloping them in flames. Two lads in front of me danced reels in the rainbow, jerking and writhing to a silent tune of death, and there was nothing I could do.

Then came the sound.

Men were mutilated and burning, and fought to rip off their clothing or douse the flames and beat at their faces, arms, legs, hair. They rushed around in circles in the roadway, screaming like pigs. A human fireball crumpled just ten feet in front of me like a disintegrating Guy Fawkes, blistered hands outstretched as he called for his mum. He fell flat and horribly still; in the heat of the flames all around me I watched transfixed for a second or two as he died. Black, choking smoke engulfed the area and I heard the voices of men I knew, friends who were crying out for help as they died in unimaginable pain. It was the sound of hell. I stooped to try and find cleaner air, but all I inhaled was the stench of burning metal and flesh and hair − acrid, gagging smells. Every breath stifled, and the heat scorched my lungs.

I remembered Yorkie and I tried to get near him, but I couldn't. Everything was on fire, even the blood in the first-aid boxes was ablaze. I knew he'd had it. I knew they all had. I didn't know what to do next. All I wanted was to get out, but I didn't know which way to run. Another friend careered past me, a human torch, his hands and face melting as he collapsed on to the red-hot deck. His skin turned from pink to grey and then to black as his body jerked on the floor. I blundered away blindly and saw others standing stock-still, mesmerized, their heads swollen like dark, smouldering footballs, their eyes piercing through their charred faces like the eyes of coal-miners, their blackened hands held in the air as if in surrender. Then they, too, started to run.

It got worse. The large consignment of petrol for the Land Rovers began to spurt out of its jerry-cans and ignite in great sheets of flame. Vapourized diesel blew back from the engine-room. Another fireball erupted, and the steady flow of fuel only stocked up the already intense heat. Our 81-mm mortar bombs started to cook. Some of them were white phosphorus. The heat increased, and the bullets and grenades on men's belts began to explode. Shrapnel and ricochets whizzed past my head as I stumbled around in the dark, dark smoke which billowed away from me and up through the open deck.

I was suffocating. I was on fire and no one could help me.

Like the scorpion that is threatened and tries to sting itself to death, I was beyond the limits of my endurance. I was in a hundred separate agonies as I ran towards the plasma boxes where I'd left my webbing − and my sub-machine-gun.

'Give me a gat,' I screamed, 'I'm going to shoot myself.'

In the dense smoke I stumbled over men on the floor who were either dead or terribly injured. From what I could see, those in the worst condition had had the same idea as me. They had guns in their hands. Those who didn't, or who were too incapacitated to help themselves, were begging to be put out of their misery.

I could not be sure who every man was, their faces were too blackened or disfigured, but some I recognized by their voices, oh God, the pleas and the screams from men I had laughed and joked with for so many years. Even more grotesque, I knew others by the shape of their teeth as the flames peeled back their lips into hideous grins. I couldn't find my gun; but if somebody had handed me one at that moment I would have used it. I would have released my friends from their torment and then I would have shot myself.

Boys were suffering too much pain, tortured to death. They had caught the full force of the initial flash fire and the fireball of exploding diesel and Land Rover fuel, and still they died too slowly. Some took as long as the time I was down there, and they were conscious for most of it. Even a minute is too long to die in, when every second wrenches you on to a different level of pain. Some died instantaneously; I wished they all had.

A movement.

A barely-felt ripple in the smoke on my face. Instinct made me turn and face the direction it was flowing from. My back was to the stern ramp. The fresh air had to be forward, through the wall of flames where the roadway widened out into the tank deck proper. I would have to run through the flames. There was nowhere else to go.

Many of the men were too far gone to reach the other side. They would have died trying to fight their way through, and they knew it. The wall of fire stood between them and escape, and they were too badly injured to make the attempt. I can only guess at their response. I know I heard the noise of ammunition going off behind me as I ran. I charged along the roadway and never looked back.

As I got closer to comparative safety I was hit by one final, harrowing image: a man, blown by the force of the explosion against a wall, and then stuck there as if he had been crucified. He wasn't dead. I couldn't tell what it was that kept him upright, but whatever it was, he was desperately trying to release himself from it with the only implement he had to hand – his bayonet. He was stabbing at his back, trying to prise himself off, trying to cut himself free of his clothes. I called to him, but he did not respond, another victim in his own personal hell. I had to run on.

I was fighting now with every ounce of strength and determination I had left, fighting to keep my legs moving and fighting against the agony in my burning, smoke-filled throat and lungs and the overpowering urge to take a deep breath. I stepped over a body; it groaned and squirmed, and I lost my footing. As I stood up I saw another soldier struggling to get out of the blazing sleeping-bag he must have been dozing in.

Suddenly I found other lads, shocked but unburned, running around getting themselves organized. I knew I had left hell; I was on the other side. Without breaking my run I allowed myself a quick breath, then charged onwards towards the exit I was looking for, knocking people out of my way if they seemed to dither. I just knew I had to help myself or I was going to die. I ran on across the base of the ship through thick, black smoke, accidentally kicking people and running over them in my last-ditch effort to save my own life.

I ran across the inner tank deck and found a door, but I had no idea how. Maybe it was just an in-built sense of direction or self-preservation, but perhaps it was my love for fresh, cool air that had somehow made me run in the right direction.

I emerged into the corridor to find bodies lying all over the floor – live bodies, unburned but in shock; they still hadn't reacted. I ran on, thanking God that many of my comrades were still alive, but at the same time doing everything in my power to get them out of my way and myself up into the open air.

I surged along the corridor towards the front of the ship. I came to another door. I couldn't open it because my hands were so badly burned, but at that moment CSM Brian Neck appeared and swung it open for me. A big Marine on the other side told me where to go.

'Keep going up the stairs until you can't go any further,' he yelled. 'That's where you'll be safe.' He looked at me with undisguised horror on his face.

I felt the draught well before I saw the final exit. The air was cool and clean and sweet as I charged up the stairs, and I felt as if I was running all the way to heaven.

10
EVACUATION

A huge pall of black smoke hung over the *Sir Galahad* in the clear, still air. It was a shock to remember what a beautiful day it was. Here, on this glorious afternoon, were all these men lying around on the deck of a blazing ship, their faces charred and black and their clothes and skin burned off. I sucked air into my lungs in great sobs as I tried to take in the scene around me.

There appeared to be no panic on that upper deck, just men giving what comfort they could to their injured mates. It was lucky we'd been trained in how to apply field dressings and administer morphine; all around me ordinary soldiers were putting the lesson to good use. One Guardsman came up to me and steered me gently towards an empty bit of floor space.

'All right mate? Sit down here now, let's sort you out.'

He found a medic, and the two of them cut my trousers and boots off and threw them over the side. I couldn't understand why, and I couldn't be bothered to ask. They jettisoned all the money in my pockets, too, and the set of poker dice that had helped me win it. Then I was parted from the gold St Christopher medal that Mam had given me for my eighteenth birthday, and – every bit as precious – the photograph of my little niece Rebecca in the bath that Helen had given me the last time I left Nelson. Perhaps in the heat of the moment it just seemed to them the right thing to do. Whatever, it was a rich, red South Atlantic that afternoon.

They ripped my syrette of morphine from the lapel of my jacket and jabbed it into my arm. Then they painted a big 'M' and the time of application on to my favourite, non-army-issue green T-shirt.

I stood up and turned to the medic to ask him a vital question. 'Have a little look, mate,' I said, 'and make sure my . . . you know . . .' But it was no good. I felt too embarrassed. I changed tack. 'I mean, are my teeth all there?'

The medic looked at me, I felt he was about to paint a big 'B' on my T-shirt as well – for Basket-case. After all, if my teeth had gone, so would have half my head.

'For God's sake, man,' I blurted, 'give us a situation report on my wedding tackle, will you?'

He lifted the waistband of my underpants and had a good eyeball. 'All present and correct,' he said. 'Looks in perfect working order.'

'Thank God for that.' At least one per cent was left. If the family jewels had been missing I don't think I'd have bothered coming back. I sighed with relief as they sat me with my back against a pillar.

Every now and again there was an explosion down within the hold, and balls of fire shot up into the sky, the shock waves reverberating all around us. There was another big blast, ammunition going off. Any second, I thought, the ship would blow itself to pieces.

The man beside me muttered something and I turned my head. To my delight, I found I was sitting right next to Pem, my section second-in-command. He was badly burned. Another soldier, with only superficial wounds, sat on the other side of him. This lad needed a couple of stitches because a painting had fallen off the wall and hit him on the head. 'Well, that's it,' he said to Pem, like someone in an old John Mills movie, 'wounded in action. That's us off home now.'

With so many of my friends and colleagues dead, it was wonderful to find Jimmy Salmon alive and unscathed. He was busy putting injured people into winches, but he found time to run over to me. 'It's all right, Wes,' he said. 'They'll get you off. They'll make sure you're OK.'

Black, acrid smoke billowed from the stern section, and huge flames leapt up from the tank deck. Ammunition continued to go off with sharp cracks. Nobody could have been left alive down there.

Sea King and Wessex helicopters had launched a rescue operation within seconds of the bomb raid. Now I watched them fly into the impenetrable smoke to rescue men from the ship and from the sea. Winchmen were lowered into the water to grab survivors and haul them aboard. Sometimes the helicopters were obscured altogether by the smoke, emerging moments later with

EVACUATION

Guardsmen and sailors dangling beneath them in the winch-strops.

The helicopter pilots were amazing, shuttling ceaselessly back and forth to bring casualties off to the battalion's aid post ashore. They performed miracles, hovering above the deck even though there was constant danger from sudden explosions of ammunition or fuel. Time and again the Sea Kings and Wessexes returned, beating their way towards us through dense smoke. Often they were hovering within six inches of the obstructions on the deck to winch off wounded men on stretchers or perched on cargo-slats.

I was dressed in just a pair of underpants and my green T-shirt as I rose up into the Sea King. I was surprised at how unfrightened I was as I went up in the winch – and at how uncomfortable it was on my back. The temperature was freezing, and the cold bit into the open wounds on my legs. I started to shiver.

Beneath us the *Sir Tristram* – which had also suffered serious damage and casualties – launched lifeboats, which began taking some of the rubber life-rafts in tow. Other rafts started drifting towards the blazing slicks, but helicopter pilots at the bow saw what was happening and, bringing their aircraft round to the stern, used the downdraught of the rotor-blades to blow the rafts to safety.

The narrow inlet of Port Pleasant looked swamped with lifeboats, orange inflatables and landing-craft. Hundreds of survivors were staggering on to land, some, I learned later, from lifeboats that had been rowed ashore with the Guardsmen singing a rousing blast of 'Men of Harlech' or some such song.

We flew straight to Ajax Bay, a trip of just five minutes. When we landed I could see a white building with a tin roof through the open doors of the helicopter. Guys in red berets ran towards the open doors to give what help they could. The lad next to me had a broken leg and they tried to remove him as gently as possible. They seemed to me to be taking a hell of a long time about it, so I just leapt on to the stretcher myself. 'Home, James,' I said.

The poor unsuspecting stretcher-bearer at the other end – his arms nearly jumped out of their sockets. But this was no time for arguing, and they carried me off towards the aid post.

We passed a group of cammed-up Paras on the way. 'Stick it to 'em for the Welsh Guards, lads,' I shouted.

These were the tough, battle-hardened veterans of Goose Green, yet they looked horrified at the sight of me. A great number of us wounded were in a terrible state, shocked, burned, maimed and bleeding.

My stretcher was placed on the floor of the large, disused out-house at Ajax Bay, nicknamed the 'Red and Green Life Machine'. I didn't feel too bad for a bit. Medics treated people all around me on a first come, first served basis, rather than according to the extent of injuries. There were so many casualties, it would have taken them all day otherwise just to do the assessments.

I swapped stories with a few of the lads. One, who had been landed at Fitzroy first before coming on to Ajax Bay, told us about the children from Fitzroy settlement who, totally oblivious of the threat of further air attacks, had come out and handed round jugs of hot tea to the injured. I'd also missed what must have been one of the greatest cracks of the whole campaign. The Sea Harriers had returned to fly the combat air patrol they'd abandoned only minutes before the Skyhawk attack, and left long white vapour trails behind them as they circled high above. Looking up, one Welsh genius had begun to sing the British Airways jingle, 'We'll take more care of you . . .' I wished I'd been there.

From the outside, the hospital had looked like a series of garden sheds made out of concrete, with a corrugated asbestos roof. Inside, it was like a deserted pavilion, with no furniture or equipment apart from two six-foot tables and rows and rows of stretchers. I lifted my head to look around. I didn't feel any pain except in my legs, which felt as if they were being dragged through a barbed-wire entanglement. I cried out in agony.

'Come on, Squeaky, you're a Welsh Guardsman,' said Dai Shaw, an old rugby and mortar colleague who was standing in the corner. 'Stick with it.'

But it was no good. I was cold, I was going into shock. I had tried to save others on the tank deck and it hadn't come off. Now I was trying to save myself, and my body was waving the white flag. I cracked, and my screams distressed my fellow casualties so much that the medics had to lash something into my leg to put me out. It was a blessed relief.

I woke up on a table. It seemed to be very dark. Someone's jacket was under the back of my head. My wounds had stuck to it.

'What's your name?' a voice asked me.

'Weston.'

EVACUATION

'Number?' I couldn't see who was speaking.

'24469434.'

'Unit?' It must have been night-time, or evening. All I could see were blurs and shadows.

'Welsh Guards. But what about Yorkie? Have they brought Yorkie in yet?'

'Who's Yorkie?'

'Andrew Walker. Guardsman Andrew Walker. Blond-haired lad, about six foot one. Have they brought him in?'

'I'll go and check.' The voice went away for several minutes, then returned. 'No, I can't find any record of him.'

'Don't bother,' I said flatly. 'He must be dead.'

All that afternoon and evening, helicopters continued to bring load after load of casualties to Ajax Bay. I could hear the sounds of the dazed and wounded as they staggered in. At one point there was a shout that all the treatment areas were completely full, but still the helicopters kept clattering overhead, and more and more stretcher-borne casualties were hustled through the main door. Medics rushed around, trying to distribute even shares of their expertise and loving care.

I was told there were 143 casualties in all, including forty-six who had died. Those who were still alive were either lying around in the buildings or standing near the doorway, blowing on their raw, damaged hands in a pathetic attempt to make them cool. Skin hung from their faces in tatters, their faces were blistered and peeling, their hair was singed. But from what I could hear, every one of them knew a mate who was worse off than himself, and who should be tended to first.

They came to cut the rings off my fingers, and a man with a very posh accent said something to me.

'You an officer?' I asked.

'Yes,' he said, 'I'm a captain.'

'God, you're ugly.'

'You're not looking too pretty yourself.'

'Sir?'

'Yes?'

'I'll always look prettier than you.'

By now my eyelids had swollen and I couldn't see a thing. But I could hear what was going on, and I knew the medics were still performing marvels. With each new arrival, they first cut away the fused and charred clothing, then assessed and recorded the total percentage of burned skin area and, where necessary, set up an intravenous drip. Then, so carefully and lovingly you could have sworn they were treating young children rather than soldiers, they spread thick, white Flamozine cream over the affected areas. 'It contains a silver-and-sulpha drug mixture,' one medic said to me by way of conversation. 'It's pain-killing and antiseptic, and promotes healing.'

My hands and fingers were enclosed in sterile plastic bags instead of the bandages I'd vaguely expected. 'This is a more hygienic way of doing things,' my medic said, 'until your hands stop swelling.' In the worst cases, apparently, the surgeons had to slit down both sides of each swollen finger to prevent strangulation of the circulation. Luckily my hands were spared, or at least I thought they were; I was swimming in and out of consciousness by this stage.

By evening, the floor of Ajax Bay sounded stretcher-deep in torn wrappers and Cellophane packets. For the medical officers, medical assistants and – more often – Marine bandsmen, it was a constant round of checking, adjusting, recording and commiserating. The Marines were simply magnificent, there's no other word for it – and that's a hard thing for a Guardsman to admit.

' 'Ere, doc,' I heard one of them call out to a doctor, 'now that we've passed the practical, how's about getting a bit of theory?'

They had to laugh. When you're surrounded by shocked, burned faces, white as ghosts with Flamozine, men with hands that are red and raw, running with weeping lymph from flash burns, what else can you do? I would always have been the last to suggest that war is a joke. I had seen it at first hand now, and I knew it wasn't. But if you put any two soldiers together for long enough, they will eventually make each other crease up with laughter. At Ajax Bay, laughter was pretty much the only thing that kept us going.

One of the Marine bandsmen stayed with me as waves of pain washed through my body. I needed a friend. He must have been there for twenty minutes or more, at a time when I'm sure he had better things to do. He held my arm until I passed out again. I could hardly believe that one man could show another so much care and compassion.

I came to. I could barely see, I could only make out light and shadow. I remembered the voice that had asked me my name and number, and I suddenly realized that I hadn't seen him, hadn't been able to see him. Perhaps I was blind. I was still heavily drugged. I went in and out of consciousness.

'I'm thirsty,' I cried out. 'I need ice-cold water.'

All I got, though, was saline solution.

I started trying to sell off my family for a can of Coke and some ice.

No response.

'Send me home,' I tried. 'My mother's a nurse – she'll look after me.'

No response.

Then an injured man right next to me started calling desperately for help. 'Nurse, nurse, fetch me a bowl,' he pleaded, 'I'm going to be sick.'

I joined in, but nothing happened. The staff just weren't quick enough, unfortunately.

'Forget it, nurse,' I shouted a few seconds later. 'He's been sick – all over me.'

It was the start of a great friendship. The Royal Engineer in question was called Mark Richards. When the bomb exploded, he had been sound asleep in his sleeping-bag on the tank deck. Unbelievably, he had slept right through the whole episode, only waking up when he felt a bit hotter than usual – to discover that his bag had been burned to a cinder. He was the soldier I had passed earlier on the tank deck.

Sounds and images swam in front of me. I wasn't too sure any more what was real and what was dreamed.

'Is it all right if I smoke?' I heard a squaddie ask a doctor.

'I thought you'd just finished,' said the medic. Everyone laughed.

I passed out again, and woke up to a sound that made my blood run cold.

'Air-raid warning green!'

Please God, no. Was it for real or was I just reliving the nightmare of the voice that had echoed down the tank deck? I didn't know. The medics began shifting stretchers. It took them a long time to get to me. When my moment came, there was another shout.

'Air-raid warning red! Get down! Get down! Get down!'

This is beyond a joke, I thought. If they're going to bomb me, let's have a straightforward kill this time round. This was getting on my nerves. I couldn't handle it. Nor could the medics. They dropped the stretcher and ran for cover. I didn't blame them. They had first-hand experience of the damage bombs could do.

Another blur. Then I came round on a helicopter. I thought I was drowning. I had a tube down my throat, and I tried to pull it out. The winchman began pushing it in again, until he realized that I was regaining consciousness, when he removed it.

Then I felt us land on the deck of a ship, and I was being lifted by kind hands.

'All right lad, we've got you now.'

I didn't have a clue where I was, but I somehow knew that I was going to be safe, and that was all that mattered.

11

ABOARD THE *UGANDA*

My mother knew it had happened to me.

'Knowing they had to take the mortars round by ship,' she said later, 'when Michael Nicholson said at twenty to six that night that it had been hit, with such graphic descriptions, I just knew it had happened to you, just knew, you were in support company, the only place you could have been was on the *Galahad*.'

For my family and many others, it was the beginning of a long and nerve-racking vigil. Unbeknown to them, General Moore had signalled the Task Force HQ at Northwood that the Argentinians believed he had lost nearly 1,000 men in the disaster and had therefore lost the whole momentum of his advance. As far as he was concerned, it was operationally imperative that the enemy continue to believe this. Northwood immediately told the Ministry of Defence that they wanted the extent of Fitzroy casualties 'talked up' as much as possible, despite the heartache it would cause. Official statements were broadcast at once that casualties had been heavy and might delay the expected British assault on Port Stanley.

'And for three hours I just stayed outside in the garden, tidying it up,' Mam says. 'I couldn't believe this was happening. Then the nine-o'clock news came and I saw it, and then I waited to watch the ten-o'clock news – and at four minutes past ten the Ministry of Defence rang and told me that you were injured, not seriously. Then two anxious days passed before the Ministry of Defence phoned me at seven at night and told me it was four per cent burns, hands and face, not serious.'

In accordance with General Moore's wishes, the Fitzroy casualty list was not in fact released until after the assault on Port Stanley had commenced. For the two long days that brought such anguish to my family, Secretary of State John Nott kept stating that to announce casualties could be of assistance to the enemy and put the men in the Task Force at greater risk. But then he completely scuppered the General's main objective by adding that 'the Task Force commander's plans have not been prejudiced by these attacks'.

'Within two hours of the call to say the burns were not serious,' Mam says, 'Captain Evans from the Welsh Guards was knocking at the door to tell me they'd made a mistake with the percentages, it was forty-six per cent. That was very harrowing. I think the twenty-four days leading up to you coming back were the most desperate days of my life. They say with the modern-day technology, satellite systems and that, they've got communication, but there was no communication for us at all.

'We fought for every bit of information that we had and it came to a point at one time that I felt, well tell me, is he alive or dead, because they told me four per cent, forty-six per cent, then seriously ill, they were lifting us up and putting us down, we couldn't come to terms with it at all. I thought, if he's dead we'll come to terms with our grief – but not the way they were doing things to us. I feel the communications were very, very bad.'

In fact I was already worrying about what my mother might have been told about my injuries, and had arranged for a familygram to be sent home from the *Uganda*, the hospital ship to which I had been transferred from Ajax Bay. 'SAFE AND WELL ON HOSPITAL SHIP UGANDA,' the message read. 'JUST A SUPERFICIAL BURN BUT IMPROVING VERY FAST. COMING HOME SOON. PLAYING RUGBY STRAIGHT AWAY. PLEASE SHOW TO SUSAN. LOVE, SIMON.'

I was really not conscious at this stage of how badly injured I was. Looking in the mirror, I could still say to myself, 'You don't look too bad at all, old son – once you get the scabs off, you'll be all right.' I was also lulled into a false sense of security by being allowed to have a bath in Savlon solution and finding that the occasion passed fairly painlessly. The only drawback was that people couldn't catch hold of me anywhere because of the burns, so I had to get myself in and out. It was wonderful to feel clean again. I didn't think to ask how bad the injuries were, and nobody told me.

I started to need special drops because my eyes were beginning to stretch wide open; the lids had puffed up and then shrunk, and I couldn't blink. The medics wanted to cover my eyes with pads, but I wasn't keen. After a week, the doctor decided to carry out some emergency plastic surgery to get the lids working again, or the eyes would be lost. The heart-and-lung specialist informed him that there were only sixty minutes in which to do the job or I'd croak. Commander Chapman carried out the task in fifty-five minutes flat, listening to Queen's *Greatest Hits* and singing along. He knew every lyric. He wasn't a great singer – but he was a damned fine surgeon.

I got my first 'Get Well' card from Nelson – from Aidie Williams and his wife, Jackie – but time passed very slowly for me. There was no television in our little sick-bay, and no other form of entertainment. For a while I was entirely on my own. The staff put on a private film-show of *Car Wash* for me, but I couldn't see a thing, even from four feet away. I began to wonder whether maybe it was all a bit more serious than I'd thought.

The *Uganda* was well-known as a school-cruise ship – I remembered that Helen had travelled on her just a few years before. I was lying in a bed in the official hospital bay, a room that she might have visited herself during her cruise.

Most of us in the room were walking wounded; only a few had broken legs or other injuries that made them totally bedbound. One chap was suffering from bad depression; all the others – Hugh Trigg, Graham Broad, Mark Richards and myself – had been injured on the *Galahad*. Then one day they brought in a Marine who'd put his cigarette out in an ashtray full of gunpowder. He'd been burned all the way up his arm and armpit and on his hand.

'Flash burns,' said the doctor.

'Very flash,' I said.

I felt sorry for the poor Marine in one respect. Being in amongst us can have been no fun at all. We had scabs, we stank of burned flesh and sweaty bodies. How the nurses put up with it I'll never know.

Everyone was cheerful to start with, on the surface at least, but once the adrenalin had stopped pumping, there were problems. We swapped stories about what we'd seen and what we'd heard. One guy, L/Sgt Martin Miles, had had a big heavy door blown on top of him, and had been trapped underneath while everyone ran out over him. Finally someone had responded to the faint cries of 'Help! Help!' that were coming from down below and he'd been rescued. He'd got away with only a chipped bone in his ankle.

There were brave men who had gone into the flames to rescue others. There were unsung acts of heroism. Guardsman Mark Davis, nicknamed Moses, who had a punctured lung, told us of the Welsh Guards medic who had gone back inside the burning ship to find him. Moses had collapsed on the stairs, his lungs full of smoke. The medic had pulled him out and saved his life. Fishing people out of the water was one thing; going unprotected back into the danger zone was quite another.

Some Guardsmen had repeatedly gone down into the fire to bring people out, only to become victims themselves. I was told that Cliff Elley, a man whom I respected greatly, was one of them. People told me that he'd been seen after the bomb went off, fit and well, but had then disappeared. He had gone back down into the flames and the flying bullets to save others.

'Play for yourself,' Cliff had said to me before that Army Cup game. 'But when you need to play as a team, play as a team.'

I had seen people erased from the future. A few seconds – that's all it had taken. Men I'd been joking with were now just memories, confined to the past. The horrors had been appalling; I knew the sights and sounds and smells would live with me for ever. 'Dear God,' I said at one low point, 'I know you probably won't recognize my voice because you haven't heard from me all that often, but please – let them rest in peace.'

I was lying in bed with just a sheet on me, my legs totally encased in bandages. After a while I asked the staff to take the bandages off. My legs didn't feel as if they were badly burned, and all I wanted was to let the air get to them so they could scab up and heal. The doctors did as I asked. They found that my wounds had already contracted an infection, and there was nothing they could do about it. I had needed blood, and during the transfusion I'd contracted septicaemia.

In my sleep I fought my way off that deck of death time and time again. My lungs filled with smoke and the smells of burning flesh and oil. My memory brought back twisted, pained, screaming faces, bodies crawling and hands melting. The explosion would happen again. And again. The nightmares began.

One night the shadow of a man appeared at the end of the bed. He was leaning against the foot of the bed, standing with one leg crossed in front of the other, watching over me. I wasn't hallucinating: at that stage I wasn't being given drugs, because my breathing was so shallow, my whole existence was hanging by a thread. Anything that impaired the functioning of my heart could have killed me. I was suffering too from the effects of smoke-inhalation.

I called the nurse in once, but she walked right through it, so I knew she hadn't seen it. I never saw it again, but I felt very calm afterwards. That spirit must have been real. Before that I'd been feeling bad pain. I had gone to sleep one night and said quietly to myself, 'I hope I don't wake up.' I did, but it was only an hour later. After the visitation, I felt more at ease with myself. I never again felt that I wanted to die, or even entertained the thought that I would.

It was only much later, in England, that Gran revealed to me that she had prayed that same night to her first husband. She had asked him to take care of me – and he had.

In my waking moments I wondered if I had done enough. It played on my mind that I'd left behind guys I had served with throughout my army career – yet I know I couldn't have done any more to help. Not having been able to save at least one of my friends hurt – and hurt like hell. I had tried and I had failed. But if I had remained with them for any longer, I would have been buried alongside them.

It was around this time that I had a helicopter visit from some of the lads in the mortars. They weren't supposed to visit – it was a breach of the Geneva Convention: if you land on a hospital ship you're not allowed back on land; in other words, the wounded can't be treated and promptly sent back into battle. Gary 'Geldof' Williams, my old room-mate, was among them, and so was my platoon commander. It was a great boost to my morale. I was chuffed to beans. It was just so lovely to see them. I still didn't know how badly injured I was. Ashore, word had gone around that I was dead; that's what all the boys had been told. It was only when the helicopter landed on the *Uganda* that they discovered I was aboard.

As the days went by there was a lot of pain: both physical pain and the pain of grief, the horribly empty realization that the dead weren't coming back. I felt as if my insides had been ripped out and I was hollow, raw; the special cord that connected me to my mates had been severed, and I bled.

I thought there was no way I could get over the pain, the

intensity of which I could not explain to people at the time except to say that in my mind it was total darkness, even in the middle of the day. Sometimes I went completely into myself. I hadn't known that I could be hurt so deeply. I had never before seen death with my own eyes, and of blokes I cared so much for. I felt cheated. You live and you love people, and they die. I missed them more than words could express. I wished I had had the chance to say goodbye.

Out of the thirty of us in mortar platoon, only eight had survived. Twenty-four other soldiers and sailors had died, and still others had been wounded. It was easily the worst disaster that Britain had suffered; a fine battalion had been dealt a terrible blow before its campaign had even begun. I was pleased when I heard that the lads got through the war without any more casualties.

On the World Service I heard that Port Stanley had fallen, and that a memorial service had been held at Fitzroy. The *Sir Galahad*, still burning two weeks after the attack, was towed twelve miles out into the South Atlantic and sunk as an official war grave. Our padre conducted the service. It was a cold, cheerless evening, and Welsh Guardsmen formed up around him on three sides of a square. As a bugler sounded the last post, the choir sang the Welsh national anthem, 'Land of My Fathers'. All that now marks the site is a lone stone cross, bearing the crest of the Welsh Guards. The stone was taken from a quarry near my home town.

The defence of freedom, I had discovered, is not cheap. My friends had paid the price. My loss was my share of that cost. But I have no complaints.

12

COMING BACK

They'd been saying to me, 'You'll be going on the next hospital ship to Montevideo, and from there you'll be flown home.'

I must have heard that one about three times, and each time they said it I pinned my hopes on a quick flight back to the UK. It never materialized, and I was starting to fret. I really wanted to get home. I'd had a total binful by this stage. I felt claustrophobic in the tiny ward, I wanted out – and when I decide I've had enough, nothing in the world will stop me from getting my way. I nagged the poor medics mercilessly. At last, about three weeks after I'd first arrived on the *Uganda*, a harassed nurse came in one morning and said, 'This time it's it – you're off.'

I knew I was going, because they pumped three pints of blood into me, ready for the journey. I climbed out of bed and helped myself be loaded into a wheelchair, and we went up on deck. A fresh breeze was gusting from the land, a mile or two away. As I turned my face into it I caught my first glimpse of Port Stanley – roofs of red and green corrugated iron, the odd column of smoke, still the occasional fluttering white flag.

'Why are we anchored so far from shore?' I asked the nurse.

'Engine-cooling system,' he said. 'It sucks up water from near the bottom of the ship. If we stay inshore for too long, the filters get clogged with silt. Depending on tides, we're only allowed a certain time near land each day.'

I breathed deeply on the sea air as I was wheeled towards the ship that was moored alongside us. A logistics ship used for charting the sea-bed, the *Hydra* was only a small craft, no bigger really than a fishing trawler. Her crew hoisted the thirty of us aboard, and we said our goodbyes to the people on the *Uganda* who had looked after us so well. Then, with the *Hydra* already slipping anchor, we were ushered down to our new home in the crew's quarters. God knows where those poor blokes kipped themselves – the only other enclosed spaces were the engine-room and the bridge.

We discovered the most extraordinary thing about the *Hydra* almost straightaway: the nurses. Those lads were as rough as they come and not highly trained, but they were absolutely marvellous to me, full of life and sparkle – even though they probably hated my guts. I was always thirsty, because of my burns, desperate for drink after drink. And though I didn't show it, I was also frightened, and I needed constant company and reassurance.

I was a stubborn swine. Even after the clout I'd been dealt, I still had the strength to walk. I'd get to my feet by swinging my legs over the end of the bed and dropping them to the floor. They would usually split at once and start to bleed, because the whole of each leg was one continuous scab. Then, with blood dribbling down my legs and a big sheet wrapped round me like Mahatma Gandhi, I'd shuffle off with one of the lads for my daily constitutional around the *Hydra*'s deck. The distance covered was probably no more than 100 yards at the most, but every time I did it I felt as tired and as elated as if I'd just run a marathon.

'Here you are, Simon,' one of the nurses said one night, 'get this down you.' He gave me an ice-cold tin of cider. It was as sore as hell to hold it between my raw hands – but I needed it.

Within minutes I was skulled. I was well bladded, singing and all sorts. They took me into the mess room where the walking wounded and crew ate, a silver heat-retaining blanket wrapped around me because my own body thermostat was out of commission. As is the custom on most naval ships, the evening horse-racing was under way. Half a dozen wooden horses of different colours are 'raced' with the help of two buckets and two dice, but don't ask me how. All I know is that one of the petty officers bought me a horse, and by all accounts the wretched thing is still running.

I was on the *Hydra* for only five days all told. 'We'll be in Montevideo tomorrow,' the doctor said on the fourth, 'but before you are transferred to the dock I want to take the slough off your back injuries.'

They took me into the medical room and sat me on a treatment table. I immediately yelped with pain. There was a slight breeze from the little ceiling vent and it was agony on the back of my head.

'I think we can sort that out,' said the doctor. But instead of just switching off the vent as I expected, he came over to me with a hypodermic and injected me with a massive dose of pethidine. Good stuff, pethidine. I felt it sweep through my legs and around my system and I was away with the fairies. The doctor scrubbed away at my back to his heart's content, raking off all the muck and scum. I could feel the pressure and motion of the instruments, and it was still as painful as hell, but I no longer cared. I tell you, for occasions like that, pethidine is made in heaven.

I was almost cocky as I sauntered back to my bunk. For me, pain was a thing of the past. I bent my legs, clambered on to the bed and said, 'Easy-peasy, this is a cinch.'

The pain returned at that moment with all the subtlety of an Exocet missile.

'Please can I have some more pethidine?' I bleated, but none was forthcoming. For the first time in my life I understood the desperation of the junky who needs another fix.

When it came to pain, I began to look for the easy option. Sometimes it was excruciating, climb-up-the-wall sort of pain, at other times it was simply unbearable. A sort of background burning was always there as well, as the nerve-endings grew back, but I had to learn to live with that. There is a limit to the amount of pain-killers they can give you before you become addicted.

'How does it feel?' the doctor asked me later that night.

'Like having a tooth drilled without an injection, for hour after hour,' I told him. 'The drill is hurting and hurting and hurting, and eventually you simply get used to it. But when other pain suddenly comes at you from left field, it takes a lot of handling.'

The doctor was good; he cared. So did the nurses. In fact, all the care we received might have been from blokes and a bit abrasive, but they did their best and their best was marvellous — especially considering they were looking after injuries they'd never seen before.

Another major plus about the *Hydra* was that we could buy duty-frees. I had no money, but one injured lad bank-rolled me for 200 tailor-mades.

'Send me the money when you're back home,' he said.

He was a member of the SAS who had somehow, somewhere managed to get himself shot in the backside. When it came to clandestine skills he was a past master, pinching bottles of whisky from the officers' mess without ever being caught, and distributing them equally amongst the lads – even the lads with tracheotomy tubes, who couldn't drink a drop. As far as I was concerned, the only problem with his generosity was that I'd actually given up cigarettes. The way I saw it, I'd had enough of smoking for a while.

We docked in Montevideo the next day and British Embassy staff brought fresh milk on board. There were two or three litres between all of us, but I somehow ended up quaffing most of it. As I told the others, it was the most delicious, refreshing milk I'd ever tasted.

'I think the trip to the airport is going to be interesting,' one of the lads said, surveying the fleet of little Chevette-sized vans that had arrived to collect us. In the end the bigger lads had to bend double to get into them, no matter what the extent of their injuries.

'Please don't put that big thick gauze pad on the back of my head,' I said to the driver of my van.

'It's to protect your head during the ride to the airport,' the interpreter explained, but I wasn't keen. In the end I decided it was unfair to keep the other lads waiting while I haggled over my medical treatment, so I let the man go ahead. He was acting in good faith, poor bloke, but I wish he'd been around later to see the effects of his handiwork. The pad welded itself to my injured head, and, I have to say, the hours it took to separate the gauze from my flesh were very special moments in my life.

I didn't notice much about Montevideo as we drove towards the airport, except that on every street corner along our route there seemed to be a burly Uruguayan soldier, armed with a machine gun held across his chest. Apparently the President was very jittery about anything happening to us while in transit through his country. That made two of us.

After a two-hour guided tour of what felt like every pot-hole in the city, the cavalcade of vans eventually arrived at the airport. We drove straight on to one of the runways and pulled up alongside an RAF VC10. For the first time in my army life I was glad to see the 'crabs'. They smiled, they spoke English – and they didn't want to stick thick gauze pads on my head.

Most of the seats on the plane had been removed and replaced with bunks along the sides and down the middle. I was put on a top bunk, at about shoulder height, because it made it easier to treat me. A medic appeared with several sheets of thin, spongy material and stared thoughtfully at my exposed injuries.

'What's that stuff?' I asked, by now a considerable expert when it came to treatments and their possibly painful implications.

'It's foam for your back and legs,' he said. 'It will make you more comfortable for the journey.'

'Don't put it on,' I said, 'it'll stick to the burns. I'd sooner take my chances without.'

But as usual, being only the patient, I was wrong. Like hell I was. That stuff would stick to me like shit to a blanket. Peeling it off again would send me to the very gates of hell and back.

Our discussion was interrupted by the sound of the pilot's voice on the intercom. 'No smoking, please,' he said, 'we are now taking off.'

That was that; no more time for argument. The foam went on. The engines whined up the decibels, and from my bunk I had a perfect view of the starboard unit as it vibrated gently, vigorously, violently – and then threw itself all over the runway.

'Ah. Welcome to Montevideo,' said the Captain.

There was an SAS major aboard who said that he wouldn't allow any of us to get off the plane. 'This is a neutral country. Under the terms of the Geneva Convention we won't be able to leave again until hostilities cease.'

We did leave the plane in the end, however, and got back into the little vans and drove all the way back to the harbour. The *Hydra* had been recalled and the crew were there at the dockside to greet us. The Embassy staff reappeared, and they had more fresh milk for us. No prizes for guessing who drank it.

We were in dock for two days while a new VC10 was sent out – long enough for the street vendors to get wise to the fact that there was a whole new market to be tapped. One guy came around selling leather and sheepskin coats. His face was a picture when he walked on to the deck and saw his potential customers for the first time. The coats were incredibly cheap and the boys clustered around. This was very bad news for one Marine, called Flatback, who had been hit in the stomach by mortar shrapnel. He had to stay curled up in a ball so that his wounds could heal; he could use his hands, but needed the other lads to lift him in and out of his bunk. They were putting him into bed when the coat-seller arrived, and in the excitement the lads all turned round and left him just hanging there. He was rescued in the nick of time.

At long last we got back to the plane, and this time we actually left the ground. I ate two meals on the trot, and drank as much Coke as I could. All that was missing from my life now was my mam and a great big juicy quarter-pound burger with cheese. We stopped at Ascension to refuel, replenish and swap crews. I slept most of the way, and the journey seemed to be over in a flash. Two other injured lads helped me a great deal during the flight – Alec Wilson of the Scots Guards and a Marine called Oscar. They were marvellous, and I owe them a big debt of thanks.

As we made our approach at Brize Norton, the pilot made an announcement: 'Ladies and gentlemen, you have just entered the *Guinness Book of Records*. The flight has taken us just sixteen hours, a new record.'

It was only later that I discovered that part of the reason for the rush was that I was on board. Apparently my injuries were so bad that I could have croaked at any moment. Well done that pilot, is all I can say now. And thanks for caring.

13

HOME

Touching down at Brize Norton was a great relief. I had come home. We didn't know quite what faced us ahead, but at least we had returned, which was more than many of my friends had done.

My first thoughts were of my family, and particularly my mother. I knew that she would be there to greet me if she possibly could, but I had no idea what she had been told. I was very apprehensive. How could she react when she saw me? I knew that I hadn't exactly been Robert Redford before I was injured, but now, with my face all burned and my body wrapped up in bandages, I looked more like an Egyptian mummy than I did her son.

I was the last to be taken off the VC10. Getting me down from the top bunk proved to be such a problem that in the end I just got down myself and climbed on to the stretcher. However critical my condition was, it seemed to me the most logical thing to do. I was then carried down the gangway and off into one of the waiting ambulances. This was a real 'welcome back' moment. When you are lying on a raw red back that has been bumped up and down for hours in a plane, and someone – however gently – tries to lift you into an ambulance, you come back to the present with a very real jolt.

Once inside the vehicle, I asked them to open the windows to get some fresh air. It was then that I heard something that made me smile warmly inside. It wasn't the sound of English being spoken, nor the sound of my mother's voice: above the noise of the rattly old diesel engine, I heard the reassuring sound of trees rustling and birds singing. There had been no trees on the Falklands and no bird-song – and none on the *Uganda* or the *Hydra*, either. Everything else around me seemed to fade into insignificance; all I heard was those trees and those birds.

I was driven from the landing-strip to the RAF hospital at

Wroughton. As the doctor travelling with me got out of the ambulance, one of the RAF boys waiting to carry me inside said, 'Welcome home, lad, we'll look after you now.' Those were the first words anyone had really said to me, but they didn't sink in properly. I was still looking for my family.

'Look at that poor boy,' my mother said to Nora, her voice full of emotion.

I hadn't heard her remark, or realized that she hadn't recognized her own son, but it was at this moment that I saw her. I called out, 'Hello, Mam.'

She turned to me and our eyes met. She was completely stunned; it was as if she suddenly couldn't breathe. She didn't say anything to me. She couldn't.

The RAF boys saw her reaction and whisked me away so that she could compose herself. When I saw her a few minutes later she was still in tears.

'Don't cry, Mam,' I said. 'I'm all right. I'm alive.'

It was there that I found out how she had learned of my injury. 'The twenty-four days since you were hit have been the most desperate days of my life, Simon,' she said. She was scarcely able to hold back the tears.

'Hi Mam,' I said again. 'Hi Gran.' I didn't realize why Mam had turned away. I was in no position to take on board other people's feelings. I was too deeply absorbed in my own pain.

There wasn't time to say more. The doctors were eager to helicopter us off to the Queen Elizabeth Military Hospital in Woolwich. I said a brief goodbye to Mam, and my stretcher was lifted through the open doors of a Chinook. They filled my ears with cotton wool for the journey, and for some reason that made me even more irritable than I already was. It was the worst helicopter-ride of my life. Chinooks vibrate violently in the middle, and that was just where I was sited. I felt totally helpless. The sheets I was lying on had wrinkled and stuck to my back. It was agony.

Just before we landed, we were given a brief that there was a news crew waiting for us, with television cameras. 'Don't say anything, lads,' we were told, 'don't react.'

Don't react? They might just as well have told me to stop breathing; I would have taken just about as much notice. I felt pretty incensed at the press trying to sensationalize, gawping at the gimps, the injured, the missing limbs, the burned and the fried and the scarred. Then I thought, you're not going to get away with this, you bastards. I strung together a few words that came out beautifully. 'Fuck off. What do you want, a freak-show or what, you fucking heathen bastards. Piss off.'

The name of the BBC producer was Malcolm Brinkworth. The auguries for a continuing friendship were not exactly promising. I had no idea then that it was his intention to make a serious documentary on how the services' medical corps coped with the kind of burns injuries war could result in. Nor did I realize that I had been chosen as the subject of that documentary because I was the worst-injured to make it home.

It was a great relief coming to Woolwich. I'd have given a lot for a decent view of the rolling Welsh countryside and a deep breath of the clear air of the hills, but I had that to look forward to. For now I was given a chance to settle after the roller-coaster journey from Ajax Bay, and in a place where they knew how to look after me.

I've always found hospitals sterile, demoralizing places, and the Queen Elizabeth was no exception. But it did have its advantages. For a start, the staff were wonderful, and there were also a number of lads down the corridor who'd been through what I had. There was one particular guy who'd also survived the explosion on the *Sir Galahad*, and whose hands were in even worse nick than mine. I'm sure the competition that later developed between us to get back in shape did us both a lot of good. Apart from that, I discovered a great source of comfort in the knowledge that we had shared something that touched and hurt us more than we could ever explain to those who hadn't been there. And many of us had known the boys who'd died.

The first specialist I saw was Colonel McDermott, a plastic surgeon who specialized in treating burns victims. Although I couldn't see much of his face behind the surgical mask on that first visit, he was a man whom I was to get to know quite well and to respect.

'How are you feeling after your journey?' the Colonel asked.

'Very tired . . .' My voice was a croak.

'Still very tired, are you?'

'Yes.' There didn't seem to be much more I could say.

'Now about these hands,' Colonel McDermott said, removing

them from the sterile polythene bags they'd been resting in like two little monsters from the film *Alien*. 'Are you getting any movement out of them at the moment? Would you like to show me what you can do?'

I said that I could straighten and bend them to a certain degree, but that movement was getting more difficult rather than less so.

Colonel McDermott decided that I should be lowered into a bath to soak off the dressings on my back and legs. I'd been lying on my back and could feel that I was stuck to the things. Nobody realized how much pain I was in. I can still hear my screams as they lifted me into that bath. They had to grab hold of the raw areas. There simply wasn't anything else to grab hold of. I was back on the *Galahad*, burning up all over again. Every single individual nerve-ending was on fire. I felt like dying. I thought, hell must be a nicer place than this.

'Jesus,' I said with some restraint as the dressings started to come free, 'I don't want to go through that again.'

The pain lessened to sheer agony for the next couple of hours. The water didn't go through the foam, so all they could do was rip it off. This time they gave me pain-killers. I needed them.

Colonel McDermott had his own sense of priorities. He decided to concentrate initially on my hands and my eyes. I was going to need both in a big way once I got back on the rugby field.

'All right, I'd like you to try moving those fingers again,' he said, pointing with a biro at my left hand and dictating to a nurse with a note-pad. 'Got some involvement on the left palm as well there, hasn't he? So that's left palm . . .'

I listened as he continued his examination.

'Mixture of deep dermal isn't it, and some superficial, but there's some new skin forming there.'

I hadn't a clue what he was talking about, and the incessant pain in my hands was the only thing reminding me that these strange, mutilated objects belonged to me. 'As long as you can sort out my eyes and my hands I don't care what you do,' I said.

'Those are first on the list.'

It must have been around this time that Mam and my stepfather, Loft, had their first chat with the surgeon. It must have been incredibly hard for my mother. She's a district nurse, and she knew from the start what my injuries meant. And yet there she was at my bedside for what seemed like day after day, smiling that warm, brown-eyed smile that had soothed me since my childhood. It was only much later that I learned that what I had interpreted as a smile had in fact been a grimace as she fought back the tears.

She never tried to pull the wool over my eyes, even when she knew that a firm answer to my optimistic questions might throw me into a pit of depression. And she was right not to. We Welsh might suffer from verbal diarrhoea, but it means we can spot bullshit a mile off.

'I reckon I'll be done for my twenty-first birthday,' I said.

She paused before answering. 'I don't know about that. You've got five weeks to go for that, Simon, and I don't know. You've got a lot of guts and determination, but whether you'll be home in five weeks I don't know.'

I was uncharacteristically quiet.

'Well the thing is, does it matter whether you're home for your twenty-first? We can bring it up here, can't we?'

But the social club in Nelson was where I wanted to be. Of course it would have been great to see Carl Dicks and Nigel Saunders and Bobby Brain and the rest of my mates in Woolwich, and they certainly would have made the journey. But it wouldn't be the same. Not by a long chalk.

They were due to operate on my eyelids for the first time on the Monday after that conversation, 5 July. I was going to have to stay in bed afterwards for five days.

'Will you remove all the pus from my eyelids?' I asked Colonel McDermott in the pre-op room.

'As much as I can. I hope they won't be as mucky as they are at the moment old son, that's true.'

I took a deep breath and told him about the nightmare I'd had ever since I was choppered to Ajax Bay. 'At the moment I'm petrified of going blind, absolutely petrified . . .'

The Colonel smiled through his mask. 'Well that's not too unreasonable, but I don't think there's any real danger of that. You won't go blind if we get the eyelids working properly. That's why we're doing this operation this morning, to make them work better. Right, can we let the lads get on with it and pop you off to sleep? Good boy. See you later.'

The idea was to remove thin layers of living skin from my thighs, shoulders and rump, with a machine a bit like a cheeseparer, then to lay it out on cotton wool before stitching some of it on to the backs of my hands and using some to rebuild my scorched and melted lids.

When I watched the process later on the television documentary it made me even more pleased that I had been under a general anaesthetic at the time. But that didn't mean that I wasn't the first to appreciate Colonel McDermott's artistry.

The object was to go for a thin split-skin graft in a fairly continuous sheet to cover my hands. The skin needed to be fairly thin to give the surgeons a surface that would fit more easily around my fingers. The thinner the skin graft, apparently, the higher the 'percentage take'. The team would then remove dead tissue from the reception sites so that those areas would put up new capillary vessels into the graft fairly quickly.

The grafts were to live on my tissue juices for the next thirty-six hours while that process was going on. Providing that the transplanted skin was kept still and in close contact with the prepared surface, there was a good chance that new vessels would grow and the graft would take. The grafted skin was stitched in place to stop it skidding about when the dressing was put on. The Colonel moulded wet wool into my hands to get the fingers and the knuckle joints fairly well extended. Apparently there is always a tendency in severe burns cases for the fingers to claw. As the wool dried out it would set into a splint.

I had been told that it is regular practice in the management of major burns to do this process of resurfacing by stages, doing as much each time as is safe with regard to the patient's general health.

The Colonel next turned his expert attention to my eyes. I had already had one emergency skin graft on the *Uganda*, and that had done a lot towards preserving my sight. The blink reflex is a remarkable thing, the Colonel told me, and it can usually outpace any foreign body flying towards the eye, or any flash. So it is very rare that the front surface of the eye is directly burned. In my case the blink reflex had closed the lids firmly.

The trouble was that in having closed so efficiently and therefore taken the brunt of the thermal injury, the lids themselves were at risk of scarring up and contracting, which would cause secondary exposure of the cornea. The Colonel wanted to prevent this at all costs, because sooner or later it would lead to ulceration and to perforation of the eye itself. And that is one way in which eyes can be lost.

The Colonel chose a relatively hairless part of my shoulder from which to take this graft. With luck this would mean that there would be little growth of hair on my lower eyelids.

These first few operations at Woolwich also brought home to me another aspect of my recovery that I had not been aware of. My body was forty-six per cent burned, and all the affected areas needed to be resurfaced with fresh skin. What I had thought of as my unscarred areas rapidly became donor sites for the areas that were badly burned. And let me tell you, having just one split-skin graft off one part of me that I'd thought had escaped the inferno was bad enough. Having that area and other areas harvested again and again for yet more skin was absolutely excruciating, and meant that those parts too became scarred. I kept on believing that it would all be all right. But the agony of the operations had only just begun.

And so it went on, an endless round of operations and physio, more operations and more physio. I saw a slightly different face in the mirror after each skin graft, and I had to start learning how to use my face and hands all over again. It was just like being a kid, experimenting with scowls and grins, moving my jaw around until even my tongue got cramp. Believe me, that was another first.

I was like a child in terms of my other capabilities, too. I couldn't even wipe my own backside. People often don't realize how soul-destroying it is to have an adult mind marooned inside a child's body. My reaction was: go away, I want to hide. That's what you feel when they're taking the extremely sticky, cling film-like bandage – called Op-site – off your raw donor areas and changing your dressings and they're hurting you and you want to go home.

Nobody understood how frightened I was, not even Mam. I was too much of a bravado merchant to let anyone see that I was scared rigid. The realization that you are badly injured is a painful, frightening and lonely process, because no one can go through that part with you. You realize on your own. Somebody could have told me every day that I was going to be permanently disfigured, and I wouldn't have heard them. I didn't want to know.

I was too busy covering up my inner battle by being childish and cracking jokes to see the pain my mam was going through. I should have stopped to realize that because she's a nurse, she knew how close to death I was. It was only much later that I discovered how many times my heart stopped beating during this period. But Mam knew. Mam was there, sitting at my bedside and watching me slowly and painfully getting worse and worse, until I finally turned the corner and started out on the equally painful road to recovery.

About three weeks later I was up and about in a big way. The combination of Colonel McDermott's skills, Mam's long vigil and my own body's downright stubbornness had produced results. I got depressed occasionally about how long everything seemed to be taking, but Mam was there to point out patiently how far I had already come. Neither of us forgot how far there was still to go.

At that stage my major ambition was to be able to pick up a pint and hold a cigarette for myself. It never occurred to me then that the ultimate targets of returning to the Army and the rugby pitch would be beyond my grasp, partly because I realized that the only way of stopping myself going out of my mind was to take things one day at a time. Life had to be lived in a series of short bursts, each one aimed at something just a little further than I could see.

Saturday 7 August was one such goal. Since before I discussed my twenty-first birthday with my mother on her first visit to Woolwich I had been determined to mark the day by returning to Nelson. It would have taken wild horses to stop me going home.

It felt great leaving hospital for the first time. Then, as we drove through London towards the M4, I started to feel conscious that people might see me. I wanted to hide. I felt embarrassed. I wasn't sure what my reaction would be if I saw people recoil from me. Once we were out on the motorway I relaxed. The journey was enjoyable, even though my injuries were sore.

Wales is my country. It's a marvellous place to come from. As Mam drove me through the valleys that day, I realized just how much I value the place and its people. There will always be a lot of me, and a lot for me, in Nelson. It's our stamping-ground, the place we jacked up our silly little plans to go somewhere and do something. I'll never really leave Wales. I'll keep travelling now, because I know there's a lot more I want to see and do, but my heart and soul will be for ever in the place I grew up.

As we passed through the familiar outskirts I thought, God, this is quiet. Then I saw a group of ladies standing on their rose gardens, all waving, and I thought, how did they know I was coming home? Then we rounded the corner and there were all these people. I was terrified. I wasn't bothered about the injuries, I just wasn't comfortable with everybody staring at me. I never had liked being the centre of attention. Still, it was the sort of welcome that confirmed me in my love for the place. Even people I had never met cheered us as Mam headed the car for home. We drove under a magnificent banner that read 'Nelson salutes you', and I hadn't had such a lump in my throat since Mam had appeared at Woolwich.

I leaned painfully across to her and said, 'Pop in Gran's house on the way, will you Mam? I'd like to give her a bit of hassle.'

The last time I'd walked up Nora's front path seemed a lifetime away. When she opened the door and saw me, there were tears in her eyes. Wearing a mixture of shorts, shirt and bandages, I must have looked a bit of a sight. She just kept shaking her head, and I thought I was going to start crying as well.

'I thought it would be a nice surprise for you,' I said.

Gran came forward to hug me.

'Don't, don't . . .' I said. I was petrified that she'd grab me on my sore places and then feel bad about hurting me.

Finally she said, 'Welcome home, lovely boy.'

'Put the kettle on then . . .'

That day was brilliant. They were all there – Gran, my grandfather, my uncle, even Helen and her gorgeous little daughter, Rebecca. We'd been through a lot of grief as kids, Helen and I, as I've said. We'd hated each other, really. But when we saw each other then, all that fell away. I knew she was disturbed by the shape I was in, and she seemed to want to say things to me, but she didn't get round to it until later. A lot later.

There was so much to catch up on, so much to tell. I sat with my family and it all came tumbling out: my gratitude, my hopes for the future – and my plan to nip down to the social club with the lads that night, even though I still couldn't pick up my own pint.

In an emotional day, perhaps what touched me most was Rebecca's reaction. She's always been the apple of my eye. She may be my sister's child, but she belongs to me, too. I was frightened she might be a bit scared of me – but kids are just as daft as ever: all she said was, 'Simon he fall down and baddie baddie.' Later she would climb up on my lap and go to sleep. It hurt like hell, but I never stopped her. She reminded me of what was real.

I couldn't really go down to the social club, not that time. I kept telling myself I would, but I wasn't strong enough. They're not the sanest bunch of boys down there, after all, though they're about the best.

When the cake appeared, I blew out the candles and they all sang 'Happy Birthday'. I looked across at Mam, and I knew she was thinking what I was thinking. Not so very long ago she'd watched a poor boy with burns she didn't recognize being brought out of an aeroplane, and she'd started to cry. And I'd said, 'Don't cry, Mam. I'm all right. I'm alive.'

All the time I was in hospital, my girlfriend, Susan Draper, visited twice or three times a week, whenever she could make it. She was like a rock to me. She would accuse me of being a Doubting Thomas when I got depressed about whether I would look half-way human, or about whether my hands would work again.

She never seemed to worry about all that. I remember her grinning at me and saying, 'You've still got all your features. Nothing got knocked off or anything. You've still got your nose, your mouth, your chin. And you're a little bit thinner . . .'

A little bit? I'd become a less-than-twelve-stone weakling by that stage.

'I can't wait to get you out,' she said. 'Get you fit and well and then we can get married.'

She knew I wouldn't do it until I was fit enough to sign the marriage certificate. There was no way anyone was going to carry me for the rest of her life.

She used to say, 'You're lucky, Simon. You came back and that's all that matters to me. You came back, you came home. It doesn't matter to me what you look like – never did before, did it!' Cheeky bugger.

By 4 November I was ready to be moved down to the Joint Services Rehabilitation Centre at RAF Chessington. There was a lot I could do now, after eleven operations, some of which had worked, some of which hadn't. I was able to do a fair bit of running, for a start, and it's not bad countryside down there. I could strike a match, light a lighter, hold a cup, hold a pint pot for my beer.

These were all little things that most people take for granted, but there were quite a few of us gathered at Buckingham Palace less than a month later who viewed them as major triumphs. We were there for the South Atlantic Campaign medal ceremony, and it was, inevitably, a very moving occasion. There was pride there, certainly, and as the Duke of Edinburgh presented me with my medal, I stood tall. But nothing could shake off the memories of the lads who weren't there, or the knowledge, as I watched my mates on parade from the sidelines occupied by the maimed and injured, that there was little chance now that I'd be joining them again.

They played 'We'll Keep a Welcome' after the national anthem that day, and I knew there would always be one for me in the 1st battalion of the Welsh Guards.

By the New Year of 1983 I was back at Woolwich for my twelfth operation. I'd grown a beard, which I was rather proud of, but the feelings of pain and dread with which I faced the latest attempt to get my hands working were much the same. The grafts across some of my fingers had grown into webs which had to be split, and because the joints wouldn't straighten properly they would have to pin the tips.

Three operations later, Colonel McDermott was ready to have a crack at my nose. As he explained to me, my skin had been contracting again and had pulled the tip of my nose up into my face. They'd sorted it out with a bit of resurfacing here, a split-skin graft there. The Colonel told me that they would need to carry on with such 'adjustments' in a series of operations over the next two years.

Sue wouldn't be around to grin at me through all that. I knew I'd miss her a lot, but I'd basically come to the decision to split at the beginning of March. Things had started to go wrong while the documentary was still being made. Sue had started taking off on me and I couldn't understand why. Probably it was because I was being such a swine to her on account of my injuries. Whatever the reason, it was as if we were just playing out the last few scenes of a black-and-white movie, and I just couldn't let her carry on like this. I had so many uncertainties about the future, it simply wouldn't have been fair of me to go on burdening her with them as well.

We'd never had any arguments or upsets over my injuries, and when I went home for the weekends with her, she used to do my dressings without batting an eye. But I had a long road to travel, and part of me insisted that whilst Wales and my family would always be there in the background, it was a journey I had to make on my own.

14

OUT OF HOSPITAL

Progress had been painfully slow. On my left hand, the fingers were stiff because the tendons had been burned off the top. I had lost my little finger because it was of no use and was in the way; the surgeons had lopped it off. Overall the hands were pretty much gnarled and scarred. The thumb was all right, just about the only working digit I had.

As I said, when my face was burned my nose shrank, because I have this awkward skin which contracts. My nose was pulled up out of shape and I looked like a male version of Miss Piggy. If you looked at me straight on, you could see right up my nostrils. Colonel McDermott's answer to the problem was to take some skin off the top of my bum and put it on my nose. After that, whenever I kissed anyone, they didn't know how close they came to kissing my backside. Little thoughts like that kept me happy.

Of all those injured on the *Sir Galahad*, I was the last to leave hospital. My body looked like a pink-and-white chess-board where patches of skin had been lifted from one part to be grafted to another. After thirty-five operations, the worst of my physical battle against the burns I'd suffered may have been over, but my battle to come to terms with them had scarcely started.

I had thought that once I was through the main surgery and recuperation, life could only become easier. Yet the opposite was true. Instead of finding that it was all over, I discovered that my biggest battle of all was just beginning – the fight for rehabilitation. The physical pain might have gradually lessened, but emotional pain was about to take its place – just as intense, and just as unbearable.

At first, the biggest challenge I had faced was getting back to being Simon Weston. But now, the biggest challenge I had in front of me was learning to live with life, learning to be a human being again. In the early days after the bombing there had always been so much going on, so many medics and camera crews swarming around, there wasn't time to think. I was far too busy working on getting better, having more operations and doing exercises, to worry seriously about the future.

Being filmed in *Simon's War* had provided some light relief at a time when it was much needed. The public response was just overwhelming. Over 1,000 letters poured in from people I'd never met. They sent money and little different things – one young lad sent me his lucky key-ring. Physically, I was beginning to feel better, but once I'd left Woolwich and Chessington and returned home, and all the attention had died down, I began to be tormented again by nightmares and flashbacks. I used to wake up in the middle of the night hoping it had all been a bad dream. There were times when I felt I couldn't handle it any more. I was off drugs and my mind was back together, and I was having to face the future and the fact that there were things I could never do again. The dream of playing rugby had long since been shattered, and I couldn't run and jump and fool about like I once could. But that didn't mean I wasn't the same guy inside.

The long, hot summer of 1983 was not kind to me. My skin had been sensitive to the sun at the best of times, but now the grafted areas were especially vulnerable. I also had a major problem with sweating. The grafted skin had no pores through which the fluid could pass, with the result that I perspired buckets through the few remaining good areas. I was almost more worried about the wetness showing through my T-shirts than I was about how people would react to my scars.

I became a nocturnal animal, coming out, like Dracula, with the setting sun. I'd go out to discos with the lads, have a ball, and creep back home in the early hours. Then I'd get up in the afternoon, have a bath, and lounge around in a pair of shorts until it was time to get ready to go out again. I put on an awesome amount of weight, mostly courtesy of lots of food, inactivity and Olde English cider.

I was desperately trying to live like a normal human being, but I had to look at life in a different way because people looked at me differently. Inside I was normal, but outside I was scarred. I wanted to go places and do things, but everywhere people stopped and stared. The fact was, most people felt revulsion when they saw me. They seemed to think that I was scarred on the brain, too. I tried not to let it bother me, but inevitably some things could not be shrugged aside. One night outside a disco in Cardiff, a pair of teenage girls stared, pointed and laughed at me. If only they could have known how much more that hurt me than any other kind of pain I had had to endure.

No wonder Nelson came to mean so much to me. I felt very privileged to live there. I could walk up the street knowing the kids wouldn't laugh or point. I could be myself. Everyone knew me, everyone understood, everyone cared. Outside Nelson, I didn't feel at ease.

Sometimes on a train people would keep on and on staring, and when they looked too long I felt like jumping up and poking them in the eye. I knew very well that if I had been them, I'd have stared too, because it's human nature. But I got fed up with being looked upon as a freak.

My ordeal came to a head in July when a bunch of us from the social club went up to Hereford on a darts trip. The evening went well, until at one point I started chatting to two girls who had seen *Simon's War*. Normally people were nothing but absolute kindness when they recognized me, but the boyfriend of one of these girls showed signs early on of feeling a bit frozen out of the conversation. He kept trying to butt in, but his girlfriend was more interested in hearing my exciting tales of derring-do. I went on and on; poor girl, she didn't know that I could talk a glass eye to sleep. Thwarted in his attempts to join in, the boyfriend eventually resorted to making witty comments about my appearance.

I didn't respond. It was the first time since leaving hospital that I'd encountered such overt antagonism, and I felt vulnerable and exposed. There wasn't much I could physically do about it anyway, the state my hands were in. But out of the corner of my eye I could see that Carl and the others were bristling.

Finally the boyfriend delved deep into his hand and played what he obviously thought was his Joker: 'Oi, when you gonna take your mask off then?'

It was one comment too many.

A member of the Nelson team, whom I shan't name, stood up, walked casually over to the table and gave the comedian a head-butt — smack on the bridge of his nose. The second wave were only a split second behind, and soon established a firm bridgehead, all over his face. I only hope it was a month or two before he went round poking fun at the disabled again.

After he had left we went up to the landlady to apologize for the broken furniture and for causing her so much bother.

'Rubbish, boys,' she said, 'I owe *you*.' She had heard the whole episode from the other bar and was just sorry that I had received that sort of treatment on her premises. She gave us all a round of drinks on the house.

On 6 October 1984 I reported back to Woolwich for yet another operation on my hands.

Being there this time was completely different. The previous year in hospital had been spent with dressings and injections and tablets and infections and worry. This was a totally different atmosphere: there was no worry, no pressure, none of the embarrassment of losing half the food out of my mouth or dribbling tea down my chin or having to ask for my backside to be wiped for me. I was free to go where I wanted to, do what I wanted to. On one memorable afternoon, about a week after an operation, I was allowed out with a nurse for three hours to watch the hospital team play rugby. It was the first day I'd ever drunk lager and I overstayed my three hours by another eight. There was ice all over the ponds near the hospital entrance when we made our way back in at 2.00 a.m., so naturally it was decided to do some ice-skating. How I escaped serious injury I'll never know.

There seemed to be quite a few loonies on Ward 13. Some were Paras, waiting for new plastic legs – probably so they could go out and kick something. They spent most of the day practising wheelies in their wheelchairs. Then there was the amazing black guy – a civvy – who wouldn't eat his breakfast until he'd had his special cup of tea. This consisted of tea, sugar and a large pinch of marijuana leaves. Often during the day he'd nip into the toilet for refreshments, and the whole ward would fill with clouds of herbal substances.

Besides doing the hand operation, Colonel McDermott had also taken out several small tiresome areas on my face where it was difficult to shave. In some places hairs had been growing inwards; in others it was impossible to use a wet razor because it would cut the skin, and an electric razor simply wouldn't penetrate. As a result I had been left with little bits of long hair, which looked pretty unseemly.

'It may be necessary to do some of the areas again,' the Colonel said a few weeks later, 'but by and large I think the whole beard area has improved so much over the time, and the skin is so much more supple now, that it'll stop pulling your face out of shape.'

I smiled and thanked him. It was then that he dropped his big bombshell.

'Now we seem to have come a long way in the two years and a bit since we started all this,' he said, and there was something about his tone that was ominous. 'I think it's useful sometimes to think where it's all leading, because the thing you've got to think hard about now is whether soldiering with these problems is really a worthwhile thing to do or whether it isn't better to consider some form of new life in the world outside . . .'

My heart sank a bit more with each sentence.

'So sooner or later I think you've got to consider seriously what the future has to hold. If your decision is to think about a new way of life, then we can call upon a lot of forces from outside – resettlement advice, assessment, aptitude tests, retraining for a new job. It's not my final decision to make and it isn't yours, but sooner or later we've got to ask people to make that assessment . . .'

I don't know why I was so surprised. It was something I had known he was going to say, but when he said it it still came as a blow. I'd accepted in my own mind a long time before that I'd have to leave the regiment, because you can't stay on in the Army with hands like mine and you can't be a lead weight around people's necks. But it still left a sick feeling in my stomach.

I left hospital a few days later and Mam drove me home. She was as sad as I was to have our secret fears confirmed, but, as ever, very supportive.

It wasn't long before I was summoned back to London to appear before the army medical discharge board. After a day of tests, I found myself seated in front of a doctor. He read to me from a prepared statement, which quoted my 'Pullins Assessment', a functional analysis, apparently, of a soldier's capacity to undertake his military duties. It took a time for what he was saying to sink in. I suppose I was clutching at straws, hoping to catch some stray word of hope or encouragement in amongst all the medical mumbo-jumbo. But ultimately what it boiled down to was that I was unfit for further military service.

'The findings of the board will be submitted to the commanding

147

officer of the hospital for confirmation,' the doctor concluded, 'and when they have been confirmed they will be forwarded to the commanding officer of your regiment for his authorization of your medical discharge from the Army.'

And that was that.

Next stop was a meeting with Major Handy, the army resettlement officer, and a disablement resettlement officer working with the Manpower Services Commission, the Army's civilian link with the job-finding network.

'We've got to forget about all the problems in the past,' the Major said, 'and think about getting you established as a civilian. For that we need some sort of background on you, thoughts and ideas of your own, and just try and work with them.'

'I don't have any ideas of much significance,' I said.

'Insignificant or not, all of us have a little dream tucked away in the back of our mind. Now's the time to pull it out and have a look at it. It may be impractical in the long run, but it's worth having a look at. What if everything was fine – is there anything you see yourself in, apart from the Army?'

'I was always into using brawn not brain, I found it easier on the head. I just enjoyed doing what I was doing.'

And it was true. I didn't have a clue what I wanted to do. Not one iota. There was more chance of me knowing what the Pope was saying in Italian. I thought I'd try for a job, preferably one that would make me a millionaire – but I doubted if that was going to come along, so I'd just plod along, Joe Soap.

Mam picked me up at Cardiff station and I was unusually quiet for most of the way home, deep in my thoughts. I didn't know what to expect in civilian life. I could only pin my hopes on the professionals – people who would resettle me and assess what I could and couldn't do. Mam felt that there wasn't a lot in Nelson for me. She thought the village had helped me all it could, that if I stayed there I'd just vegetate. And yet I wasn't prepared at that time to venture further than the village. I didn't intend to move away from Wales, because I liked it. I'd been away from Nelson once and I'd nearly never come back.

I was twenty-three, and I wanted to enjoy my life to the full. Just because I'd been injured, I didn't intend to lie back and sit in a corner like a hermit and let the world pass me by. But I still had to come to terms with getting up every day and looking in the mirror and saying, 'That's you, you're still ugly, you still look the same way, you haven't changed.' I still looked like a panda with those white eyes in the middle of a red face and my Miss Piggy nose. The scars would settle in time, but I didn't quite feel ready to go job-hunting. I guess I was afraid of employers' reactions.

The fact is, it's just not socially acceptable to look the way I do. Some of my friends cried when they first saw me, and they're a pretty tough bunch. Inside I was still the same old Simon Weston; it was just that everyone looked at my face first – and I knew only too well what they saw.

You try to put up a front, but it does drag the stuffing right out of you. All of a sudden, reality caught up with me. The physical pain had gone, but it was replaced by a pain that was much harder to cope with, mental anguish. It was doubly hard when I realized in my heart of hearts that I wasn't going to go on doing all the things that had been such a large part of my life. I wasn't sure that, at the age of twenty-three, I could come to terms with that.

At home I was grounded, and the frustration was enormous. I had twenty-four hours a day to think of myself and nothing else; I began almost to look forward to going back to hospital for my next operation as a release.

I felt as if I'd been chased to the top of a tree by all the fuss and the publicity and had fallen out of it – and kept on going when I hit the ground. I had to climb out of the hole I was in even to get back to ground level, and then I had to learn to climb the tree all over again – but this time at my own pace.

In the outside world, people were still saying to me, 'How are you? You're wonderful, you're a hero,' and then they'd pat the old boy on the back and buy him a drink. And I'd wake up in the morning feeling awful, and I'd look in the mirror and I'd think, what's the point? I got more and more lazy and lethargic. I was drinking myself into oblivion.

At home, it was love, the greatest of human emotions, that was slowly killing me. Drink was a kind of escape from the suffocation, the total lack of independence. I was being a swine, I knew it, but subconsciously I was sending out a message: get away from me, leave me alone. I'm not ashamed of my behaviour. It wasn't something I could control.

I stopped caring about myself and about everything. I didn't wash, I didn't brush my teeth, I just wanted to sit in my room alone all day. In the evenings I would go out and drink ten or fifteen pints of cider and get so drunk that the next day I couldn't remember a thing about what had happened – and worst of all, I didn't care. I was turning into the village idiot. I grew fat and scruffy and, for the first time since the bombing of the *Galahad*, I lost my will to live. I felt that for me there was no future, no light at the end of my little tunnel.

Mam was devastated. For her it was pure hell. She had been told when I was injured that none of our lives would ever be the same again, and I'd lived to make her remember those words. I was a complete swine to her, but I couldn't explain why, not even to myself. Maybe it was just because she was there.

She didn't know what to do for the best. I was so obsessed with myself and my despair that I stayed in my room all day, not talking to her, not talking to anybody, even when my food was brought up to me. She'd go down to Gran's sometimes and come back with her eyes red from crying, but even that didn't get through to me.

The depression didn't lift. I was like ten bears with sore heads. I was rude to my family, rude to everybody. I was nasty to Mam, not worth the ink on my birth certificate.

When people came to the house, I smiled for them, I said the things they wanted to hear, but it wasn't what was going on inside. Only Mam knew of my great sorrow at having lost my mates, and of the terrible guilt I felt about them being dead. Over and over I blamed myself for being alive while they had died. On the very blackest days I wished that I had gone, too. 'Mam,' I remember crying at the foot of her bed one night, 'it's so much harder to live.'

'It's courage of living, even surviving the way you did,' Mam said to me, but her words didn't get through.

Gran, too, had a go at bringing me to my senses. 'Don't you dare say that you should be dead. Not when we've grieved and worried and waited for news of you. Your voice is coming out of your face and that's what we want, it's what we've always heard, bless your heart.'

One night after I'd had too much to drink again I went into Mam's bedroom and stood over her, sobbing. 'Don't you realize how my hands got burned?' I cried, putting my hands out in front of her.

'Well, you got burned with the bomb.'

'No, Mam. There were boys there and I was trying to push them out, and why do you think my hands are all burned? Because when you go down you clench your hands, but I tried to push them out and they wouldn't come, Mam, they just wouldn't come and they were on fire and I had to stop it and all the skin was dropping off my hands – and those boys died and I ran, and I should be dead with them.'

'Simon, you had the courage and you ran. They just couldn't.'

I'd come so far, and to her all my progress seemed to be slipping away. What worried her more than anything was that I'd go down so low that I'd never climb back up. At the end of her tether, she decided to get in touch with my other 'family' to see if they could help.

The Welsh Guards couldn't have responded more quickly. An officer called at our house a few days later on what I thought was just a passing visit. We swapped pleasantries to start with, and then in the course of the conversation I was asked if I'd like to go to Germany to watch the team play rugby.

'Yes, sir,' I said. No hesitation.

Just the thought of going cheered me up. I travelled on my own and collected my usual round of stares. But this time I didn't care. Depression is a circle and you're a pea in the centre, rattling around. You're stuck. But there is a chink in that circle, and everyone has a key to open it. My regiment was my key. And when I got there and discovered that they hadn't forgotten me and they were still my mates and treated me quite normally, I was cured.

Nobody in Germany was going to suffocate me with kindness.

I drew strength from the lads and the way they ignored me. 'Want a game of cards, Squeak? You deal.' 'Get us a cup of tea, Squeak.' It was the reverse of everything I'd got used to. It was great, I was even coming out with the old excuses – 'I would make the tea, lads, but I've got to sort my jeans out' – not the new, contrived ones based on my disabilities. The boys even told me I was wrong sometimes. To patronize someone because of their injuries is the worst thing you can do, because you create a beast – a beast you can't control. What do you do with it when it's become a drunk, an alcoholic, a drug addict?

Nothing was done for me unless I asked. Nobody mollycoddled me. If I wanted to speak to the lads I had to go to them, they didn't come to me. It was the best therapy I could ever have had. They were used to seeing injured soldiers all the time. They weren't going to bend over backwards for me.

I was in Germany for nearly three weeks. When I came back I was a changed person. There was this scarred boy coming back a scarred man. And it was thanks to the lads and their no-nonsense, no-pussyfooting attitude.

There was one incident in particular that had a profound effect on me. I had gone to watch the lads play and I met the man formerly in charge of the Welsh Guards rugby team, Glynn 'Chalky' White, a gravelly-voiced legend, in many people's eyes probably one of the greatest Welsh Guards who's ever lived.

'Hello, Squeak, how are you?' he boomed as I went up to him.

He stretched out his hand in greeting and I went to shake it. But as I had got into the idle habit of doing, I didn't bother to raise my thumb. I was presenting him with what must have felt like a stump.

'Shake my hand properly!' he commanded.

I was mortified. I had allowed myself to be disabled in a handshake. It was a moment of truth, another lesson learned.

I came back from Germany in time to see the second documentary about me, *Simon's Peace*, which was first shown in June 1985. On top of the visit to the regiment, it was just the slap in the face I needed. I stopped drinking so heavily after seeing the big fat slob on the screen, guzzling a bottle of sherry, the village drunk. For the first time in almost two years, I felt motivated. The best motivation, of course, is anger, and I felt angry with myself for having got into that state.

The root of the problem had been that I had desperately needed to regain my independence and, in turn, my self-respect, but everyone had been too involved to realize that. Mam's life had revolved around me totally, from visiting me every day in hospital to bringing me home and doing everything for me.

In June Mam and Loft made themselves take a holiday. They flew off to Jersey and had a wonderful time. When they got back, I was on the doorstep with my apron on.

'I coped perfectly all week,' I laughed. 'Now, is anybody ready for the Sunday lunch I've cooked?'

In throwing off the role of 'patient', I had turned the corner. But I still had to face some cold, hard facts about my future. In spite of the surgeons' skills, my limitations were severe. Both my hands –

one minus a finger – were crippled. In short, I could no longer do the job for which I was trained, and I knew it. What chance would I have of finding work in civvy street?

The kids, as ever, were rays of sunshine. Richard would get his little fat arm and wrap it half-way round my neck and give me a kiss. Rebecca would come home from school and come straight in to see me. She must have been able to remember me vaguely from before I was injured, because if she was shown a pre-1982 photograph of me she would say, 'That's Simon.' They didn't notice my scars as they scrambled and crawled all over me, kissing and hugging me. They just saw me as someone they loved. For them, at least, it was as though the *Sir Galahad* horror had never happened.

I stayed at home for a few more months, and later that year I was discharged from the Army with a lump-sum payment and a disability pension. I had already received a handsome payment from the South Atlantic Fund. The Army offered me a job as a storeman, but I wouldn't consider it. 'Thanks,' I told them, 'but it would drive me round the bend sitting in stores all day, having been so active. Anyway, I wouldn't be happy because I couldn't hold rank. I couldn't tell men to do something I couldn't do myself.'

So there I was, for the first time in eight years, no longer a serviceman. But at least the wishing and the hoping were over. I was resigned to my lot. There was no more the Army could do for me and no more I could do for them. I couldn't have been a storeman or a porter; my pride couldn't have stood it. I walked out of the office that day with my head held high, as high as the Guards had taught me to hold it. I might have been walking into an uncertain future, but I was walking tall.

15

TENERIFE

In January 1986, shortly after passing my driving test, I was offered an all-expenses-paid holiday for two in Tenerife by a generous lady well-wisher. I accepted, and Carl Dicks came with me. It was the first holiday I'd had since I was injured – and it certainly proved to be a move up in the world from staying in guest houses in Blackpool with views of the gasworks. We had the free run of the lady's luxurious apartment in Playa de las Americas.

Carl and I did the usual British touristy things for the first day or two – sightseeing, drinking, eating out in restaurants every night, walking up and down the beaches eyeing up the lovelies. Often we danced away into the early hours of the morning, just generally having a wild old time and making new friends.

We met a girl called Maggie Reed, just twenty-one years old, who was on holiday with her sister, Nikki, who had Down's syndrome. They were being hassled by a group of Spanish lads who were trying to chat up the pair of them. Carl and I dragged them out on to the dance floor and had a great time. Maggie so impressed me, taking her sister away on holiday like that on her own. She has been a very special friend ever since.

On about our fourth night on the island, Carl and I went to a party. We took a short cut through a garden, and in the darkness I skipped over a hedge and a low wall on to what should have been solid ground on the other side. Instead I found myself plummeting twenty feet down into an alleyway filled with building materials. I landed badly on a pile of rubble and what felt like cacti. Carl ran for an ambulance and I was carted off to hospital. The doctors X-rayed me but, despite the pain I was in, found nothing broken. They then spent a couple of hours pulling long thorns and pieces of masonry out of me and covering me in iodine. I felt in absolute bits. Quite apart from having done physical damage to my hip, my knee and my shoulder and collected countless cuts and bruises, I wasn't exactly happy to find myself back in hospital.

I must have dozed off. When I opened my eyes it was morning, and a beautiful nurse was coming into my room. She had short, fairish hair and the most lovely brown skin I'd ever seen. She went over to the window and pulled open the curtains. Light flooded into the room as she turned to look at me. When she saw my face she gasped.

'Hello there, lad,' she beamed, 'what are you doing here, then?'

She was from Sheffield, and remembered me from the documentaries. We got on like a house on fire, and spent a while chatting about this and that – and about how best I could go about discharging myself. It was a lovely, clean hospital and the staff were marvellous, but if there's one thing I can't stand it's listening to piped Spanish music. Later that morning, as Rodrigo's *Concierto de Aranjuez* came around for what seemed like the tenth time, I headed for the admissions desk to sign myself out. Then, after a fruitless search for a taxi, I set off on the mile and a half hobble back to the apartment. I had a joyous reunion with Carl over a bottle or two of Tenerife beer, and we decided to try and have a quiet time of it for the rest of the holiday.

Just a few nights later, however, disaster struck again. Carl and I got parted in a crowd, and as the night was still young I thought I'd try to find him rather than just head back to the apartment. My eye was attracted by the flashing sign of a discothèque, and I decided that that was where Carl must have gone.

I went down a flight of steps and approached the pay desk. There were three charming characters in attendance: a skinny, weaselly type, very smooth and Latin-looking, wearing a leather tie; a much bigger bloke; and a little dumpy security guard, whose belly spilled over a California highway patrolman's belt from which hung a large, leather-clad truncheon and a gun.

'What's the price?' I asked the one with the leather tie, quite civilly I thought.

'500 pesetas,' he replied.

'OK,' I said, putting my hand in my pocket.

'700 pesetas,' he said as I pulled out my money.

'What?'

'1,000 pesetas.'

'Hang on, what's the form here, mate?'

'1,500 pesetas.'

'Come on.'

'Ha ha ha,' he laughed mechanically, pointing at my injuries and jabbing me on the chest in a Latin gesture of contempt. 'Malvinas, ha ha ha, fuck English.'

Now the last thing I wanted was to get into a fight; I'd just finished two and a half years of major surgery. But I wasn't just going to walk away from this.

I caught hold of his tie. I don't know if it was because it was his best one, but he screamed. He was up in the air, he was running around. Then all hell seemed to break loose. The big bouncer grabbed hold of me from behind, and in a textbook move that would have made my unarmed-combat instructors proud, I brought my elbow back hard into his stomach like a piston, turned, and threw him to one side. The weasel lunged forward at me again, and with the state my hands were in there was little I could do to defend myself but head-butt him. He fell screeching to the ground, and I began to think it might be time to leave.

Unfortunately, I didn't see the little fat security guard come up behind me with his truncheon. I felt him, though; he hit me fair and square between the shoulder blades, and it hurt. I spun around, angry and dazed, and found myself staring down the business end of a Beretta pistol.

I made a dash for the stairs. I couldn't believe how much longer that staircase had become. I took the steps two at a time, jet-propelled by the image of my mind's eye of the Beretta's muzzle. At the top it was a simple case of 'Legs, do your stuff . . . Come on road, my best friend, get shorter!'

I ran all the way back to the apartment and slammed the door hard behind me.

'Do you mind, Wes,' Carl shouted from his bedroom. 'I'm trying to kip in here.'

16

DOWN UNDER

In the summer of 1986 I received a letter from the Guards Association of Australasia. One of their committee members, Dennis Turner, a former Coldstream Guard from New Zealand, having seen the documentaries had floated the idea of my doing a goodwill tour, at their expense and as their guest. Would I like to go? I replied almost by return of post that I'd love to, and the next thing I knew, Don Cross, one of their officials, had come over to Britain and set out an itinerary for me.

I was to fly to Perth on my own. The Guards Association had paid for the flight, on Malaysian Airlines, and a British expatriate in Melbourne had very generously had me upgraded to business class.

It was my first trip of any significance, since being injured, on my Jack Jones. Mam, Gran and Grandsha drove me to Heathrow. I was only going away for six weeks, but Gran was all hugs and kisses and tears. I love my family desperately, but they do fuss a lot. I just wanted to get the goodbyes over with and get on the plane. None the less, it was quite a moment when we parted company and I disappeared into the departure lounge.

The flight was less eventful than my last long-haul one, the record-breaking VC10 run from Montevideo to Brize Norton. We arrived in Perth at about 2.00 a.m. after flying via Paris, Dubai and Kuala Lumpur. I was wearing a peaked cap with a seagull on the top of it, which I'd got off a Varsity reporter on a train one night. The contingent of representatives from the Guards Association of Australasia was parade-ground smart in blazers and ties. They put me at ease at once when they presented me with a slouch hat that carried all the Guards badges.

Mam's cousin Colin was also there to greet me. When all the handshaking was over, he drove me to his place to relax and to enjoy the first of many generous Australian welcomes. At the slightly more respectable hour of 5.00 a.m. we drove over to my uncle Arthur's, where I was to stay for ten days.

Don Cross had set a busy schedule. The Royal Marines were in town, and the following night we had dinner with them and went on board ship. It was the first time I'd been on a Royal Navy ship since the Falklands, but I can honestly say I didn't feel one jot of emotion – except to marvel at how big everything was, and what good drinkers the Marines are. The next morning I woke up not only jet-lagged, but lager-lagged too. Luckily I was chauffeured everywhere in Neil McLean's magnificent white Rolls-Royce. Neil used to live next door to my cousin Colin, and had volunteered his thoroughbred motor. He looks just like a young Tommy Steele, and he's the sort of chap who wouldn't do anyone a bad turn if he could do them a good one. Neil is a superb character. I'm proud to have spent ten wonderful days in his company.

There were more dinners to attend, more speeches to be made. I gladly filled in the odd gap in the set programme with a few charity 'appearances', which I was delighted to see resulted in several colour televisions being donated for a children's burns unit.

Then began the real whistle-stop tour, taking in chiefly Victoria, Sydney, Brisbane and Adelaide. Everywhere we went, I was bowled over by the friendliness of the Aussies. I met the British White Crusader team, who were in Perth to compete for the America's Cup, and went out and watched them from the tender. We lunched on champagne and wonderful cheese rolls. The French team provided one of the biggest laughs of the day. Their boat was called *French Kiss*. The boat had a little rubber power-boat, which they had called, rather wittily, *Kiss Me Quick*. The French, it seemed, had quite a good grasp of English idiom. But not enough, unfortunately, to stop them also proudly painting on the team helicopter, in large red letters, the name *Kiss Me Chopper*.

In Adelaide there was a big Guards reunion dinner, where I eventually had the pleasure of meeting Dennis Turner, the former Coldstream Guard who had had the idea of inviting me over in the first place. This was followed by a week of sightseeing trips and visits to the wine-growing district. In Melbourne I met another expatriate, a Welshman, who had very kindly stood me all my internal flights. I also stayed with someone from the Household Cavalry who I'd actually once propped against. The marvellous Ivor Gamlin conducted me around New South Wales and the fabulous Blue Mountains. They were covered with snow, and they reminded me of Wales. I walked and I walked and I walked.

In Sydney I visited the harbour bridge and the opera house, and they were every bit as magnificent as I'd imagined. Other highlights, in Perth, were meeting Lewis Collins in the bar, after watching him in a play called *Death Trap*, and visiting the famous Yanchep Inn, which people drive thirty miles to just for a drink. On my visit I was presented with one of the biggest barbecued meals a former sixteen-and-a-half-stone prop forward could ever have hoped to set eyes on. The interesting thing about the Yanchep is that it's owned by a Welshman. I don't remember much about the next day.

For the first time since I'd been injured, I began to relax on my own and to enjoy meeting new people at gatherings. I had begun to realize that I could face up to others on my own terms and be me, Simon — not just a burned face. I had more self-confidence now to cope with all the functions, all the dinners, all the fresh faces to meet and new hands to shake. It felt good. And I really owe a lot to Neil McLean and Don Cross for all the help they gave me.

After ten days in Perth, ten in Adelaide, five in Melbourne, ten in New South Wales and twelve in brilliant Brisbane, it was time to fly back to Perth. The Welsh Society of Perth came to a final Guards farewell dinner. We sang a few songs, and eased our way through the biggest bit of beef I'd ever seen in my life. My thank-you speech came from the bottom of my heart, because I couldn't remember when I'd had such a good time, amongst so many good and generous people. Australia had actually given me more than they perhaps ever knew. I was almost sad to be returning to Britain.

I came back to Britain for three weeks, because I'd promised an ATC corps that I'd go to their Christmas party. Then, on 17 December, I got on another plane and flew all the way back down to New Zealand.

While I was still at Woolwich, it had been arranged for me to join Operation Raleigh as a signaller when I was fit and well again. I had gone to their London headquarters for an interview, not realizing at the time that because of who it was who had actually nominated me, it was just a formality. At Anchorage airport I discovered that I was on the same plane as Colonel John Blashford-Snell, the creator of Operation Raleigh.

'I never did find out who nominated me,' I said to him conversationally.

'You didn't? Well I shouldn't really tell you this, but I'll give you a clue. It is someone very closely associated with your part of the world, who has followed your progress with a lot of interest and concern.'

'My mam?' I ventured. 'My gran?'

'No. As a matter of fact, it was the Prince of Wales.'

I was rather quieter than usual for the rest of the thirty-six-hour flight.

There were about seventy Operation Raleigh venturers on the flight, all between the ages of seventeen and twenty-four. From Anchorage we flew on to Tokyo on Japan Airlines, who taught me that I don't like cold noodles and raw fish. We milled around at the airport for six or seven hours waiting for our next connection, eating as much as possible and gradually getting to know each other better. We stopped again in Fiji, where most of us grabbed the welcome chance to have a shower.

When we finally flew down into Auckland there wasn't a cloud in the sky, and all you could see were houses and green, and more green, a bit more green, and then a bit more green. I'd never seen so much beautiful countryside in my life. New Zealand is absolutely gorgeous. It must rate as one of the most unspoiled countries in the world.

We had three or four hours to kill, so a few of us took a taxi into town. We did a bit of sightseeing and went down to the harbour before returning to the airport and boarding our flight to Christchurch. I got on the plane and sat down, and a stewardess came round with sandwiches. The next thing I remember is waking up as the wheels touched the ground. My sandwich was still intact in my hands. It was the first time I had ever slept on an aeroplane, and my mouth tasted like the Odor-Eater in a desert dispatch rider's boot.

I was met at the airport by my uncle Arthur's daughter, Heather. I spent Christmas with her and her wonderful family and was then driven down to Te Anau in Fjordland for the start of my phase of Operation Raleigh.

After being shown to the tent that was to be my home for the next two or three months, I was introduced to my fellow members of staff. However, as I quickly discovered, there was nothing for me to do. I had been sent out there as a signaller, but because we weren't Post Office registered I wasn't allowed to use the equipment. I filled my time with familiarization courses and sessions in first aid and search and rescue.

My first project proper was with the team cutting a track around the Kepler Mountains. I was sent there to keep the peace; the team was divided equally into meat-eaters and vegetarians, and they didn't get on. One girl wouldn't cook meat because she didn't eat it herself. Such were the concerns of these pioneering spirits from the other side of the world.

Next was Breaksea Island. It was wet and horrible, and I was bitten remorselessly by sandflies. I was notionally in charge of the venturers there who engaged on a rat-eradication programme. The idea was to create a flightless-bird sanctuary. The vegetable v. meat debate had mercifully been left behind, but food problems of a different sort now took over. All our rations were dehydrated, and after a few days of the diet our location earned a new name. We called it Break Wind Island.

It was on Breaksea Island that we were flooded. One afternoon, after it had been raining hard for three days, all the members of the party were spending a few moments relaxing. I decided to have a short snooze, and went to lie down in the tent, only to be woken up by shouts from outside.

'Wake up, Wes!' called Tony Horgan, an ex-Army cook. 'The tent's flooding.'

'What do you mean?' I said.

'We're sinking.'

I sat up and jumped off my bed – into about a foot of water.

'Don't bother,' said Tony. 'We've sunk.'

Looking out, I faced a scene of devastation – and all our bits and pieces were floating away towards the beach. It reminded me of the small flooded trench in the Falklands. If it wasn't fire, it was water.

I shouted to the other venturers to help, and they all rushed off in different directions. I expected them to return armed with pots and pans to help me bail out. Instead they came back carrying armfuls of cameras to capture the disgust on my face. Some friends, I thought.

I would say that I learned from my four months with Operation Raleigh rather than enjoyed them. I learned that I didn't like sleeping rough any more. I learned that I didn't like mosquitoes and sandflies and I didn't like being floated out of my tent. But I did feel a great sense of satisfaction after a long bout of 'bush-bashing' – blazing a trail through miles of dense vegetation. It was really hard-going even for the fittest members of the contingent, let alone for the less able-bodied. I was knackered by the end.

One of the most significant events of the whole trip occurred on Breaksea Island, when I came across someone I recognized at once as a kindred spirit – and he wasn't even a Welshman.

Paul Oginsky was twenty-five years old and came from Liverpool. He'd worked as an electrician at ICI and British Nuclear Fuels before deciding to devote his time to working with people. He had gone back to college and qualified as a sports manager. He'd worked voluntarily with various outdoor-pursuits organizations, often drawing on his experience as a keen member of the TA Parachute Regiment (for which I held nothing against him).

Paul had been invited to join the Liverpool Action Group (funded by United Biscuits and the European Social Fund), which had been set up to study ways of remotivating unemployed people. Subsequently Paul had led and participated in many courses in this field, including Operation Raleigh. We were thrown together when we were stranded on the island for several days, and immediately discovered a common interest in working with young people in depressed areas of Britain. It didn't take us long to outline our new joint venture, which he persuaded me to call Weston Spirit. It was a great idea – but I still had quite a while left in New Zealand in which to think it over.

After the end of phase party I hired a car with Paul, Lionel Fairbrother and Mick Curtis, all of them TA Paratroopers, and we toured South Island for five days, sleeping in the car. Dunedin proved to be a town of special significance for me. It was there, for the first time, that I found the courage to put on my bathing-trunks and 'go public' with my scars. I had worked out for myself a long time before that your scars are what you've got, they're not what you are. That hadn't made it any easier to expose them to public scrutiny, but now, at last, I'd learned to come face to face with my fear of being stared at. I was egged into it by the no-nonsense attitude of the other lads, but I have to say as well that the New Zealand kids at that swimming-pool were fantastic. They just ignored me; they were far too interested in their own fun to take any notice of a crinkle-cut chip from overseas.

I went back up to Christchurch with a guy called Ian Latimer, a New Zealand army captain a year or two older than me. Ian shared a house with a New Zealand army nurse, who had spent time in England on an exchange programme with the British Army, at a military hospital in London. The night I met her she walked into the room, did a quick double-take, smiled and said, 'Hello, Simon.' She'd been one of my nurses at Woolwich.

I was guest of honour at Ladies' Night at the 2nd/1st New Zealand Infantry barracks just outside Christchurch one night. I'd never been anywhere where officers drank so much beer. I travelled to Auckland next, where I stayed with Frank Sharman and his wife, Trixie, and then on to Wellington to stay with the tremendous Triggs, who had first written to me after I was injured. Ken Trigg, an ex-Coldstream Guard, is married to Odette, a Swansea girl, and they have a gorgeous daughter, Tracy, who in the short time I was there became like a sister to me.

Paul had been staying at a deer farm in Tapukki, and I went down there to meet him. I arrived wearing a cowboy hat, riding a hobby-horse and armed with two water-pistols. I rode around singing 'Do not forsake me oh my darling . . .' We saw a sign one day that said 'Happy Sandwich Day', so we went round saying 'Happy Sandwich Day' pleasantly to everyone we met. We didn't realize it was the name of a local restaurant.

We flew on a twin-prop plane to Rotorua. The first thing we'd notice there, people had warned us, would be the pungent smell of the region's sulphurous mud-pools. We smelled nothing – mainly, I suspect, because of the degeneration of our nasal faculties after so many weeks on Break Wind Island.

The Maoris honour people whom they class as warriors or brave, and for some reason they had decided that I qualified for a special welcome. It frightened the life out me, all the tongue-wagging and paddle-waving.

Soon after the ceremony had begun, it started to rain. 'This is a good omen,' one of the elders told me. 'The gods are weeping with joy for you.'

It was a wonderful welcome and a ceremony I'll never forget. I touched noses with a number of people that day. How many Maoris do you know who have touched a Welshman's bum with their noses?

And then, all too soon, and after marvellous hospitality from Don Colquhoun, Paddy Keegan and Dennis and Kath Turner, it was time to board the plane for London.

On the first leg of the long flight home, Paul and I talked more and more about our plans. We shared an awareness of some of the problems faced by people living in the depressed urban areas of Britain. So many young people seemed to be drowning needlessly in a sea of apathy, and we wanted to do something about it. We devised a way of attracting the most positive of these youngsters and stimulating their enthusiasm to motivate others within their communities.

Our plan was that through the medium of residential courses in rural settings, these young people would learn skills in group work, leadership and community awareness. They would be given the chance to develop their initiative and confidence in a supportive atmosphere, where the emphasis would be on a balanced programme of action and reflection. The courses would serve as a beginning, not as an end in themselves. Participants would be supported on their return home in the development of local enterprise projects, which would identify needs and seek solutions.

Well, that was the grand theory. Paul and I parted company in Japan, where he was to spend some time staying with a Japanese venturer, while I returned home to think about what we had discussed. The plane finally came down through dense clouds and landed at Heathrow. I was glad to be back in Britain. I'd been away six months – and half a year is a long time to be away from Wales.

Helen was there to greet me in my car. I drove all the way home.

17

WESTON SPIRIT

Paul telephoned me after I'd been home for a week or two and asked me whether I still fancied putting Weston Spirit into practice. I said yes, but not without a little stab of reluctance: moving to Liverpool meant moving from Wales. It was a wrench, but I felt propelled by the thought of what we hoped to achieve. Hope we had plenty of; all we needed were funds, offices and expertise.

We approached Merseyside Council for Voluntary Service (MCVS) for advice and support. They offered us a project base in one of their broom cupboards. As soon as we had managed to relocate some large papier-mâché animals, we were in business.

MCVS also agreed to provide other office facilities free of charge, which included the first office desk I had ever sat behind. Paul and I wrote down all we knew about setting up organizations, which took us about ten minutes. Never mind, we soon found many people who offered us good advice – most of it conflicting. We were getting nowhere fast.

Merseyside Youth Training produced a Weston Spirit letterhead, and Paul and I started writing to people to get things moving. One of our lucky breaks was that because of my history and the documentaries, the media needed little prompting to take an interest. I appeared twice on the BBC television programme *Breakfast Time*, and plugged the venture in many other television, radio and press interviews.

Paul and I were joined by another Merseysider, Ben Harrison. All three of us now set about the leviathan task of setting up a charity from scratch. Needless to say, we jumped in feet first and made immense cock-ups. We made the mistake of trying to do everything ourselves. But in this life you get nothing for nothing. If you want everything of quality you have to pay for it. Our major error was that we thought penny-pinching was the way to success.

You have to be seen to be doing the work before anyone else will throw in their lot with you.

Donations and offers of help started to trickle in. The Post Office decided to help, and found us a marketing company. Falcon Cycles donated bicycles for a proposed sponsored bike-ride from Mexico City to Toronto.

Dealing with the problems of setting up an organization absorbed a lot of time, and the launch of Weston Spirit kept getting put back and back. We wanted to do something more immediate, so we decided to run a short course along Weston Spirit lines. Ten trainees from Merseyside Youth Training were selected to take part. A course took place in Derbyshire, and was a great success. The trainees returned to set up a scheme called the Liverpool Youth Venture Project to involve young people in their communities. News of the success of the course spread. Other youth organizations enquired about courses, and more plans were drawn up.

When we began we didn't believe we had the answer to the problems of the inner city. We believed we had the answer to a small part of them. That's always been all we're offering – to re-enthuse youngsters rather than just watch them go on having this apathetic attitude, the influence of peer pressure, most of which is of a destructive nature. I'm not claiming to be a child psychologist, I just want to give these young people a chance. I now believe that if there is a reason why I was injured, then it was to become reasonably well-known and therefore good at opening doors. I've bounced back; God, have I bounced.

I never thought I'd sit behind a desk in my entire life, or go to committee meetings dressed in a suit and tie. I have been a soldier, a player of rugby and a trench-digger, and I have never experienced this type of lifestyle before. It's a lot harder than it looks. I feel I've got a lot out of it. I've learned a lot.

If setting up this venture has taught me nothing else, it's taught me that patience is a virtue – and that God helps those who help themselves. Everything might well come to him who waits – but you've got to be doing something while you're waiting.

By the end of 1988 we had raised over £50,000 and run six successful courses. The response from the youngsters who have taken part has been fantastic. They have taken on the Weston Spirit mantle and are the best advertisement the organization could ever have. I am very proud to be associated with them.

As long as each day remains a challenge, that's all that matters to me. It means a great deal to have achieved so much so soon, and I hope it will mean a great deal to a lot of other people who would not otherwise have had the chance to realize their ability to succeed. Getting the show on the road involved a lot of hard work and a lot of frustration, but at the same time it was great experience, and through it I met a lot of wonderful people.

But there was still one outstanding item on my personal agenda that just had to be faced, and that was the tricky question of what to do with the rest of my life. Weston Spirit had given me a reason for being around, but I didn't plan to be actively involved for ever. I was still only twenty-seven. I had a mortgage. Eighteen months is long enough to go without a wage packet. I had to start earning. My whole future was ahead of me, and it needed to be planned.

That was why, when a letter arrived one day from the Douglas Bader Foundation, offering me an interview for a flying scholarship, I grabbed the opportunity with both hands. It meant I could put off making any career decisions for at least another month or two.

18

FLYING

I turned up at Biggin Hill on the appointed day, still not knowing who had sent in my application form for me. To this day I don't know.

There were twenty-two of us down for selection, including one lad with spina bifida, who already held a private pilot's licence and who wanted to get his commercial pilot's licence. The Civil Aviation Authority had said he needed to be an instructor first, and the Douglas Bader Foundation scholarship was paying for him to do just that. It's a marvellous institution, operating on the principle that if Bader could fly as a disabled person, then why shouldn't others? Over the years they have helped countless disabled people to realize that, quite literally, the sky is the limit.

The selection procedure consisted of batteries of tests, followed by intensive interviews for those who passed. The tests for us were the same as those given to RAF candidates. Some were like space-invader games, where you had to try to keep a dot in the centre of the screen, or chase a white dot up a wiggly line of red dots. Some involved mathematics. Equations, I love them like a broken leg. I go dyslexic when I look at numbers. I sat there with this test paper in front of me and I just got bored. When I reached the most important question I answered it by pure guesswork: I just chose the formula that looked the sturdiest, with a little c on the top and a bold H inside some brackets on the bottom.

Next came the medicals. The tests on my eyes were extra rigorous. They were concerned about the effects of the bomb flash on my sight. 'I'm happy to say you have absolutely no scarring on the eyeballs,' the doctor told me. Unbelievably, it was the first time anyone had actually said that. I could drive a car, I could lift weights, so I wasn't worried about my hands; but my eyes were a different matter.

The medicals were conducted in the same block as all the other tests and interviews, in the general admin centre at Biggin Hill. There was a big waiting-room with a television, usually used for running RAF videos. The intellectuals amongst the candidates sat on the edges of their seats and talked earnestly about flying and current affairs; I slumped back on the couch and watched *Brookside*. I wanted to relax. I was as nervous as hell.

We all knew the interviews would be the toughest part. My initial grilling was carried out by two RAF officers. I enjoyed the chat, it was like talking to a captive audience of two. I hope the two officers enjoyed it. They may not have learned much about current affairs from me, but they certainly could have found out a lot more about what was going on in Brookside Close.

Next, after an interval of four or five hours, came the Big Interview, in front of a board of about twelve people. I didn't enjoy the wait: I could hear the previous chap making the whole board laugh, and I suspected it was going to be a tough act to follow.

It was. When summoned, I knocked on the door and walked in. The room was small, with one big, long table and plain plastered walls, the sort of room you see in films of courts martial. The jury were seated around the table, and my chair was vacant in front of them, waiting for the accused. I was conscious of every step as I walked towards the sea of unsmiling faces and sat down.

I usually find that after a minute or two of talking to a person I know how to adapt to them. With a dozen people, you can't do that. I was absolutely stuck. It was like being in front of a firing squad. There was no smile when they asked a question, no hint of a sympathetic tone. And they were such eminent people – doctors and commodores, and Sir Alastair Steadman, head of the International Air Tattoo. I felt under pressure and exposed. (I discovered later, after I had left the room, that my jeans had worn through on the inner thighs, and I had been sitting there with acres of flesh visible through the gaps.)

'What are you doing living in Liverpool?' they asked me.

I was allowed one or two minutes on the topic, before another question came at me from left field, one I really should have anticipated.

'Why do you want to learn to fly?'

I'd never actually thought about it before. 'Ah,' I said, as profoundly as I could manage. Then I had to stop and think.

When I was a kid and living on the RAF base in Lincolnshire, there was an open day. One of my earliest memories is of looking inside a helicopter. Later, when I joined the Army, I was put in 3 Company, the heliborne company in Berlin. When we trained for Northern Ireland, and while we were actually at Bessbrook, we were in helicopters five out of seven days, doing between two and four helicopter journeys a day. I love them. They're great machines – especially when they're evacuating you from the battle zone to the safety of a hospital ship. I'd often thought I'd like to learn to fly them, and over time it had become one of my great ambitions.

That was essentially what I said to the board. I saw the fixed-wing flying course as a stepping-stone. In truth, learning to fly wasn't something that was at the top of my agenda, but the opportunity had arisen and I had to take it. As Mam had said, 'If you don't have a go, you'll never know.' I was going ahead because it was another challenge.

Basically the job of the twelve-man team seemed to be to take me apart. They wanted to know everything. It was a horrible experience. The people asking the questions were actually very nice people; it was the situation I couldn't handle. It was the first time ever that I'd been under pressure of that sort. Perhaps they were trying to simulate flying conditions. If so, they succeeded. The whole interview was a real gripper.

Afterwards, I was fairly certain that I'd failed – especially when I discovered the holes in my jeans. But at least I thought I'd given it my best shot. If I hadn't passed, then it was because I wasn't good enough.

The results were due about a fortnight later, but I found mine out early. I was in London for the Man of the Year reunion, and had lunch with a close friend, Dame Felicity Peake, who had had a very distinguished RAF career.

'You're a dark horse,' she said with a smile.

'Why's that?'

'I had dinner with Sir Alastair last night and he told me you've won one of the scholarships . . .'

I phoned Biggin Hill the moment I got back to Liverpool. I was going away the next day on a Weston Spirit course and would be out of contact for a while. I didn't want to miss out. They confirmed my acceptance. Chuffed? Having achieved this on my own was almost as good as being carried shoulder-high around the Arms Park.

I arrived on time at Kidlington, but was late getting to the admin block for registration. Someone had forgotten to tell me that the press were there. They wanted a photograph, and asked me to look interested in things I didn't have a clue about. I hadn't even been taken up in an aircraft then. It was the first of many such intrusions. All through the course, I kept being interrupted by press calls. I answered them all because I thought it might inspire someone else to apply the following year.

Kidlington is an old wartime airfield, with miles of little roadways and a mass of disused buildings and hangars, some dating from the Second World War. The RAF school is at a place called the General Aviation Centre — a rather grand term considering it then consisted of a pile of old huts. Next to it is Langford Hall, where most of the Muslims learning to be commercial pilots live, and opposite is a fascinating old dome, where the rear gunners of Flying Fortresses used to practise their skills.

To my utter delight, I came across Noel McConkey again. I'd met him at selection, and I was over the moon that he'd passed too. Noel was blown up by the IRA when he was a member of the RUC. He lost both legs, one from above the knee, one from below, and one arm from above the elbow. For me, Noel is the epitome of bravery, the one living man I admire above all others. Whatever he says is said with feeling. He's a straight-talking man, and that's what's always endeared him to me the most. But that Irish accent — even after seven weeks, I still found it hard to understand; and to make matters worse, he speaks very softly. Noel hails from Coot Hill in Eire, but volunteered to join the RUC. He was blown up, and was then forgotten. A terrorist can go to Queen's University and do a law degree, but because Noel, coming from Eire, wasn't a British subject — even though he'd served in the RUC — he didn't qualify for a scholarship. He even had to pay £75 to become a British subject. That's the absolute pits. Anyway, Noel is not a bitter man, so I should follow his example. Let me just say that it is a joy being around that guy. He is much more disabled than me — but I'd only do things for him if they were things he could have done for himself anyway and I was just speeding things up to get to the pub.

My room at Kidlington reminded me of the depot at Pirbright. It was a classic army 'bunk', with a bed — basic, sleeping-uncomfortably-on-for-the-use-of — a table, a wash-basin, a cupboard, a light and a shelf. The only thing I didn't notice that day was the enormous in-flight refuelling aircraft parked not fifty yards from my window.

I did notice it at 6.30 the next morning. That was when the jet engines fired up and the wash propelled half of Oxfordshire's dust and dirt in through my open window. Thus was the pattern set for the next seven weeks.

I very quickly got fed up with all the reading and writing we had to do. It reminded me of school, and I hadn't exactly excelled at bookwork then. How do you make aerodynamics interesting? I mean, air-flow over a wing — where's the interest in that? Some of the people we came across spoke English, but a lot of them spoke aeroplanes. As Noel said, they walked around with little aeroplanes in their heads. 'Yeah,' I said, 'without pilots in them.'

Noel and I both found it very hard to stay in studying at night, and we started to take most of our meals out in pubs. We fast obtained the reputation of being fond of our alcohol, but in fact all we needed was a couple of pints away from aeroplanes. The weekends were different: then we sank a sensible few, because by then we'd had a whole week of fuel mixtures and ailerons. Flying is great fun, but if I was told I could never do it again, although I'd be very sad, I wouldn't fight it in the same way that I would fight, say, a driving ban. When I do get my licence I shall be very pleased — it will be an achievement. But I don't *need* to fly, not the way some of the students did.

After two or three days I felt like packing up, because I was so affected by motion sickness. Turbulence is very similar to wave movement: it makes your eyes roll to the top of your head. I didn't feel I was learning anything, because I was so busy thinking about not being sick. On the third day of the course it rained. 'We'll be up again tomorrow,' I said to myself, 'but if you still feel sick at the end of the week, we'll kick it.' From that moment, everything was fine. It must all just have been psychological — either that, or something to do with the strength of the coffee. You could creosote a fence with Kidlington coffee. There was so much caffeine in it, I was getting aches in the back of my head. I gave up drinking it, and never had another recurrence — except when doing an exam. Then I'd get a pain in the front of my head – either because my brain had migrated, or because it had been stretched and was at last starting to be fully used, like an air-bed filling with air.

Flying with an instructor can be really tedious. On your own, it's great – there's no one there to criticize. Without someone looking over your shoulder, you can sit there quite happily and convince yourself you're doing things rather well. I was naturally apprehensive to start with; it was the fear of the unknown, like diving into a black hole in the sea. Thinking in three dimensions – sky, horizon and ground – was totally alien to me. There are millions of pilots around the world, and they all say, 'You can land, you can put a plane down.' Of course you can eventually, but what if your instructor has a heart attack during your first lesson? I'm not a religious person but I did start to think about who might save me.

On one occasion we stopped flying even though it was clearly a suitable day for it. We knew something was up, and our suspicions were confirmed when we were asked to change into our best bib and tucker. Noel and I put on our RUC and Welsh Guards ties – but everyone else was wearing an International Air Tattoo tie, so we had to do likewise. We assembled at the bar, and at 11.30 precisely a helicopter swooped down in front of us and landed. I recognized the pilot at once – even though he was slightly shorter than I would have expected for a king.

Like five other places on the course, mine had been financed by His Royal Highness King Hussein of Jordan. And now, in the midst of what must have been an immensely hectic schedule while he was in this country, he had taken the time to come to lunch and meet his protégés. We felt unbelievably honoured. Even though he'd sponsored the places, he hadn't needed to take the trouble to come and see how we were getting on.

The King strode into the bar, shook hands with us all and had a word or two with everyone. Then the lunch gong sounded. My throat went a little dry when he came and sat at my table. Luckily Noel was there to engage him in some conversation. Poor King Hussein, I doubt he understood a word of the Irishman's banter.

There were three others at the table, including two injured lassies. We all talked about the King's son who was in the Jordanian Army, and about flying. I couldn't believe we were there chatting to one of the most powerful statesmen in the world. Most of the people at that table would have had to struggle to pay for even a single flying lesson. King Hussein had his own air force.

His Majesty leaned across and asked me a question about the Falklands. I started talking about the *Sir Galahad* and the events at Fitzroy, a subject I wasn't usually short of conversation on, but as I spoke a strange thing happened. For the first time in six years, I suddenly didn't feel particularly forthcoming on the topic; I felt conscious of the fact that at most gatherings of disabled people I had always been the best-known – since the documentaries, I'd been right up there alongside Niki Lauda and the Elephant Man as one of the world's great disfigureds. It seemed that I always got pushed to the forefront, but now I suddenly felt that it was someone else's turn.

I let the others take up the thread, and in the same moment I decided to write this book. If I am entering a new phase of my life, I thought, one in which memories of the Falklands will play a progressively smaller and smaller role, then perhaps I should commit those memories to paper before they fade for ever.

A few days later, I was out on a practice session with my instructor, Liz, when suddenly she spoke to me over the headset. 'Pull up outside the tower.' Her voice was calm. As the plane came to a halt in the correct spot, she climbed out and spoke to me again. '. . . If you're in doubt when you're coming in, or you're too high, or too fast, or the wind is too strong, then call the tower, "Yankee Whisky – going round," and make another circuit.' She wished me luck, and disappeared into the old, concrete control tower.

The word 'solo' never passed her lips.

I remembered my checks, eased back on the brakes, and the Cherokee leapt forward towards the distant horizon.

19

LOOKING BACK

Wherever I go there are always questions about the Falklands war. It is inevitable, the question and answer session about what happened at Bluff Cove. With the marks of my own experience stamped across my hands and face, it is only natural, and such questions deserve proper answers.

For me and many of my colleagues, as we went down to the South Atlantic, the war was a distant dream. It was our duty to go. We were sailing south in the belief that it was only fair and right to protect the freedom of British subjects. If we didn't stand by them in their hour of need, we would be failing them. If we believed in freedom ourselves, we had no choice.

I had joined the Army and had signed on the dotted line. I had to obey orders. I had never thought that I would actually go to war – but then, who had?

The tragedy that struck the Welsh Guards was the result of a gamble that did not come off. It was the 'Bridge Too Far' of the Falklands war. It still seems amazing to me that in a conflict in the scale of the one in the South Atlantic, the bombing of the *Sir Galahad* was the only really major set-back that Britain suffered. The losses of the *Sheffield* and others were disasters, but the *Galahad* incident was a horrible taste of what might have happened on an even more ghastly scale if the Argentinian air force had attacked the Task Force convoy before it entered San Carlos Water on 21 May, or if their bombs had exploded in greater numbers, or if any of the ships that were in fact sunk had been crammed with troops as the *Galahad* was. We were lucky.

The tragedy will never go away. Nor should it. People still ask me, 'Don't you feel bitter about what happened? Don't you want the people who were responsible brought to some kind of justice?'

My answer is always the same: 'Where do you begin to apportion the blame? With Galtieri's mother?'

It was a sad and unfortunate mistake which could have been avoided. The controversy about who said what and to whom, and why things weren't done or weren't in place, has raged ever since. I am not about to add fuel to an already well-stoked fire. All wars involve gambles. Unfortunately there are always people who suffer: the troops themselves and their families and loved ones back at home. I have been through my own private hell, and so has my family. But I am not bitter.

For the sake of your sanity, you cannot point the finger in situations like these. The much-publicized row between Major Southby-Tailyour of the Marines and Major Sayle of the Welsh Guards is now history. I don't feel bitter towards Major Sayle, nor do I want to blame him. All that would do would be to give me someone to feel anger towards, and I don't want to feel anger any more. He wasn't a very well-liked man, but that is irrelevant. He was in command and we were his troops, and no amount of bitterness or wishful hindsight can alter that. And no amount of ifs, buts and maybes will bring back my friends and colleagues who died on the ship. It is all over. It is finished. There is new life to be lived and new blood to be bred from. I only hope that those in a position to ensure that such events are remembered and digested do so, and that efforts are made to see that they do not happen again.

It is a well-worn cliché that something good always comes of adversity. In my case it is true. I have learned a great deal about myself and about other people and their motives from what happened. I have learned that coming to terms with a tragedy is not helped by feelings of revenge. Revenge isn't going to restore my face, hands and body to what they once were. Revenge isn't going to help the families who lost loved ones cope with the tragedy. And a spirit of revenge isn't going to inspire us to use what we have all learned to help others who suffer similar sadness and adversity. You don't have to be in a war to get killed, maimed or burned.

You can't live your life concerned only with yesterday. Yesterday is dead and buried. Bad or good, it is only about memories. You have to go on with life, with today and tomorrow.

I only hope that I can keep faith with my new feelings, my new ideas and my new spirit, that I can put them into practice and lead a more fulfilled and more rewarding life than I could have done before. I am a changed man. I am more tolerant, more aware of others and their troubles. I am more able to give of myself and to do what I can to help other injured or disabled people cope with the difficulties they face. I hope that I can also provoke healthy and able-bodied people into thinking about their own reactions to and prejudices about disfigurement. Accidents don't happen just to other people.

In this sense I am content with what happened to me. I know it must sound strange to other people, but now at least I have been able to share my story with others, in the hope that they too can perhaps draw some strength from it. It has been a gamble for me, writing this book, putting myself on the line. I only hope that, unlike Fitzroy, this one pays off.

20

LOOKING ON

I'd be coming up to the end of my time now, if I was still in, just six or nine months left to push. If I'd been an NCO, I'd probably then have signed on for another three years – and what a great three years they would surely have been. It's sad for me to have to accept that I don't think I'll ever find another job that could give me so much excitement or such a wide variety of friends and acquaintances, or be as challenging or rewarding. I miss the Army desperately. I'd give anything to be a soldier again.

What the future holds for me as a civilian, it's hard to tell. I know I get frustrated easily if I've got nothing to do. I'm always on the look-out for something that excites me and keeps me interested. There are so many things I'd like to do; whether I'll have enough time to do them, I don't know. And whether I'm sensible enough to allocate my time properly is something else again.

I want to take up sub-aqua, I want to complete my flying course, I want to drive round Australia. But perhaps I'll just fade away and run a corner shop. After all, I'm just an ordinary guy who happened to have the good fortune to survive a tragedy and to have a documentary made about me.

My long-term ambitions are probably the same as those of most guys – to have a house where I'll be happy, a wife I love, a couple of kiddies, one cat, one dog, one goldfish. And a job. But none of these things is in the wind yet. I never had a trade. All I've ever been is in the Army, or injured. I can't be a soldier again – quite apart from my injuries, I've forgotten most of my training. But I can talk. Perhaps I could read kiddies' stories on the radio. 'Listen with Squeaky' – it's got a bit of a ring to it.

Basically, I suppose, I just want to be the happy-go-lucky lad I once was, cracking jokes and having a drink – Simon Weston, village lad. But I have to be realistic. My needs are a lot different now, and so are my expectations. It doesn't excite me any more to think of going to Cardiff for my night out. But I haven't outgrown my childhood mates; I still enjoy their company immensely. They're still the best friends a man could ever want. They were there when I needed them, and they've never gone away.

I've bought a house in Liverpool, but my real home, as it is for anyone else who's been loved and cared for, is *home* – the place I was brought up in. My Liverpool house is just a staging post, a place for me to further my life in, so I can go on to do what I really need to do and to achieve what I want to achieve.

The passage of time has helped; so has having so many understanding friends and relatives, and living in such a wonderful village. But the occasional set-back still occurs. When I was driving up from Wales recently, I overtook two pretty girls on the motorway. I was rocking and bopping as I drew level, and I looked across and smiled. The girl in the passenger seat stared back at me for a moment, got her friend to look at me as well, and pulled a face that clearly said, 'Ugh!'

Reactions like that are instilled into us when we're kids. People have such misconceived ideas of what's attractive. Finding a girlfriend is going to be twice as hard for me as for someone who looks 'normal', but that's fine, I can live with that; it just means that when I do find someone to settle down with, I'll know I've found a bloody good one. And as Gran and Mam taught me a long time ago, if you're any sort of person in your own mind, and you can believe in yourself, you can go out and achieve so much. People should never give up on that.

The way people express their sympathy can sometimes niggle. There's patronizing sympathy and there's constructive sympathy. Take it from me, if a disabled person needs something, he or she will ask for it. If they can do something themselves, they will. There are disabled people who are disabled only when it suits them; they're abusing the system and they get my back up.

Ignorant people can't be blamed. People can't help ignorance. And at least being ignorant is better than being patronizing. Nothing is more hurtful than being on the receiving end of patronizing remarks and behaviour, and it can be hard sometimes not to be rude in return. I always make an effort not to be intentionally rude, except when I've had a drink or two. But even then I'm more likely to be boring than offensive. That's all right in my book. You don't get shot for being boring. You just get ignored.

I'm very glad to be alive. Perhaps no one can understand that unless they've been there and come back again. I knew one chap who'd been severely injured, and I said to him, 'God, you're lucky to be alive.'

'No,' he said, 'I'm lucky not to be dead.'

That struck me as very poignant. It made me think. Which way of looking at it is true in my case? The answer: that I think I'm lucky to be alive.

There have been times when I've wanted to top myself. Up to the time the first documentary was made and screened, I was all right. After that there were the days when I didn't want to wake up, when I was fed up with being pestered, when I wanted to be a private person again, keeping myself to myself. But then I had to remind myself that I had agreed to be filmed. No one had forced me to go on television or the radio or to give press interviews, or, come to that, to write books. If you can't do the time, don't commit the crime.

I used to find ways to deaden the emotional pain. It amused me to think that I was walking around in public with skin on my nose that came from my backside.

'What's the matter with you?' my mother or my gran used to say. 'You've got a face like a bum.'

Never was a truer word spoken. But at least I could walk around and say, 'Yes, but this bum can still smile.'

At times I felt so sorry for myself that I wanted to end it all. How was I ever going to get a girlfriend? How was I going to survive outside the Army? There was nothing left for me to do. I hated myself. I hated everybody. When I felt like that, I discovered that there's always someone who can help you. In my case, it was a specific group of people – the Welsh Guards. I needed to go back there, to be with them, to realize I wasn't a part of them any more. They helped me by letting me see that I was still a Guardsman at heart, I still had that something that made a bond between us. But once you've gone you've gone. The regiment doesn't stand still for people who aren't 100 per cent. It can't afford to.

All those things are hard to come to terms with. Personally, I don't ever want to come to terms with the fact that I've been disabled. If you come to terms with it, you've got nothing more to fight against.

I've drawn so much from knowing that there are many others with far worse disabilities than my own. I was very fortunate in that when I was injured I was injured with a group of lads, my mates, my regiment. I wasn't on my own, I was fighting my battle with them.

I had other sources of strength to draw on, too – my family, my village, my friends. Through their love they gave me spiritual strength. It was a power I could tap into when my own fuel tank was empty. They didn't care how much I took; that's where I got the spirit to go on.

To other people who are badly burned, disfigured or disabled I would like to hand on a word or two of advice – things that I had to learn the hard way. Never look at yourself. Look at others, and think to yourself how much they have achieved. Ask yourself, why can't I? What's so different about me that I can't do the same? There's no excuse for not trying. I was frightened to at first. Then I saw what others were achieving, and the soldier – and the Welshman – in me said, let's have a go.

As long as you are prepared to put up with what you've got, to meet it head on, then others will also meet it head on. But if you take a back seat, then other people will allow you to do just that. People will only give you so much sympathy. There's only so much time they have to give you. Then they got bored with it. Then it's you on your own. The more you pity yourself, the less people will want to have to do with you.

Try not to feel too sorry for yourself. Try to help yourself by helping others. Because when you're helping others, you forget about what's wrong with you. Give help and information and you'll be amazed by how much it helps *you* to get better.

To the temporarily able-bodied, I would say this. Please never tell someone like me to 'pull yourself together'. That's the most unhelpful statement in the world. Nobody *wants* to be ill or depressed. If there was such an easy way out of it, believe me, people would take it.

Nor should you suffocate injured people with kindness. If they need help, they'll ask. And if they're too proud to ask, then let them struggle until they do ask; too much pride can kill a person as surely as too much love. My own family nearly drove me to despair with their kindness. You have to sit back sometimes and let people struggle through. Don't pamper people who are injured; give them room to breathe. Above all, never look down your nose at a disabled person. Remember that there but for the grace of God go you – and I.

The documentaries helped me so much because they allowed people to see my plight. People could then understand what I was going through. Hopefully I can now lead by example, by going on from strength to strength, by continuing to achieve, by showing others that everything can be overcome. That's why being in the public eye means so much to me, because by being publicly candid about my personal battles I know I'm helping others. I get letters from people who say, 'You've helped me so much – without your strength and courage I couldn't go on.' Maybe that is why my life was spared on the *Galahad*.

At first I hated going out and being stared at. But the only hint I can offer other disfigured people who are about to venture out in public for the first time – and it's scarcely a comforting one – is that the world will kick you in the teeth every time. If you go down on your knees, it'll kick you in the teeth. The only thing to do is to get back up, get stuck in, and kick it straight back.

Get up, take it on, take it day by day.

Don't try rushing it. Don't try thinking you're going to be Paul Newman or a Hollywood starlet. You're not. Forget it. You're scarred. I still dream of not being injured. I dream of having good hands. I dream of fixing plugs without difficulty. But dreams are in the subconscious. It's only in the real, conscious world that you are going to find fulfilment. So accept that you're disfigured and that you're going to stay disfigured. Don't try thinking you're going to wake up as someone beautiful tomorrow, because you're not. You're never going to wake up and find it's all gone. It might improve with time, but it won't go away. But that still doesn't stop you from being a person, it still doesn't stop you from being accepted, or from driving a car, or from getting a job or falling in love or getting married or doing any of the other things that will make life worthwhile for you.

People like people, and if you've got a personality, then people will accept you. Keep being you and it'll work. The only way we can get disfigured people – myself included – to be socially acceptable, and beat off this notion that everyone has to look like

Lucy and me on our wedding day, 12 May 1990.

With James, July 1991.

With Lucy and James, July 1991.

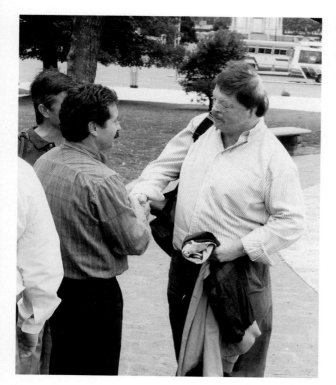

Meeting former Argentinian pilot Carlos Cachon in Buenos Aires, November 1991.

Carlos and his wife, Graciela.

Left to right: me, 58 Hughes, Yorkie and 11 Hughes, 1981. All three friends died in the fire on the *Sir Galahad*.

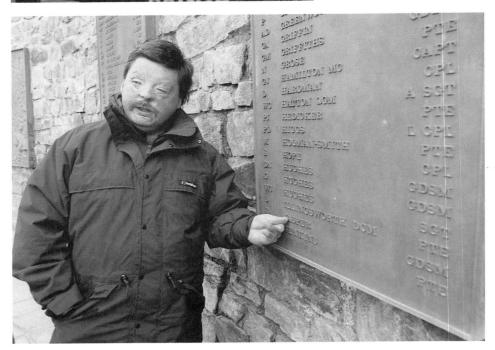

At the Stanley memorial which lists, among the dead, 58 Hughes, 11 Hughes and Yorkie.

The *Sir Galahad* shortly after the fire, June 1982.

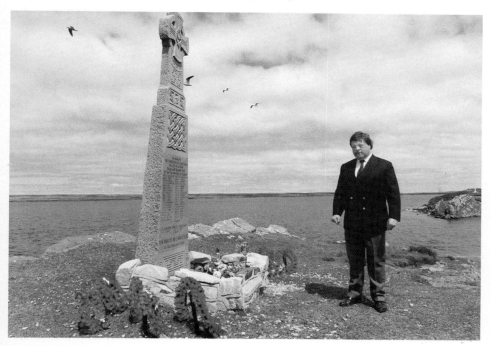

At the Welsh Guards' memorial, Fitzroy, overlooking the bay where the *Sir Galahad* was hit.

With John and Gary at the Stanley memorial.

With Gary on Tumbledown.

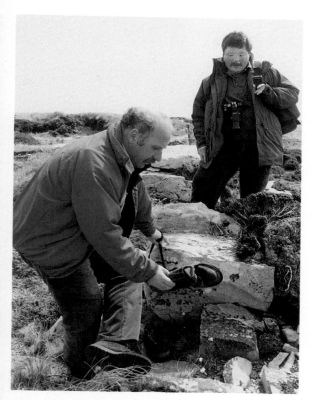

With John – and a pair
of Argentinian boots –
on Wireless Ridge.

In Stanley.

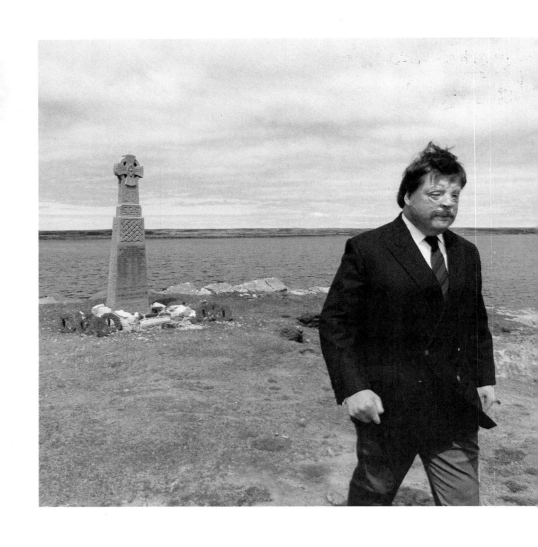

the front cover of *Vogue*, is to get out there and live our lives in the best, fullest, most active and enjoyable way we can. And that is not something we can do sitting alone in a darkened room, without mirrors, watching television.

I'm relaxed about girls now. Two or three years ago I was really bothered about the whole subject. Getting a girlfriend was the ultimate. I felt inadequate, and the problem got magnified in my mind. I spent a lot of time brooding over whether a girl would want to touch me, or see my scars. After all, we're all the same. We all live with preconceived images of what we want and what we should be and what we're going to get.

I've had my fair share of girlfriends since I was injured. I haven't done badly, I haven't done exceptionally well. I'm no Casanova, but I've had my fair share of fun. I'm not desperate any more for a long-lasting relationship; if one comes along, then one comes along. I would like to settle down with someone I love and who would love me back. Someone I love enough to make me want to settle down. Someone to have fun with. But I'd hate it to happen overnight. I'd want a girl to be 100 per cent sure. Eventually I would like a family. I'm a Grade A, Class 1 wimp when it comes to kids. I love them, they're sacred.

The family is a great institution, and if the love I've had from mine is anything to go by, every home should have one. I would like to be able to come back from work and know that the woman I love is there. We'd cook huge meals, watch the kids come in from school, watch them growing up. That's the sort of thing I'd like to happen, one day. One day.

The world did not stop for the Falklands war. It hesitated, perhaps, for five or ten minutes each day as people switched on for the latest bulletin. The war changed the lives of the people who went down to the South Atlantic, it changed the lives of the families of those who are buried down there, but the world kept right on moving.

We did not take part in a holocaust. It was not a war that will be remembered for ever. It was just another conflict, and now is just another already half-forgotten story, a more and more distant memory of Union Jacks and cheers of glory. But for many the price is still being paid; their war is still going on.

My story, like those of other Falklands veterans, is not going to be recorded alongside histories of the two World Wars or the

American Civil War, wars that raged for years and years and cost hundreds of thousands of lives, and in a way, I am glad. The Falklands war will die a natural death.

It is not something that I want to be reminded of every day. I have only to wash my face or clean my teeth for that. And at night I have only to close my eyes to see Yorkie and Cliff Elley and all the others, laughing and joking, just seconds before that Argentinian Skyhawk released its load.

Even six years on, it's still sometimes hard to believe that they're dead. But then, to remember the manner of their deaths, to think of the flames and the smoke and the screams, is to go beyond grief. At the time, I didn't know that I could be hurt so completely and so totally. I felt fury at their loss. Outrage. Emptiness. I hadn't had the chance to say goodbye. I still miss those boys more than words can express. Their deaths left a hole too deep to fill.

Gradually, of course, with support, and kindness, and most of all time, I have come to feel that life is worth carrying on. But the hurt is still there, and the sadness.

Not a day passes when I don't think of them, but at least through me and others their memories are kept alive. I know now that there is a sort of life after death, because no one can erase those boys from my mind. I will never forget them. Nor will I forget those awful moments on the *Sir Galahad* that wiped so much fun and goodness off the face of the earth. I am prepared to live with those memories. I only hope that others can learn to live with their prejudices against the injured and the burned and let us live in peace.

POSTSCRIPT

As I said at the beginning, I am a man at peace. I hold no bitterness. And yet there has always been an area of my early life that for a long time I felt was unresolved and unhealed: my relationship with my sister, Helen. God knows, we fought like cat and dog when we were kids, and as far as I was concerned, everything between us ever since had been soured – or at least overshadowed – by that early animosity.

Then, a day or two before this book was due to be delivered to the publisher, a long letter thumped on to my doormat in Liverpool. I recognized the posh grammar-school handwriting at once. Here are some of the thoughts I want to share:

'Dear Simon, I know I only saw you yesterday, so you'll wonder why I'm writing to you. I don't really know myself, except that I feel the need to, because I somehow feel the time is right to tell you some things that I've often wanted to but never have.

'We didn't get off to a good start, did we kid? Let's be honest, we hated each other's guts. Every time I caught a disease, you'd catch it, and then, little bugger, you'd pass it back to me. I broke your arm once. Another time, your nose. Later, I slammed the door and ripped the toe-nails clean off your foot.

'You were just as bad. You'd charge around the house after me with a red-hot poker, or throw the carving knife at me – remember? You detested me, and I'm not really surprised. I was a right madam, Simon, thinking I was better than everyone because I went to grammar school. But if you can believe it, I loved you, even at the same time as I loathed you.

'Being in the Welsh Guards gave you an air of superiority. You stood tall. You were something special. I loved you. So much had happened, you were now a man, I had changed. I'd had everything chucked at me that I could take; I still cry about it now.

185

'I didn't follow the Falklands campaign, I didn't want to know. I was in bed when I heard the phone ring. Steve answered it and I heard him say, "Oh my God." He came upstairs to tell me the news. "Simon's been injured," he said. "He was on a ship and it's been hit. I'm sure it's not bad. Get dressed and we'll go down to Nelson."

'We couldn't get the car started, and we had to go by bus. It took an hour to get there. Mam was hysterical up in her bedroom. I felt so weak I couldn't go in. Someone said to her, "It's OK, it's not too bad. Four per cent, hands and face, it's not serious."

'We went down to Gran's, and Loft tried to comfort Mam. A little later he phoned us to say, "Get up to the house, get up to the house. We've got some bad news. Simon is very ill." When we got there, Loft said, "Simon is dying."

'Mammy was so upset, I was hysterical. She said. "Get her away from me." All I could think about was that you were going to die. Then, a few days later, I remember us receiving your telegram. It wasn't from you, they weren't your words; they were fine, they all made sense, but they weren't your spirit.

'We waited for the first plane, but you weren't on it. Then we went up for the second, but again nothing happened. Eventually you came on the third, but the family wouldn't let me see you because I was pregnant. They thought it was wrong. I'll never forgive them for that. I cried and I cried and I cried. The more I thought about it, the more I felt I had to see you. I phoned Dad in Scotland and asked him if he'd take me. In the end he did.

'We went to the hospital. You'd just had an operation, and I saw your feet. "That's Simon," I said to Dad. "I know he's going to be OK. There's nothing like his feet." I knew it was you. "Oh God," I said, "it's wonderful, he's back." Then I started looking slowly up your body, until I got to your face. "Oh Jesus," I wept into Dad's shoulder, "look what they've done to him."

'I had to get out. Dad took me outside and sat me down. We'd only been in for two minutes, so we went back in after a while, after you'd had a little sleep.

' "Don't get in the way of the fan, Helen," you said to me, "because I get too hot."

'You couldn't see my heart, Simon, but it was bleeding. I'll never forget, I stood up and looked at you. This handsome, wonderful-looking guy had been decimated. Your hands were in bags.

' "Come over where I can see you," you said. I looked at your eyes, and you looked at mine, and it was as if you were reaching out with your hand, grabbing hold of my heart. "I'm coming back," they were saying. The eyes were right inside me.

'Rebecca came in one day, a lot later, when you were home. You were tired. She came up, your hands were so sore. She said, "Baddie, Simon," and she touched your fingers. You let her. She climbed into your arms and went to sleep. You must have been in agony, but she meant so much to you that you let her.

'I felt it was cruel. I couldn't see the point of it all, I just couldn't see it. At any time during the first year, if I'd been left alone with you, I would have killed you, because I loved you. I wanted you dead for a long time. The first year was awful. I just wanted to smother you. I grieved for the boy who'd died, much as I loved the man who'd come back. I grieved for the brother I hadn't had for long, and now they'd taken him away.

'But I love the man who came home almost more than my own children, I love him more than anything. That's why Richard is called Richard Simon, and why he's a bit of a devil and can get away with anything, because he reminds me so much of you.

'So what I suppose this whole letter is about is that although I realize you're happy now, I only wish I'd had time to show the person you were before how much I loved him. I couldn't talk to you about any of this without crying, and that would turn you off straightaway. I just want you to know how deeply I care for you. You're more than a brother. You're my confidant. I love you, and I love you as you are.

'Your bitch of a sister,
Helen.'

I folded the letter carefully back into its envelope and poured myself another cup of coffee. I sat for a long time at the kitchen table, deep in thought. It was late and I was in a hurry when I finally left the house that morning, but I couldn't help noticing that the air was a little fresher, the trees were greener and the birds were singing even more brightly than usual – just like when a stray dark cloud that has blocked out the light of a summer's day is finally blown away, leaving only a brilliant, sunny sky.

GOING BACK

RETURN TO THE FALKLANDS

SIMON WESTON

with John Man

To my lovely wife, Lucy, and to Mam,
for understanding and not fudging.
I love you both.

ACKNOWLEDGEMENTS

My grateful thanks to Gary and John for their unfailing support and wonderful sense of humour, both on the visit and on our return from the Falkland Islands.

To Malcolm Brinkworth I give my sincere and affectionate gratitude, because without him this meeting would never have taken place. Thanks, mate.

CONTENTS

1   I Had to Go Back   1
2   The Reasons Why   29
3   Buenos Aires   45
4   Meeting My 'Tormentor'   57
5   The Ranch   79
6   To the Falklands   95
7   San Carlos   111
8   Goose Green   125
9   Fitzroy   137
10   The Argentinian Cemetery   147
11   Attack and Defence   153
12   Tumbledown   159
13   Wireless Ridge   171
14   An End and a New Beginning   181

1

I HAD TO GO BACK

September 1991

The first I knew that something was happening was when Lucy nudged me awake.

'Simon, rub my back,' she said, with a sigh of pain.

'Do you think this is it?' I asked, blearily. It was 3.30 a.m.

'I don't know,' she said, as I got to work. 'It's never happened to me before.'

She was late starting labour, so there'd been plenty of warning. The bags were all packed. To be on the safe side she phoned the midwife, while I took a shower.

Just as well – by the time the midwife arrived, half an hour later, Lucy was getting real pains. We were off, through a soft summer dawn – it was 29 July – to Caerphilly Miners' Hospital, and straight into Delivery.

After Lucy had changed and had an examination, the midwife said it could be a few hours yet. A few hours! Lucy had suffered quite enough already. I wanted things to get a move on. My nerves were shot to pieces, so I went out to get a cup of tea. In one of the corridors I was surprised to meet a member of staff who had once been a military nurse and knew several people who had treated me after the fire. That helped pass some time.

Back in the ward with Lucy, they said things were coming along nicely. God, it was hot in there. Lucy was doing her breathing, grabbing lungfuls of gas and air, not saying anything, just concentrating, while I stood beside her, stroking her forehead, glancing occasionally out of the uncurtained windows, watching the light strengthen over the bushes and trees in the hospital gardens. The doctor came in, a soft-spoken Asian lady who kept Lucy informed of progress.

Suddenly – in a restrained and ladylike voice – Lucy swore, and grabbed me round the neck. The baby's head had started to crown. Then her hand shifted to my chest and grabbed my shirt. All of a sudden I seemed to have no chest hairs left. This was major pain time, and not just for Lucy.

Inside, too, I was all knotted up. I'd heard all the horror stories about what can go wrong. I was as worried as anyone else about whether the baby would be normal or not. On top of that, I had my own special worries. One part of me knew there was no way my genes could have been affected by the bomb, no way that my scars would reappear on my baby's face. But logic had nothing to do with it. There was another part of me that feared the worst.

And I was in fits wondering whether it was going to be a boy or a girl. I really wanted a son, at least the first time around. The idea of a daughter left me feeling very insecure. I felt I could cope with a son, someone to pass on my own experiences to, someone to encourage on the rugby field.

I glanced down. It wasn't as easy as I'd hoped. The doctor was using forceps. There was the head now, and then the back, all bloody, and Lucy's hand was beating at my chest and throttling me, and then the little bum looking like a twin-cheeked chocolate éclair, because the baby's bowels were obviously in fine working order, and then, as the little thing slid round . . .

A boy.

I tried to tell Lucy, but found I couldn't speak at all. It was

2

the matron who said, 'Oh, you've got a boy,' as she lifted him to clean him up.

Lucy was relaxing at last, groggy with the effort and the gas. 'It's a boy,' she said softly, and then kept on repeating, 'It's a boy. It's a boy.'

The matron handed him to me. He was perfect, from his damp fuzz of hair down to his wrinkled feet and button toes.

And I still couldn't talk.

I'm not someone who's usually lost for words, but I *couldn't say a word*. My mouth was opening and closing like a goldfish, my eyes were full of tears, and there was a lump in my throat the size of a beach-ball.

People who say childbirth is the most beautiful thing they've ever seen must be sick, honestly. The sight! The pain that she went through! God! No way in this world would I ever go through anything like that! Yet it was one of the most amazing and wonderful events I've ever witnessed. I wouldn't have missed it for the world, and if we are lucky enough to have more children, I won't miss their births either.

Standing there, holding James, with tears blurring the sight of him, was the most moving experience I'd had since I got injured. It had been nine years since an Argentinian bomb had blown away my old life, along with almost half my skin; nine years in which I had been patched back together, recuperated, left the Army, travelled, done things I would never have dreamed of, discovered the rewards of helping others as I had been helped, become a husband and, now, been given the joy of becoming a father.

James was a seal set on a new life.

You'd think I'd have been all set to live happily ever after. I was grateful, don't get me wrong; if this was all there was to life, it was OK by me. But there was something missing, a restlessness that I felt in still moments, a hidden unhappiness revealed by the nightmares that still occasionally came at me, something that had to be explored. I knew I wouldn't be able to do my best by Lucy and James unless I found out what it was, and coped with it.

Superficially, of course, in body and mind I was in great shape, compared with the mess I'd been in when I emerged from hospital in 1983. I still have a rebuilt nose and a moustache that won't grow straight, a face like a badly-chewed pasty (in the words of one of my closest friends) and a head that looks as if I've just been scalped. It always makes me smile when I have a haircut and the barber politely shows me the back of my head in the mirror. There's no hair there at all, because the skin came from some other part of my body and it's as tender as a baby's. If it gets exposed to the sun by mistake, it turns an instant tomato-red.

But at least I *have* a face – not all that pretty, but one I've become used to, which is why I can joke about it, and why it's good for friends to joke about it, too. I don't want you to think it was an easy journey, though, as anyone who has a facial injury – especially a burn – will tell you. Face and hands – these are the bits that really define you as an individual in the eyes of other people, the bits that everyone notices, that can't be covered up. It was a long hard struggle to accept that the face staring at me from the mirror was not a mask hiding the real Simon Weston, but *part of* the real Simon Weston, the new me. What you see is what you get. People stare, but it doesn't bother me now. If they don't like the way I look, that's their problem.

For years there hadn't been much more to improve on, except the middle finger of my left hand, and even that was in better shape now.

My hands had become a mess in the few seconds after the bomb, when I grabbed one of the lads who was on fire. The left hand was the worse of the two. The little finger had been burned off and the others were badly distorted. The middle finger was bent over backwards and twisted, and was always getting in the way. So at the end of 1989 they decided to operate. It may sound only a small thing after what I'd been through, but it hurt like hell. In fact, at the time I thought it was the most painful operation I'd had, probably because I'd forgotten a lot of the suffering and because I wasn't used to it. They broke the finger and shoved a pin up it to keep it straight. It swelled up and got infected, and gave me the most excruciating pain for about four weeks.

But that was over now. So physically I was about as perfect as I'd ever be. Well, to be honest, I was a bit overweight, but that's never a major worry with me because I'll always have my prop-forward build and I can always weight-train and run my way to fitness if I want to.

Emotionally, too, I had come a long way. Once, I'd been a happy-go-lucky squaddie whose main ambition in life was to fill in my pools coupons every Friday. The fire burned away all that. For a while afterwards I felt as though I had been left with nothing, and I sank into depression and drink. Slowly, with a lot of medical and psychiatric help, I emerged.

In all this I was lucky – lucky to have survived, lucky to have the help I did. Even the *Sir Galahad* incident itself had its lucky side, though it took me a long time to see it. It gave me a unique opportunity to change. I decided I didn't much like the person I had been before. I could do better.

When I joined the Army, I joined to see the world, to fire a gun, to wear a uniform. I was nothing but a big kid, thinking only of myself and the next pay cheque. It was like going from one school to another, to a school uniform with pay. We could jump in the mud, drink, do all the things mothers disapprove of, get fit, play sport, get paid, eat, always have a bed to go to at night, get paid, have a beer, get paid, have friends, get *paid* – for being in uniform, can you believe it? For being like a big kid (albeit a professional one)!

Because you have to have a certain childish mentality to be in the armed forces, especially in Northern Ireland, where we felt we could do with all the laughs we could get. Once, Tommy 'Mad Mo' Morris put on an NBC (nuclear, chemical and biological suit), installed himself in the pit beneath the 'thunderbox', the six-holes-in-a-plank toilet, and ignited a thunderflash. Boom! Six bare-arsed squaddies tore out into the field, swearing they'd never eat Army curry again. That, I'm sorry to say, was high-level humour by Army standards.

And the discipline! Just like school. At school you get told off for having dirt on your blazer or your tie undone. It's no different in the Army. The only difference is that in the Army they fine you rather than give you lines.

When I got injured, my life changed at a stroke. The bomb wiped out the life I'd had before. In the Army, at least I'd been a kid. After the fire, I became a baby again, totally dependent on others. I couldn't eat, move, even relieve myself, without the help of others. Outwardly – physically – the best I could look forward to was being someone totally different. There was no help for it: I had to change inwardly as well. I resisted, of course. But as time passed I saw that there was a way to gain some benefit from what had happened. I had been given an opportunity not many people get. Because I looked different, nobody was going to stop me from acting differently. There were no expectations to fulfil. I could be a different person. In metamorphosis, I could, with luck, find liberation (big words for a Welsh squaddie, but that was part of the change, too).

So if my time in the Army extended my childhood, the injury was the beginning of a different sort of growing up. I can imagine more comfortable ways of growing up. If I could have had the choice of being injured or not, I would never have been injured. But since I *was* injured, things couldn't have gone better. I gained the courage to show myself in public. I started to work with charities. I was the subject of three television documentaries, and wrote a book about my recovery, *Walking Tall*.

I owe part of the change in my life to public exposure. It wasn't my idea, but I'll always be grateful for the way the documentaries and the book forced me to change, to grow in confidence. For months after the injury, I could do nothing at all except talk. That was an education in itself. Then later, for the book, which was 'ghosted' from my tapes, I spoke for the first time about the fire on the *Sir Galahad*. It meant reviving bitter, horrible memories, but it was also a release. I began to let go of the past, and it began to let go of me.

The response from the public was the best medicine anyone could have, an inspiration, repeated hundreds of times. People said I'd given them the strength to face tragedy, but their courage strengthened me in return. The letters amazed me — thousands of them, bag-loads of them, some from people eager for me to turn to religion (one was even signed 'Jesus'), but most from ordinary people who'd been feeling bad about themselves, or about something that had happened in their lives. It was good to know that my survival allowed them to see there could be a way forward.

I'll let one letter stand for hundreds, one that I find particularly moving, not just for what it says but for what it leaves out:

6 June 1985

Dear Simon,

Thank you for allowing us to meet you in your television series and the magazine article. You not only went to protect us in the Falklands as a soldier . . . but you saved two people this week.

My youngest daughter and I thought that we had to end our intolerable situation, which has lasted for four years, but much, much longer in a lesser degree.

As we discussed our plan, *Simon's War* came on the TV. We did not sleep that night. No one — not even two other daughters and two grandchildren — was able to do for us what you have done: made us realize that we have to live, and not only that – be brave and positive, and keep going, and stop the luxury of our self-pity.

We know it will not be easy: but with you out there, your terrific spirit, your humanity, you are our talisman.

The way back for us in trying to become human beings again is to think of others apart from ourselves, and we will think of you, Simon, and concentrate on your well-being, your future, because you are worthwhile.

We wept for you, and with you (I know it sounds trite, but it is true). If only we could have helped you and your dear mum and dad, but we didn't know. Now that we do, our lives have been changed. Your destiny altered ours. Thank you and God bless you.

I knew my role in their new-found courage must have been marginal. The spirit must have been there in the first place for my experiences to bring it out. I didn't believe I was anything special, and I don't now. But even one letter like that would have been enough to make me think I was doing something right. I couldn't help feeling a new sense of responsibility to those in physical or emotional need.

The reactions never stopped amazing me. One man on holiday in Spain said proudly that it had taken him three days to read the book – and it was the first book he'd read all the way through. Friends who heard me on the radio and television accused me of taking elocution lessons. I began to reassess myself, and the experience gave me a sense of new-found freedom. I felt as if I'd been lobotomized at birth and somebody had just given me my frontal lobes back.

Of course, it wasn't all down to me. The press played an important part. I've never really understood why they focused on me, but I was working for charity a good deal, and perhaps that made it easy for people to like me. Anyway, to be fair, as much as the press have been bad to other people, to me they've been brilliant. Without the press, I'd be a nobody, and a lot of deserving charity cases would be worse off.

The response to going public confirmed me in my decision to get involved in charity work. It wasn't a simple decision. When I first got injured I didn't want anything to do with it, because I suppose I felt I was a charity case myself. It's a hard thing to face up to the fact that you're disabled, especially when you're twenty-one, all strength and vitality and rugby and beer. I certainly didn't want to admit that I was a part of what a lot of charities are set up for, and that I might remain so, for ever.

It was only when PHAB – Physically Handicapped and Able Bodied – in Devon approached me that I began to see that I could do some good. They don't ask me to do too much now, but whenever they do, I'll help if I can, because through them I stopped being a charity case myself. They hold a special place in my heart.

The other charity I will always feel close to is the one named after me, the Weston Spirit, set up to encourage and enable young people to overcome adversity within their inner-city environments. Our office was in Liverpool, based in the MCVS (Merseyside Council for Voluntary Services). It was a terrific boost to the charity, and to me personally, when Prince Andrew agreed to sponsor us. He even came to Merseyside, to the pools company Vernons, who had agreed to provide work experience for our youngsters. He flew up from the West Country by helicopter, after half a dozen other engagements, gave a twenty-minute speech and showed he was interested, friendly and well-informed. I was just amazed at the quality of what he gave us – and all while he was on leave from the Navy. How he managed it I don't know, but I'll always be grateful.

Through PHAB and the Weston Spirit, I came to see that by using publicity I could get across a simple message, one it had taken a long time for me to learn (thanks again, Mam), but one that had really helped me when I finally did learn it. If I had to sum it up, it would come down to two words: be positive. If you're not positive, you're never going to get anywhere. People are often too ready to blame lack of achievement on lack of money, on the lack of other people giving them something, instead of creating something for themselves. People who do that sometimes miss the whole point of being alive.

I also happen to believe that sport can play a crucial role in the creation of a positive attitude. I'm biased, of course, because I enjoy sport so much. I think that if young people took part in sport to vent their aggression, they'd be a lot less likely to get involved in trouble. It's not a matter of expense. Youth clubs and councils will usually provide if only . . . OK, this is not the place for a speech, but I do feel strongly about it.

I remember one occasion that really summed up the benefits of this approach to me. Lucy and I were at a running track in Blackpool, presenting prizes at the annual meeting of the Sports Association for the Disabled. In the 100 metres there was one little girl with cerebral palsy who could not co-ordinate her limbs well enough to run. She set off, arms and legs everywhere, obviously excited by the race and the challenge. Within a few paces she fell over. I thought that was it for her, but she got up and continued, and I saw she was laughing. Then she fell over again, and got up again – and again, and again, at least ten times, and every time she did it she laughed, and nothing in this catalogue of failure held her back from her goal, the tape. I watched, enthralled, gripped by a whole spectrum of emotions – wanting to cry, wanting to laugh, wanting to rush out and carry her, wanting to run with her. At last, alone, way behind everyone else, she made it, triumphant. She had won her own personal race. That, I thought, was how I had to live my life.

It works both ways. I get back as much as I give. Every now and then, something happens to remind me that I have this link with thousands of people I'll never know. Once, in an Indian restaurant, a drunken Scotsman behind me started to throw punches at waiters who were trying to ease him out. He was so Brahms and Liszt that a few of his punches landed on my shoulders and spilled curry down my shirt. Another Scotsman intervened and ushered the drunk outside, recognizing me as he did so. When he returned he came across to me, held out his hand and in a broad Glaswegian accent apologized for intruding, saying, 'Scuse me, pal, hope you don't mind me being totally *stereotypical*.' I found that a wonderful turn of phrase, and it made my day.

Usually, it's small things like that which add a glow to the day — a passing remark, a shy request for an autograph from some ten-year-old kid. But there was one memorable encounter with some people a little higher up the social scale.

Lucy and I were at the Imperial War Museum, which had just been newly refurbished. It was quite an occasion. Royalty was present *en masse*. We were wandering round a war-weary Land Rover when there was the Queen, right in front of us. Quick as a flash, an aide introduced us, and she moved graciously on, leading a little crowd of notables. Then, as if they were just part of the crowd, Prince Andrew appeared, with the Duke of Edinburgh. Prince Andrew had served in the Falklands, and we had met at the Weston Spirit. 'I know this chap,' he said, and introduced us to the Duke, who asked about the injuries and my recuperation. I told him the story of how the Army doctors had grafted on undamaged skin taken from remote parts of my anatomy, ending with the news that a slice of backside had been used to rebuild my nose. 'So now, when a woman kisses me,' I finished, 'she doesn't know how close she is to kissing my bum.' It was an old joke, which Lucy had heard too often, but it must have been new to the Duke and the Prince, because they bellowed with laughter.

All this was brought into focus for me during my three years in Liverpool. I had needed to leave home for personal reasons —

I had gained a good deal of confidence, but needed to stand on my own feet at last. And after all she'd been through, my Mam needed *her* independence. After helping to establish the Weston Spirit, there seemed no reason for me not to stay on. I bought my first car – a low-slung, moonstone-blue Ford Sierra Cosworth, complete with tail-fin and spoiler, a great car for a fancy-free bachelor. I took out a mortgage and moved from lodgings to a little two-bedroomed semi in the suburb of Woolton, and set about making a new life.

But what did that mean? I still had no real idea. One thing I did know, was that I needed challenges, any sort of challenges. I liked being alive again, but I knew I couldn't expect to go through life wrapped in cotton wool. As the actor Anthony Quayle said, in his last television interview before he died, 'If you haven't got any danger in your life, hurry up and find some.'

One challenge that had already come my way was when I was offered the chance to learn to fly, financed by a Douglas Bader Scholarship under the control of the International Air Tattoo. It was a wonderful offer, and I'll always be indebted to the man who inspired the award.

As an ordinary soldier who had got injured, it's good to have extraordinary people to look up to, in particular disabled people who show through their lives how much can be achieved. Douglas Bader not only had guts, strength and competence, but he also knew how to use publicity to help people. It wasn't the fact of his injury that set him apart, but what he did with himself afterwards. He was the first double amputee to drive and fly, and certainly the first to go straight back into conflict. The late, great Douglas Bader was, is and always will be the man who, in my eyes, achieved the most for others as a result of being disabled. If I'm ever a quarter the man he was, then I shall feel I have achieved something in my life.

Anyway, I was just three hours away from qualifying for my pilot's licence when something happened that brought me up short. I was doing solo circuits around Liverpool airport in a strong wind. As I came in to land, the wind kept pushing me up and down, so that I had to keep changing my angle of descent. I was afraid that I would either overshoot or hit the ground with a bang, and decided to go around again. Next time the same thing happened. By now I was sweating buckets (that's one problem of being burned, by the way – it upsets the cooling mechanism). My imagination started to work overtime. If you come down wrongly, you come down hard, and there's little protection. The third time around I made it, and sat there with my heart racing, dripping sweat and muttering, 'No more.' Flying had not become an obsession with me and now I knew it never would. I didn't need that kind of risk-taking in my life.

But it did prepare me for a second challenge, which I might never have accepted if I hadn't done some flying. In the summer of 1989, someone organizing an air show at the US Air Force base at Fairford in Wiltshire called me up. He asked me if I would do something to raise money for the International Air Tattoo, the people who had given me the flying scholarship. I wanted to help. Besides, King Hussein of Jordan would be there. He sponsors six of the IAT scholarships, and I had met him once before, when I was learning to fly. All I had to do, according to the man, was some 'wing-walking'. It sounded pretty scary. He tried to reassure me: it didn't involve actually walking on a wing. I just had to stand there, tied on to the wing, upright.

I wasn't very reassured because I have a terrible fear of heights. As a kid, I had to be rescued off cliff-faces more than once. As soon as I look down, I'm finished. At a book-signing at Lloyds of London, I had to go along a glass walkway high above the main floor. There was nothing but glass between me and death. I fixed my eyes straight ahead and concentrated on putting one foot in front of the other. My fingers still tingle just thinking about that, not to mention my absolute major fear – parachuting.

Still, I do have this weakness: I will do almost anything for charity. If somebody were to offer me money for charity to jump out of an aeroplane with a parachute – mind you, it would have to be a *huge* amount, and I'd need a very big nappy – I'd do it.

So, of course, I said yes to the wing-walking. Well, I told myself, it can't be too risky – after all, the pilot will be wanting to get home to his wife and kids.

The day came. It was a sweltering summer's day and I arrived, with nerves twitching and sweating profusely.

It was a surprising experience. I found myself zipped into a windproof suit, immersed in a helmet and goggles, looking like Biggles, standing on the top of this high-performance biplane, strapped to a strut sticking up from the fuselage. We trundled out ready for take-off. The soft breeze swept away the summer heat, and all at once, I began to feel more secure. We took off. No panic, I suppose because there was nothing against which to measure our height. I even managed a few quick nervous little waves as we swept over the crowd.

It was coming into land that scared me. The plane seemed to crab-walk sideways towards the runway, and I'm sure the only reason we straightened up was because I was praying so hard. As we trundled to a halt I felt quite elated. I only realized what I'd been through when I stepped down. My knees were locked back, solid with tension. I felt as if I looked like Douglas Bader himself, clumping stiff-legged across the tarmac. Later, as promised, I met King Hussein. I'm sure he was as charming as ever, but I can't remember a word he said because he was with Queen Noor, who is an *extremely* attractive lady.

The next challenge was both more dangerous and more demanding. It started when I was on the TV show *Wogan*, when Terry asked me if there was any dream that I really wanted to fulfil. As it happened, I had always wanted to drive a fast car, ever since I was a kid, and I said so. I had my Sierra Cosworth, but I meant a *really* fast car, on a racing circuit. A few days later a PR company contacted me. Did I fancy trying my hand at racing to raise some money for the Weston Spirit?

My Mam and Gran were against the idea. 'What do you want to do something so bloody stupid for?' Gran had said, with her usual force. They were afraid of my getting burned again, especially as my real grandfather, Gran's first husband, had been mad keen on cars and had died in a motor cycle accident. But that didn't bother me much. I knew that racing drivers were well protected by fireproof suits and had no intention of refusing.

I found myself learning to race in a Ford XR3i on the Oulton Park circuit in Cheshire. I wasn't a natural by any means. My distorted hands were clumsy on the wheel and gear-lever. The first time around I could have been beaten by an ice-cream van. But I persevered, for two days a week, over a couple of months, getting to know the course and the machine, getting the feel of high-revving gear changes and learning to anticipate the critical moment when the back starts to slide as you go into a corner. It was a thrill, the double challenge of doing something so precise at such a high speed. Concentration and practice had their effect. At the end of the two months, I had knocked fifteen seconds off my lap time, and was within a second or two of my instructor's. I was ready for my first race.

It was October 1989. I was to drive a Sierra Cosworth in the Firestone Production Saloon Cars Race at Thruxton in Hampshire. I had my own Sierra Cosworth, of course, but this was different. The time leading up to the race was without a doubt the most nerve-racking of my life. I had really put myself on the line this time. Up in a plane, I was on my own; here, I would be in full view of both the public and the media, testing my new skills, challenging myself to overcome my disability, knowing that failure would set back the chances of other disabled people who wanted to race. The day before I could hardly eat. That night, I don't think I slept. When I arrived at the pit – far too early – I was like a new boy at school, with no idea what to say, where to put my clothes or when to change; all this, thirty-one other competitors, and twelve laps to go.

Well, I didn't disgrace myself. After an unnerving start – there was a crash on the first lap that put one driver in hospital – I managed to stay on the road, and came in twenty-fifth. It was enough to encourage me. I was no Nigel Mansell, but I knew I could improve.

Over the next year I competed in sixteen races, half a dozen of which I failed to finish. My disabilities didn't seem much of a hindrance after all, even though once my co-driver broke the gear-stick, leaving me to handle a jagged piece of metal that stripped the tender skin from my palm. I even managed to come in third on one occasion – not great, but not too bad for a beginner.

So in many ways things were going well. I was involved in charity work, and physical challenges had been overcome. But there was another sort of lack to be made up – nothing to do with my body, or me as a public figure, or achievement, but me as a person, the inner me.

Let me backtrack:

Immediately after the fire, I was terrified I'd never have a girlfriend again. I can joke about my looks now, but there was a time when every glimpse of myself in the mirror was enough to send shivers down me. I was frightened I looked so terrible that no one would ever look at me or touch me again. Time brought reassurance. In Liverpool I'd had a few girlfriends, and regained belief in myself as a man – but only to a certain degree.

I had developed a long-term, deep-seated urge to make a family, have children, put down roots, find stability. By the time I had started racing I knew that this, too, was at least a possibility.

A year before, in the summer of 1988, I was in the office when a girl walked in who I had never seen before. I couldn't help noticing her, because any man would. She had deep dark eyes like little pots of coal, and a gentle easy manner. There were only about half a dozen people in the office, and I knew all the others, so I naturally introduced myself. Her name was Lucy, and she was working part-time for Merseysports.

At that stage, neither of us gave the other much thought. I was just off to learn to fly; she was going to the United States to spend the summer working for Camp America. We parted as casual friends do – a little kiss on the cheek, a quick 'Look after yourself' – without any idea we would meet again. Even if I'd thought about it, I wouldn't have thought about it for long. I knew I was no humungous catch – scarred, bald, gammy hands, bit of a beer belly, and certainly no confidence I could get a pretty, spirited young girl to *marry* me.

In the autumn, when we were both back in Liverpool, we bumped into each other again at a Weston Spirit get-together. Soon after this she heard I had a terrible cold, and decided to see how I was.

It so happened that I had someone staying with me – Jane, a woman whose husband had died in the Falklands. I didn't know her well, but I'd invited her to stay, just to lay a few ghosts to rest. We were talking over a cup of tea when there was a knock on the door. It was Lucy.

She seemed embarrassed at finding Jane there. Suddenly, touched by her thoughtfulness, I realized that I wanted to see more of her. I had to do something, right then, to show her there was nothing going on between Jane and me, and yet not be rude to Jane. So I suggested we all go out for a Chinese meal. Luckily, after a little polite prevarication, Lucy agreed.

Then afterwards, just as she was going, I suggested she come with me and a couple of others to a football match – Newcastle United v. Manchester United – at St James's Park, Newcastle on Sunday, two days later.

It was a miserable day – rainy, windy and bitterly cold. We walked for ever from the car-park. During the match, a fight broke out behind us. I joked that Newcastle was often like this: you went for a fight, and sometimes, if you were lucky, a football match would break out right in front of you. That day, we were borderline lucky: it was a dead boring nil-nil draw. The only thing that lifted the day for me was that Lucy seemed happy to snuggle up to me. I fancied her something rotten.

That was really the start of it. Lucy seemed not only to like me – she liked football! It was obvious she would never *really* appreciate the finer points, because she was an Everton supporter. Being a Manchester United fan, of course, *I* could tell her what real football was all about. But if she could put up with rain, cold, aggro and a draw, she had to have something.

It didn't take long for me to realize what an extraordinary and wonderful person she was. Fortunately for me she wasn't bothered by my looks – mine or anybody else's, as far as I could see. It was a wonderful thing to be appreciated for myself rather than as 'the Falklands veteran' or the 'media personality'. She seemed always to look right through to the heart of people. As long as they were decent, she was nice to them. She didn't judge, and had no hatred for anyone except people who hurt children.

Soon I realized that knowing her was changing me. Like most men, I started off just being proud of her, with a 'look-at-this-girl-on-my-arm' attitude, as if I ought to be owning her. But I quickly realized I would never own Lucy, and that was one reason I had begun to fall in love with her.

After three months – in March 1989 – she moved in with me; and three months after that we got engaged. It was a funny time. The first book had just come out, and I didn't want any more publicity. On the other hand, once we knew we were going to get married, I wanted to mark the occasion. So one evening, when we went out for supper at an Italian restaurant with a couple of friends, I ordered a bunch of two dozen roses to be delivered. It took some elaborate planning, because I had bought the engagement ring – having managed to discover Lucy's size – and smuggled it along with me. Once there, I got the restaurant to hide the ring in the roses, then deliver them to Lucy while we were still eating. Of course throughout the meal I could hardly eat for nerves, but when the roses came, when she opened the note, when she saw the ring, when I saw her expression – just pure delight – I knew I had done the right thing.

Then, somehow, the press had got hold of it. All the newspapers wanted to take photographs. We refused. Reporters camped on the doorstep for several days. It was the first time that I appreciated how intrusive they could be. They seemed to assume they owned us. Lucy once had to walk straight past the house and on to the neighbours' for a cup of tea until they had gone. Two of them were really sleazy-looking guys from the tabloids, one with hair slicked back over the collar of his leather jacket, the other in a suit with tie skew-whiff, his collar undone and a note-pad in the pocket. *Stereotypical*. They were trying to get a story on Lucy and her ex-boyfriends, but she'd never really had any. There was no story, and eventually they went away.

So we managed to keep our privacy, up until the end of the year.

Around this time my professional life, such as it was, took another turn. Out of the blue, the BBC in Cardiff asked me to present a radio show entitled *Summer Gems*, which featured well-known Welshmen. I had to choose ten records and say what they meant to me.

I must have done something right, because two months later the BBC approached me again. Would I like to host my own show? Well who wouldn't? Soon, every Saturday, I had fifty minutes of music and a chat with a celebrity going out over South Wales and part of the Midlands. I enjoyed the work and loved having the chance to talk to people like Lenny Henry, Gary Glitter and Elkie Brooks about what interested them, and me, and (with luck) the listeners. The radio show was also the only bit of real routine I had in my life – something I was beginning to miss.

The only problem was, it meant driving 500 miles a week between Liverpool and Cardiff. It was expensive, and a strain, especially with the marriage getting closer.

This wasn't the only strain. I still haven't really forgiven Malcolm for what happened. My old and trusted friend, Malcolm Brinkworth, who had been largely responsible for the three documentaries, informed me that he was making a film about charities and wanted to include the Weston Spirit. Would I take a bunch of kids through an assault course up at Purbright?

Well, I would do almost anything for Weston Spirit and for Malcolm, so of course I agreed, never suspecting a thing. I cheered the kids over walls, along horizontal ladders and through rubber tyres, while the cameras rolled. Then, with the performance over, I was relaxing with the kids when I saw a strangely familiar figure approaching me.

It was Michael Aspel, and one of Malcolm's crew was a Thames TV cameraman, and This, out of the blue, Was My Life.

I was totally gobsmacked.

'You bastard!' I shouted at Malcolm. Trusted friend, indeed! He knew I hated surprises! 'You bastard, you lied to me!' Then I turned to Michael. I must have looked outraged, because he told me later he thought I was going to put one on his chin.

As it happened, despite my apprehension, everything was fine. We would have spoken to King Hussein directly from Jordan, if the satellite link hadn't broken down. And when Lucy came on, it was more than fine. This was the first time we really made a public statement of the engagement.

The next problem was the marriage. It occurred to me that it would be perfect if we could be married in the Guards Chapel, in London. It may seem strange these days for an ex-soldier to remain attached to his old regiment, but I certainly was, and still am. The chapel was the only place that seemed to hold any religious significance for me, because it spoke of things that will always be real to me – the boys I served with, especially those who died. Somehow, my old boss Brigadier Johnny Rickets heard of the engagement and my dream, and said he'd fix it.

We were married on 12 May 1990, the eighth anniversary of the day on which I sailed for the Falklands aboard the *QE2*, and almost twelve months after becoming engaged. My best man was Jimmy Salmon, who helped save my life on the *Sir Galahad*, and the service was conducted by the former Welsh Guards padre, Reverend Michael Walters. Lucy's chief bridesmaid, Susie Fowler, was a dream in a peach-coloured dress, and she had three other bridesmaids and my seven-year-old nephew Richard as a page-boy.

Everything was perfect – the service, the band, the wine, the food – except that nerves turned the whole thing into a nightmare for me. I'm still not too certain about some of the details. If there hadn't have been a video and so many pictures it would all have remained a blur.

I remember getting changed in the sergeants' mess and then nipping downstairs with Jimmy for an ale – anything to take my mind off what was going to happen. Then there we were the two of us, Jimmy in his red Welsh Guards tunic wearing his Northern Ireland and Falklands medals, me in morning dress, being greeted by friends and relatives.

Already there was a crowd outside the railings. I was thankful that the security was good. Even so, two respectable old ladies who had come up from Brighton specially for the occasion had managed to slip past into the chapel, uninvited. No one minded, and they have provided us with a few laughs since, seeing them on the video tiptoeing here and there, trying to avoid the camera.

I remember standing, shifting my feet in an agony of apprehension, staring up at the golden mosaics behind the altar – the chapel was bombed in the war, and this was the only surviving bit of the original. I remember staring at my fingers – one of them was plastered, because I had somehow managed to cut myself that morning. I remember wondering: did I take the price off the bottom of my shoes, for when I kneel down? I remember the Trumpet Voluntary and Lucy appearing beside me. I had been told not to look at her, but I couldn't resist a sly peak. She looked a dream in great swathes of ivory.

Then a little bit of drama. We were well on our way, with the Rev. Mike doing his stuff, and me wiping the sweat from my forehead, trying to concentrate on Mike's words of wisdom. He was giving us a talk about marriage having its downs as well as its ups, and had just mentioned 'the pressures that cause us to stumble', when, as if on cue, *whump*! there was a heavy thud from behind.

We turned, and there was Susie out for the count. She'd fainted, poor girl, right on Lucy's train. Wondering what was going to happen, I looked anxiously at Mike. He could see that Jimmy was already helping her up and that she would be all right. 'Don't worry,' he whispered, 'the funeral service is on the next page.'

A few minutes later, with Susie back in action, we were on our way out, down the banner-hung nave, with the band playing the Pomp and Circumstance march. We posed briefly for an army of photographers, and led off into the hall nearby for a sit-down meal.

It was magnificent, I know it was. I just wish I could remember it. But I had a speech to make, and I knew I was going to be terrible, and I was terrible, and the whole experience was too wonderful and too nerve-racking for me to take it in.

So it was a bit of a relief to return to motor racing. Not for long, though.

It was almost the end of the season at Oulton Park in October 1990. It had been raining, and the surface was still slick. I was coming off a bend called Druids, at over ninety m.p.h., swinging a bit wide. I put two wheels on the grass, and then turned a little too sharply to regain the road. The car skidded, spun sideways, and hit a retaining wall of Armco, which smashed the back end off. I ended up 300 metres down the road. I don't remember the crash itself. I must have blacked out. I honestly believe that if you die in a crash, you know nothing at all about it.

I came to, hearing one of the marshals telling me, 'Stay where you are.'

'You've got to be joking!' I yelled, in less polite terms, because there was one thought in my head – fire! – and I threw myself out in a forward roll away from the car. I sat on the Armco and took off my helmet, mildly shocked and so embarrassed I hardly registered the bruised ribs and aching, whiplashed neck.

That ended the season, and, for all I know, my short racing career. There was no sponsorship for the following season, and I couldn't say I was sorry. I had enjoyed racing. It was nothing to do with being attracted to danger. It is far safer than people think, and no more dangerous, statistically, than rock-climbing, hang-gliding or microlighting. But I'd done enough to know that it wasn't going to be a career. It demanded total commitment to the machine, to technique, to the team behind you. Hours, days, weeks, years of concentration. That's what it takes to be a winner, not just talent. Even if I had had the talent, I knew I would never have been able to commit myself to the life.

Anyway, I had a new and better life now. Lucy and I had settled into marriage. We might have been in Liverpool still if it hadn't been for that weekly journey to Cardiff – that, combined with a puzzling, worrying sequence of not-so-petty crimes.

Although I didn't know it at the time, the trouble had started one day when I was in the office. Someone had come in and said they'd seen a youth tampering with my much-loved Sierra

23

Cosworth. I ran out but was too late to catch the culprit. He had used a screwdriver to break a door-lock and one of the alarms, but had failed to get in. There was no reason to think there was anything sinister going on – the car was a highly prized item worth stealing. I just put it down to bad luck.

But over the next few months, there were four more attacks – another on the Cosworth and three on two other sponsored cars – both 4 × 4 Sierras – one of which was actually stolen, and subsequently recovered after a police chase. In all, there was several thousand pounds' worth of damage. OK, they weren't my cars, but I had to pay the insurance on them, and I began to wonder if it was the cars themselves they were after, or what they thought might be *in* the cars? And why would they think there might be something in them worth stealing? Did they know they were my cars? Was this personal?

The thing that really set me worrying was when they had a go at Lucy's 1.4 Orion (my Sierra was in the garage). It was the cheapest out of sixteen cars on the street. There was a 1600 injection Orion in front of us, a brand new 1800 Sierra behind us, and further down the street stood a Lotus and a brand new XR21 among others, all much more powerful than Lucy's Orion, which contained nothing more than a cheap radio-cassette player. And it didn't only happen once. There were three attempted break-ins in three weeks. The house was an ordinary little two-bedroom semi, but I was beginning to wonder: if this is personal, how soon before they get inside the house?

So we decided to move south, back to the valleys, back to my roots. We chose a plot of land on a new estate, on a hilltop high above a hamlet, even before the foundations had been put down, and moved in October 1990. My home village, Nelson, was only a mile away. I felt a renewed sense of belonging, being cradled again by crags and ridges and grassed-over tips, while over the hill were the familiar lines of terraced houses I remembered so well from my childhood.

Practically, as well, it made a lot of sense. Lucy now had neighbours to talk to, and we were closer to some of my oldest friends. Mam and Gran were nearby. Mam is a district nurse, which was a great help when James was on the way.

Then along came James, and a new meaning to life, and deeper questions about my past, present and future.

One thing I was sure of: charity work was something I would always do, if I had the opportunity. I enjoy fund-raising for charities. I enjoy the challenge, the satisfaction of working with people, and for people, and the exhilaration of reaching a target. It really gives me a high, an uplifting burst of feeling in my stomach, as if I were a child again, suddenly discovering I've done something well.

There is one group of people I feel great empathy for: burns victims. Being burned myself taught me how easily you accept humiliation, how much you want to hide, and how important it is to show yourself. Only by making that statement can you accept yourself as you are, and make other people accept you. That's one of many reasons I'm grateful to Malcolm – the documentaries showed a burned person beginning to live a normal life. It really made a difference to the way the public perceived injuries that had just been ignored before. Now people often say to victims who are recovering after being caught in fires, 'Oh you've been burned – like Simon Weston.' By providing a point of reference, that helps both sides – the scarred and the healthy – to accept the wounds and the problems. That's one development I would never have predicted, and one thing that makes some sense of my injuries.

It's not just burns victims, though. As a burns victim I'm also one of a larger minority, the disabled. Because I know the good it can do, I'm always ready to take up a challenge on their behalf. They should know it's OK to fight, and that standing up for a cause can bring results. People shouldn't take it for granted that someone else is responsible. 'It doesn't affect me; I'm nineteen; I can drink fifteen pints of lager; I'm great and stuff the world' – this was me, once, and look what happened. So many go through life without even *thinking* about disabled people – yes, they exist, but they belong somewhere else, to somebody else, in a home. But take a group of people in any pub – out of every hundred, there are two or three who are registered with some form of disability. They should be seen with more than a sympathetic glance. People should say, 'That is me, or a friend, or a relative, in a few years' time.' They should realize that everything they do now for others could help them or their relatives eventually.

So often now I see issues, small and big, that need action. Take disabled parking. Often people who are themselves not disabled but who have a disabled partner or relative display the disabled person's car sticker, even when they don't have the person with them, because this way they can park the car more easily. But it's not right. They ought to get fined for doing it. The law ought to be tougher. I believe it's something to fight for, or at least *part of* something to fight for.

That's why I was so pleased to be given the opportunity to get involved with the Royal Star and Garter Home, the organization that looks after disabled and injured ex-servicemen and women. They've been in existence seventy-six years now, and they need cash to refurbish their main building in London. I was happy to help. It's a wonderful cause – two world wars and over seventy smaller conflicts have involved hundreds of thousands of men and women who never know when they might need help. One day – who knows – I might be one of them.

The place is full of amazing and deserving characters, like the man who woke up to find he had a form of multiple sclerosis. It took him seven years in the Royal Star and Garter Home to learn to walk again. Then there was Owen, who had been captured by the Nazis, been force-marched through snow, contracted frost-bite, and had both feet amputated by the Red Cross. Another old bloke, Horace Ham, is ninety-five. He was wounded on the first day of the Battle of the Somme in the First World War, and returned to the front to do twelve 'over-the-tops'. After the war, for the next seventy years, he was fine. Then, without any family left, he needed someone to provide him with some care. There he was, with a room of his own, still able to keep his independence and to enjoy his game of snooker.

But however rewarding charity work is, it isn't enough to build a whole life on. I had no professional direction. Challenges had been met; but they were not enough. There were causes to fight for; but I wasn't sure what my role could be. I wasn't sure I could raise cash, hire and fire, get sponsors, do all the things that professional charity-workers do. I felt restless and unfocused. Becoming a father had forced me to think about all this, and the future. If I couldn't work out my own destiny, what hope had I of helping others? Of guiding James?

And it wasn't just a lack of professional direction. The truth was there were hidden fears gnawing at me, fears I had no idea how to face, but that had to be faced sometime. I knew I would never be able to move forward, to build on whatever I had achieved, for myself, for others, for Lucy, for James, unless I faced them.

I had never imagined the road to recovery would be so long, or that it would ever lead me back to a wind-whipped shore eight and a half thousand miles away.

But the time had come.

I had to go back to the Falklands.

2

THE REASONS WHY

October 1991

There was nothing new about the idea of going back. I had
first expressed a wish to return to Malcolm, not long after
the war.

I could have gone years earlier. I had received half a dozen
offers to go back; they were there almost from the word go.
But at that time I would only have considered returning with
the boys, with a big bunch of Welsh Guards, so that we could
honour the lads in the best way possible – partying all the
way there and all the way back. That's how they would have
mourned us, and that's how they would like to be mourned –
with a lot of alcohol, a lot of laughter, a lot of sarcasm. It's
the soldier's way of dealing with impossible emotions.

Once a friend was kind enough to fix up the flights for me,
on my own. Mam asked me what I'd do if I went. I said I
wanted to go to San Carlos, where I had first landed, to the
huge freezer plant, used as a hospital, where I almost died,
and to the shore where they put the boys to rest. I said I'd
like to walk the final few hilly miles over Mount Longdon,
Tumbledown, Wireless Ridge – the places that had given their
names to battles, and become household names in 1982 – to

Port Stanley, because I had never made it all the way the first time.

'Take some daffodils,' Mam said, because it was spring when we had this conversation. 'Throw some daffodils in the water.'

'I wouldn't do that, Mam,' I said. 'The boys would rather have cans of beer.'

In the end, even though I had the chance, I didn't want to know. It wasn't right for me then. In fact, it was so far from what I wanted that I forgot the whole conversation. It's only Mam who remembers.

Somewhere along the way, though, I began to change. Gradually, almost without realizing, I found I needed a different way of coping, something more personal, something deeper: a return.

But not *just* a return. Malcolm and I agreed that it would make a subject for a fourth film – the last one, definitely the last – but we both knew for different reasons that there had to be something more.

I already knew what that 'something more' had to be. A strange idea had resurfaced, one that had been with me for years. It was this: that one day, somehow, I would meet the pilot who had dropped the bomb on the *Sir Galahad*.

I never took the possibility seriously, until talking to Malcolm brought it sharply into focus. With his involvement in the making of the documentary, I might be able to achieve my ambition.

By 1991 it had become a reality. Malcolm knew the pilot's name – although to me it didn't yet mean enough to stick in my mind – and believed that the meeting could be arranged. For him, as a film director, the time was right. The tenth anniversary of the war was approaching. For me, the time was not perfect, not with James so small and growing so fast. But I knew there never would be a perfect time. I made my decision: better now than never, better face what had to be faced, if the rest of my life was to make any sense.

Backed by the BBC, plans hardened; we were to set off in early November.

I was so wound up it was hard to believe. I would sit in my chair, holding James and wondering about things that my teenage self would have thought totally weird. Where was my life going? Why this urge to return to the scene of destruction, death and horror? What good would it do me – or anyone else?

You might say it would have been better to leave well alone. The same thought occurred to me, many times, with increasing force.

In October, there was a commemoration ceremony for three of the lads who died – Cliff Ellie, Brian Jasper and Ian Anthony Dale – all in my platoon, and all from the same school, Hawthorn High in Pontypridd. I didn't know them well, but each had a memory attached to him. I used to play rugby with Cliff. After the bomb struck, he ran back into the inferno to do what he could to help, and never came out. Brian had left the Army once, and had recently rejoined. He had had two little girls, I remember. Ian had slept next to me on the way down on the QE2. I remember him telling me that his wife was pregnant.

It was a moving service, with a couple of hymns and the unveiling of simple plaques in the foyer. As I looked across at the families, as I talked to them afterwards, I began to feel more and more like a traitor. I was less than a month away from meeting the man who had caused the death of their sons. Was I really doing the right thing by going back? I didn't want to offend any of the friends or relatives. They, and hundreds of others, remember every single day that sons, fathers, husbands, cousins, uncles, friends will never return. I didn't want to make those memories more painful than they already were. Nor did I want them to think I was being disloyal to the dead. Certainly, I didn't want anyone to think I was forgiving the pilot on their behalf.

But my intentions wouldn't be enough. I came away believing as firmly as I have ever believed anything that, if I went, if I met the pilot, if I treated him like another human being, I risked losing the respect of many people both in military and in civilian life, especially those who had lost friends or relatives.

Did this mean I shouldn't go? As I thought about it, I realized that I could not be responsible for the way other people reacted. I would simply have to take whatever came at me, and try to make people see that this was something I had to do for myself, however hard it would be, and whatever the risks, because otherwise I wouldn't be able to live my life to the full, and then I'd be no use to anyone.

If there would be anything to forgive, I hoped I would be forgiven. If I managed to find anything positive in the experience, I hoped that I would be able to pass it on.

Why was I going back? It was a question I asked myself every day now.

I didn't particularly *want* to go back. There wasn't a lot there to see. It wasn't as if I was about to bind myself permanently to that place and that time, like an old soldier from the First World War returning to the Somme. A glimpse of bare hills and a forty-five minute shopping spree in Port Stanley, and that would be it, right?

It's simply that I *had* to go back, just this once. There was something in me that *needed* to go back. There was something missing, some lack, something to be completed. But what?

I had thought and thought about this. And I didn't know. I wished I did, but I didn't. All I knew was there was a feeling of emptiness. There were times when I thought, 'I'm throwing my life away, because I'm not achieving enough.' Then I went through a phase when I was working non-stop for about six or eight weeks without a day off. I was here, there, a school to visit, a launch, an opening, a speech. I couldn't wait for a rest. Then I got my rest and I thought, 'I'm wasting my life away again.' I was never satisfied – fed up with doing too much, and fed up with not doing enough.

Restlessness and confusion. Same as many people my age. But why should feeling restless and confused have made me want – no, *need* – to go back? It seemed to be time to look deeper.

Perhaps I had to experience something I never properly experienced at the time. I was never a part of the war. I didn't even hear any guns fired. The closest I got to action, before the bomb struck, was when I was on the *Fearless* and saw two Sea Darts zip up towards two Argentinian Canberra bombers. One plane blew up. That was it. The sum total of my experience of action, until I was just about to go ashore at Fitzroy.

I never even saw much of the spot where I was injured. A quick peek above deck, a glimpse of treeless hills, a shiver in the gusty wind, and I was back below, in pursuit of warmth and a cup of tea. I was never a part of the injury process, because it was over so quickly. I heard the air-raid warning, squatted down, and then it was boom, whoosh, and I was out of it. It must have taken no more than twenty minutes, perhaps half an hour, to get me off. It was so quick I never really had a chance to understand, to assimilate.

Perhaps there was unfinished grieving – for myself, and for my friends.

There was reason enough for grief. I had been injured. I had lost my friends. I had lost my youth. I had lost my middle twenties. I had lost my job. I had lost my sport. I had lost what might have been, what I might have become – my future. Having come out the other side obviously I've gained in certain aspects, but the losses – I still feel them tremendously. They don't go away.

But the sense of loss was disturbing. It lacked a focus. I'm not an angry person, so I didn't blame anyone for what had happened. Right from the beginning my Mam worked at building on only positive feelings in me. I had no one to blame but myself, she said. It was my decision to join up. People get hurt in war. It was no good moaning – I had to take responsibility for my own fate. I wondered: was it not having someone to blame that made me feel this strange, unfocused restlessness?

Certainly, perhaps most of all, I still missed the boys who had died. I had joined up with some of them. Some of them had come to my house. I remember once, just before we left for the Falklands, arriving home in a one-ton vehicle with three other lads. One of them, Gareth Hughes, was a Welsh Guard (the other two were REME – Royal Electrical and Mechanical Engineers – blokes). Gareth was the driver. We were on our way back from Cardiff to our base in Brecon Beacons, and were eager for some home cooking. 'Seems like more boys here than there are in the whole Army!' Mam had said, and whipped up masses of egg, corned beef, chips, and apple tart. We ate her out of house and home, then roared off, more worried about running out of diesel than about leaving my Mam destitute and starving.

Now all I've got is the memory. I never had a chance to say goodbye. Saying goodbye is part of grieving. You need that sense of occasion, a little bit of time to realize your loss – something spiritual, if you like, though I am not a religious person at all.

The first time I really began to understand what had happened was when my Mam came to see me in hospital with a list of those who had died. She'd been to the memorial service. On the service-sheet were the names of everyone who had died. When she saw me, she laid it on the line, reading the list, with me crying like a kid from beneath my newly made eyelids. She was afraid that if she didn't confront me, I would never take it on board, never be able to grieve, never come to terms with the loss.

Perhaps that hadn't been enough.

The grief came through in odd little thoughts. My penknife, wallet and poker dice were all lying on the sea-bed in Port Pleasant. My rifle – that must still be aboard the *Galahad*. My pack. My book – I was making my way through a paperback, *The Legionnaire*. Small things that represented a huge part of my life. The *Galahad* is a war-grave now – she was sunk two miles out to sea – but it might help to see the spot where she was hit.

I thought I'd been through the whole grieving process. You'd think nine years would be long enough.

But perhaps the grieving couldn't be complete until I'd come full circle.

Perhaps I also needed to reassess the whole experience of the war in some more objective way.

Strangely, I couldn't feel bitter about what had happened. It would be easy if we could sit around pointing the finger and blaming. But in war, sacrifices are made, lives are lost, things are asked of normally placid, decent men that would never be asked of them at other times. This is true on both sides.

When I thought of the Argentinians, I didn't think 'enemy'. I know there are people and armies who love the power and authority they've been given, or they've taken. The Khmer Rouge and the East German Stasi, for example, both seemed to enjoy destroying people's lives. But I didn't feel it was like that with the Argentinian armed forces. I thought they were misled. The media were state-owned, and those in power could tell people what they liked; there weren't many dissidents to counter them. The war we fought was the creation of one man and his government trying to alleviate their problems. It looked easy: thirty marines, 1,800 people, a few windswept hills. They never thought Britain would send an army 8,500 miles to protect a few sheep farms. A major mistake. I couldn't hold anybody, except a few of the leaders, responsible for being caught up in an error they had no control over.

Fine, I could understand the Argentinians being a bit aggrieved – they started it, and we finished it. That's war. There's got to be a winner and there's got to be a loser. Of course, in a way, everybody's a loser in war. But in limited, military terms there has to be seen to be a victor. Luckily – and there was a lot of luck involved – it was a conventional conflict, solved conventionally, by the seizure of arms, equipment, and men. We won, they lost.

And I was still convinced it was a just war, if any war is just. I hate, loathe and detest warfare, yet I was not ashamed to say I was a soldier who loved the Army, and that I had fought in a conflict I believed to be right. Most of my mates felt the same.

Once you're in a situation of war, there's nothing else you can do about it. You can't afford to think about the arguments for and against. You have to go there and do your job, otherwise you're dead. You don't want to take life, but if you have to, you will. There was an aggressor who needed to be stopped, in the only way possible – open conflict. Politics were beside the point. We did what we did because at the time it was the right thing to do.

None of us wanted to be there. None of us even knew where Argentina or the Falklands were. None of us was really interested in Argentina, apart from the fact that it had a football team, and that the Argentinians weren't too bad at polo and hockey. Other than this nobody knew a great deal about them, and not too many of us cared.

But when you sign up for the armed forces, you sign on a dotted line. In between each dot is an unwritten rule: you're signing up to kill or be killed, to maim or be maimed.

It's a tragedy of life that armed forces are necessary. But they'll remain necessary until all political disputes are settled and all terrorists content. Until then, mothers' sons will die.

By the time this book comes out, a lot more mothers' sons will have died. Whether they be Catholic or Protestant, British or Argentinian, Israeli or Arab, Croat or Serb, every soldier is some mother's son, and he deserves to live.

That's how I felt about the Argentinians. I felt sorry for the way they were lied to and the way that they were forced into war – how could anyone force a teenager to go to war? On the *Canberra*, there were five captured Argentinians, the youngest of whom (we were told) was just thirteen. I was on board ship with wounded kids of seventeen and under. Tragic.

But life is not a cute business in which we can all go around patting each other's faces with buttercups. The hard truth is that a teenager with a machine-gun can be as deadly as a marine. If he's wearing the opposition's uniform, and he's got a gun in his hand, you have to assume that he's prepared to kill you. That's where kill or be killed comes in. It's you or him.

With hindsight, you can say things should have been different. The politicians should never have allowed the conflict to escalate. But, as I saw it, there was no point feeling bitter even about the politics of the war. Neither at the time nor afterwards did I believe that political cynicism influenced our government's decision to go to war; it was not making a deliberate attempt to win an election by its action. Of course, the Conservatives awarded themselves Brownie points after the event. But one thing about Mrs Thatcher – she is a mother. She turned out the Air Force to find her son when he was lost in the desert. She took a lot of flak for doing so, but she did only what any mother would have done, given the power. I couldn't see her callously sending off a load of mothers' sons to battle, just to win an election.

This is what came to me when I tried to assess the war objectively. But perhaps it would all change when I went back.

Perhaps I needed to go just to meet the man who had done this to me, the pilot who had dropped the bomb. Maybe it sounds perverse, this urge to meet the man who had killed my friends, who had burned my old life away together with half my skin, but I wanted to talk to him, to find out how he felt about it, to look into his eyes, to see if there was a soul in there.

Now I had the chance, and I was scared of what I would feel when I met him. But it also challenged me, and offered the opportunity of some form of release that I couldn't understand.

Why scared? I didn't know. I didn't resent or hate him. I suppose I should have hated him. He had taken away my friends. I tried to find reasons why I should, but I couldn't, and I was sure I wouldn't unless he turned out to be a hateful personality. I was not going to dislike him just because he was doing his job, doing what a serviceman does in a battle. And there was nothing to forgive, because there was nothing to blame him for. If I'd had the chance to do it to him, I probably would have. How could I hate him for doing something that in ordinary circumstances he would never have done to me? But the circumstances were extraordinary, and he was carrying out his orders, doing his duty; you can't blame a man for that, even if it means killing forty or fifty men.

Sometimes I wondered if he was like me at all. Quite possibly that pilot had not lifted a finger in anger since. Perhaps, like me, he was more than happy to live peacefully. Perhaps, like me, he had found it a wonderful thing to say 'Good morning', 'Hello', 'How are you?' After being in action, there's a daily joy in the simple assertion that you're at peace with the world. Most people take such things for granted, like driving the same route to work every day for twenty years. Not me. I was still delighted just to be alive. Perhaps the pilot felt like this, too.

Or perhaps not. Perhaps this guy with a background so different from mine was an arrogant sod proud of his kills, some vindictive lout who went around crowing about the number of Welsh Guards he had taken out, someone I would be happy to part from his teeth. If I imagined him to be like that, yes, I could feel anger stirring. Then I hoped he would be like that, because it would be good to have a go, to take revenge for myself and my mates.

But it didn't last. My mood would change, and next time I would think: perhaps he was a slum kid, making good in the Air Force, the pride of his parents; or from some cowboy ranching family on the pampas; or maybe he was from Patagonia, from one of those pioneering sheep-breeding families who had moved from Wales a century ago. Maybe we had ancestors in common. Now there was a strange thought.

Anyway, he must be intelligent, tough, expert, to make a pilot. Was he married? Did he have kids? What was he feeling when he took off that day? Two very different people, linked by a brutal destiny, our lifelines suddenly snapping together. We were bound, and divided, by a terrible event. He had been only a few feet from me as the bomb flashed past me. At what point did our fates interlock? When did the damage he did to me and my mates become 'inevitable'? From the minute he climbed into the cockpit? From the minute he was born?

So back and forth went my thoughts — now calm, now with a twist of anger — though I knew that was only my imagination at work. But always there was an edge of fear to the thought of meeting him.

And when the tension built, I thought: well, after all, there's nothing extraordinary in what I'm about to do. Similar things have happened countless times, in countless wars. It gave me solace about meeting this guy, that English and German officers, fairly soon after the war, had felt more linked by the experience imposed on them than divided by their old enmity. British and U-boat sailors, British and German pilots — they couldn't forget, but they could forgive. The strange thing was, when they met, they found that there was nothing, in the end, to forgive.

It sounded easy when I said it. The trouble was, it didn't reassure me. I was still scared, scared that it was all a bit too easy. I felt like a kid whistling in the dark to keep away the bogey-men, to keep away the thought that when I met him, he would turn out not to be simply a pilot, but a tormentor, a sadist, a torturer. Then the fear would return, fear that emotions I could only guess at would leap up at me from the darkness, and no amount of whistling could keep the fear away.

Perhaps in returning I was looking for some way to cope with emotions about my survival. I often wondered why I hadn't died in the fire. Why me, and not the others? Could I have done more to save them?

Perhaps I'm a born survivor. Perhaps my unconscious had told me that if I were going to die, I'd better make sure I died in Wales. Perhaps, as my mother says, I just hated the idea of dying in water. Perhaps I came back just to annoy my mother and to spite my mate Carl, who'd get the 400 LPs I'd promised him if I didn't make it. But joking about it didn't help make sense of anything, and sense is what I needed.

When I remembered the few seconds immediately before and after the bomb struck – not that I did so often those days – I could see myself heading for my mate, Yorkie, who was fast asleep. I was going to shout in his ear, slap him on the back of the head, and wake him up. Lazy sod, why should he be asleep when I was awake?

Now, because I was running towards Yorkie, when everyone else was concentrating on getting ready to go ashore, perhaps that was the tiny injection of aggression I needed to do what I did. I remember the intercom squawking 'Air raid!', me squatting down in self-protection, the extraordinary grey streak of the bomb as it whipped through the ship before my eyes, the sudden rainbow flare of the explosion, the burst of flame, the moving fireballs of my mates, the choking smoke, swollen heads, blackened flesh, burning clothes, my own hands beginning to melt as I watched, the man I tried to help, falling through my hands, slippery as a roasting chicken, my skin flaking off on his uniform, uselessly, and then the terrible sprint through smoke and flames to the fresh air. I would have died if I'd stayed to help him. But I still have nine fingers, and he's dead.

Could I have done more and still lived? Might I have saved lives, even if it meant losing my own? I was with mates, and I knew their lives depended on me, and mine on them, and yet, when the moment came, I had failed them.

Those few seconds, when I ran – was I driven by self-preservation, or cowardice? Perhaps I did what I could. Perhaps nothing would have made any difference. But the fact of my survival made me doubt, and from the doubt sprang guilt, and the guilt was still with me. It will be with me for ever.

The only way I could cope was to make sure that I lived my life for a purpose.

So my feeling of emptiness had to have something to do with my future. There's a lot that I'd like to do. I'd like to win at something sporting, to own nice things, to earn well, do college courses, travel, do well on the radio – not that I'm a Steve Wright or a Simon Bates or a Dave Lee Travis, not a pushy, drive-hard-till-you-drop sort of person. But I needed to do *something*. I'd like to be free to discover what, and this trip was about achieving that freedom.

This in its turn had something to do with being in the public eye. This part of my life bothered me; it didn't seem real to me. I don't think of myself as being well known. I don't like being told I'm famous. I don't keep mementoes. I don't read much about myself. I never watch anything about myself on TV. At heart, I don't think I'm that media-worthy. I may do something that catches the imagination of the press now and then, but apart from this, I think I lead far too boring a life for them. This is what I wanted – an ordinary family life.

One thing was for sure – it had been a very strange experience, being me over the last ten years. All this talking and writing, especially as it was all about someone so young, and someone who had done so little. There's nothing unique or clever about being burned, or about my recovery. What was I going to do – *not* recover? It was as if I was two people: the public me – the way I had lived my life since my injuries, the way I had coped with my injuries – and the private me; but yet not two people, because the private me *was* the public me. I had just carried on doing what I enjoyed doing and what I thought was right; it wasn't worth all the attention. I was fairly certain the general public would one day have had enough of Simon Weston.

This isn't to say I knocked the publicity. I hated to think that all that experience might come to nothing. I wanted to be able to put it to good effect. But how?

I felt my life was an alphabet, with bits of the beginning and lots of gaps. If I looked hard between A and C I might find B. Then I'd have to find other letters, and then see if I could spell anything. I never was much of a speller, so I worried. What did I do today? Was it right? Was it useful and meaningful? Or did I just waste today, throw twenty-four hours away? All I knew was that somewhere along the line achievement was really important. I just wished I knew what it was I was supposed to achieve. If I didn't go crazy, maybe I would find some answers.

Later, with a little bit of luck, perhaps I would be able to transfer some of that understanding to my son. I would love him to understand the things that have baffled me, see some of the things I've seen, learn some of the things I've learned, know some of the people I've known. I hoped and prayed this was to be a journey that would benefit the two of us.

And ultimately I had to come away from the Falklands laughing. Whatever else I felt, if I didn't come away laughing as well it would haunt me for the rest of my life. There would be a few tears when I got there – bound to be – but unless I came away with some laughter there would be something left undone.

There was only one thing for it: to go.

3

BUENOS AIRES

15 November 1991

It was going to be a demanding trip, to say the least.

For me, it was a direct challenge, and I had no idea how I would take it all: meeting people we had been at war with; travelling, with all the tensions that involves; new places; new food; new beer (now that could be a real worry); and, most significantly, the strain of meeting the pilot and going back to the scene of my injury.

But I would also be part of a process – the making of a documentary. This involved a dozen people, a lot of money, a lot of preparation, and a lot of pressure – on me, and on the others, particularly Malcolm. We would be going with a television crew: a cameraman, an assistant cameraman, a sound man, an assistant producer and a production manager. This would be the first time a documentary about the war had involved both British and Argentinians. If the logistics were tough, the political arrangements were horrendous. The little I heard of them made me amazed that anything had been successfully organized at all.

Then there were the others: my co-writer, and a journalist from the *News of the World*, which had bought the serial rights and was eager to keep an eye on its investment; and, later, in the Falklands, a photographer was to join us.

Finally, there were the two Falklands veterans, who were vital both to the film and to me. I knew their support would be important, and I was sure I would benefit from a good dose of cynical Army humour. Their presence added a whole other dimension to the arrangements, because one of them was still serving. There had been little, if any, contact between Argentinian armed forces and our lads.

My own personal journey, the film, the book, the squaddies, the travel, the politics – the overlapping interests involved meant conflicting pressures for everyone. What could possibly go wrong? Practically anything – and everything.

It had always been important for me, and for the film, to take other military people with us. At first, I had wanted to make the trip with some other Welsh Guards. That had seemed right – Welsh Guards honouring other Welsh Guards. But very few of the Welsh Guards had been involved in fighting. Like me, they had had a limited war. It was important for the documentary that my companions should have wider experiences than mine, not identical ones.

But they couldn't be too different. I had no interest in going down there with pilots or sailors or SAS men. They would have to be from the regular Army, so that their experiences would balance mine, as well as extend it. And they had to be squaddies, not officers, so that they could convey the feel of war at its most basic. We could take no more than two or three men.

In the end, Malcolm had chosen two: Gary Tytler, then a lance-corporal, now a colour-sergeant from the 2nd Battalion, Scots Guards, and John Meredith, a platoon sergeant, later a warrant officer, with the 2nd Battalion, Parachute Regiment, usually referred to simply as '2 Para'. Both had seen the war through to the end, in vicious hand-to-hand fighting, in freezing, wet and windy misery.

I knew we would get on, right from the first meeting in the pub at the bottom of my hill. We talked about mutual friends. The Army is a small world, and we all knew both Welsh Guards and Scots Guards, who train in the same depot. John remembered many of them from a drill course at the depot, and he had also been an instructor at Brecon, where the Guards do their NCO training. I knew some Territorial paratroopers that John knew, because Paul Oginsky, co-founder of the Weston Spirit, was also a TA paratrooper.

That first meeting was a bit strained, because there was some filming going on as well, but it was enough for me to see they were both great lads, and supreme professionals. We bounced off each other and shared the same sense of humour, though they were both very different from me and from each other.

Gary was lean and fit, with a steely gaze and a trim moustache, the image of the fighting man. He had joined up at fifteen, left later for five years, then rejoined. He was quietly spoken, with a brilliant turn of phrase, but there was a menace to his quietness and humour. God help anyone who came up against him. He had fought virtually the length of Tumbledown on the bitter night of 13/14 June, and had been mentioned in dispatches for showing qualities of leadership at a crucial stage. He had fighting stories to make your hair stand on end, and to make you disgrace yourself with laughter, sometimes both at once.

John seemed a very different type. He had the army in his blood. His father had been in the Royal Welsh Fusiliers and the Paras, so John knew what the life meant long before he joined up at seventeen. He had served for over twenty years. Now around forty, he had left the Army just over a year before and had put on a bit of weight. At first sight, he gave the impression of a jovial father-figure. There was nothing jovial about his looks ten years earlier, but there was something to the father-figure image – his job had been to make sure his men were working as a team. He had to know not just how to drive them, but how to encourage them and how to protect them. He also had to fight with them. While Gary was helping to seize Tumbledown, John and his sixteen men had helped to take Wireless Ridge, a couple of miles away.

Like me, they were to meet Argentinians who would be as far as possible their opposite numbers, men who had tried to defend Tumbledown and Wireless Ridge. I had quite enough to worry about with the planned meeting with the pilot, and wasn't so interested in these other guys. But Gary and John were looking forward to meeting them, if only to ask a few professional questions. They didn't have the same sense of apprehension as me. After all, they hadn't been wounded, didn't have my emotional burdens, and didn't have to worry so much about a public image.

Well, so they thought. They were both so direct and so vivid in the way they talked that I was fairly sure they would have a public image after the documentary, even though they had none before.

16–20 November 1991

Buenos Aires turned out to be a major surprise. I didn't know what to expect, nor did Gary or John, but we certainly expected some sort of reaction to the presence of British servicemen among former enemies. And my image of the city was of a ramshackle, filthy South American capital, labouring under an oppressive government, where people were starving because of explosive inflation.

One first impression confirmed part of my image. As we drove in from the airport, a roadside sign stated: 'The Malvinas are Argentinian!' So apparently the political issues behind the war had not changed. Perhaps we really were among enemies.

Later, a glance at a map confirmed what the sign claimed: there were the Falklands, coloured a soft pink, labelled 'Islas Malvinas'. The capital, in huge letters, was not Stanley but

'Puerto Argentina'. The map stated that the islands were under 'military government', along with South Georgia and the Sandwich Islands. I suppose that meant *Argentinian* military government, because the islands were part of Argentina's most southerly region, the 'National Territory of Tierra del Fuego, Antarctica and the islands of the South Atlantic'.

After we'd checked in, some of the team went to phone home from an international communications office near the hotel (if you phoned from the hotel your bill looked like Argentina's overdraft at the World Bank). On the list of international codes, there was no number for Britain, Great Britain, England or the United Kingdom. It was obviously omitted by official order. It seemed a bit petty, especially when the girls on duty told you without a blink. Ordinary people didn't seem to have a problem dealing with the Brits.

There was something odd about these experiences. Politically nothing was settled. The Argentinians simply knew, as a matter of fact, that the Falklands belonged to them. On a personal level, there was nothing offensive about this claim (nothing all that surprising, either, when you realize how close the islands are). No one throws it in your face, or makes a fuss about it. It makes no difference to the way ordinary Argentinians relate to ordinary English people. But it struck me as a bit odd that we won, they lost, and yet the conditions that led to the war are exactly the same as they always were. If ever another madman were to take over, he could use the same arguments to start the whole thing up all over again . . .

Well, perhaps I had it wrong. I was wrong on practically every other count. The Buenos Aires we saw had little in common with the city I had imagined. The airport was bright, airy, efficient and clean. On the way in from the airport, as open grassy expanses gave way to buildings, there were some areas that were obviously shanty towns, and maybe the outlying suburbs were not up to much. But the road was a newish motorway, and it led straight to the heart of a city that was more like central London or Paris than the poor, blighted, filthy place of my imagination.

A walk around town confirmed my first impressions. The place looked pretty clean, cleaner than London. And the traffic! I was lucky not to be impaled on a bumper. God alive, I thought as I dodged my way over a pedestrian crossing, these Argentinians seem determined to do for me one way or another, if not ten years ago, then now. Mind you, the cars seemed a bit old-fashioned. As far as I could tell, the locally-made ones were mostly Austin Marina bodies with a variety of accessories to give the impression of different makes.

And the shops! There were some places that would make you think you were in Kensington. The buildings are solid, ornate nineteenth-century European style. There's a branch of Harrods, a Cardin, a Gucci, and everything at prices that destroyed any hopes of picking up high-quality stuff cheaply. I thought at least that cheap leather would be easy to come by. This was the land of gauchos and beef. But no; even the leather was much the same price as London, and it was probably the same leather, too.

One thing I was almost right about: the inflation. There *had* been inflation you wouldn't believe – 5,000 per cent. That had meant prices doubling every week. But by some trick, inflation had stopped dead in its tracks a year or so earlier. How had it happened? The people I asked couldn't explain. One man – intelligent, well-travelled, with excellent English – said, 'This is magical realism', and left it at that.

Anyway, no problems. The local currency, the austral, was pegged to the dollar, and everyone was happy to take either dollars or 'australians', as we nicknamed the Argentinian money. The only real difficulty was that the chronic inflation meant that there were 10,000 australians to a dollar. You needed a backpack to carry enough of them to do serious shopping, and a computer brain to remember how many zeros to knock off when working out the exchange.

One thing I will say about Buenos Aires: the women are

gorgeous. They seem to go with the centre of the city – classy, wealthy, sleek, well-dressed. It was impossible to put the world to rights here, at least not when you were spending a happy hour nursing beers at a pavement café. Gary, John and I tried it. I was the soul of discretion, of course, but Gary, in the middle of some anecdote, would break off as if he had just seen a Pucará coming in for the attack. 'Bloody hell,' he would mutter, eyes tracking some vision over my shoulder, 'I could get used to this place.'

One thing I found very odd. On every block there were newspaper kiosks, and almost all of them displayed the most mind-blowing pornographic magazines I have ever seen. It wasn't a question of taking a quick peak behind a curtain – they were right out there for anyone to see. Very odd that such things should exist in a Catholic country, odder still to display them.

This place never seemed to sleep. My room overlooked a main avenue, and the traffic would still be going at three in the morning, horns beeping. Parties would go on till late, and then the shops would open early, with people polishing up the windows and kids hauling crates of Coca-Cola about.

It was hard to realize at first that the atmosphere wasn't always so relaxed. Not so long ago, Argentina had been a police state. Apparently, every Thursday the central square in Buenos Aires was still taken over by the mothers of 'the Disappeared', protesting that even the present government was not doing enough to find relatives spirited away to their deaths over the years of dictatorship, or doing enough to punish those responsible.

Then we heard a story that revealed something of the hidden tensions. A man had been driving along with his ten-year-old son. A policeman stopped him, drew a gun and demanded money. The man refused. The policeman shot him, twice, in front of his son. There were many other witnesses. The next morning the son was on a breakfast TV show that seemed to specialize in gruesome, tear-jerking stories about violent deaths, if possible involving children. It appeared that no one had seen anything after all. No one was prepared to testify against a policeman for fear of what might happen. It was the sort of story, common enough in South America, that made you glad to be living in Britain.

One day, we took a spin round the city in glorious sunshine that threatened to sizzle the skin off the top of my head. The city was a continuous surprise, if only because it was so European. A few huge avenues were named after dates that had something to do with the declaration of Argentinian independence from Spain early last century. One of them has fourteen lanes, which makes it the widest avenue in the world, according to our driver, Oscar. He was full of information – and misinformation. At one point the 9 July Avenue swirls past a huge monolith, a sort of Cleopatra's needle. What was it? 'Oh, that's there so the avenue has something to go round,' Oscar informed us.

We circled a huge park dotted with big trees with exotic blue blossoms – jacaranda trees – and drove past the largest opera house I've ever seen. It takes up a whole block, and seats 3,500 people.

'President Bush was there on his state visit,' said Oscar proudly.

'I didn't know he could sing,' I said.

I was beginning to feel a bit sleepy. There's only so much tourism you can take, especially when it's hot and you've indulged in the local brew the night before. There seemed to be nothing much about the place to show that it was in South America rather than Europe. I was beginning to think fondly of home. Lucy and James. A good English breakfast. Where in Argentina would I find a good sausage or a rasher of bacon?

Then Oscar promised to show off something that would revive my interest – the home of the footballer, Diego Maradona. It turned out to be a massive, modern, angular block of metal, concrete and darkened glass. He lived in *all that*? Well, not exactly. He owned it all, but it was a block of apartments, and he lived in one of them. We didn't call in. It reminded me of what I was missing: a good football match. Now that would be worth staying on for.

At this point, I must have dozed off, because the next I knew we were down by the docks, in a working-class area of old timber and tin shacks, cheerfully painted in greens and reds. One street was obviously set up for tourists, with artists displaying paintings of gymnastic locals performing the tango. A young woman, accompanied by an old man on a guitar, was singing in a wavering voice.

Round the corner was something I really needed: a bar, offering shade and refreshment. It had an odd sign – a cut-throat razor and a pair of scissors. Perhaps it had been a barber's shop once, a sort of Argentinian Sweeney Todd's. It overlooked the dock, which reeked of low-tide mud and was lined with hulks that looked as if they'd been left over from a Second World War movie set. The bar, a simple, two-room place, run by a wiry man with a thin moustache, had walls covered with a strange collection of objects – old 78 records, bits of rigging, and old paper currency promising to pay the bearer huge numbers of noughts.

The owner, Jorge, surprised me by asking me and the lads to write our names on the wall. It seemed an odd request. Had he recognized me from somewhere? For a moment, I was nervous. We were among old enemies, weren't we? And no one was supposed to know I was there. But it was OK. Oscar had let slip that we had fought in the war. Jorge hadn't heard of me, and was delighted we were there precisely because we had fought.

'It was a crazy thing, the war,' he said, as if apologizing for the leaders who had caused such an unnecessary division between friendly peoples. 'I am glad you are here, so we can meet.'

He scrawled on the wall in Spanish: '*Aquí hubieron ex-combatientes Ingleses, amigos nuestros.*' – 'Here were English ex-combatants, friends of ours.'

Gary, John and I set aside our hesitation and signed our names. It was obviously the right thing to do, and was appreciated, because when we came to pay, Jorge wouldn't hear of it. 'It is between friends,' he said.

I sometimes wonder: was that little statement on the wall of a dock-side bar the first public, written sign of reconciliation by ordinary men like us?

We didn't have much time to enjoy Buenos Aires, but there was one evening that proved truly memorable. Well, not memorable in detail, because the details were wiped out in a haze of noise, beer and laughter, but memorable in mood.

We had been filming in a local restaurant, found by Gabriel, a towering, tousle-haired film maker who was helping to organize some of the trickier sequences. The place was filled with wooden tables and beams and dangling plants and nooks and crannies, with a dance-floor to one side.

The filming ended. Drinks arrived. The mood became jovial, not to say a little raucous. Soon, Gary was a little the worse for a few ales, and involved in a deeply earnest discussion with Gabriel. At one point, when Gabriel wrapped a genial arm around his shoulders, he pretended to take offence — 'Now listen. The effing Malvinas are effing British. You effing remember that.' Gabriel responded with a grin and a hug and the gift of a tiny toy guardsman from a collection of toys in a side-cabinet. (Why a restaurant should be selling toys I didn't know.)

Anyway, Gary was mortified. 'What can I do?' he muttered. 'He gave me this — after what I said to him! Got to give him something in return.' Urgent and wild talk about early morning trips to Harrods, and sending for a courier to bring a suitable gift from home — anything. In the end Gary stripped off his T-shirt, and offered it as a gift. Gabriel re-dressed him, and reassured him. All Gabriel wanted was to see us happy. This was thanks enough.

Meanwhile I had got talking to the son of the restaurant owner, who turned out to be a rugby fanatic. Somehow the suggestion arose that I should try to arrange for a team of local teenagers to come down from Wales to play against a similar bunch in Buenos Aires. I was able to take the letter of invitation away with me, and handed it over to the local lads when I got home. This left me with a really good feeling, and strengthened my belief that sport can break down barriers. I just hope it comes off.

On our last evening we were invited to a high-class restaurant, Michelangelo's, which is famous for its tango-dancing cabaret. I knew nothing about the tango, but it was supposed to be worth seeing.

The restaurant was a terrific place, created in the huge brick vaults of what had once been a storage cellar, and then a convent. The vaults had also at some time been used as a torture chamber and a smugglers' den. It was supposed to be haunted. Anyway, it had a great atmosphere.

There are lots of stories about its lurid past, though the pamphlet they give you and the plaques on the walls destroy the mystery of the place. At least, they do if you only read them in the English translation. One story concerns the Ghost of Michelangelo, the spirit of a smuggler who had hidden among the crates, intending to stow away on an outgoing ship. This is his terrifying tale, in the English version:

During the nights, he got on here, or according various, someone one night, intented, using this tunnel to get on board as a stowaway. But being hiden, foll on him many bulks that produced him slowly dead by asphyxial. From there, his spirit goes around permanently in this house. Many nights, he shows his appearance with clear steps, with going up and down the ladders, with permanent mumbles.

After being scared out of my wits by this, you can imagine how reassured I felt to get into the cabaret, a little theatre upstairs that made me think we were in for a strip show. It was like nothing I had ever seen before, live or on film. Accompanied by ageing musicians with mournful expressions, extremely fit men and women performed cowboy dances, doing amazing things with *bolas*, the balls on ropes that gauchos use for tripping up cattle. They swung them in blurs, struck the floor with them, tap-dancing with their high-heeled boots at the same time, in a whirl of limbs and ropes. The star of the evening ended up whirling his balls around so close to his head that he whipped sweat off his brow. This is not a trick I'll be practising in a hurry.

These dances were mixed in with tangos, all in old-fashioned 1930s dress. They always looked discreet at first, but then, when things livened up, the main purpose seemed to be for the boy and girl to entangle limbs and trip each other up. It looked like the mating-dance of two mad octopuses. They wound their legs around each other as if heading for a vicious fall, and then escaped with astonishing speed and flexibility. It was great, but once was enough. I don't think I'll be trying to open a tango bar in Nelson.

Besides, by then my mind wasn't as much on the show as it might have been, because I was distracted by what had happened over the previous three days.

No doubt about it, the purpose of my trip had already been fulfilled, and no number of ball-swinging gauchos or loose-limbed tango dancers would have been able to change my mood.

4

MEETING MY 'TORMENTOR'

17 November 1991

The meeting with the pilot – Carlos Cachon – was to take place in an apartment owned by the parents of one of Malcolm's TV contacts, Claudia – Gabriel's dark-haired and very chic wife. It would be as private, quiet and discreet as was possible, given that we would be meeting in front of cameras.

I was incredibly nervous. I chose some lightweight clothes, because I knew I would be bothered by the heat, then chatted stupidly in the van about anything, just to forget the knot in my stomach. We drove to an area of solid, ornate blocks – one building was an embassy – that wouldn't have been out of place in Kensington. A lift took us up to the apartment. Vanessa, the assistant, rang the doorbell.

The sound of the bell brought a sudden thought: 'Is he *here*?' What if he opened the door? No, that was ridiculous. Besides, I knew that Malcolm would not do that to me. But the thought made me horribly aware of my own nerves. It was not as if I were meeting a monster, or something that would hurt me, but . . .

Yes, it was. That's exactly what it felt like – like being a child in the middle of a nightmare. I knew it wasn't true, I knew it wasn't like that, but the knowledge didn't save me from the feelings.

The door opened. The mood lifted a fraction.

God, what an apartment! Claudia's mother had been born in Russia, and been brought to Argentina as a child after the Revolution. Her family had become rich. They all seemed to be good-looking, widely travelled and multi-lingual. The apartment reflected the life style.

An entrance hall contained an English antique desk covered with two or three dozen silver-framed family photographs. I was led round a corner, past a huge living area. I caught a glimpse of a library, which led into a dining room. An old French tapestry on the wall. Shelves of leather-bound books. Two exotic eastern sculptures of mythical animals. Flowery wallpaper on the ceiling. Great folds of yellow curtain across the windows. Thick, light green carpets, deep chairs. The place seemed to show the finest things that Argentinians could aspire to — rich furnishings, a European heritage, intelligence, education, social standing.

No doubt most Argentinians did not live like this. But it showed how good life could be if the country were properly run. No wonder there was anger at the former leaders for making such a mess of things.

But I wasn't there to admire a rich interior – though I did later – and I was far too nervous to concentrate on it anyway. We went past the living area, on along the white-painted corridor, round a corner – this place was a maze – and into a smaller room, a study overlooking a private garden. There, the film crew was all set up, lights and cameras ready. Outside the picture window was a balcony enclosed in wire, either to keep children in or thieves out, perhaps both. A solid leather sofa, with bookshelves on either side. An *Encyclopædia Britannica*, and rows of *National Geographics*.

I sat down, and took a sip of mineral water, wondering what on earth was going to happen next. Brian, the cameraman, did some shots of me sitting down. I stood up, paced around, drank some more water. Of course, the whole thing had been carefully planned. The pilot had been collected, and was waiting nearby until I was in position, and the cameras were rolling.

You might think it was an artificial setting for such an emotional meeting. True, there have been many times I have felt as if I was being pinned down and examined by scientists. But not at that moment. I was so wound up I couldn't think of anything except the immediate future, and that was blank. I was frightened of how I might react if the pilot turned out to be a cold fish, with no emotion in his eyes and no soul. I wondered if I were about to make an idiot of myself, even disgrace myself by doing something stupid. If he were to try to make everything all right with some glib remark, I knew I wouldn't be able to restrain myself. I'd walk out, ruin the film, ruin my friendship with Malcolm, destroy my chances of coming to terms with the past, take back home the burden I had brought . . .

The crew made cheery remarks, and I tried to pretend I was being the true professional. But I wasn't. My mouth was dry. I could have done with a beer – anything – to relax me. It reminded me of being a kid, waiting to see the headmaster, knowing something was going to happen, probably going to get the cane, but not sure what for.

And then, there was the assistant producer and interpreter, Benetta, showing in my 'tormentor'. But he didn't look like a tormentor. He didn't look much like a pilot, not at all like a man with the power to kill forty-seven men and injure ninety-seven others. He was shorter than me, athletic-looking, but very much lighter build than me, with brown puppy-dog eyes and a moustache. I thought: I could crush this little guy.

He looked at me, and I could see the shock. He sort of held back, just for an instant. I thought at the time it was the shock of seeing what he had done to me.

I felt a sudden rush of anger. It was as if the sight of him suddenly opened the doors to past experience. Not that the memories themselves came pouring through – there was too much else going on for that. But it was as if I knew they were there, and this man was the key to them, and the pain. This was the man who had caused the flash that singed off my eyelids, the fire that scorched my skin and burned away my hands, the man who had done as much, and worse, to my mates, who had changed my life and ruined scores of others. I didn't want to remember – I had come here to put the memories behind me, once and for all – but here he was, the man who had recreated my life, threatening me with the past I had come here to forget, expecting me to treat him like some kind of a friend. There was a part of me – Simon Weston, the twenty-year-old Welsh Guard squaddie – that wanted to hate him, needed to hate him. I saw how small he was, how insignificant; I saw how easily I could smash in his face.

He came forward with his hand out, eager for the meeting.

Carlos was the son of a rep. who sold the products of a factory in the south, in Mar del Plata. They weren't a rich family, but Carlos was bright enough to consider becoming a doctor. When he was sixteen, and about to start the long business of medical training, one of his friends decided to try for the Air Force. Carlos went along to keep him company, just for fun, not with any idea of committing himself to a new career.

Not long afterwards, a letter arrived informing him that he had passed the Air Force tests. Ironically, his friend had failed. On impulse, Carlos gave up his plans for a medical career, and accepted the offer. He qualified as a pilot in the early 1970s, when he was approaching thirty.

By then his life had taken another turn. On his seventeenth birthday, just after he started his Air Force training, he was invited to a party where he met a petite, dark-eyed fourteen-year-old. Her name was Graciela. The next morning, he was feeling so groggy from too many vodka-and-Cokes that he could remember nothing much except her name and the fact that she was extremely pretty. That was enough. He tracked her down through a mutual friend, and began to date her. They were married six years later. So they almost grew up together. Or rather, as Graciela put it, 'we stopped growing together'.

When the war broke out, Graciela and their two young children, a boy aged five and a girl aged three, were living in a military apartment in San Luis province, in central Argentina, while Carlos, now a first lieutenant, was in Río Gallegos in the south, the closest Air Force base to the Falklands, 350 miles due east.

It was a tense time. Carlos would give Graciela a daily phone call to tell her he was all right, but he could not divulge any details. They were just brief calls – 'I'm all right. How are you?' – 'We're fine' – nothing but simple reassurances. Until the call arrived, though, she had no idea if he had come through that day unscathed.

Once, before the time of the daily call, Graciela was returning from a shopping trip when she saw the local priest stop outside her apartment block. The block contained four flats, two up and two down. She and the children lived upstairs, to the left. She guessed what the visit meant: one of the four men whose families lived there had been killed. Her heart in her mouth, she watched him. He started to climb the stairs. For a terrible moment she thought he had come for her. Then she saw him turn right, not left . . . She was seized by a wave of relief that she had been spared, and horror that her friend's husband was dead.

Carlos had flown two missions before the day of the raid on the *Sir Galahad*. His 5th Hunter Group – initially twelve Skyhawk A4Bs – flew over 100 sorties during the war, sinking three ships and damaging six others. It was dangerous and demanding business. In all, ten Skyhawks were shot down and nine of the group's pilots killed. They had to come in so low and so fast that there was always a risk of doubt about identification. On 1 May 1982, when the British forces were expected any day, Carlos had bombed one of his own ships, the cargo vessel *Formosa*. Luckily, the bomb didn't explode – 'Intelligent bomb!' he commented with a wry smile when he told the story later. (Frequently bombs failed to explode, because the planes dropped them when so close to their targets that they didn't have time to prime themselves. If it hadn't been for this, we would have lost many more ships.) On another occasion, he was about to bomb a British ship when he saw that it was the hospital ship *Uganda*, and pulled away just in time.

On the day of the *Sir Galahad* bombing – 8 June – there were eight Skyhawks in his flight. It was chilly, with scattered clouds and showers. The planes were each laden with three 250kg bombs – not a full load, but they needed extra fuel for the trip. During the forty-minute flight out to the islands, they would refuel over the ocean, at about the half-way point. Three of the planes had problems refuelling, and had to turn back. They included the flight leader. The task of leading the squadron now fell to Carlos, flying only his third war mission. He heard the order come over his headphones – 'You're in command! Take them to glory!' – and felt a thrill of fear. Later he was to find this reassuring. 'No one who is normal would be unafraid. Now at least I know I'm normal!'

The mission was clear enough: he was to attack ships lying in Port Fitzroy, one of the two parallel inlets to the south of Stanley. He came in fast from the south-west, flying low, to avoid the British radar. The height, the speed and a succession of localized but violent rainstorms wiped out all fear and kept him at a peak of concentration. He spotted Port Fitzroy, zoomed over the inlet from the west, and . . .

No ships! He had been wrongly briefed. Banking hard over the sea, he headed south, and was already on his way home in his mind, when: 'There they are!' came a voice over his headphones, referring to two grey shapes, *Sir Tristram* and *Sir Galahad*, lying to the west, in Port Pleasant. He banked again, lined up on the *Sir Galahad*, dropped down to within a few feet of the surface, and came at us.

At that moment, I had just been asked to get a cup of tea by Corporal Pemberton. 'Ah, come on, Pem, ask someone else will you?' I said. If only I'd done as I was told. That's what you get for disobeying orders. It was then that I started jogging back along the deck to slap Yorkie awake, and heard warnings being shouted.

After a few seconds over open water, Carlos released all three bombs. By the time one of them struck, engulfing me and a hundred others in flames, he was pulling up over the ship, and aiming for home. He had no idea if the bombs had actually exploded – he couldn't look behind him to check – but he was certain, absolutely certain, he had hit his target. There was no way he could have missed. He felt a surge of exhilaration. He had achieved what he had been training for, and as he said, 'In war that's all that matters.'

Radio silence on the flight back meant he had no idea if he had been successful or not until he landed. Then one of the others who had been behind him congratulated him: '*¡Bueno impacto!*' There was no rejoicing. His commander, who had known him for ten years, merely said: 'I would have expected nothing less from you.'

The exhilaration did not last. The war was over a week later, and he had to come to terms with defeat, the death of friends and political upheaval.

And there was more. He knew his bombs had wrought terrible damage, and it bothered him. A week after his return he began to get cramps in his back, and he would wake in the early hours in pain. The pain shifted to his mind. He felt an emptiness that could only be filled by knowledge of the effects of his action.

Only years later did he begin to find what he was looking for. He saw a photograph of the *Sir Galahad* in flames, and was horrified. But he never knew how many people had been killed or injured. For years he had wanted to meet someone from the other side, if possible someone from the *Sir Galahad*, to express his sympathy, make a human contact, find the human face behind the smoke and flames. Much later, he even saw a picture of me, though he had no reason to remember my name. This strengthened both his feeling of horror and his need to make contact, to be able to speak to a British person and explain that he had not acted out of anger or bitterness, that there had not been anything personal in his action.

So when Malcolm approached him, it was like an answer to a prayer, or, in his words, 'It was like touching heaven with my hands.' He had left the Air Force years earlier to earn a better living as a salesman, working as an agent for a manufacturer of packaging and boxes. He and his family had returned to an apartment in Mar del Plata, where his parents came from. Malcolm not only convinced him that the film was going to tell a little of the truth about the war – something that had been avoided in Argentina – but he also offered the chance of finding some kind of release, a minor version of the kind of release I was seeking.

So when he came in and looked at me, the shock I saw in him was not the shock of revulsion at seeing a burned face, but the shock of recognition. There was a human face behind the flames he had caused, and he had already seen it.

His hesitation when he saw me lasted only a second. Then he held out his hand.

The rage that was building up in me was only part of what I felt, though it took a long time for me to begin to understand my own confused and compressed feelings.

Those were not the eyes of a killer. There was a warmth in them, a sadness, a sincerity, and a trust that I would not have betrayed even if we had been alone. Although one part of me felt the surge of anger, instantly other parts of me rushed to control it. I don't think any flicker of what I was feeling showed in my expression or actions.

I took his hand. 'Hello,' I said.

'Hello. How are you?' he replied, in English. 'Nice to see you.'

The contact brought a sense of relief. The same hand that had released the bomb into the side of the *Galahad* was in mine; yet this man I called my tormentor, as if he was some sort of sadistic giant, had a gentleness about him. He felt the clawed fingers and the lump in the middle of my palm, but there was no look of surprise or shock on his face.

I let go his hand.

The rage was still there. But I would never have forgiven myself if I had given in to it, because I knew how wrong it would have been. It was OK to feel the anger; but it was good – very good – to know that I was in control. Simon Weston, the twenty-year-old squaddie, was long gone. I was a thirty-year-old husband and father, with ten years of change and experience behind me, and whatever I had become, it was not all bad, and the man sitting down beside me was part of that change.

It was Carlos who spoke first. He had something to say, and he wanted to say it in English. He looked at me, 'I'm sorry . . .'

'Don't be sorry,' I said quickly. I was afraid he was about to apologize for his actions. No apology was necessary – or possible. If he tried to, I was afraid my anger would explode after all.

' . . . for you and your family,' he went on.

At once, tension ebbed. That was not an apology, but an expression of sympathy.

'Well, maybe so, but you didn't do it on purpose,' I told him. 'You didn't do it deliberately, to me personally.'

He stared at me. I had reached the limit of his English.

'*Yo entiendo* . . . I understand English . . . more or less . . .' he hesitated, and Benetta began to interpret.

This released Carlos to give a little formal speech of welcome, and then, without thinking, I began to speak. I had no plan of what I was going to say, only a general idea that I wanted to ask a couple of specific questions about the raid. As it turned out, I didn't get around to these for a while. I told him I hadn't come here to shock him or give him a hard time, that all I wanted was to put to bed some ghosts inside me, that this was probably the only way I could complete my grieving. I hoped he understood.

He didn't, and it was too long a speech to come across well in translation. Neither of us was used to talking through an interpreter. We never learned to slow down, or to talk in small speeches. Poor Benetta was fighting to hold an avalanche of words in her head. The messages Carlos and I were trying to send each other were in constant danger of being lost.

No, Carlos wasn't shocked. He was pleased. He said he'd wanted for years to meet someone who'd had a far harder time than he had. He said the war was an accident for him as well as for me, and that this was an opportunity to erase scars and grief.

Good sentiments. I warmed towards him. I could feel the resentments of the last ten years beginning to slip away. He was just an ordinary bloke, after all. There was no anger left now, only a desire to make him understand why I had wanted this meeting, why I had wanted to make contact, person to person.

'This is a time when men who fought can say "Ten years is enough." We shouldn't be allowing politicians or politics to stop us from being human beings. We have to say, "It's over." It's over. I don't blame you for what happened, although you led the attack. I don't blame you for that, as I know that in war nothing is personal. It can't be.'

With hardly a pause, I plunged on, expressing sympathy for him as a friend of grieving families, and for the families themselves, and saying I hoped the documentary would contribute to better understanding between us all.

It was too much. My words were getting through, but I could see that my feelings were being lost in translation.

Still, he responded. His heart was in the right place. He said, yes, it was true, he'd been on a job, and had been well prepared for it, 'but it is now our responsibility to regain some human value from it all, and neutralize the consequences of what had happened.' That's why this was an important moment; we could work together for reconciliation.

I wasn't so sure about this. I was there for my own reasons. I didn't want to get into things like reconciliation between nations.

'I think it's a responsibility of ordinary people,' he went on, 'to help our diplomats to break down the barriers that lead to war . . .'

Perhaps so, but I would feel easier if we could talk about more down-to-earth matters. Besides, it was the end of a reel. There was a brief break. Carlos chatted in Spanish to Benetta, and seemed to gain in confidence. Then I brought the conversation back to us. Had it been hard for him to come here?

No, no, no. For many years he had wanted to meet someone he'd fought against. A dream had been realized.

In turn, he asked me how my life had been since the accident. A considerate man was Carlos, but where could I begin? Best not try. Best stick to the present.

'Bloody hard!' I said with feeling. 'But I don't think it could have been harder than coming to meet you today. Not so much for me, but because I know that the families and the loved ones of my friends and my comrades who were injured will see this. I just hope they will be able to take away from this film a feeling of tolerance.'

I don't know where the idea of 'tolerance' came from, but it suddenly seemed a key to a lot of things. I wanted many people to show tolerance: me in my response to Carlos, the families at home in their response to both of us, the British and Argentinian governments in response to each other.

On I went: there was no blame on either side . . . We, too, were only servicemen doing our jobs . . . Nothing I could say would take away his grief . . . This was doing a lot to relieve my own personal anguish . . . I didn't know where I was going with all this, and I couldn't even remember having said it afterwards, but, at last, in my own way, I was getting to the core of it.

I said I hoped the film and the book would allow people to see Carlos as a person, as I was doing right then. 'One of the things I wanted to do,' I went on, 'was to look at you and see if you had life in your eyes, because, believe me, in the last ten years, I've wondered – I've really wondered. And there *is* life in your eyes, and you're *not* the spectre that's been haunting me.'

Benetta was going crazy trying to make notes and keep up with me, and she did brilliantly. She spoke for as long as I had done, and when I heard the word *fantasma* – spectre, ghost – I knew she had captured what I wanted to say.

I don't know if Carlos had really understood. He was talking about the Argentinians believing the war to be rooted in a just cause, and remembering the heroes of the war, and the need to get beyond that, to the human, and the personal . . .

Perhaps my attention was beginning to wander, or perhaps I was beginning to get a little impatient, for I suddenly switched to a technical point. 'How did the intelligence people know that my ship was where it was?'

He didn't know. He had just been told the ships were there. But it led, he continued, to a 'difficult, sad moment'.

The understatement of the decade! 'Carnage,' I told him. 'As bad as it could ever get for any human beings.' But I didn't want to dwell on the horrors. He could see well enough what it had been like from my face.

Had been like – that was the point. Past tense. If we were to put the war aside, there had to be some give and take, a little humour. I told him that he and his men had been good pilots – even the British pilots had complimented them. 'You could do your job well. I wish you hadn't been able to map-read so well!'

A laugh, then back to another specific question: had all his men got back safely? Yes, they had, though the next mission – arriving at the Falklands when we were ready for them – had lost all of its eight Skyhawks. (In all, the Argentinians had lost seventy-five planes.)

I sympathized with him. He had lost friends, as I had. We were both losers. 'Although Britain was seen to win the conflict, nobody won,' I said. 'We have the victors and the vanquished, but there's nothing victorious in what happened – just a great deal of sadness.' The best the Falklands War could achieve was to force negotiations – a hollow conclusion, when negotiations would have been better from the start. 'If more people were willing to face up to their fears, the way we are meeting today, perhaps none of it would have been necessary, and you would still have your friends and I would still have mine.'

War was a terrible thing, I continued. We both knew that. Would Carlos let his kids join the armed forces?

Yes. Carlos would be happy if his son were to choose the forces as a career, happy whatever choice he makes, as long as it is done with honour. This was the only way to act, in whatever circumstances.

Honour seemed to be super-important to him. At the time, as a pilot, he had had no choice. Honour lay in doing what he had done. Now, though, it was possible to find honour in a different type of action, by influencing politicians to talk to each other. 'I believe in my soul that those islands belong to Argentina, and perhaps you feel equally strongly that they are British, but that need not enter into the relationship between us.'

We were getting into a difficult area, because he was forgetting a point I felt strongly about. In fact, it was the core of the whole dispute, as far as I was concerned, and it inspired me to make the longest speech of the afternoon. I suppose I felt there were some principles at stake on my side as well.

The question had to come down to a choice by the people who lived there. He would surely understand that. 'You're re-experiencing democracy and freedom, which is wonderful . . . In Buenos Aires, you can see people with a great deal of freedom and a great deal of happiness, and I don't think anybody had a right to take that away. If any one person were to take the rights of the other away, I think that would be wrong. Ultimately, that's what I believe I was there for – to protect the freedoms, the democracy of those people who live there.'

As I often do when I'm trying to make a strongly-held point, I began to repeat myself: 'I believed that it was right then, and I still believe it was right to react in the way that we did, and I still believe that the solution that we ended up with was the only right one, because *nobody* has the right to take anything by force.'

Then suddenly I saw another dimension to the question of ownership. How could a country 'own' land that was not its own? I started to become philosophical: 'Ultimately none of us owns anything,' I continued, 'because we come into this world with nothing, and we go out of it with nothing, so we've owned nothing, we've just enjoyed it for the time we were here.'

I paused. I wouldn't get anywhere with this. Back to practicalities. 'I honestly believe that if we're ever to resolve the differences over the Falklands, we have to get the people who so-called matter – the politicians – round a table.' That at least we could agree on. 'But ultimately the decision on who has sovereignty has to come down to the people who live there, and call the place their home. That's the way I feel about it, and those are the reasons I was there.'

Probably I should have stopped there, but other thoughts came to me, in a steady stream. Argentina claims we stole the islands in the first place, but that means we're going back a couple of centuries, and what happened then can hardly have any bearing . . . At this point, luckily, the film ran out, and I sat back, exhausted, uncomfortably warm with the lights and the concentration, and let Benetta do her best.

I hope she spared him. I doubt if we would ever have agreed on the question of sovereignty. Each of us claimed to be for 'democracy', just as everybody believes he or she is on the side of good or has a sense of humour, but we still wouldn't have agreed. I believed in the rights of the Falklanders. He would have said that as the land was Argentinian, it was the people of Argentina who should decide. Deadlock. It was best to avoid it. Arguing would solve nothing, and no one would care anyway.

But at least we were on firm ground about the futility of war and the need for contacts. When we started up again, we were on to easier, more personal topics – kids, and the importance of sport. 'I just hope that if our sons ever meet,' I said, 'it will be on a field of sport and not of combat, and that they can enjoy a beer, a *cerveza*, after the game. And it won't matter who wins or loses on that day.'

I was beginning to feel we had gone as far as we could, and found myself working up to a finale, speaking about my hopes that such pain should never be experienced again, and the role of our kids in making sure that it wouldn't be, and not wishing Carlos any evil, and hoping there would be a decent political solution that everyone could be pleased with, including the Falklanders.

The heat was beginning to build up more under the lights, and I was looking forward to a drink. There was only one more thing to be said. 'I certainly won't forget this moment. It's done a lot for me – *what* I don't know, but it's done something already . . . I hope that you enjoy the rest of your life, because I think that after this meeting, I certainly will, and I wish you all the best. Take care.'

There. That was it. I shook his hand again, and waited impatiently for Benetta to finish interpreting. But Carlos wasn't ready to stop yet. Perhaps touching my hand again

71

sparked a new thought. '*¡Mira, Simon!*' – 'Look, Simon!' –
he said. It was the first time he'd used my name. He did
so, I think, because he suddenly needed to acknowledge my
injuries directly. 'Look, Simon . . . You may have discovered
over the last few years that there are in your body things more
important than your hands. Your mind, your heart, your eyes,
which are expressive, your mouth which can express feelings –
those things are all more important than your hands. I think
it's a disability you have already overcome.'

Nice thought. Now it really was time to end, and I said so
with a glance at Malcolm.

No. Carlos had started again, expressing the hope that this
would not be our last meeting. I played this suggestion a little
cool. It was a long way to come, so it was really in the lap of
the gods.

'That's about it,' I said again. 'I can't say any more.'

Carlos, too, relaxed. He mentioned football, and rugby. He
said he played rugby – full back. I'd been a prop forward, and
pointed out my greatest qualification – 'No neck!' We agreed
it would be a good thing if more conflicts could be settled
by sport.

'Perhaps in a thousand years we'll evolve to that point,' he
said with a laugh, but the laughter was becoming a little forced
on both sides.

'All right. That's it.' I looked at Malcolm: why the hell was
he still filming?

'*Bien*. Let's go.' Carlos knew it was over, too. We both stood
up awkwardly.

'Yeah, I think so.' And then to Malcolm again: 'I think you've
seen the end. Are you satisfied?'

'It's your meeting,' he said, from beside the camera.

I was at a bit of a loss. The camera was still running, and
the heat of the lights was killing me. 'What are we doing now?
Have you got some coffee lined up or something?'

'Whatever you want to do.'

'Let's have a cup of coffee because I'm parched.'

'He was trying to give you an invitation earlier,' Malcolm said.

'An invitation to what?'

'To meet.'

I was confused. I knew that there was a plan for the other lads to meet up with their opposite numbers, and that perhaps I was expected to be part of that. But I wasn't too clear about what exactly would happen, or what my role might be. There simply hadn't been time to think about it.

Just then the idea of an invitation didn't register because there was a brief flurry of words in Spanish and English, and before I knew it the suggestion was made that Carlos should introduce his wife. I didn't know she was there until that moment.

At this I could feel a part of me – the old, unreconstructed Simon Weston – really backing off. I wasn't there for social reasons. I really didn't have all that much interest in meeting Carlos's wife. I had got what I wanted from the meeting. Not that it was a big deal. I certainly wasn't going to be anything but polite.

Then I realized: the camera was still running. At this point I began to feel the whole thing was getting out of hand. Meeting Carlos's wife had nothing to do with the relationship between me and Carlos. It was tacky. More than that, it might actually detract from the meeting in some way. 'Do we need to film this?' I asked.

Malcolm nodded.

'Why?'

'It's what's happening.'

'I know it's what's happening, but *why*? I don't mind meeting his wife, but . . .' I saw Malcolm's face. He was going to go on filming, no matter what, unless I threw a tantrum. I had seen enough to know that. And, damn his eyes, I respected him enough and trusted him enough to respect my wishes, even then, to let him do it. And he knew it.

Purely not to offend Carlos, I gave in: 'Oh, yeah, go on – go fetch her.' Carlos vanished, and Malcolm took the opportunity to probe me about the meeting. Well, I felt good about the meeting, and said so. But was I relieved? How could I answer that truthfully?

I didn't have to. Carlos was ushering in Graciela. I had to admit it, she was a real charmer – petite, even smaller than Carlos, with coal-dark eyes and short, straight hair. '*Es Simon,*' Carlos said.

I shook her hand.

'*Simon,*' she said. '*¿Qué tal?*'

We started a stilted conversation, the three of us, with Benetta's help. For the first time Carlos asked about my private life. 'Your wife,' he asked in English, 'in London?'

I explained that she was in Liverpool right then, with my little boy's grandmother, but that we lived in Wales.

Carlos asked their names. I told him. He told me how long he and Graciela had been married. We all agreed that time marches on, and that this was all very nice etc., but what we really needed was a beer or three, because it really was *very* hot in there.

And still the camera ran.

Then I found myself chatting about the politics of the Falklands again, which was not something I had ever wanted to get into, so I brought the conversation back to the two of us – Carlos and me – and the frustration of not being able to be more relaxed together. 'It's language, that's all that separates us now.'

Graciela nodded. 'We have to promise that for the next time we'll have to learn to communicate.'

'If you come to my house,' Carlos added, 'and you're not speaking Spanish, I won't give you anything to eat!'

I laughed. 'Nothing to eat! Oh, boy! That's a major problem!'

Then Carlos surprised me by offering me a little Argentinian

Air Force calendar marking the tenth anniversary of the war. It contained twelve pictures honouring, not to say glorifying, the role of the Air Force. He leafed through it for me: a Pucará blowing up a helicopter at Goose Green, a Mirage engaging Sea Harriers, Skyhawks attacking the *Coventry*, and – for September – a view of Carlos in his Skyhawk blowing up the *Sir Galahad*.

'That's us. The *Galahad*,' I said. 'Thank you.' I doubt if I kept the irony out of my voice. It was a very strange present. I mean, if you had almost killed someone by mistake, would you give him a picture of the deed? It was so strange that I forgot about it instantly. Call it an emotional defence mechanism; call it instant forgiveness, because I'm sure he meant no offence. He happily handed out the same calendars to everyone, with obvious pleasure. Anyway, I somehow managed to lose mine very soon afterwards.

Now it really was over. We all wanted something to eat and drink, and there was nothing else to say. It had all happened in slow motion, like a dream, when all the time my feelings had been tripping over themselves to get out. There were things I still needed to say on camera, so while the other two moved away, down the corridor, I stayed on and spoke about my feelings – my initial anger, and then my immense relief at having met Carlos – to Malcolm, and to the camera.

But there were other hurdles yet, before I could relax into the sense of relief.

For one thing, as we were talking afterwards in the gorgeous sitting-room, Graciela and Carlos actually invited me to stay in their apartment in Mar del Plata. I was well out of that. My emotions were so overburdened I could hardly take anything more. Certainly the idea of *staying* with them was too much.

Luckily, it was not up to me. Our schedule was just too tight, and I was able to refuse graciously.

Then, when the time came to say goodbye, Carlos took

me completely by surprise. He wrapped his arms round my shoulders and hugged me. God, that gave me real problems. I'm not a hugging sort of person, and I don't know people who make a habit of hugging. Hugging women is one thing, but hugging men? Well, it's not me, or part of my culture.

On top of this, all my old worries about meeting Carlos came rushing up inside me. I had already shaken hands with the man who had killed my friends, and I was as certain as I could be that their families would not thank me for it. I had spent two hours talking to him, face to face, man to man, without expressing the grief and anger the families must feel. They wouldn't thank me for this either. But at least they – or some of them – might understand my reasons for wanting the meeting. What I was sure that they would find impossible to accept was any sign that I could instantly forgive and forget. That's what the hug signified for me. It was not something I could do.

Yet, on another level, I liked him. The warmth, the sincerity, the depth of sadness, the shared experiences as husband and father, the shared experience of being caught up in the vast machinery of warfare – all this had drawn us together as human beings.

So, rather than reject him, I allowed him to hug me, and found myself responding – clumsily, without any depth of feeling, but still responding. It was either this, or push him away, and after what we'd been through that would have been wrong as well. I thought: thank God it's not on film.

There was a lot to work through. For me, that takes time. I'm not good at putting feelings into words instantly. But one thing was certain: once I was out of the apartment, back in the hotel, having a beer with the lads, I felt as if a huge weight had been lifted from me.

I was thankful that the strain of the meeting was over, of course, but it was more than that. It felt like the strangest thing, as if I were flying, as if I had been suddenly reprieved from a life sentence, as if suddenly someone had given me the most wonderful present.

I made a start at getting to grips with all this immediately after the meeting with Carlos, when I was talking to Malcolm. I talked of my initial desire to find something to hate in Carlos, my discovery of his professionalism and his humanity, the strangeness of discovering that the man who had caused so much damage to me should have a wife and family, the extraordinary difference I felt between 'before' and 'after', between 'then' and 'now'.

A chapter of my life was now finished. I had changed – I could feel it already. I was pleased with the realization that I had controlled my anger. I felt a new tolerance growing in me, especially towards Carlos. I could see that what he had done was a limited part of his life. There was so much more to him than being a fighter pilot who had bombed a ship ten years earlier. I had seen my tormentor, and I was free of him.

'I hope they'll understand,' I said to Malcolm, and to the camera, speaking to the public and the people back home whose reactions I feared. 'It's not about politics, it's not about money, it's not about being unfaithful to the families, or to the memories of my friends and colleagues who died. It's about me, Simon Weston, the man, the person, the human being who is dealing with his own problems his own way, because he had an opportunity to do these things. I hope people will be more tolerant with me than perhaps I have been with myself for the last ten years.'

Yes, I could afford to be kinder to myself, and to others, from now on. No need any more to force myself to carry the burden of the past. Never again need I fear facing anybody. I said it was as if I had been holding myself to ransom for years, 'not ever meeting the person who held your body in torment'.

Then, as I thought back over the day, it struck me what an odd image this was. It confused Carlos with me. Should I believe what I almost said: that I, not Carlos, was the tormentor I had been longing to escape? I seemed to have come all this way to find Carlos, and succeeded in finding not just him but a new self as well.

Whatever it was that had been oppressing me, I was free of it, and I felt great. Now I wanted to get away from Argentina, on to the Falklands to meet whatever awaited me there, and then hurry home.

5

THE RANCH

19–20 November 1991

Two days later, there was to be a different kind of meeting – a group meeting between English and Argentinian veterans. It was to take place at a country estate belonging to Gabriel, our fixer. Carlos would be there, along with Gary and John's opposite numbers, one of whom had fought on Tumbledown, the other on Wireless Ridge.

Admittedly it would extend the range and significance of the film, but I really didn't want anything to do with it. If I had felt good the previous night, it was nothing to how I felt the following morning. I felt so good I found it hard to believe, and harder still to put into words. There was something magical about the feeling, something mysterious. I simply knew that my release from the past was almost complete, and there was nothing in the future that I couldn't handle – good or bad.

This was the feeling I wanted to be left with. I didn't want to be bothered with anything else, and certainly not the business of once again being at the centre of attention. I knew that's what would happen, not just because I look different, but because it would look good on film.

There was another reason for me not to be part of the meeting.

Gary and John had begun to share their pasts with me. They
had had much more experience of war than me, and I enjoyed
hearing what they had seen and done. So it seemed only fair that
they get as much out of all this as possible. When they met their
opposite numbers, the mood would be totally different from the
meeting between Carlos and me. No one in that group would
have the emotional burdens I had – and Carlos had. They would
be discussing their military experiences. That was how it should
be. It would spoil it all for them if I were to come barging in. I
had made my decision. 'I'll be fine wandering round in town,'
I told Malcolm. He was not happy, because he had some idea
of the sequence of shots he wanted, and it included me.

No way. What had I got to gain from meeting Carlos again?
I had achieved the peace I had come to find. I didn't want to
risk undoing the good work of Sunday. Carlos held no further
interest for me. It was as simple as that.

Malcolm knew me better than to try to make me change my
mind, but he asked me if I would go along in the car, just so
that we could be filmed arriving as a group. After that, if I
didn't want to be included, that was up to me. Fair enough.
I couldn't see the point of it, but I owed him all the help I
could give, as long as it didn't undermine my own peace of
mind. Besides, when I thought about it, I didn't mind going
along for the ride. This would be my first – and perhaps only
– trip outside Buenos Aires.

Still feeling a little wary, but nevertheless determined to stick
to my decision, I joined the others for the trip into the
countryside.

It gave me a glimpse of a world very different from the
sophisticated centre of the capital, of something rather more in
line with my preconceived ideas about Argentina. Old colonial
houses and modern blocks gave way to shanties, the motorway
gave way to an ordinary road, populated by noisy, ramshackle
trucks, cheerful bulbous-nosed buses and old jalopies. The

countryside was green and lush, but no one seemed to care for it much. The cars, the roads, the houses in the few villages we went through – everything had a rough, unfinished look about it. It wasn't surprising, really, when you considered the huge size of the country in relation to the size of its population – ten times the size of Britain and only half the number of people. I hadn't realized how big it was. The distance we travelled that day hardly showed up on my map.

About thirty miles into the country, we pulled in past a line of dusty houses. There was a line of cars with plastic bottles on their roofs – our driver said this meant that the cars were for sale. Down a side road, where grimy children seemed to be playing near an open sewer, I caught a glimpse through the doorway of a tin shack. Two women were sitting silently looking at a child on a table in front of them. I don't know what they were doing, but the scene – the filthy children, the sewer, the tin shack, the little silent group – was a picture of abject poverty. Opposite was a railway with a fine old engine that looked as if it was a survivor from the 1930s.

Lunch-time. Led by our assistant, Vanessa, we trooped into the weirdest restaurant I'd ever seen. It was like stepping into a shadowy old junk shop. The high walls were covered with a wild collection of objects: the heads of an ostrich, an ant-eater and a boar, snake-skins, old telephones, a radio set, a telescope, whips, a model ship with a dragon's mouth, old rifles, and ancient advertisements for stage shows; there was even a stuffed frog holding a little guitar. From the roof swung a chandelier made of a wagon wheel, with ostrich-eggs dangling from it.

Vanessa thought it was fascinating, but I looked around at the dusty objects, and the dusty bar and tables, and thought: if I want to eat in a pigpen, I'd rather find one for myself. I began to wonder if I was going to survive . . .

. . . especially when we were given the opportunity to try the local delicacy. A plate appeared, piled high with little bits of grilled meat. Now, I've done a bit of travelling and I know that sometimes you are offered things that should never be eaten. I know for instance that it's more than your life is worth to eat mutton-bird in New Zealand, although the Maoris consider it a great delicacy. I had a feeling this was another of those occasions.

Yes: those tasty-looking little morsels were the saliva glands of cows. Thanks, but no thanks. I had the queasy feeling that one bite of saliva gland, and I'd be up on the wall along with the armadillos and the snake-skins. I'm sure I was right, too. The following day a lot of our group went down with severe cases of Galtieri's revenge. It was entirely their own fault. They should never have eaten bits of a cow that were never intended to be eaten. Luckily, the restaurant did a very tasty steak and chips, and the local ale wasn't at all bad.

We carried on into wilder regions, turning off the main road into an unpaved side road. We rattled along, sending a cloud of dust up over scrubby pastures. We passed the rusty wrecks of several cars; they looked as if they had broken down, and had simply never been collected for repair. A swampy area had been used as a rubbish-tip. There was a scummy pool of water in the middle, in which three grimy-looking kids were fishing. I wondered why such an empty area had to be so messy.

Off up another side road – this whole farming area seemed to be divided by a grid of dirt roads – and then into the entrance of a dirt driveway, at the end of which stood two houses surrounded by trees. Several cars and vans were parked in the driveway. I spotted the film crew, ready for us, and beyond, across a lawn and in the shade under more trees, tables and chairs. A crowd of people waited, among them the Argentinian ex-soldiers whom Gary and John were to meet – and, I supposed, Carlos.

Well, I didn't want to know. I had made my decision, and I was going to stick to it. The cameras turned towards us; Gary and John got out. I stayed in the van, and relaxed, without even watching as they strolled over to the meeting.

I was on my own, and all attention was somewhere else – it was great. My mind drifted over the meeting with Carlos and how I felt about it. I could see the two houses through the trees, one belonging to the owner of the farm, the other where the farm hands lived. Nearby was a barn and the wreck of an old tractor. It was very peaceful beneath those trees. They were very tall and were covered with a loose sort of bark that was peeling away from the trunks. I wondered vaguely if the locals had some use for the bark. Silence, except for the buzz of a fly in the midday heat.

I sank into myself. The pressures I had felt from Malcolm and my resentment at being here vanished. I felt again, even more strongly, the extraordinary feeling of release from tension. It wasn't a question of forgiving Carlos for what had happened, because there was nothing to forgive. I had been right: he had only been doing his job, and any professional – me included – would have done the same in those circumstances. Nothing to blame him for, nothing to forgive.

I could see that he was a good man – a man whom I couldn't possibly hate, a man whom I couldn't help liking. No, 'liking' was the wrong word – I couldn't bring myself to say I liked someone who had done what he had done. Besides, liking can only come from really getting to know someone, and Carlos and I had only exchanged a few stilted speeches through Benetta.

Still, I had achieved what I had come for. I had at last seen through impersonal horror, and found a human being. All sadness, worry and guilt had fallen from me.

A strange image came to my mind, something I had heard about and never understood, something to do with Zen Buddhism: the sound of one hand clapping. It hadn't made sense before, and it didn't make sense then, certainly not to someone who's idea of perfection was a perfect pass or a perfect goal, but there was something about the image that fitted my mood.

Afterwards, when I got home, I discovered that the image did after all make a strange sort of sense. Apparently one way to pose the problem is like this: what is the proper response when asked 'What is the sound of one hand clapping?' The proper response is to extend your hand in friendship. That was what Carlos and I had done. Perhaps only a Zen master could describe the feeling of release that we experienced.

I felt everything had been changed. The past was slipping away, and I could look forward to a new life. I was eager to get on with it, to get back to Lucy and James, and to face whatever had to be faced. I began to imagine changes – trivial, silly things. Perhaps I'd start by sorting out my wardrobe. I'd plan things better; get a dog; take more exercise.

Yes, I would experience a new sense of enjoyment. But it would be serious as well. I was as sure as anyone can be that there would be some public criticism of me for meeting Carlos. Somehow it didn't bother me. I would be able to handle it. I would have friends who would understand, my family would understand, and I would have a new sense of self-respect. All of this would carry me through. Even if nothing of the public Simon Weston were to remain, the private Simon Weston would be there, stronger than before.

I felt as if all these years I had been trapped inside a shell, a cocoon, and I was now ready to emerge into something new and fresh.

A bird screeched in the tree above me. I looked up. I had been on my own, in a sort of a trance, for almost two hours. In the distance, between the tree-trunks, I could see a truck on one of the dirt roads, sending up a cloud of dust.

Three men, the drivers of the cars and vans, were strolling towards me. One of them was sucking what looked like a silver tube which was stuck into a silver container. I wondered if this were some kind of drug. The one with the silver pot stuck his head into the van and held out the pot with a grin. It was filled with a slurry of green leaves, as though a very large plant-eating animal had just thrown up in it. Tea-break, South American style.

I took a tiny suck through the tube. Ugh. It had an acrid taste, like drinking cigarettes. I grimaced, making the men laugh, and handed the pot back.

The mood had been broken. I got out and wandered round. A hundred yards away, Gary and John were deep in conversation with the Argentinians, surrounded by the film crew. I noticed that the trees were part of a large garden that gave way to fields on either side. Along one side there was a tennis court.

I began to wonder if perhaps I was acting like a difficult child by not joining in. But no; no one over there would benefit from my presence. I was willing to do almost anything for a charity, or for the family, or friends, but there was no point my being there. Gary, John, and the Argentinians had all fought the war through to the end. I hadn't. They had things to talk about that I could not share. I would just destroy the purpose of the meeting, as well as possibly shattering my own sense of well-being. I strolled back to the van.

Malcolm came over, with the cameraman, Brian. 'What do you want to film me for?' I asked.

'I need it. So that people can make sense of why you are not at the meeting,' he replied.

Fine. I knew he wouldn't try to spring any surprises on me, and returned to my own inner peace and wandering thoughts. The family. My Mam. The need to make them all proud of me. The desire to put the last ten years behind me. I didn't have to keep reliving it, repeating those old patterns. If James was interested in what his dad had done, it was all there — on film and in print. I'd have moved on to other things: radio, perhaps; charity work; sponsorship; who knows what. 'Today is the first day of the rest of your life.' I liked that saying. Right then it really seemed like an important truth.

Just then a face appeared round the door of the van. It was Carlos.

As I learned later when I spoke to people who had talked to Carlos and Graciela during the filming, Carlos had been very puzzled by my absence, and perhaps just a little hurt.

He knew I was there, of course. He and Graciela had genuinely hoped I would be able to visit them in Mar del Plata, and were looking forward to seeing me again. He couldn't understand why I simply sat back there on my own. It was not the way he would have behaved. While the ex-soldiers talked over the campaigns, while the cameras rolled, he had been assuming that I would at least put in an appearance when people turned to the food and drink.

When I didn't appear, his vague sense of unease suddenly hardened into determination. He respected my decision. He knew that things were difficult for me – that much at least was explained to him – but, as he said later, he 'couldn't bear to see Simon sad'. He just wasn't going to let me get away with being so remote and stand-offish and, well, just plain British.

He felt the moment was right – he said it felt like 'the moment of take-off'. So, without even telling Graciela, he walked over to the van.

It was the first time we had been together alone, without an interpreter. I had picked up a couple of Spanish phrases, but neither '¡Manos arriba!' ('Hands up!') nor '¡Dos cervezas!' ('Two beers!') seemed very appropriate just at that moment. Carlos's English was very stilted. This didn't bother him. He was determined to give more of himself, and to get more from me, and he wasn't going to be put off by the small matter of language.

Slowly, painfully, he made me understand that he had left the Air Force, that he was working as a packaging salesman, that his children were a boy and girl, now aged fifteen and thirteen. Equally slowly, I told him about Lucy and the baby.

'The baby,' he said, 'is boy or girl?' Odd that we had talked for almost three hours the day before and hadn't exchanged many details of our children.

'Boy.'

'His name?'

'James.' Hadn't I told him that when we first met? I couldn't remember. I added that it was the name of one of my closest friends – my best man, Jimmy Salmon, who had helped save my life on the ship.

But I don't think he was listening. '*Increíble*,' he said. 'Name of *my* son is James – Santiago, Saint James.'

I stared at him. 'That's really strange,' I said.

Then for some reason, I suppose because other names are more important in his culture than mine, he asked: 'And the second name?'

'Andrew.'

His eyes widened further. 'Andrew,' he repeated. Then slowly, hesitantly: 'My daughter – the name of my daughter is Andrea.'

Now we were both staring and shaking our heads, almost lost for words. All I could say was 'Weird . . . freaky . . . incredible.' All he could say was: '*Increíble. Certamente.*'

There didn't seem much else we could say. What had been the chances of us choosing almost identical names for our children? Astronomical. Unless it wasn't chance, unless there was something else that connected us besides the bomb. This thought only made the coincidence seem even weirder.

Whatever it meant, I had to admit that Carlos's initiative had forged another link between us. It hadn't spoiled anything for me; and it had done something more for him. The sadness I had seen in his eyes two days earlier seemed to have gone, and I saw laughter there.

As we drove back an hour or so later, I thought: this time it's definitely over. I had done everything I had wanted to. I was free. No more Carlos. No more filming. For God's sake, it was time to move on, get to the Falklands, and get back home to Lucy and James.

Wrong again. Back at the hotel, to my surprise, there was Carlos, with a couple of the other Argentinians, sitting in the lobby. They were staying in town overnight. 'See you in the morning,' Carlos said cheerfully.

What was happening in the morning? Oh, yes; Gary, John and I were going to do a little more sightseeing. We had been having lunch in a café in Buenos Aires when Malcolm mentioned that the memorial to those Argentinians who died in the Falklands War was not far away. We said to each other, 'Oh, be nice to go along and have a look.' Not a big deal, just a brief, informal visit, just the three of us, so that we could pay our respects as private individuals.

However, unknown to me, another idea had emerged. The meeting at the ranch had gone well. Someone had let slip that the lads and I wanted to take a look at the memorial. Now the Argentinians were going to join us. Malcolm liked the idea. It would make another good sequence.

A personal meeting between myself and Carlos was all very well. A meeting between veterans on both sides was fine – ordinary blokes talking military matters informally without too much emotion. But this . . .

I imagined the three of us standing shoulder to shoulder with the other three in front of their equivalent of the Cenotaph, and the whole thing looking like an official statement that the war was over and the breach healed. I had a vision of Carlos and me being seen as symbols of peace and reconciliation. It seemed to me the whole thing would be well out of order, not just for me – John was out of the Army, but what would the Army families and the Army itself think of Gary? In his view, it would go down like a 'shit sandwich'.

Once again Malcolm reassured me. There would be no filming of us all together unless we were happy about it. No one would try to manipulate us into doing anything. Certainly there would be no suggestion that this was in any way official. It would be informal, discreet and personal. We would be in control.

OK. We decided we could live with that.

Next morning, off we went in the van to Juan Martín Square, a rolling expanse of well-tended grass dotted with trees. The day was cool and overcast, but the square was alive with parents, children and dogs.

At one end, set into the slope of a low hill, was the memorial, a curving wall of pink marble facing a flag-pole. Beyond the flag-pole was the road marking the end of the park, and after this a tall brick tower. It all looked quite new. Into the memorial wall were set twenty-five black plaques, with about twenty-five names on each: 'Those who fell in the struggle for the Malvinas and South Atlantic Islands'. There were 655 names there. This was the official number of Argentinian losses.

Our Argentinians were waiting for us: the veteran from Tumbledown, Carlos Vazquez; Juan Carlos Diez, who had been wounded on Wireless Ridge, and who claimed to have 'English blood' in him as the result of a transfusion in Stanley; Carlos Cachon, of course; and Ignacio Gorriti, an infantry company commander most of whose regiment had been captured at Goose Green.

And Juan Vallejos – a tall bloke with a moustache – who had also been on Wireless Ridge, but who was looking a bit out of place. I discovered why. It had been important to track down a man called Juan Vallejos, because, like Juan Carlos, he had been part of the only Argentinian counter-attack, just before they surrendered. He had been injured, had lost a leg, and now had a wooden one. The assistant producer and interpreter, Benetta, had gone through agonies, working through a maze of government departments, first to find Juan Vallejos – he was stationed somewhere on the other side of the country – then to get permission for him to be filmed, and then to make arrangements for him to fly to Buenos Aires. He had arrived on the morning of the meeting out at the ranch. Benetta had gone to pick him up. He came striding towards her. No wooden leg. By a weird coincidence, there had been two men named Juan Vallejos on Wireless Ridge. This was the wrong man. This one hadn't played an important part at all. Moreover, the poor guy had been so heavily warned not to say anything compromising that he was a bag of nerves – so scared he never really unwound.

While John did his best with his opposite number, Gary was soon deep in conversation with Carlos Vazquez. It was all quite informal, and the tension over filming vanished. It was also important, particularly because of Vazquez. Later I was to learn a good deal about him and what he had to say from Gary.

Vazquez, now a senior officer, had been a sub-lieutenant commanding a platoon on Tumbledown. He looked the image of the hard-bitten veteran – lean, short hair, moustache, muscular. But there was much more to him than this. He was also extremely emotional, most unusual for such a senior professional. He had reason. He was a man with a mission: to make sure that the truth was told about the Malvinas campaign.

He said the government had constantly sought to blame the Army for the defeat. Documentaries and articles always harped on about the inadequacy of the soldiers. No one looked at the politics of the defeat, the failure to look after the troops during the war, the lack of information, the terrible reception the men had when they returned. The truth was constantly covered up. Even the memorial itself – built only a couple of years earlier, right by a busy road, and set in full view of the 'English Tower', a building donated by the British government in the last century – was typical, he said, of the official but underhand campaign to denigrate the Army and cover up the impact of the defeat.

His main point concerned a tragic and disturbing subject: the 655 names on the memorial. 'But you know as well as me,' he said to Gary, 'that there were thousands of dead.'

Thousands. Gary was sure he said 'thousands'. To back up his point, Vazquez went through the names of those who had died in his platoon on Tumbledown: nine names – but he had lost seventeen. So he alone knew of eight men whose deaths had not been officially acknowledged.

Like a hidden sickness, the question of the Argentinian dead kept coming back – then and later. Almost half of the 655 were on the *Belgrano*, leaving only about 330 killed in the war itself. This didn't seem very many. Everyone 'knew' that many unrecorded Argentinian bodies were buried in trenches and dumped at sea. Perhaps there was a lot of rumour in the talk, because Argentinians have reasons to be suspicious of official statements concerning the war. But it was certainly well known that many bodies were never identified; and there were a lot of recent conscripts. It's easy in war to lose track of who's been sent where.

Carlos and Graciela were obviously pleased to see me again. And once more, despite my initial hesitation, I couldn't help warming to them, and greeted them like old friends. Soon Carlos was giving me much the same message as Vazquez was giving Gary. He also said he knew of ten dead whose names did not appear on the list. Did *every* survivor have a list of unrecorded victims? If so, the numbers could quickly add up to 'thousands'.

I wondered what all this meant for ordinary Argentinians. What must the families of those who died feel – especially those whose deaths went unrecorded – knowing their sons and brothers and fathers had fallen in a useless, hopeless gesture? And what of the survivors? The poor kids who fought there must have come back in humiliation, to a country that couldn't or wouldn't offer them the support they needed. I wondered what I would have felt if I had been rejected instead of looked after, and what the other two lads would have felt if they had been badly led doing a useless job – and lost? What sort of scars does all this leave on a country?

After looking round the memorial with Carlos, I described some of my own experiences in more detail. I mentioned the kids I saw on the *Canberra*, the youngest of whom was only thirteen, we were told. Carlos couldn't believe this, and I'm not sure I do, but the boy certainly looked no more than thirteen. I told him a little about the bomb, and how I got off the ship; my time in hospital; my recovery.

Then we moved on to less heavy subjects. Carlos told me severely I would really have to learn Spanish.

'Hey,' I said, 'I know some already: *¡Dos cervezas!*'

'That's good,' Carlos laughed. 'You come again – and next time, you bring Lucy.'

'It's a deal.'

'But only if you promise to learn Spanish.'

'Well, I can't come back if I don't!'

'Right! Besides, you won't eat otherwise!'

Then, for a second time, Carlos hugged me goodbye. Pat Hill, the *News of the World* reporter, seized his chance and took the photo that later appeared on the front page of his paper. I wouldn't have chosen to embrace Carlos, certainly wouldn't have chosen that sort of exposure. But I knew Carlos now, I wasn't surprised, and the anger and confusion I had felt at our first meeting were things of the past. Something had shifted in me over those two days, thanks in part to Carlos himself. I can forgive myself for accepting his gesture. I hope the relatives of those who died at Carlos's hands can forgive as well.

Finally, one of the other Argentinians, Ignacio Gorriti, who spoke quite good English, handed me some dried flowers. 'I have a request,' he said. 'Would you place these in the British and Argentinian cemeteries in the Falklands?' I said I would be delighted. I had no problems about placing flowers on Argentinian graves. It would be an easy enough task, and it was only right to help them honour their dead. (He, too, mentioned that he knew of half a dozen names missing from the list of the dead.)

At the monument, a score of people had gathered to commemorate members of their families who had died in the war. It wasn't a regular event. Perhaps they had made a special journey together from a country area. They placed wreaths, then broke into an out-of-tune version of the Argentinian National Anthem, ending with a ragged cheer. It all seemed normal enough, but they were the lucky ones – they had the names up there to act as a focus for their grief.

What of the others – hundreds of families perhaps – whose sons' names were written nowhere, who could never come here, whose grief would never find a focus and a natural release?

EAST
FALKLAND

WEST FALKLAND

LAFONIA

South Atlantic Ocean

Ajax Bay
San Carlos Water
San Carlos
Sussex Mts
Cantera House
Mt Usborne
Camilla Creek
Burntside House
Darwin
Swan Inlet
Goose Green
CARLOS FLIGHT PATH
Mt Pleasant Airport (MPA)
Bluff Cove
Stanley
Fitzroy

Miles
0   5   10

Mt Kent
Mt Longdon
Wireless Ridge
Two Sisters
Tumbledown
Mt Harriet
Sapper Hill
Mt William
STANLEY

Bluff Cove

Port Fitzroy

Fitzroy

Sir Galahad, Sir Tristram
on 8 June 1982

Port Pleasant

Miles
0   5   10

6

TO THE FALKLANDS

21–26 November 1991

It was a relief to leave Buenos Aires. It's a great city, but I've no plans to go back there. I had done what I came to do, and was eager to get on with the second half of the trip.

We were flying the long way round, via Chile. Before the war, there were direct flights from Buenos Aires to the Falklands, but not now. Air links, even non-government ones, are political statements, and there's a long way to go yet before either side is ready for that. So there we were, after a 600-mile jump over the Andes, dropping down to Santiago, with a few hours' break before the next leg of the journey southwards, into colder regions, almost to Cape Horn. From there, a small commercial flight, which makes the journey only twice a month, would take us back east to the Falklands.

Landing in Santiago took me straight back to Sicily, where we had landed when I was on my way to Kenya with the Welsh Guards. The same dry heat, the same dry hills, the grass scorched brown by the sun. I would have to look out for the top of my head. In this heat, I'd turn into a tomato in minutes. There seemed to be a strong military presence, from the planes and helicopters on the runways to the uniformed characters wtih machine-guns staffing the airport buildings.

This was an international flight, so we needed to clear customs. This brought an unexpected problem. Did I have anything to declare? Any food? Any fruit?

'No, only some dried flowers.'

That did it. The box containing the flowers for the British and Argentinian graves was opened. The man popped one of the dried seed pods, and shook his head. It was against regulations to bring the flowers in. Malcolm and Vanessa explained their purpose, but it did no good. The flowers had to go.

I was keen to take a look at the place, even if it was only for a couple of hours. Several of us took a cab from the airport and told the driver to run around town, then stop somewhere in the middle for a beer.

We found ourselves winding up a steep road up a mountain. The driver, who was beginning to be a fund of information, said he was taking us up to a virgin. I was beginning to think the Chileans were very hospitable people when I saw what he meant. On top of the mountain was a huge statue of the Virgin Mary. The road led to a couple of shops, and a few stalls where Indians sold carpets, ice-creams and mock swords made out of the 'swords' of swordfish. A radio was blaring out 'Who's crying now?' It was the sort of tourist trap you see the world over.

But the main feature of the place was its stunning view over the city. It lay in a plain between mountains, some of them snow-capped even in that heat. I was doing some videoing, and beginning to think I'd better find some shade, when I noticed the driver pointing. He was pointing at a stadium. I thought he was about to tell us something about the local football team, but no – this was the place where thousands had been killed under General Pinochet. 6,700 the driver said.

It was extraordinary. This sense of violence just below the surface seemed to be something typically South American.

During the next hour, as we flipped briefly around town, had a beer, and drove back out to the airport, we seemed to be in a stable, peaceful country. Yet only a year before it had been in the grip of a regime that had made thousands disappear, just as in Buenos Aires.

The driver said 50,000 had vanished in the country as a whole. He had friends who had been tortured and knew of families that had been destroyed when a son or daughter 'disappeared'. He said they had been taken into the countryside, shot and buried in trenches – killing fields that had still not been identified. Who had been involved? As far as I could gather, an intelligence service formed from four forces – the Police, the Air Force, the Army and the Marines. A year previously the reign of terror had come to an end; yet no one had been prosecuted. The killers were wandering around free.

The next leg of our journey was a longer one. Chile is a very strange shape – very long and thin, squashed between the high Andes and the coast. We'd already crossed the continent from east to west. Now we were heading 1,000 miles south, along the Andes.

Duncan, our assistant cameraman, looked down with a professional eye on the awesome snowy peaks below. He was a surprising bloke – wiry, with long curly hair down to his shoulders. Back in the Michelangelo in Buenos Aires, the waiter had called him 'Señorita'. Nothing effeminate about him, though – he was incredibly fit, and incredibly strong, because he is one of the best sports climbers in Britain, ranking in the top five. He worked as an assistant cameraman just to finance his climbing habit. We were flying over some of the most challenging climbs in the world. Like Mount Fitzroy: a peak battered by fearful weather, combining the most difficult aspects of both the Himalayas and the Alps. It had been climbed for the first time only in 1968. One day, Duncan would like to have a go.

Our stop-over was a windswept little town called Punta Arenas, set on the Straits of Magellan, which slice right across above Cape Horn, joining the Atlantic to the Pacific. Here, too, the military were everywhere: fighters, cargo planes, bunkers, dummy bunkers, helicopters, AA emplacements, rocket sites.

After checking in – the hotel was very good, better than the one in Buenos Aires – I took a walk with Gary down to the shore. It was a pretty miserable place, with an icy wind slicing up from the south. Two jets screamed low overhead, reviving memories of Argentinian planes on the Falklands. A huge high-sided cargo ship, perhaps an accommodation vessel for oil-workers, was manoeuvring slowly into dock. This was where the explorer Ferdinand Magellan had passed through on the first round-the-world voyage in 1520. No doubt it was better than going round the Horn, but someone (it turned out to be Duncan) had captured the spirit of the place by scrawling in the sand a huge arrow pointing south labelled 'Hell', and another pointing north labelled 'Home'.

We strolled up a hill, and looked around. I could see instantly why so many people had never been there. If I never saw the place again, it'd be too soon. To the north, the Andes run out. The hills are low, barren of anything except scrubby grass, and a few small wind-blasted trees and gorsebushes.

'Looks like the remains of a nuclear explosion,' I said.

'No,' Gary commented. 'It's not that nice.'

There is nothing much to the south – the other side of the straits – except lowlands stretching down to Cape Horn. After this, it's a stormy run down to Antarctica.

Below us, the town was a boring grid of streets; low buildings, lots of corrugated iron roofs painted blue, green and red. But it was a surprisingly active place. 150,000 people live there. The cars looked in better shape than they did in Buenos Aires, and the hotel was good, so there had to be some money about. Some of it must have come from the military. Chile and Argentina are not on the best of terms, and the land is divided oddly. Chile controls the Straits of Magellan, while Argentina has half of Tierra del Fuego. So the southern tip of Argentina is sliced off by Chile. They are still in dispute over a few islands on the cape. The town is also a main jumping-off point for expeditions to the Antarctic, especially for the Americans and British. And there is oil in the area, though I didn't see any obvious sign of it.

Next morning, we were off again in a twin-engined Otter. I'm a little nervous of small planes, after my experience trying for my pilot's licence, and there were things about this flight that made me wonder if we were going to make it. We'd just started to taxi when we came to an abrupt halt. A fire-engine roared out to meet us. No need to evacuate, though – the pilot had forgotten his passport.

We took off. The brown grass and distant grey hills dropped away as we headed north and east along the edge of the Magellan Straits. Below, cold waves broke on grey shores and a lone road cut across the drab landscape. In the distance, northwards, through rain that looked like a gauze, snow-capped mountains loomed briefly, and southwards harsh and treeless lowlands ran towards Cape Horn.

The landscape changed. A scattering of lakes appeared, looking like bomb craters. The sun broke through, splashing gold on the browns and greys. There wasn't a single house. A finger of land jutted out into the sea.

Suddenly the coast veered away northwards. We were over the southernmost part of Argentina now. Not much farther north was Río Gallegos, the base from which Carlos had taken off on his bombing missions. I could see blue-grey mudflats, grey sand, the brown of dry grass, and the green of shallow water. The colours swirled around each other like an abstract painting. Then we flew on into cloud, and South America dropped away behind us.

I settled back. My major concern was that ice was forming

on the wing-strut, just outside my window. Then, despite the 'No Smoking' sign, the loadmaster said it was OK for Gary to smoke. As he lit up, Duncan gently opened the door to the cockpit. There, in full view, was the spare fuel tank. Gary opened his eyes wide, and hurriedly put out his cigarette.

After this there were no further problems, at least not until we got there. I imagined that it would probably be an emotional experience, revisiting the places where my past was lost; but I had no idea what to expect, and so I had no reason to anticipate. I had not read much about the war, and certainly never read anything about the Falklands. I felt drained of emotion, waiting for whatever was coming next.

Now we were dropping slowly down through the clouds. The first bit of the Falklands appeared – a flat, grey streak, hardly rising above the water. Then more small islands, and a coastline with inlets and peninsulas. Beneath the clouds, through flurries of rain and patches of mist, I saw a drab, treeless expanse of moorland. We had come 8,000 miles to fight for *this*? It was hard to understand, as crazy as if Argentina had decided to send a task force to the Shetlands.

Another stretch of water. A rocky coastline, sand dunes covered with rough grass, then more of the camouflage colours of the grass and peat landscape. Perhaps we had just crossed the Falkland Sound that divided East and West Falklands. We must have flown close by the place where I had first come ashore. I could see tracks across peat, peat cuttings, a few sheep.

Then suddenly, a line of houses, Nissen huts, some trailer homes, all scattered along the edge of a large inlet. It looked like a village on a Scottish sea loch.

We banked. Below was a wreck. For a moment I wondered if it was left over from the war. No – it was much older, a rusty hulk, perhaps from the late nineteenth century. Then a muddy chaos of building works. We swung into land – and there, right in front of us was a communications mast. The engine revved. We rose, sank again, and landed.

A small white building, blanketed in rain, announced 'Stanley Airport'.

We climbed down into driving rain, directed by weather-beaten men in waterproof clothing. They wouldn't have looked out of place on a North Sea trawler. Someone pointed out a cable dangling from the tail-plane. Was that the Otter's radio aerial? Or had we picked it up from the mast behind us? God, every time I came here something nasty seemed to happen.

'Bloody weather you brought with you!' said a bearded figure with a grin, recognizing me. It was good to hear an English voice again, after all that Spanish.

'Not much different from the last time I was here,' I replied.

'Well, it must be you that brought it, then.'

We hurried into the little white house to find ourselves going through customs, of all things. It seemed odd to be arriving on an international flight at such a small place.

Then on, in four-wheel-drive vehicles, into Stanley, with our driver Tony, a softly-spoken bloke of about thirty. We had landed close by the town, in the old terminal. A new RAF and Army base, built up since the war, was situated about thirty-five miles away. This provides the only direct air link with Britain.

God, what a miserable arrival: rain, bitter wind, flurries of sleet, even a quick hailstorm. In the first few hours we seemed to get a dose of the worst of British weather. And this with summer around the corner. John and Gary assured me that it could change equally quickly for the better, but I hardly dared believe them. All I could remember – from that wet and windy trip on the *Galahad* ten years earlier – was the grimness.

At first glance, Stanley didn't offer much to lift the spirits. It's situated on a rise that skirts Stanley Harbour, an estuary five miles long and about half a mile across. It really is a small place, no more than a village, with around 2,000 people mainly living in wooden prefab houses imported from Britain. There are four pubs, two hotel bars, a disco, no cinema, a supermarket, and a few smaller shops, all stocked with basic corner-shop goods, and that's about it. You can hire videos, but there isn't much else to do with your spare time.

Mostly it has the feel of a 1950s suburb, with the houses crowded together – odd when you think of all the space round about. There are a few lines of terraced houses straight out of the 1930s. Some new houses were being built, in more modern designs, so I supposed the population was growing.

The grandest house is the governor's – a graceful Victorian building defended against the everlasting wind by evergreens. Apparently it takes a good deal of tender loving care to grow trees there. There are a few in Stanley, one at the other end of the estuary, and that's about it. I didn't see any others anywhere.

It was odd to come half way round the world and arrive at a place looking like a slice of Scotland, with bacon, sausages and eggs for breakfast. This was welcome, and I was sure I would get on with the people, but I couldn't imagine I'd be able to generate much affection for the landscape or the town. Still, I didn't want to make up my mind yet – the fact that people chose to settle here must mean that it had something going for it.

We were staying in two hotels, a larger one, the Upland Goose – named after one of the island's best known birds – and a little place converted from a private house, Emma's.

Both gave a view over the estuary. A grassy bank guarded by a couple of ancient cannons looked across the inlet to a range of low hills forming part of Wireless Ridge. The slopes were covered in yellow-brown patches of grass broken by grey stone that burst through to make a rocky spine. Lower down, smaller stones had been made into huge grey letters that picked out the names of ships – *Barracuta, Beagle, Protector, Endurance* – the Royal Naval vessels assigned to the area over the last century. (Darwin had come here in a ship called *Beagle* on his round-the-world voyage in 1834, but this was a different one.)

Away to the left, if the weather was clear, you could see the sharp cone of Mount Kent and the lower, ragged heights of Tumbledown – names from a past I was close to, but never a part of. This time around, I would be.

As we were stuck in Stanley for a day or two, the first thing I wanted to do was to check up on the only contact I had in the Falklands – Ann Green. Her son Paul had been in the Guards with me, and was one of those killed in the *Galahad* fire. I knew Ann had moved down to the Falklands after the war, and thought I might be able to persuade her to put on a kettle for me, if I could find her.

It didn't take long. Tony knew her, because she lived two doors down from him, a short windy walk from the hotel. I strolled round to find her. The house, a couple of hundred yards up the slope from the shore, looked like a seaside boarding house, with a glassed-in verandah, except that it had a corrugated iron roof. It overlooked a kids' playground and a few Nissen huts and garages.

When I knocked on her door, it was just on the off-chance of finding her in. But there she was, delighted to see me, and more than happy to make a brew. We had met briefly at a service in St Paul's Cathedral in 1985, at the dedication of a war memorial.

Pretty soon we were deep into our memories, looking through Ann's photographs with her daughter, Carol: Irish Guards trooping the colour one hot summer's day around 1980 – I could remember watching it from the street; my squad training – old friends, far-off times; Windy Miller, who took a burst of shrapnel in the face in Northern Ireland; Maxy MacDonald, one of my instructors; and, of course, Paul himself, looking as rough as I remembered him.

Ann had had five kids in all – the oldest, Carol, then two boys, Paul and Michael, then twins. Paul could be a pretty difficult character, not to say violent, as Ann will admit. I never knew why until then.

He'd been badly burned when he was three, and as a kid he always wore long shorts to cover his scarred thighs. Later, there had been emotional fits, suicide attempts, psychiatrists' reports, and small-time trouble with the Police until he joined the Welsh Guards. When I knew him, he was still trouble, but by all accounts he was a lot quieter than he had been. Ann said he loved every minute of the Guards, enough to inspire his brother Michael to join as well, with tales of regular money, and drinks, and loads of girls.

She had seen him and Michael off on the *QE2* on 12 May, with the sun shining and the bands playing and everyone cheering and crying. 'I couldn't take my eyes off Paul,' she said, 'Michael was standing right beside him, but all my vision was full of Paul's face. I had this feeling then that this was the last time I was going to see him again.'

'Yes,' Carol added. 'Michael always used to say, "Don't worry about me. I've got a return ticket." But with Paul it was, "What will be, will be."'

When Carlos made his approach, Paul was playing cards down on the tank deck, a few feet away from me as I was making for Yorkie. One of Paul's friends – who later told Ann what happened – had just appeared to find him, telling him there were some blue movies being shown upstairs in Accommodation.

'I'll be up when I've finished this hand,' Paul said.

Just about then, the alarm call came, and I squatted down on the deck, and Carlos's bomb came across in front of me. Paul must have been almost as close as I was to the explosion, but why he should have died while I lived I have no idea.

Back home, Carol was in the middle of her engagement party when she saw a little black car pull up outside the house, and an official-looking man get out. She knew at once.

'I've some bad news,' he said, at the door.

'It's Paul, isn't it?'

Yes. He had been reported missing, but Carol and Ann were

certain of the truth, even before the message came through the next day: 'Presumed dead'.

Yet, despite the despair inside her, Carol kept on with the party. Paul had paid for half of it, and a small voice inside her said: if he comes back and finds I've cancelled the party, he'll call me a silly cow and give me a clip round the head.

A year later, in May 1983, Ann was on the Ministry of Defence trip to the Falklands for families of the dead. She was still deep in grief for Paul, and you would have thought she'd have felt nothing but bitterness. Far from it – she fell in love with the place. She loved the peace, the silence, the wildness, the cleanness, the safety, the freedom from the stresses of life back home. She loved the people – two jumbo jets filled with relatives arrived in Stanley, yet everyone was made welcome in someone's home. She was overwhelmed by the generosity, the gratitude and the sympathy.

When she visited San Carlos – where the first landings had taken place – it was a beautiful day, and the hills that looked so drab when it rained were golden in the sunlight. It was certainly not the grim, wet and icy lump of moorland the press had depicted. A thought came to her: if this place is worth dying for, it's worth living for.

As soon as she got home she decided she would like to emigrate. Her friends were shocked. They told her she was sick, she only wanted to be near Paul, she should face reality, and anyway the Falklands was a lump of rock in the middle of nowhere. She knew better on all counts, and the family backed her. A letter to the Falklands landed her a job as cook in the Upland Goose Hotel. By November she was on her way. She'd never regretted it.

It was strange how Paul's death had changed Ann's life – and Carol's. She was an announcer on the local radio, something she would never have done if she'd stayed at home. Ann looked as if she had come through some rough times, but I'm sure she had made the right move.

Hers was a story that made me think there might be a bit more to the islands than met the eye.

That evening, me and the lads found a local, Deano's. It was home from home – noisy, crowded with young people – mostly construction workers and squaddies in jeans and T-shirts – hazy with smoke and beer. I don't indulge all that much now, but there was nothing else on offer in Stanley, and it was good to have a few ales with Gary and John.

Besides, I got a pretty good reception. Several people recognized me, so we weren't short of company. A DJ told me all about the local karaoke evening – we attended one later, and it was a trial, with the same performers doing the same songs week after week. One young lady wanted to have her picture taken with me, together with her friend; but her friend was so shy she could hardly speak, let alone get into the picture. It took all my powers of persuasion to get her to stand beside me, to look up and smile. By the time we were done, she seemed happy, which made me happy for her.

The noisy conversation also gave me a chance to learn a little more about the place. One piece of gossip was interesting. Apparently everyone here, too, 'knew' that many more Argentinians had been killed than their government would admit to. There were stories of Argentinian troops burning bodies on a headland near Stanley and dumping bodies at sea. This was another reason for taking seriously all that talk about thousands of Argentinian dead unaccounted for.

Deano's attracted some pretty odd characters – and some surprising ones. One was the harbour owner, with a neck thicker than mine, carpet-beater hands, and eyes that looked as though he'd been on a three-week piss-up. Another had a ring in one ear and low eyebrows. His name was Paul – Paul 'Scouse' they called him, because he was from Liverpool. His story was one laugh after another.

He might have looked rough, but he was a military policeman.

He was in the Falklands as a punishment. As a *punishment*? For what? For being drunk and disorderly and conspiring to assault. It transpired that he had been out on the town with a mate when the mate was picked up by the local police. Then they picked on Paul, simply because he was in the area. Paul kept quiet about his occupation. At four in the morning, he called his solicitor. They sued for wrongful arrest. Politically this was not a good move – not good for relations between the military and the civilian police. So he was posted to the Falklands to keep him out of harm's way.

No sooner was he down here than he heard he'd won his case. He was richer by two grand. More than that – he *loved* it. This coarse-looking, ear-ringed street-fighter type had fallen in love with the wild life. He was mad keen on photography. He chattered away like an even rougher version of David Bellamy about white-sand beaches, and nesting penguins, and killer whales, and pregnant dolphins, and the red-banded caracara – whatever that is. He was involved with a girlfriend, and had just requested that his punishment posting be doubled.

Work? Not too much of that. He had seven cases in four months, all of them civilian, except for one. He'd found a private asleep on guard duty out at the Mount Pleasant base. There were rockets, vehicles, God knows what in the compound. Some drunk might have sneaked in and driven off with a Rapier.

How much was all this stuff worth, anyway?

'120 million pounds, Corporal.'

What?!

Paul's face registered genuine horror. He'd recommended a court martial.

It was partly because of Paul that I went on my first trip outside Stanley. Tony took me out past the wreck we had seen from the plane – a rusty hulk that the SAS had hidden in for a couple of weeks to spy on the Argentinians in Stanley – to a beach called

Gypsy Cove. It was a delightful spot, with sands as white as the Caribbean, deserted (of course) and sheltered. Offshore lay the ominous dark strands of the huge, rubbery kelp that gives the islanders their nickname – 'Kelpers'.

The only Falklanders around, though, were the birds, mainly upland geese and penguins. The penguins, very smart and dignified, paraded into the shallows, surged about like seals, and stared out of their burrows, cocking their heads from side to side as if they couldn't believe their eyes. They acted as if they had never been disturbed in their lives.

There may not have been much in the way of entertainment in town, but at least we had the wit and wisdom of the photographer, David Thorpe, who had joined us in Stanley. David was a delightful character – professional, yet never intrusive or demanding, and also very funny. I could do with all the laughs I could get.

He was not, at first sight, someone with film-star qualities. Let's say he was no longer in the first flush of youth. Not too tall. Like me, he didn't suffer from a flat stomach. No denying his charm, though – easy to talk to, a fund of anecdotes from a varied life, and an obvious delight in his family. We were chatting over supper at the Upland Goose, and I said how nice it must be to travel so much – the people, the women . . .

He surprised me by saying that, yes, travel always restored his faith in his own sexual prowess.

And him a family man. Oh, dear.

He caught my eye. 'Let me tell you about Dr Feinstein's Law of Sexual Polarity,' he said, and began to explain, in a street-wise London voice so deadpan it took a while for me to catch on.

'Wonderful thing, the unconscious.' His tone was slightly superior, as if he was telling me something I really ought to know. 'If anyone enters the room, you're unconsciously aware. Beautiful woman comes in. Before you know it, you check her out. It's an automatic response. Stands to reason.'

I nodded. I couldn't think what he was getting at. He carried on.

'It's the same when a man goes into a room. The women notice. But with women it's different. They guard their reactions, don't they? With me, though, the effect is really dramatic. When I go into a bar in a hotel abroad, I'm on expenses, the places are pretty good, inevitably there are one or two beautiful women there. Inevitably, something very extraordinary happens. *Not one of them looks at me*!'

I gave him a sympathetic smile. Now we were getting to the sob stuff. Middle age creeping on, no longer attractive to women etc.

He took a sip of wine. 'At first when this happened, I was hurt, because I thought they hadn't noticed me. But that didn't make sense. Of course they'd noticed me. Of course I had registered in their subconscious. So why didn't they look at me? Was it because I wasn't worth looking at?

'No. Deep down. I knew that was ridiculous. I mean, there would be a reaction sometimes, wouldn't there? Law of averages. Then I realized what was really going on. *I was too attractive for them*! The impact of my personality, my looks, my animal sexuality – it was all too much. They knew that if they once looked up, if our eyes once met, they would be lost. At my feet. Their world in ruins.

'There was only one possible response: they had to pretend to ignore me. It was the only way they could avoid becoming my complete slaves.

'Of course, it's all done at the unconscious level. If you tried to get them to admit the truth – I'd never do it, because it would be cruelty, wouldn't it? – but if you tried, they would deny it. Well, they'd have to, wouldn't they? You can laugh,' he added, seriously, 'but it's quite true.'

'And now I know the truth, it's a great source of strength.

Every time I go into a foreign bar, and the women all ignore me, I know what's going on inside them, and I feel this warm glow of male pride.

'I could have any woman I want, any time. But it's better this way. I like to see proof that I'm getting more attractive with every passing year.'

He drained his glass, and pushed back his chair. 'That's why I love foreign travel. It's a continual boost to the ego. Wonderful thing, the unconscious. 'Night.'

Slowly, I was beginning to get an inkling of what the Falklands were all about.

Before the war, the Argentinians had been on their way to taking over the place. The British government hadn't really been interested. The Argentinians had the air link, they were the obvious trading partner, and they had put some cash into the islands' economy. The islanders had no alternative but to respond. Many people told me that if Argentina had continued to play it cool, it would have been given the place within a few years.

As it was, Galtieri simply shot himself in the foot. The islanders had always considered themselves to be as British as me. Whatever the official attitude, they were legally British. We had no choice but to respond. After this, there was no way that Britain could be seen to be betraying the islanders.

As a result, the islands had never been so secure. There had been only forty marines there in 1982; now there were almost 2,000 troops, a huge base and a growing economy. The governor had just opened up the islands for oil exploration. This would lead to a mini-boom. Soon there would be more people, more houses and more jobs.

Was this good or bad? I had no idea yet, but I was beginning to look forward to finding out.

It might not be a place I would choose to live in, but it promised to be a more interesting one than I had imagined.

7

SAN CARLOS

26–27 November 1991

I had always said the first place I wanted to visit was San Carlos, because that was the first place I came ashore – well, the only place that I remember anything about. I knew there was a memorial there – probably nothing much more than a cross and a few words on a headstone – but I didn't expect the visit to be all that emotional, because nothing much had happened there for me. It would be an easy way to start re-experiencing the past.

The night before, over an ale or three, somebody had asked what I was doing next.

'Going to San Carlos.'

'Oh, going camp, are you?'

I gave him a look. Was he looking for a slap in the gob, or what? Damned cheek. I didn't think I had been acting particularly effeminately. But no – it transpired that all areas outside Stanley are referred to as the 'camp', short for the Spanish *campo* ('field' or 'countryside'). Well, all right. Yes, I was going camp.

San Carlos lay on the other side of East Falkland, only sixty-five miles away, and half of that was paved now. But according to Tony, our main driver, the last few miles were a rough ride over moors and mountains. This last section might take three hours or more, depending on whether we bogged down or not. There are Welsh Guards who could probably beat a Land Rover over the same course.

We headed out in a convoy of three four-wheel drive vehicles. Two of these were modern long-wheel-base machines with bulbous tyres; one was older, with a short wheel-base and an unorthodox solution to the problem of peat and mud – its owner, Tony, had welded another set of wheels on to the back wheels. This one was being driven by Gary.

There was even a minor challenge about the first few miles, out to the RAF and Army base at Mount Pleasant Airport, or MPA as it's called. The road leading west between mountains and the coast was mostly gravel. It was solidly made, with a good curved surface to provide run-off for the rain. But the combination of slippery gravel and a sloping surface made the going a little dicey, especially as the engineers had dug huge six-foot ditches on either side. It felt more like navigation than driving.

On several occasions we skirted mine-fields. The Argentinians had laid tens of thousands of mines, some on the west coast, but most around Stanley. There were many types, from small three-inch anti-personnel mines to anti-tank mines; so many that it would take years and millions of pounds to clear them. The engineers had done their best, and then simply fenced off the rest. Maps are easily available from the Royal Engineers HQ in Stanley, where the types of mines found are on display.

There are 115 marked mine-fields, many contained within miles of fenced-off areas that are marked on the map in red – 'known to be still mined'. They look large when you see them, but in fact they can be measured in acres rather than square miles. Along parts of the coast, explosive devices have occasionally been found washed up by the tide. The Engineers are careful – *all* the remainder of the islands are marked blue, which means 'may still contain unexploded bombs, ammunition, missiles etc.' Very few areas are marked green, meaning they've been 'exhaustively checked', which is as good as saying they're guaranteed clear. In fact, I don't think there has been a single mine-related incident since the war. It's quite a record.

If you knew nothing about mines, you might think that the peace might occasionally be shattered by an exploding penguin, but in fact it takes a certain pressure to detonate even the most sensitive anti-personnel mine. I saw the carcass of a sheep in one mine-field, but I think it had died of boredom. The penguins and seals are certainly safe.

Anyway, there we were, driving on ball-bearings above six-foot ditches past mine-fields, in a fog of dust thrown up by the car in front.

Every now and then we were threatened by death-defying sheep. They are as silly on the Falklands as anywhere else. They see you coming and start running away ahead of you. The car catches up, the sheep panic and decide just as you draw level that it's safer on the other side of the road – and cut straight across in front of you.

Dust, slippery gravel, sloping roads, six-foot ditches, kamikaze mutton and mine-fields: God help the Argentinians if they ever try a quick run in from MPA.

We were heading west, across the gentle lower slopes of mountains that were familiar from the war: William, Harriet, Challenger. The flanks of the hills were camouflage colours – patches of dark green heather and lighter green and brown grass, all flowing down from the light grey spines of rock. These were the same colours that had depressed me when I first saw them from the plane, but the day was clear, and the air so clean that distant summits stood out as sharp as nearby rocks, and the sun and clouds scattered patches of shadow and light. Perhaps it wasn't quite so grim as I had first thought.

It might have been a part of Scotland, except for something that I had never seen before. Not surprisingly, as it turned out, because it, or rather they, are special to the Falklands. Now and then, the grassy slopes on either side of the road were divided by odd outcrops of rock. After we had passed several, I recognized them as the 'rivers of rock' that I'd heard someone mention in Deano's. Now I remembered – we'd been told about them when we were coming south on the *QE2*: watch out for the rocks; you could break a leg on them if you try to walk over them, and there are sometimes huge drops down into God knows what.

They were puzzling things. The rocks all seemed to be good-sized boulders, all within a certain range of sizes, none of them small enough to lift by hand, and none much larger than a car. They were mostly lying in channels, like rivers that seemed to be leading down from the bare upper slopes. But sometimes they spread out into little plains, like rock lakes. Some seemed to have been lying there dead for thousands of years, and were covered all over with heather and grass. But others were uncovered, as if they were still moving.

As an ex-soldier my first thought was: bloody awful ground to fight over. Somewhere to our right was Tumbledown. Imagine crawling over thirty yards of this rubble, on a freezing night, carrying a rifle with bayonet attached, trying to keep quiet, when every move makes a scrape and a clang, and there are enemy trenches ahead, and flares above and snipers up on the higher ridges.

But I couldn't help wondering about how they had been formed, these 'rock runs', because you see them on all the hillsides. I had never bothered about geology, so I guessed that they must have been made by ice – perhaps by Ice Age glaciers. Perhaps in winter this was where ice formed, and where water flowed in spring. But nothing seemed to make much sense, and no one I met knew the answer. And why aren't there rock runs anywhere else – in the Brecon Beacons or in Scotland?

Over to the left, towards the sea, there were three or four houses, the first signs of life outside Stanley. Bluff Cove, home to perhaps a dozen people. Beyond lay Fitzroy, and the inlet where the *Galahad* had moored. Well, time enough for that later.

On, through dust, across white tussocky grasslands, towards MPA. In all those thirty-five miles there was just one roadside building, a hotel, of all things, presumably catering for civilians who came in on the RAF flight and wanted a real taste of the wilds before hitting the dizzy metropolis of Stanley.

MPA itself was an eye-opener – we stopped there to buy some dried flowers for the memorials, replacements for those taken by the Chilean customs. The place was a square mile of runways, hangars, offices, shops and living quarters, all neat greens and whites, with tarmacked roads, each named with solid British signs in solid black British typeface. One of our few overseas outposts – and a new one at that. A self-contained world for 2,000 people.

What was it all for? Simply to make sure the Argentinians didn't think of trying it again? Or was it all part of a longer term, strategic plan, to do with future investments, oil and minerals, and defending British interests in Antarctica and South America? Perhaps, after the war, men in dark suits had let their minds wander to what might happen if we were to find oil there, and the Russians got nasty or South America really went down the tubes. Perhaps they had had words with their pals in Washington. It might be useful for us and the North Americans to have a big, secure base in the South Atlantic. Perhaps, also, it might be useful to have huge expanses of harsh landscape for training in. Perhaps a lot of things. One thing was for sure: no one was going to pull out of there in a hurry.

After this the road turned into a track. It had been a track for many years, but just then it was hard going, because a new road was being built across the peat and grass. In a year or so the run to Goose Green would be a doddle. But right then it was an obstacle course. We slalomed around bulldozers and scrapers and piles of gravel and top-soil. We accelerated briefly along newly scraped mud. We crawled over untouched peat. We hopped in and out of the vehicles to open and shut sheep-gates. The rough pasture stretched away unbroken on either side. We had swung away from the mountains – they now ran far to the right, over five miles away, not that you could judge distance in that sparkling air.

There was something else about the plant life here, now that I saw it close up. The surface was covered with plants I had never seen before. Known as 'balsam bogs', they consisted of thin twigs densely matted into pin-cushion shapes. They looked like giant puff-balls. They were quite solid, but not solid enough to support you, and certainly not solid enough to offer resistance to a Land Rover's wheel.

Twenty miles and a couple of hours later, Tony led us down off the peat on to hard sand, because it was an easier route when the tide was out. The coast stretched away to the left. We could see a collection of white-painted houses, with red and green corrugated iron roofs. Then up, with the ribbed wheels taking a good grip of the soft soil, and on to a ridge.

We were on a land bridge, a mile wide and five miles long – a strip of land that prevents East Falkland being sliced in two. To the south, the island opens out again into its other half, Lafonia.

On the land bridge itself stood two little settlements: Darwin and Goose Green – the houses we had seen further back. This was familiar territory to John; it was the scene of his first battle, and the first big one of the war. But this wasn't our destination yet. We were heading on around the coast, northwards, beyond the end of the road, up over the Sussex Mountains, to San Carlos.

Now we were really getting into the wilds. The convoy of three vehicles forded a stream, axle-deep. John remembered wading through it when he led his platoon towards Goose Green. He had good cause to remember it. It had been night, and very cold. Already his feet were wet, and now he had to get a lot wetter. 'As I crossed I could feel I was slipping deeper, deeper, deeper. Aaah! Don't let me get wet nuts! Too late. I was expecting two little frozen lumps to appear out the top of my collar.'

We headed uphill over the thick cushion of peaty soil. Although San Carlos had been occupied for a century – every now and then we saw the course of an old wagon-track – no one had pioneered a track for motor-driven vehicles. Each driver was a pioneer, searching out his own course. It was no good following someone else – the wheels often cut through the surface ploughing up mud that was best avoided by anyone coming after.

It required a strange kind of skill, heading steadily uphill over the broad tussock-covered flanks, swinging the wheel back and forth to avoid soft spots and outcrops of rock and small ponds of black, peaty water. Often it was impossible to see why Tony chose one direction over another. There seemed to be no difference between this yellow patch of grass and that.

Our lads were good, but they didn't make a big deal of it. Sometimes locals did the same run in the dark, when things could really get tricky. 'You think you know every blade of grass until something goes wrong,' the hotel-owner in San Carlos told me after we arrived. She had been stuck coming this same route a few days earlier, until an SOS call on the radio summoned help from San Carlos. It took a few hours, but another vehicle, with a winch, sorted her out.

Not many cars came this way, perhaps half a dozen a week, but this was enough to show how fragile the wilderness was. There were tyre-marks from weeks, even months, earlier. The old wagon-track was a permanent scar, with no signs of growing over. If more cars came, the whole mountainside would become a churned-up mass of peaty mud that would never be allowed to heal. One day, there would have to be a road. Then what? More settlers, and an end to a century of isolation?

This was the land John had advanced over ten years earlier.

We stopped briefly at one site he remembered, Camilla Creek. Back then it was a house. Now the house had gone. There was nothing but some bits of concrete and a few poles, the wind that whipped away your words as you spoke and clouds blanketing the summits of the hills.

We began to weave along the spine of the Sussex Mountains. The views became ever grander, though clouds were now lowering over the high ground. I still wouldn't have called it beautiful, because it's not my sort of landscape, but it was definitely spectacular. Below, the tongues of land licked round inlets and lagoons. The sea was untroubled by the gusting wind, perhaps because it was protected by the shores of West Falkland, easily visible less than ten miles away.

Further along the ridge, San Carlos Water came into view below us, a grey mirror of sea reflecting a grey sky. The bank of mountains ran on and curved behind the inlet like a protective arm. Somewhere on the lower slopes – invisible – was Ajax Bay, where I was taken after I was injured.

We stopped again. John had spotted another of his sites – a shallow trench with stone and peat walls. This miserable shelter had been his home for two or three days at the beginning of the war.

Like everyone else, they had made the mistake of digging in. This was when they discovered that the peat was like a sponge – it oozed. Dig down, and what you had was not a cosy protection but an ice-bucket half full of water. That was when the lads started getting trouble with trench-foot. No one ever found a decent solution. When you set up a new position, you had to dig in immediately, just to be sure of some sort of protection. But as soon as you could, the thing to do was build *up*, make thick wind-proof walls of peat turf and put a cape over the top. Then, if you could get dry, you could remain snug for hours. All around were the results, still visible ten years on.

We eased on down to San Carlos. I had spent eight days in the area, but my memories were all of carrying packs, brewing tea, cold feet and miserable nights, the long hike up the Sussex Mountains, and back down again when the powers that be decided we wouldn't make it on foot.

I recognized the jetty where we had landed, and the white house with the red-painted roof near which we had had our horrible exposed latrine. I remembered the trench I had shared with Colin Parsons. I even found it before we left San Carlos the next day, up under a ridge, close to a bridge. Still there after ten years! Well, not so much a trench, hardly more than a shell-scrape – just enough to get a bit of shelter in case of a bombing raid. But by then we knew there were no enemy soldiers around, and the thick clouds meant no chance of bombs, so we felt safe enough to brew up. All around, in the bitter night, stoves flickered.

The countryside looked much as I remembered it, though I'm sure it was nicer then. There had been a mud slide in the ridge above the little scrape. You could see the ripples in the side of the hill. Another ten years, and the scrape will have vanished, so if anyone wants to do any archaeological research at this extremely important site, they better get a move on.

The settlement itself, which I had never seen much of ten years earlier, looked surprisingly civilized. Good green grass, not the straggly pale yellow stuff of the slopes above. Three houses with red, green and blue roofs of corrugated iron. Hedges glowing with yellow gorse flowers. One of the houses was the Blue Beach Hotel, where we were staying, but this wasn't our first objective.

First came the memorial. We parked, unloaded, and followed one of the locals right on past the hotel, past a second house, along a track lined with gorse, through a gate, and into a field that sloped down to the sea.

I hadn't any idea what to expect, so I was taken totally by surprise, both by the sight, and by the sudden rush of emotion.

Ahead of me as I walked down the field, with its neat

wooden fence, was a little inlet of San Carlos Water. This was Blue Beach where the first troops – 'A' Company of 40 Commando – waded ashore from their landing craft early in the morning of 21 May. Offshore, in the darkness, waited the two assault ships *Fearless* and *Intrepid*. As the sixteen landing craft, with their 1,200 troops, chugged towards the shore, no one knew what to expect. There was a quick, intense fire-fight going on to the left, as Special Boat Services cleared about 100 Argentinians up on Fanning Head, which guarded the entrance to San Carlos Water. Intelligence reports said there weren't any Argentinian troops at San Carlos itself. And there had been lots of diversionary raids – one of them on Darwin, on the other side of the Sussex Mountains – to confuse the enemy about our intentions. But Intelligence might be wrong, and the Argentinians might not have been fooled. Perhaps it would be like the Normandy invasion: enemy planes, bombs, bullets, mine-fields, the lot.

As it happened, there was no one there. Total silence.

Men of 40 Commando had walked up the same track to the manager's house behind me, to ask the manager, Pat Short, if there were any Argentinians about. Pat is still there, in the same house. He told the story later. John Thurman, who had visited San Carlos a few months earlier, was told to knock on the door, so that at least Pat was confronted by a familiar face. Pat, the first Falklander to be liberated, seemed not at all surprised to see men armed to the teeth, their faces blacked for night combat.

'Hello, Pat,' said John. 'Do you remember me?'

Pat peered into the darkness at the shadowy figures with their camouflaged faces.

'Are you . . . British?' he asked, warily.

'Yes. It's John. John Thurman.'

'Oh, you've come then,' said Pat. Not over-emotional, the Falklanders. A Commando who was there later said he was sure that 'if we had been grass-skirted Chinamen with daggers in our teeth, the reception would have been the same'.

At the top of the field, just where the first position had been established, was the memorial. It was then I began to feel I was in the presence of something special, and the feeling grew as I approached.

The setting was truly beautiful. A five-foot wall of light-coloured, yellow Falklands stone had been built in a circle, with a gate facing downhill, towards the inlet. The two arms of the inlet swung out to sea on either side. Across the bay, the great grey bank of the Sussex Mountains loomed, their upper slopes shrouded in mist.

Behind the memorial circle stood a Union Jack fluttering from a flag-pole, and behind the flag-pole there was a huge bank of gorse, bright with yellow flowers. The only sounds were the gusts of wind, the cries of sea-birds, and the steady slap-slap-slap of the flag-pole rope.

But it wasn't the setting that really got to me. It was what I saw when I walked through the gate. I was in a small cemetery – beautifully trimmed lawn, a few graves, and a flower-bed of daffodils tucked in under the wall, protected from the wind and cold. At the far end, the stone wall rose to form a higher section about ten feet high holding dark marble plaques. I went straight up to it to see exactly what they said.

Words engraved in the marble paid tribute to the Task Force, but in particular 'to the abiding memory of the sailors, soldiers and airmen who gave their lives and who have no grave but the sea. Here beside the graves of their comrades this memorial records their names.'

I was totally unprepared for the effect these words had on me. 'Those who have no grave but the sea.' That could have been me. I stood there, with tears in my eyes, utterly destroyed by the emotion.

I scanned the names. Many of them were familiar: Ian Anthony Dale and Brian Jasper, whose memorial service I had been to three weeks earlier; Paul Green, Ann's son; Gareth Hughes, who had driven the one-ton vehicle that time when we ate my Mam out of house and home; Colin Parsons, who had shared my trench under the ridge not half a mile away; my best friend, Andrew Walker – 'Yorkie'. My name would have been almost next to his, third from the end.

And there was an unexpected name, 'Scouse' Farrell. He had been in the Medical Corps, but had been seconded to us. He'd joined my platoon just before we landed. He was the first to get trench-foot. He was a lovely guy, full of humour, and God, did he need it – we gave him hell. He was there to look after us, and he couldn't look after himself! Tore him apart, we did. Really made him feel at home. He took it well. Once he'd been on the receiving end of a few well-directed insults, he knew he was one of us.

I looked around again, feeling the wind bite at my face. For a minute, locked inside my own emotions, I had forgotten that this was more than a memorial to the Task Force and to those who had been buried at sea. It was a cemetery for fifteen men whose families had wished their husbands, brothers and sons to be buried here rather than be taken home.

As I wandered around, with Gary and John, the graves, the flowers, and the words on the simple crosses brought another rush of emotion. Here, with a small flowering bush growing on it, was the grave of one of the best-known victims, Lieutenant-Colonel Jones – always known simply as 'H' – killed while leading the attack on the hill above Darwin. One headstone read: 'Colin, we believe life and death are one, even as the river and sea are one.' Another recalled a family saying: 'Darling, you must have been a very good penny.'

One simple memorial said, 'To our dearest husband and father', from a wife and two children. That did for me. I stood there, hiding the tears, thinking, 'I could have been here, alone.' I imagined James fatherless; Lucy alone. What could be worse than being alone – me here, them there? It was too close to bear, almost as if I should have been here, buried or remembered on the plaque.

Gary and John are hard men, but they too felt the power, the *rightness*, of the place. There were no Scots Guards buried there, but there were four from John's unit, 2 Para – three killed at Goose Green, and 'That's for Fred Slough,' said John, pointing. Francis Slough – 'but we always called him Fred' – had been in John's platoon. He was shot on Wireless Ridge, within hours of the end of the war.

Once, it would have seemed odd to me that families should have chosen to have their loved ones buried abroad. I would like to think that if I'd been killed on land, my family would have brought me back to Nelson. But having seen this place, I could understand. There are memorials to British soldiers all over the world, all well looked after by the War Graves Commission. But there is something special about San Carlos. It is a perfect site, and a perfect memorial, beautifully kept by the man who has the best reason of all to undertake the task – Pat Short, the first Falklander to be liberated.

Even in the rain, with the wind gusting cold down from the Sussex Mountains, this place would be beautiful. On a day like this, it was pure magic.

Quite simply, the memorial deserves to be there.

8

GOOSE GREEN

28 November 1991

Returning over the Sussex Mountains the next day, it was John's turn to re-experience the past. Through him, a few hours of vivid, on-the-spot anecdotes, and his dead calm professionalism, I became at last a part of the war.

John, along with the rest of 12 Platoon, part of 2 Para's 'D' Company, was among the first to see action on land. The landings had gone well, despite fierce assaults by the Argentinian Air Force. A dozen Argentinian planes had been shot down for the loss of two ships (*Ardent* and *Antelope*), with four more out of action or damaged. Not bad, considering 10,000 tons of supplies and 3,000 troops were ashore, most of them well dispersed over the cold, wet and windy slopes of the Sussex Mountains to avoid air raids. Now there was nothing to do except wait for transport overland.

John's twenty-six lads, as wet and cold as the peat they dug in, were beginning to suffer with sore feet when the order for action came. They were to clear an area round one of the lonely outposts, Cantera House, on the coast six miles south. This was part of a policy of 'aggressive patrolling' in defence of San

Carlos, but it would also put them within striking distance of Goose Green if necessary. Goose Green, the largest community outside Stanley, was the Argentinian base closest to San Carlos. From there, if anywhere, retaliation would come.

Forward observers had reported seeing three armoured vehicles at Cantera House. They could carry up to thirty-two men each, so there could be quite a force there – more than a match, perhaps, for twenty-six keyed-up young men in their first action.

'Right, lads.' John was a tough task-master, but it was all for their own good. 'Take a brew kit, and only one day's supply of food.'

They were issued three days' rations, but John thought it best for them to lighten their loads. Besides, they would hardly eat in action, and if there were no fighting they'd be resupplied soon enough. Out went everything except dehydrated rolled oats, chocolate drink and apple flakes. Mixing that lot together made a slurry that would keep them going for at least two days. No bergens, no waterproofs because of the noise the material made, and no sleeping-bags. If it rained, they would walk wet, and sleep wet. They'd carry 300 rounds each for the GPMG (general-purpose machine-gun), 100 rifle-rounds each in a bandolier, and another 200 in magazines, grenades, some M66 anti-tank rockets, and spare radio batteries – in all, about sixty to sixty-five pounds per person.

They set off towards dusk on 24 May. It was good to be on the move at last, escaping the drudgery of defence routine. The CO, Lieutenant-Colonel 'H' Jones, came by to send them off. This worried some of the lads – if the CO comes by, well, it's going to be pretty sticky, right, Sergeant?

'Shut up, Minnock, and keep packing.'

There was nothing sinister about 'H's presence. He was a demanding, but fair-minded commander who would want to make sure his men went off properly equipped, properly led and properly motivated.

As night fell, they were taken by helicopter a few miles south, and dropped by a pilot so nervous he went thudding off into the darkness without leaving them their grid reference.

A brief conflab followed with the platoon commander, Jim Barry, to find out where they were. John had known Jim just three months. He was only there by chance. He was a yachtsman, and had been about to go off to compete in the America's Cup, when the Paras' departure from home altered his plans. It had been a close thing – the platoon already had a replacement commander, Jonathan Page, who was put in charge of fire support when Jim Barry returned.

Their position seemed OK. Some small lakes nearby told them they were near enough where they were meant to be – about three miles from Cantera House.

Jim Barry set his compass. They set off. Rain came, driven into their faces by the wind, limiting vision to a metre or two. They were shadows staggering and sliding over the rough ground with their burdens. It was impossible to tell how far they had travelled, until they hit a fence line that should – according to the map – lead them near the house.

The rain eased. There was the dull grey shape of a house. But was it the *right* house? One way to check was for the forward observation officer to use the radio to ask the artillery to fire one round at the house, which was pre-recorded on the artillery's computer-controlled sights. It would be safe enough – one artillery round wouldn't tell the enemy of the Paras' presence.

'Shot out!' came over the radio. 'Forty seconds!' John and Jim Barry fixed their binoculars on the shadow of the house. The seconds ticked by. Then, a good kilometre over to the right, a boom and a flash.

'If that's where Cantera House is, then we're half a k. out to sea,' muttered Jim Barry.

The artillery was way off beam. This was a great boost to confidence. Anyway, the shape ahead had to be Cantera House.

They began a silent approach, planning not to open fire unless fired on. Assuming they weren't seen, they could get in really close, and the shock of the close-quarter assault would win the fire-fight. Divided into sections, each section moved forward, 'went firm', allowed the others to come through, moved forward . . .

The house was empty. Not a trace of the enemy anywhere.

That night, there was no fire, no hot food, no brew, no dry clothing to sleep in, but at least they had cover. Next morning, new orders: they were told to meet the rest of the company and go on to clear Camilla Creek, four miles on towards Goose Green.

They had hardly got to the rendezvous, when the operation was cancelled. More new orders: return to Cantera House. This meant reclearing it, because enemy soldiers might have moved in – another silent approach. Empty, of course. Another night without decent food, dry clothing, or dry boots.

Next morning, three of the lads were casualties – two with bad feet, one with a sprained knee. Jim Barry requested a helicopter. No joy: the weather was 'too bad'. This was rubbish. The day was clear and everyone could see helicopters over the mountains. No use arguing. John and Jim Barry marched the platoon back up the hills, arriving at the top at dusk. The three injured men, all limping in pain, were out of the war. A fourth developed appendicitis that night. Four down, in a minor strategic cock-up almost certainly due to vacillating plans about whether to raid Goose Green or not, while waiting for air transport to get the troops into the Stanley area.

By now, though, plans were hardening. The day before, the *Atlantic Conveyor* had been sunk, together with huge supplies of stores and eight of the helicopters that were going to be used to airlift troops across country. After this, the decision was made that some Commandos and Paras would march overland, while others would be airlifted or shipped as transport became available.

This meant new orders for 2 Para: back down the mountains again, on foot, across eight miles of moorland, to Camilla Creek, then on another four miles to capture Darwin and Goose Green.

It was a risky operation to attempt. The land bridge was only a mile wide, so there would be no outflanking manoeuvres. There was hardly any cover. Planes based at the local airfield at Goose Green would give the Argentinians air cover. There were also Goose Green's 100 civilians to consider. And no one had a clear idea of how many Argentinian troops there were. (In fact, 2 Para was vastly outnumbered, as they discovered later.)

One day's march took the Paras to Camilla Creek, where they stopped for the night, and the following day. That evening John and his platoon, in reserve with the rest of 'D' Company, tabbed over to the operations 'start line' just north of a house called Burntside. The farm itself was being held by about thirty Argentinians who were living in a sheepshed, leaving four civilians in the house. John heard 'A' Company attack – quick rattles of fire, then silence. The Argentinians fled. No one was hurt. Everyone moved on south through the darkness, with two companies taking a shoreline each, and John's company still in reserve.

It started to rain again. 'A' and 'B' Companies assaulted positions on the right and left. Almost at once, John's lot were brought into action too. The Argentinians saw them in the light of the gunfire, and the first bursts came at them, whipping overhead, and slapping into the grass and peat around them.

It was not close-quarter action yet, but it was the first time under fire for most of them. It took Jim Barry as platoon commander and John himself as platoon sergeant to shout and kick the young lads into remembering their drills: 'See the flashes . . . Trench to the left, another to the right . . . Return fire!'

The drills clicked in. Crack-and-thump: this gave the direction of a shot, the crack of the faster-than-sound round passing overhead, followed by the thump of the gun firing. While one section kept firing, forcing the enemy to keep down, a second section advanced until they were close enough for two men to go in with grenades. At the yell 'Grenade!' everyone hit the deck, boom, a burst of fire, a shout of 'Trench clear!' and on to the next, in a rain-sodden confusion of shouts and fire-bursts and exploding artillery rounds, trench by trench, each one demanding an approach to within a couple of yards, with bullets from your own men zipping in on either side, and flares flaming overhead.

Beyond this first position, at the top of a rise, the immediate limit of exploitation, John, carrying an M79 grenade-launcher, reorganized the men as they came through, checked ammunition, counted heads . . .

There was a section missing.

John went back the way he'd come to look for them, passing through company HQ, failed to find them, and was on his way back when, by the light of mortar flashes, he saw four helmets in silhouette moving along a fence.

Back in company HQ, he asked his company second-in-command, Captain Adams, 'Have we got anyone on our right?'

'I don't think so.'

'Well, there's somebody there.'

Adams ordered up a mini-flare. Four Argentinians stood up. Could be they were trying to surrender, but no one was about to ask questions. John fired his M79.

John took one of his lads over to check the damage. Two had been killed outright, one was injured, and one had got away. The bodies and the wounded man were searched for maps and ammunition — they used 7.62mm ammo, same as the British, so it was standard practice to take it.

The private turned one of the dead men over. He had lost half his face.

'I think he's still alive, Sergeant.'

'Don't be daft. If you think he's still alive, give him the kiss of life.'

John counted twelve trenches 'taken out', before they were held up by the main Argentinian defence line, which straddled the isthmus between Darwin and the ruins of a building known as Boca House. 'A' Company were to take Darwin, 'B' Company the Boca House end and 'D' Company to remain in reserve. The whole operation was meant to be over during the night.

But it wasn't that simple.

Darwin now is a nice little place – half a dozen houses on a level stretch of grass in the lee of hills. The coast bends round into a bay, and on a rise approaching the settlement is a solid dry-stone corral built last century to hold cattle during round-ups. A quarter of a mile to the south is a sharp little hill with a monument on the top.

It was here that 'A' Company's advance stalled, and here that Lieutenant-Colonel 'H' was shot leading a renewed attack on the Darwin end of the defence line. John knew nothing of what had happened, except that the CO was 'down.'

By now 'B' Company, advancing down a bare slope on the Boca House position, had also been stalled.

Boca House then was no more than a few stones. Now, there's nothing at all, except a rolling expanse of well-nibbled grass, smooth as a golf-course, backed by a long gorse bush. Tony, our driver, said the gorse marked the line of an old wall built by gauchos in the last century to keep cattle from escaping during round-ups on Lafonia. The Argentinian position – a trench surrounded by peat walls – was a hundred yards behind the gorse.

Soon after, as daylight came, John's lot started to move round along the shoreline to outflank Boca House. A narrow path allowed John's platoon to advance round the edge of the line, and up through a mine-field. The mines were tagged with orange wire, which would have been invisible at night. Now, in daylight, they were clear enough, and it was safe enough for them to pick their way through. Suddenly there was a blast that flattened everyone. John looked round, his head ringing. One of the boys was sitting up, with some orange wire round his boot and a crater to his side. He was shocked, but not hurt.

'It wasn't me, Sergeant,' he said mournfully.

'It *was* you.' Already some of the others were going across to help him. 'And where do you think you lot are going?'

'To help him, Sergeant.'

'Leave him,' said John flatly, walking gingerly forward. 'He tripped it. He can sort himself out.'

By then, the Argentinians had begun to surrender – about twenty of them, leaving a dozen dead.

The focus of battle moved on, to a building on the outskirts of Goose Green – the school-house; and to the airfield – a flat expanse of grass that spanned a gentle rise ahead. Someone noticed a white flag flying from a peat-wall position on the edge of the airfield. After checking with his commanding officer, Jim Barry said he would take the surrender. Perhaps John should have questioned him (he blamed himself later for not doing so): if the enemy wanted to surrender, they should have been told to come forward. It wasn't up to the Paras to approach. On the other hand, a surrender would save a lot of lives. John simply told two others – Knight and Godfrey – to accompany Jim Barry, with four others to the rear in support.

From a hundred yards away, he saw the men vanish into dead ground and reappear on the rise beyond. Jim approached the position. He seemed to be talking to the Argentinians. Then two other Argentinians approached. Jim was just turning round when from somewhere came a rattle of fire, then another burst, this time from the other side of Jim. He, Knight and Godfrey went down, seeking cover probably – couldn't be too sure from this distance.

Bursts of heavy, accurate small-arms fire made those watching duck down.

'Return fire!'

'But they're shooting at me,' one of the younger lads said plaintively.

'I'm a lot closer than you are, Spencer. If I shoot at you, I'm going to hit you, so bloody well *return fire*!'

John levelled his rifle and fired. No use at this range. The next moment one of the others, Roach, came crawling back over the rise from dead ground. 'I think I've been hit,' he said.

'You *know* if you've been hit.'

'Well, I *think* I've been hit.'

A quick check revealed that a round had split the back of his windproof trousers, and nicked him – the only thing wrong with him was a draft in the basement.

Then Chevill came crawling back. He really had been hit, seriously – once through the shoulder and once in the hip. John delegated Wilson and Roach to give first aid, took a GPMG from one of the gunners and opened up. Several Argentinians fell. He returned the machine-gun to the gunner, told him to give him covering fire, and ran, doubled over, to Knight and Godfrey. As he did so, Barton lobbed a grenade from the M79, and the survivors at the Argentinian position ran off.

Knight and Godfrey were OK.

John crawled up to Jim. He'd taken a burst in the chest. He was dead. John had seen death before, many times, and felt nothing of the shock felt by the inexperienced. Personal feelings had no part in what was going on. But something changes when you lose a commander and a friend. In this case, there was an icy, controlled anger, not just at the loss, but at the circumstances of the loss. Jim Barry had died trying to take a surrender. John hadn't been much of a one to sympathize with the Argentinians before; he would be even warier of such feelings now.

Behind him, the school-house was burning well. Ahead, it was a clear run into Goose Green. From there, he had a good view of the twenty or thirty tin-roofed houses and barns that were scattered along a stubby peninsula and around the shore.

There were no more defensive positions. The battle was as good as over.

They could have gone on, but for some reason were ordered to fall back along the airfield, and dig in, as a protection against the few rounds still coming their way from the village.

It was here that Burridge and Minnock had lucky escapes. John had just told them to reposition themselves. They had begun to stand up, with Burridge moving minutely faster than Minnock, when a bullet whipped above Minnock's back, and then actually sliced straight through Burridge's shoulder harness holding his ammunition, medical kit and poncho. It left a ten-inch graze across his shoulders. A tenth of a second later, the bullet would have cut his spine. As it was, he just went down a lot quicker than he stood up, with a yelp. He took a replacement harness from one of the casualties.

John checked numbers: Jim Barry, Paul Sullivan, and Nigel Smith dead; Chevill wounded.

And Fred Slough and Sheepwash were missing, complete with GPMG and ammunition. No one had any idea where they were. Odd. They could hardly have got shot or blown up in full daylight without anyone noticing.

There was nothing to be done about them, partly because of bullets still flying around, and partly because of action overhead. Three Harriers roared over to bomb positions ahead. An Argentinian plane flew past and fired a burst that cut harmlesly through the position, scaring the life out of the wounded Chevill. Chevill was groggy with morphine and had a saline drip attached to his backside, but he took off across the grass with his trousers round his ankles. They had to catch him to bring him back.

Later, a Pucará came over and dropped napalm, but missed by a long way. Everyone opened up, hit the plane and forced the pilot to bale out, right into the arms of the Paras. (In fact, Carlos had told us in Buenos Aires that the pilot, Cruzado, had been his instructor.)

The next morning, Fred Slough and Sheepwash turned up. An officer had needed a couple of gunners and ordered them to follow him to take out some artillery pieces. Of course, they'd obeyed without question. If John could have got his hands on the officer concerned, he would have done him serious injury. Worse still, they hadn't got anywhere near the artillery, and the officer had left the two squaddies to their own devices. Knowing that if they were to try to return, they might not be recognized, and be shot, they had spent the night under a gorse bush.

That morning came the surrender – a huge crowd of Argentinians gathered on the airfield, 1,200 of them, an astonishing number, three times the whole Para battalion that had assaulted them. They were shepherded into a barn, its black roof overpainted with huge white letters: 'POW'. Barn, roof and letters were still there, untouched, ten years later.

For his young platoon, based in another barn not far from the POWs, just by the airfield, it had been quite a baptism. They'd started out with twenty-six men. Now they were down to twenty. But the action brought benefits. They were battle-hardened, and had mostly proved good lads. John had seen a couple of weak links – the clowns who needed kicking to get them moving. One lad had been badly affected by the action and the deaths, and needed to be kept working for three days solid to prevent him from falling into depression. No one moaned any more about humping ammunition instead of food. All were bitter at how Jim Barry had died, which meant they would not be inclined to be soft on the enemy next time around.

So it wasn't surprising that, once they had dug in to defend Goose Green, they should develop the easy callousness and black humour of all squaddies everywhere.

'Now I understand the theory of crack-and-thump, Sergeant: the crack is when the round hits you – and the thump is when you hit the ground.'

When sixteen Argentinian bodies were lined up on the

ground, boots were seized and tried on – for feet permanently swollen now by wet and cold – and macabre jokes made.

'Hey, look, the Isle of Man sign – three legs, all which way!'

'This guy's face!' – a bullet had passed straight through, causing it to collapse in upon itself – 'The Argentinian girnie champion! Bung a fag in his mouth, and let's have a picture!'

For a few days, they could rest. There was whisky and rum from the locals in exchange for souvenirs from the stockpile of Argentinian weapons, and food brought in by the helicopters, and fags, and sweets.

John, though, needed to stay alert. It was a team he was running, and he had to watch out that everyone was treated fairly. Take the question of sweets. Cigarettes arrived for the smokers, with a random variety of sweets for the seven non-smokers – Mars bars, Twixes and Yorkie bars. He had to remember who had had what, or it was: 'Sarge, why can't I have a Yorkie bar? I had a Mars yesterday.' One day, John meticulously sliced a single Yorkie seven ways to share out with the Marses. Next minute there was a shout: 'Who's eaten my chunk of Yorkie bar?' Uproar. Near mutiny. It sounds petty from lads who had just been through a battle, but they'd not had much for too long, and every little bit counted.

This apart, they were very different young men from those that had set out from Sussex Mountains a few days before.

They would need this hardness on Wireless Ridge, two weeks later.

9

FITZROY

29 November 1991

The return to Fitzroy had been my main aim ever since I knew I was going back to the Falklands. I was sure it would be the most moving part of the trip. I was afraid of the emotions that would hit me when I looked out over the bay where the bomb had struck, and when I saw the memorial to my mates in the Welsh Guards.

I wanted it to be a very private moment, between me and my past – between me and the lads who had never come back. I was pretty sure I wouldn't be able to prevent the tears coming, and equally sure I didn't want this on camera. I had been exposed too much; I didn't fancy the idea of breaking down with the camera focused tight on my face. So, even before we set off from home, I told Malcolm: 'If you want this on film, you've only got one chance. No close-ups, no repeats.' I didn't want anything cheapening the moment for me. As always if I expressed myself forcefully enough, he accepted.

That morning we made the now familiar journey towards Mount Pleasant Airport, doubling back towards the coast a few miles outside Stanley.

For a couple of miles, it was a rough old track, following

the ruts of other Land Rovers, through farm gates, until we rolled into Fitzroy — a dozen scattered houses, a few sheepsheds. One of these, I supposed, was the one I'd been put in briefly after the bomb had struck, but I had no memories to help me identify which. Then on, feeling our way over boggy ground, past the inlet to the south of Fitzroy, up over the grass and bumpy pin-cushion plants on to a rise.

There below was the harbour, Port Pleasant, with a little bay, overlooked by several monuments. Behind us lay Port Fitzroy, the inlet that leads to Bluff Cove, bridged at its narrowest point as a short cut between the two settlements. I had seen virtually nothing of what had gone on ashore, but since then, having seen it, having listened to Gary and John, the past has become part of the present.

John and the other Paras knew there were no Argentinians around when they arrived. They knew because of a now-famous phone call made from Swan Inlet — half-way between Goose Green and Fitzroy — by a small group of Paras who had helicoptered along the coast, flying below thick mist. They were told that the Argentinians had destroyed the Fitzroy-Bluff Cove bridge, and pulled out. They were back at Goose Green with the good news an hour after their departure.

Using the only surviving Chinook to back up their own Scout and SeaKing helicopters, 2 Para were ferried by air from Goose Green, saving another miserable, foot-sore march overland. It was a speedy and dramatic operation — the Chinook took eighty men — that was over in hours. 2 Para were now just thirty miles from Stanley, but exposed, out on a limb, and in need of reinforcements. All the stores and heavy equipment needed would come by sea.

John's platoon dug in. After a dry night, they were ordered to the shore. Then, naturally, Sod's Law came into force — it chucked it down. By the time they arrived at the shore they were soaked. A landing-craft ferried them across the inlet to Fitzroy, where they sheltered in sheepsheds.

They were comfortable enough, warm, and well fed. They'd left most of their kit and bergens behind, but all this gear would be through soon, along with a whole mass of extras inherited from the casualties. A pal of John's from a posting in Kenya the previous year, Taff Reese, had asked him for a roll mat. John had promised one as soon as the casualties' stuff came through.

On 8 June, around midday, Taff had just arrived to pick up his mat, and John had just given it to him, when the jets came over. Nothing particularly odd about this – there had been a good deal of friendly flights over, and there had been no warning of an Argentinian raid.

Meanwhile, more troops were arriving by sea. It was a grim journey. Gary was among the Scots Guards taken half-way by *Intrepid* – not all the way, because this would have left the vessel exposed at dawn. Instead, he and the other Scots Guards were transferred into an open landing-craft twenty miles out to sea, and endured a nightmarish journey – seven hours of spray, rain and wind – round the coast.

Landing in darkness, they tabbed through another downpour to sheepsheds in Bluff Cove. Here, the next day, conditions improved. The sheepsheds offered a dry base. From here, the Guards were circulated out to two entrenched positions: one on a nearby rise overlooking the bay, and the other off in the opposite direction, on low ground. Even outside, they kept warm, because they were expecting air attack, and spent a couple of days building peat walls ten inches thick, which was what it would take to resist thirty-millimetre cannon fire.

They all told each other it was only a matter of time before an attack. The Argentinians were that close, up on Mount Harriet, eight miles away.

Next in line round the coast from San Carlos were the Welsh Guards in *Fearless*, yours truly included. Some 250

Welsh Guards made the same horrible journey in landing-craft. Luckily (or unluckily as it turned out) for me, I didn't have to endure this. There weren't enough landing-craft for us all, so we returned to San Carlos in *Fearless*. The next day, we boarded the *Sir Galahad*, already being loaded with Rapier rocket-launchers, vehicles and men from Field Ambulance and 5 Brigade's medical unit.

The two Welsh Guards commanders were told the destination was Bluff Cove, off Port Fitzroy. The ship was then to return to Port Pleasant to unload the Rapiers and Field Ambulance.

This was where *Galahad*'s troubles started.

We were soon aboard, but it took another six hours to finish loading. This time I spent happily settled on the open deck, which was like a car deck on a Channel ferry. By now it was well into the night. There was a risk we might not make it by dawn, so the orders changed: now we were to head for Port Pleasant, which would save travelling the last few miles.

But then what? Were the Welsh Guards also to land at Port Pleasant, ten miles from our final destination? No one said, and no one realized the hole in the plans.

We reached Port Pleasant after the 150-mile journey round the coast at about 8 a.m. It had been a clear, moonlit night, and it was a clear, bright day. There was no sign of any Argentinian aircraft – perhaps their spirit had been broken.

The day before there had been six landing-craft at Port Pleasant. By now, though, there was only one, plus a small pontoon raft.

The majors in command of landing operations at once saw the danger of leaving us all aboard. They had a solution: we could pile on to the raft and get towed ashore. Then we could tab across country to Bluff Cove.

This would have meant a tiring march and separation from our heavy equipment. Besides, we had been told we were getting a ride all the way to Bluff Cove. Our commander, Major 'Gunner' Sayle – always known by his nickname because his initials were G.N.R. – didn't want us messed about like this and exposed to danger out in the open without our defences.

Only at noon was a decision made: we would all be ferried round the corner in the landing-craft. But again we were delayed, because the Field Ambulance claimed priority. Another hour was lost getting them ashore. This at least gave the blokes ashore some defences – the Rapier rocket-launchers.

Then, to cap it all, came another problem. The loading ramp of the landing-craft became stuck. We would all have to climb down into the craft, after our gear was loaded by crane. Another delay.

We had been sitting there, in the clear light of day, and in full view of Argentinian troops up on Mount Harriet, for five hours – time enough for a message to get to Stanley, to Buenos Aires, and to Carlos's group in Río Gallegos.

Like a true squaddie, I was keen to get back down below to have a cup of tea. Tea and sticky buns – what could be better than that, instead of being outside getting our arses wet? We knew we had been on board a long while, but it really didn't register that we were in danger.

If only I could have had a quick word with Gary, dug in on his rise three miles away to the north. He knew well enough, because the day before two Skyhawks had had the cheek to try to shoot him up – him and a few others. The first time over, they were past before the Guards could grab weapons, but they were foolish enough to come around for a second go. Everyone and everything opened up: machine-guns, rifles, pistols, the lot. The first plane ran slap into a wall of metal, wobbled, smoked and crashed into the sea. The second plane veered off double quick.

The next day, 8 June, was even better for air attacks. It was the first really pleasant day Gary had seen. Compared with the misery of previous days, this was like midsummer. The guys took turns to dry out shirts and boots in the sun, ready for action at any moment, because in weather like this it would be crazy for the Argentinians not to attack. It was 'any minute now' right through the morning. Gary knew there was a resupply ship of some sort over the hill in Port Pleasant, but it never occurred to anyone that there would be troops on board.

So it was no great surprise when Carlos popped over the hills from the west and zoomed the length of Port Fitzroy. Of course, he was after ships, not troops, so he and his squadron were out over the water, and not at too much risk from the Guards' small-arms.

Seconds later, Carlos was banking to the right out over the sea when he spotted us, and turned into his bombing run.

When they heard the *boom!* the Paras in John's shed ran to defensive positions outside. Carlos was gone, but John and the others were in time to open up on the last three, forcing them to bank away. Scots Guards and Paras alike saw the smoke of the *Galahad* rising over the bay, but no one except those on the spot knew until much later that troops had been still on board. When they learned, it came as a huge shock. As Gary said, everyone knew – the soldiers knew, the civilians knew, even the *sheep* knew – that the Argentinian planes would be coming.

I changed into white shirt, Guards tie, blazer with Guards buttons, and grey trousers. I was determined to do this properly, and waited slightly apart as the crew set up the camera.

There were five memorials in all – three on the slope to my right, one straight ahead, and another the other side of the little bay. The number surprised me. I had been expecting just one – the one directly below me, which I could see was in honour of the Welsh Guards, because it was topped by a Celtic cross, with arms of equal length set in a circle.

Malcolm caught my eye, and nodded. As I started my march down towards the Welsh Guards' memorial, I found my mind still on the camera behind me. A silly thought struck me: what if I tripped, rolled down the slope, made myself look a complete idiot on camera? I squared my shoulders, and kept a measured pace.

Approaching the memorial I forgot the camera. Sadness touched me – a foretaste of what I expected when I saw the list of names. The wind was gusting from the south, over the low ridge the other side of the bay, but there were enough breaks in the cloud for occasional filtered sunlight to take the chill off and touch the dull brown landscape with gold. To my left lay the open Atlantic, and to my right lowlands rolling over towards Mount Pleasant. A bird high above me uttered shrill peeping cries.

Strangely, at this point, it was not sadness that filled my mind. I found myself staring round curiously, my mind filling with questions. Where exactly in the bay had the *Galahad* been lying? Where was I brought ashore? Where were we supposed to land? I couldn't remember. It had all happened so quickly. Perhaps I'd never known. Now I never would know. It struck me as odd to have come all this way, to be so close to the past, and yet not to be able to answer a few simple questions.

The memorial stood on a rocky headland some twenty feet above the little cove, which dropped away to the right. The stone was Welsh, too, I remembered. It came from Gelligaer Quarry, a mile or so up the road from Nelson. Twelve wreaths lay at the base, left over from Remembrance Sunday almost a month before.

Below the cross was a braided pattern, and below that again ran the names.

I started to read the names:
Burke, Carlyle, Dale, Dunphy, Edwards
– the old familiar names –
Elley, Gibby, Grace, Green, Griffiths.
How old was the oldest then – on 8 June 1982? Twenty-four, perhaps? 'They grow not old –
Hughes, Hughes, Jasper, Keeble
– as we that are left grow old' –

143

Kedghane, Marks, Mordecai, Newbury, Nicholson
– but they would have liked the chance to grow old. I
was lucky –
Parsons, Phillips, Poole, Rowberry, Sweet
– I would see my son grow up –
Thomas, Thomas, Thomas, Thomas
– I would grow old –
Walker (Sleep on, Yorkie)
– be remembered by my children, by my children's children –
Ward, Weaver, Wigley, Williams.
And no 'Weston', because I was lucky – I would be in
a country churchyard back home, not here listed in stone
between Weaver and Wigley, not two miles out to sea and
half a mile down.
'*Yn angof ni chant fod*' read the inscription underneath –
'We will remember them'.

I was alone with the memorial, the water and the moorlands.
I felt the wind through my blazer, and looked up. It was much
the same now as it was then: blue sky, scattered cloud, bit of
a wind.

I turned away, and walked along the path that skirted the
little bay. A lone cormorant watched from the rocks, and the
waves gently lapped the white sand. I looked briefly at the other
memorials: one to men of the Royal Fleet Auxiliary, and three
private crosses – including one to Gareth Hughes, the driver
of my section.

One final look out to sea. It was strange – the rush of
emotion I had been expecting had not come. There were
no ghosts, no sudden memories. I still couldn't work out
where we had been lying. I didn't see the two ships lying
out there, the landing-craft shuttling back and forth. No
screams, smoke, explosions. Anyone standing at this point
on 8 June would have seen Carlos's Skyhawk streaking in
from the left. It would have been easy enough to imagine it

– but I didn't. Meeting Carlos, experiencing the shock of the San Carlos memorial, remembering the landing – all this had already almost completely eroded the burden of the past.

No, my past was not here after all. My purpose in coming had been mostly fulfilled before I ever arrived.

10

THE ARGENTINIAN CEMETERY

29 November 1991

A task remained to be done, a promise to be fulfilled: back in Buenos Aires, Ignacio had asked me to honour the graves of his countrymen buried on the Falklands. The flowers themselves had been seized by customs in Chile, but there was nothing to prevent me fulfilling the spirit of the request, except one thing: Malcolm wanted to film me doing it.

Once again, I found myself caught in a conflict between what I wanted and the demands of filming. I didn't mind at all about placing flowers on Argentinian graves, if I was doing a favour to Ignacio. Standing in for those who couldn't make the journey themselves – that was fine, as a private individual. But it wouldn't *look* all that reverent, because that wasn't how I felt. I didn't want to give the impression that this was me, personally, honouring the graves of those who had killed our lads. If I did, I was sure there were many people back home who would find it offensive.

Malcolm said that it was my decision, and I was in a quandary.

It had turned into a beautiful day as we retraced the now familiar track towards Goose Green and Darwin, but still I felt

147

the pressure building. Once again, I was two people: a very private person committed to my own personal journey; but also a very public person making a film, and very committed to the person making that film. I didn't know how I was going to handle it.

For the first time, the sun shone hot from a clear blue sky. Tony turned off the track and led us off over the grass for a few hundred yards, rolling down into a shallow valley, sheltered from the breeze. We lay out on the long, clumpy grass. A line of hills blocked the view ahead. A jet from MPA cut across the sky, low down, following the crest of the hills. As its roar died away, silence returned. Apart from an abandoned house a few hundred yards away, there was neither sign nor sound of another human being.

We were back on the track again, swerving around road-building equipment and piles of newly scraped earth. The government was spending a fortune on this road, and it wasn't even going to stretch all the way over the Sussex Mountains to San Carlos. Apparently, it was ending on the west coast, a few miles north of Darwin. There was going to be a new ferry terminal for the link to West Falkland. But at the moment there were only a few dozen people in this part of East Falkland, and not many more across the sound in West Falkland. Who would be using the road? Tourists? Oil-workers?

In any event, the road was part of coming change. Change wouldn't be all bad. Not long ago, kids in the 'camp' were raised only to work. I heard of one man, only fifty years of age, who had started work for the Falkland Islands Company at the age of nine. For five pounds a month, he lived on an outlying island with a couple of teenagers for months at a time. He had virtually no education. There was a travelling teacher, but he never went out to the island.

Yet he and his wife still loved the isolation they were used to, and the road would mean an end to all that, at least around here. Today's kids are drawn to Stanley, because that's where the work is. San Carlos has shrunk. The patterns of sheep-farming are changing. Perhaps when the road is built San Carlos will die completely.

I wouldn't like to live like this, but there was something special about this isolation. I could imagine hordes of tourists tearing about the hills in cross-country vehicles. This is one of the world's last truly wild places, and there's enough of the romantic in me to feel a little sad at the passing of a way of life – and the passing, perhaps, of a wilderness.

To our right now, a high peak was coming into view, a flat-topped ridge of rock. The last time we made the trip it had been covered in cloud.

'Mount Usborne,' said Tony. It was 2,300 feet high – the highest on the islands. He said there was a big black lake behind it that was very beautiful and hardly ever seen by anyone. He planned to explore it some day.

We dropped down towards an inlet of the sea. Up to our left, on top of a bluff, lay the Argentinian War Memorial. Its position was well chosen, because it looked over the inlet to Goose Green and Darwin, the scene of the Paras' success in the first land action of the war. To our right as we slowed at the bottom of the rise lay Burntside, the start line for the Battle of Goose Green. There were some workmen converting it into lodgings for road-workers. It wasn't surprising it needed work, when you consider what happened there in the war.

We swung left, up a steep rise, and on to gently sloping grassland. There lay a small field of white crosses, surrounded by a white fence, squared off – a neat splash of white against the carpet of grass.

Though this was one of the few places you could drive without fear of becoming bogged down, the setting was wilder than San Carlos – and just as spectacular. The cemetery tilts inland towards the long flat ridge of Usborne and the Sussex Mountains. Over to the left there was a slight dip. This was where we had meandered over to San Carlos. Usborne was fifteen miles away, but you could see its grey flanks as clearly as if you were looking through a telescope. In between, and to right and left, swept the brown and yellow grassland.

The cemetery itself holds 230 crosses, in neat rows, all heading little gravel graves divided by well-trimmed grass. At the top of the field stands a larger white cross.

It was a peaceful setting, enough to make me feel a proper respect, even though these were Argentinian graves. As the engines died, however, an incongruous sound rose above the breeze. Three burly men were re-laying one of the grass verges. One of them, a bearded character in a rasta hat from St Helena, was singing his head off to the radio. It was playing the Monty Python song from the film *Life of Brian*: 'Always look on the bright side of life'. Gary and John had not been all that keen on the idea of coming here in the first place. Now the awful, cheery song –

> Always look on the bright side of death,
> Even when you take your ultimate breath

– inspired in them a brief and tasteless reversion to squaddie black humour. I understood. They had fought against some of the men buried here, and almost certainly killed several of them personally. ('I think this is one I prepared earlier,' muttered Gary.) They had seen some of their own comrades killed, possibly by bullets fired by one of the dead Argentinians. Everything had been done in the line of duty, and there was no hatred in them, but the idea of honouring enemy graves didn't seem right, especially as Gary was still serving.

Fortunately, I had good reason to disown them, because one of the grave-diggers, a Geordie, recognized me, and asked me to pose with him while his mates took a snap.

The crew was getting ready. The radio was switched off. I walked among the graves. There had been an official visit from family members in Argentina back in March. Despite the wind that battered this exposed spot, most of the crosses still had dried flowers fixed to them and beads draped around them. Odd, because over half the graves had no name. On most crosses, the words in English ran: 'An Argentinian soldier known only to God'. It seemed the visiting families, unable to find a grave with their own son's name on it, had simply adopted one.

John and Gary knew well enough why so many hadn't been identified. It wasn't simply that the bodies had no name-tags; quite often, there hadn't been enough of the body left to make up an individual. And if there were only 230 buried here, what had happened to the bodies of the other 100 identified on the memorial back in Buenos Aires? Were they the ones that people said had been burned over near Stanley? And again the thought came to me: how many others had there been burned, buried in trenches or dumped at sea? This was the only grave for Argentinians on the islands, yet Argentinians had died in many places. There must, at some time, have been many, many more.

Anyway, it was good that the powers that be had done their bit for these kids, whoever they were. Each one had been some mother's son, and he hadn't deserved death on a cold and barren place he had never wished to visit, let alone fight for.

Now Malcolm wanted to film, and my inner conflict gripped me again. I was keen to fulfil my promise to Gorriti, but was very wound up about being filmed doing it. The other two lads didn't have any problem – when Malcolm asked them, they chose not to accompany me. It was down to me, and I simply couldn't find an easy solution.

In the end, I did it both ways – and neither way. I was going to fulfil my promise. I couldn't allow the presence of a camera to prevent me from doing that. And I felt under too much of an obligation to Malcolm to refuse to be filmed.

I picked up the dried flowers, and walked up the centre of the cemetery, collar up to protect the back of my neck from the sun. At the cross, I was a little reassured to see that I was not the first from Britain to honour the Argentinian dead. A poppy wreath, with the crossed swords of the British Army, had been nailed to the cross. I should, perhaps, have laid the flowers gently and stood for a moment in silence. If the camera hadn't been running, if I hadn't felt any pressure, I'm sure I would have done.

As it was, with a quick gesture that expressed the turmoil I felt, I dropped the flowers down at the foot of the cross, then turned and walked away.

11

ATTACK AND DEFENCE

29 November 1991

A funny thing happened back in Stanley that evening. After the double strain of the visits to Fitzroy and the Argentinian Cemetery, I could have done without it.

Gary and I had been having a drink or two up at the Victoria. It had been a good evening, with everyone very friendly, because by now a lot of people knew me. 'But Simon,' Gary would say, acting surprised, 'what I can't understand is – how do they *recognize* you?' Cheeky sod. Anyway it was getting towards closing time, and they're super-strict about that down there. I don't know why – perhaps it's one of the few things they can be strict about. We had promised to show ourselves at Deano's as well. As Gary was deep in conversation, I said I'd hurry on down and get our orders in before closing time.

So there I was at the bar, on my own, ordering, when it happened.

Now, perhaps I should have been warned. There had been a lot of conversations, so many I can't remember, and I'd been free enough with my opinions about the Falklands. Naturally, I had never said I found it a heaven on earth. No one took offence. But there had been this one guy who, after talking for a bit, said: 'You're so friendly!'

'Is that a surprise, butt?'

'Well, yes, sort of. I heard someone say you were a bit anti.'

A bit anti? I had probably said at some point that I didn't think the place was me, that I found it a bit bleak, and a bit small, and I didn't think I'd be coming back. I certainly never intended to give offence, because all the people I'd spoken to had been wonderful. In that case, it was nothing, over as soon as raised. But later I realized: there are always people ready to take offence. I was talking to one of them right then.

'You won't have time to drink up,' said the barmaid aggressively, when I ordered.

'Oh, I think we will.'

'Who do you think you are,' she said with sudden anger that had me staring at her open-mouthed, 'coming down here, pretending to know all about us? I saw more action than you did anyway.'

She slammed the drinks down, took my money and backed off, leaving me to take the glasses through to another room, to Gary, who had just arrived.

'I do not believe what that bird just said to me,' I muttered, and passed on her words. As I did so, I really began to see red. What the hell did she mean, she *saw more than me*? She could have been no more than a kid in the war. Gary was trying to play it cool, but I was getting more and more steamed up.

The police were outside now, to ensure closing, and we were soon leaving. To do so, we went back through the bar, and there she was.

'Hey,' I said. I couldn't help it. I had to say something. 'There's no need for that sort of talk. There's . . .'

'You saw nothing!' She was shouting now. 'I was at Goose Green, and I saw more of the war than you saw!'

I really lost my rag then: 'You call being burned like this *"nothing"*?'

'You didn't even *meet* any Falkland Islanders!' she went on. 'There were other soldiers hurt besides you, you know. Why should you get all the attention?'

I couldn't believe it. I didn't ask to go down there, I didn't ask to get burned, didn't ask to have the documentaries made about me. I find myself a public figure, and people ask me questions, and I reply as honestly as I can, and be as friendly as I know how, and then it all backfires, out of the blue, as if she couldn't bear the fact that I was a real character, with my own opinions. Now she saw that I was a human being, not some simpering wimp, some injured dog she could slobber over, something seemed to explode in her. Here she was blaming me, full of resentment, not a flicker of sympathy or gratitude – to me or all the other lads – that she and her family had been rescued from Argentinian rule. Not that I expected garlands of love and joy, but I certainly didn't deserve to be virago'd and castigated by a barmaid who'd been a kid at the time.

There was no arguing with her, no point in arguing. I couldn't accept this right then, and kept trying to get through to her, but at least Gary could see sense, and somehow got me to leave. 'Why did she *say* that?' I kept repeating, 'Why did she *say* that?' I couldn't understand what she was talking about. The anger I felt was as much surprise and shock at her unfairness. God, I had seen action! I had suffered! True, I hadn't actually killed anyone – was that what she blamed me for? True, I'd tried to save lives – would she have been happier if I hadn't? Or was it the fact of my survival that bothered her? Would she rather I were dead?

Back at the hotel, Malcolm and the others began to talk me down. It took a while – an hour, two hours, I don't know – but gradually I relaxed. With their help, I saw that my feelings – anger at being insulted, self-righteous indignation at being unfairly accused – were not the point.

'Use it,' Malcolm kept saying of the whole episode. 'Use it.'

Eventually I saw what he meant. I could never have argued her out of her anger even if we'd talked all night. She had something in her mind, and she was sticking to it. I should have seen that. Besides not being a killer, and surviving, my third mistake – joking apart – had been to take her seriously. I should never have got angry, should never have engaged. There would always be people out there wanting to have a go. Anyone with experience of being in the public eye ought to know this.

Especially me, especially now. As Gary said, 'You better get ready for it, because you don't know what will be coming your way after the programme goes out. You ought to be able to take this sort of thing, and let it roll off.'

True, very true. I would have to do better, because it would happen again sooner or later.

1 December 1991

Sooner, as it happened.

Two days later, a Saturday, Gary and I had been to the disco. It must have been about 1 a.m. We were on our way out, along with a cheerful crowd. The mood was good, as usual, because most of the crowd knew us by now, but outside the door – Gary remembered later – there were two girls looking daggers at me. He could see something was up. And this time it wasn't quite out of the blue – we had seen the two of them before, at one of Deano's karaoke nights. They were loud, very loud. We came surging through the door, and suddenly I was aware of this massive yeti creature in front of me. Faith, her name was. I swear she was almost as big as me, with short fair hair and jeans, looking a good deal tougher than her squaddie boyfriend.

'Hey,' she said. 'You saw nothing! You did nothing in the war! What makes you so great?'

She was drunk, and spoiling to have a go. Obviously she

and the barmaid had got together, because their words were so similar. And obviously she was expecting to get the same sort of reaction from me. People crowded round. Gary, who knows what's what in close-quarter combat, wasn't going to give me a chance to repeat my reactions of two nights before.

'Don't you talk about the war,' he said to her. 'You may have been in it, but Simon's wearing it.'

'Only his head and his hands,' she shouted.

'And his back, and his stomach and his chest.'

'Don't give me that shit!' She turned to me: 'What do you want, sympathy? You're rich, you are! You drive a BMW and a Mercedes!'

'Well, actually, he drives a Peugeot 205,' said Gary mildly.

'I don't want to hear that!' she yelled. 'You only look like that because you want to!'

'Oh?' To my relief, I realized I was not in the least angry. It's wonderful what a little training can do. 'You think I wanted to have forty-six operations?' I asked calmly. Not being angry was a relief. I could see her for what she was. I could see the viciousness and anger in her; I could see how simply accepting the attack would make it harmless.

'My sister's a nurse and she told me you can change your face.'

'You're right,' I said. 'You're absolutely right.'

'She knew someone who was burned, and he looks perfect now!'

'You're right,' I said again. Obviously she knew nothing about plastic surgery. I knew now there was no way she could get to me. 'You know all about my life. You know me better than I know myself.'

Poor girl, now she was looking foolish, and she knew it, and this made her really wild. 'You just keep looking like that to *make money*!'

'You know best,' I repeated reasonably. Two nights earlier,

the accusation would have stung me. Tonight, it stung someone else.

Gary saw this girl nearby draw her arm way back and throw a punch like he'd never seen anyone throw before. Her fist must have travelled six feet. Before I knew it, this fist flew past me and landed Faith a crack in the chops. Anyone else would have fallen. I would have, probably. But Faith just rocked back, and then lunged forward.

I looked round. My protector, Cathy, clearly had it in for Faith anyway, and had been driven into a fury by the suggestion that I was cashing in on my face. She was much smaller, but looked pretty ferocious. Gary caught hold of her, and held her back, swinging her round and buckling her knees, and then protecting her with his back from Faith's retaliation.

Now Faith was grabbed by some of the crowd, and started thrashing about, like a caged animal, shouting 'Let me get at her! Let me get at her!' and Cathy was looking as wild as a tiger, but Gary was already handing her over to her boyfriend and telling him to take her away.

Faith suddenly seemed to decide enough was enough, and started to back off. She made a final lunge, to be blocked by Gary. 'Stop it,' he said. 'It's not worth it.'

There was one final explosion when Cathy reappeared holding a bottle, looking as if she really meant business, but Gary sorted this out as well. Then Faith was on her way, almost as if nothing had happened, and Cathy was lost in the crowd with her boyfriend, and everyone started to disperse. People were apologizing for the whole thing, hoping I didn't think this was the way all Falkland Islanders behaved.

No apologies needed. I was beginning to see the funny side. Faith had been so wild she had made a complete fool of herself. As we walked back to the hotel, I began to feel sorry for her. I would be on my way home soon, but she would have to stay on in a small community where everyone knows everything, living with the consequences of what she was and what she had done.

12

TUMBLEDOWN

2 December 1991

Gary and John had begun to fill the last hole in my experience.
The stream of jokes and stories had reminded me of life as
a squaddie; I'd seen Goose Green; but I still hadn't really
understood what they had been through. For this I had to
wait until our last day, when the filming was over, and we
had time to walk the windy battlegrounds of Tumbledown and
Wireless Ridge.

The plan had been to attack Stanley on 8–9 June, but the
Galahad disaster, among other logistical problems, forced
delays. Delay was dangerous. The Argentinian troops were
well dug in, well prepared and their base in Stanley was
close. They could wait; we couldn't. Our men were at the
point of a supply line stretching back to San Carlos, and
beyond to ships at sea, to Ascension, to the RAF bases in
England. Delay risked injuries from exposure and losses of
food, equipment, ammunition and men, all of which would
be hard to make good.

The plan called for a two-stage battle: Longdon, Two Sisters
and Harriet to be taken on one night. Then, with artillery

carried forward in support, 2nd Battalion Scots Guard were to take Tumbledown, with the Gurkhas following through to take Mount William. In the north, 2 Para were to take Wireless Ridge. The whole plan was risky. If it were to fail, exposure would take its toll. There were few reserves. Failure at this point might mean negotiating a settlement with the Argentinians.

Longdon, Two Sisters and Harriet all fell on 11–12 June for the loss of twenty-three men. A good start. A day's delay followed, to allow time to complete reconnaissance, but already the RAF, the Navy and artillery were battering Tumbledown and Wireless Ridge. The Scots Guards were helicoptered up from Bluff Cove to dig in behind a low rise known as Goat Ridge. Gary, second-in-command of his section, which was part of Left Flank Company, which was one of the battalion's three companies, was one of the first arrivals. Just before dropping into the dead ground below Goat Ridge, he was heartened by the sight of Tumbledown, two miles ahead, lit up by explosions. The Argentinians would be lucky to have any survivors at all up there.

As the Wessexes thumped back and forth, artillery and mortar shells rained in. Surrounded by the roar of planes and the boom and crash of artillery, the Guards dug hard, fast and deep. It rained, near-freezing rain. Not that you notice being cold and wet in the middle of an artillery barrage. No one cared about the water in the trenches any more – better wet than dead.

Once the trenches were dug, the Argentinian artillery would not have been a major worry. You could hear the explosion in the gun, and would know that forty seconds later the shell would land. Plenty of time to take cover. Except that every ten minutes a helicopter would land, ironing out the sound of the gun firing. By pure luck, only one man was injured.

Tumbledown was out of sight, but the Guards were well briefed about what lay ahead. The mountain was a long spine of rock, 650 feet high, its upper slopes made of sharp pinnacles jutting up from an extraordinary, steep shield of rock, smooth as a tortoise-shell. At its edges, the shell broke into huge boulders that gave good cover. Below, a succession of tortuous rock rivers divided rough fields of grass and peat. Other troops lay invisible in dozens of trenches and foxholes. The Argentinians were well entrenched – or rather had been, before the bombardment. From the sound of things, there wouldn't be many of them left.

After dark, the battalion moved up to the bottom of the ridge, waiting, with all three companies – Left Flank, Right Flank and 'G' – in position. They fixed bayonets: they'd heard the story of a guy without a bayonet coming up against an Argentinian, squeezing the trigger, only to find his magazine was empty. Click. The Argentinian picked up his weapon and shot him dead. No Scots Guard was going to make that mistake.

From a mile away, the sound of battle – a diversionary attack to the south, towards Mount William. It was then, waiting, as the cold began to seep into him, that Gary's feelings sharpened. Fear was part of it. Like everyone else, in case anything were to happen to him, Gary had written his last letter home, and given it to a mate. Anyone who says they don't feel fear at this point is a liar. But there was more than fear – there was anticipation and excitement. He was just lying there, looking up at the clear sky, having a last fag, when a shooting-star flashed overhead. He'd seen a couple before. There's nothing mystical about Gary, but the stars suddenly seemed like good omens. He felt he would be OK. He was eager to get into action.

After half an hour or so the move came, in silence – radio silence as well. Reports of progress would be carried by runners. The commander of Left Flank, Major John Kiszley, stepped forward, and shadows shifted in the darkness. You only knew the operation had begun when the man next to you moved. The recce platoon eased forward, leaving torches pointing back and down to mark the way. 'G' Company led on, across the official start line – a fence – to take out the first heavy machine-gun post, leaving the three platoons of Left Flank to follow when the position was clear.

Almost at once, the British artillery, mortars and machine-guns opened up from behind and from Mount Harriet on the right, to give any survivors on Tumbledown something to think about while the infantry moved silently forward.

A shadow – a runner reporting back. 'G' Company had reached the machine-gun post. No one there. Great. They'd all been killed, or fled. Perhaps the whole mountain had been abandoned. Left Flank moved forward to 'G' Company, through them, and on.

But only for fifty metres. The enemy hadn't all gone. They were right there. Gary and the rest of his company were almost on them when they were seen.

Suddenly, a new and shocking reality. Games, rehearsals, training, talk, briefings, all the knowledge, nothing prepares you for the reality. From a few yards ahead, a single burst of fire, and then twenty, thirty bursts, a wall of red-hot tracer. The only response – flatten yourself. Find any possible cover: a stone, a mound of earth, anything. Novices instantly learn a new skill – how to collapse your chest one extra inch. White light above. You see the enemy, they see you. A shooting gallery. Bullets inches above your head, rocks cracking into shrapnel beside you, a man shot through his cap-star a few yards away.

Incredible. All that bombardment, yet they had survived – more than survived. Gary showed me why. He led me up into the high slopes, right under the edge of the strange smooth shell of rock. There was a cave, still littered with boots, cartridge cases, wire. It was a natural air-raid shelter. In fact, all along the mountain, the boulders and crags had all made superb shields. Despite the massive twenty-four-hour barrage, the Argentinians had sustained only one casualty. All that sophisticated weaponry, all that money, and at the end of the day, it was down to the man with a bayonet.

For long seconds, a minute, two minutes, nothing but shock, noise, confusion. Then the training began to work. Shock died. Adrenalin flowed. Exhilaration, and fear, and so many emotions, and you couldn't afford any of them, because the only way to survive was: return fire. Crawl forward. Form sections. *Win the fire-fight.*

To help, according to the textbook, the company commander would call in a 'creeping barrage', with artillery landing shells fifty metres ahead. Then the Guards would advance, and take the position trench by trench, foxhole by foxhole.

But no textbook ever prepares you for what actually happens. Artillery rounds ahead, yes. But there were rocks. Metal shrapnel, rock shrapnel. Men being hit by shrapnel, Jesus – their *own* shrapnel. A rogue barrel landing shells in among their own men. All the barrels were controlled by computer. The only way to discover the rogue was to retrain the lot at a safe spot and test-fire them in sequence. That would take time.

No more artillery. The attack lost momentum, perhaps the most crucial element in any attack, and stalled, halted, broke into a collection of half a dozen small battles. Now it was down to section commanders to win their own fire-fights.

The enemy soldiers in the rocks above and ahead were jubilant. These were the men under Carlos Vazquez, who had talked so graphically and emotionally to Gary in Buenos Aires. In the darkness between flares, one over-confident character even shouted out in English: 'Surrender to the Argentinian Army!' He stood up to shout it, making himself visible in night-viewing devices. Idiot. A hail of fire, a scream, and down he went. He must have been dead on arrival at the floor of his trench.

A trench thirty-five metres in front of Gary and his section. But the trench had a wall of rock. Automatic fire couldn't get through. He needed an M66 anti-tank rocket to destroy the trench. But the guy with the launchers was behind, pinned down by enemy fire. No help from the section to the left

– out of shouting range. And the section commander didn't want to move.

Gary said to him: 'Look, we have to take them out.'

'No. Leave it! Leave it!'

He only wanted to survive. But they all wanted to survive, and to survive some action had to be taken. If you don't get them, they'll get you – in this case, by cutting between the two sections. Each second's delay increased the danger.

Impossible to move, must move.

'We *have* to take them out!'

'Then you'll have to do it.'

Everyone looking at him, the section's No. 2. The looks said: what do we do? Suddenly, he was alone. No one to help, no one else to look to. The immediate, urgent desire: to keep down, hide, vanish. Fear of moving, because it risked death right now; but not moving meant death later; *if you don't get them, they'll get you.* Must lead, must lead by example. Can't move, must move . . . until one thing broke through – fear of showing fear to others. Only one thing to do: face the fear. Survival, his survival, the survival of them all, depended right at that moment on his bravado. No, not bravery, he was no braver than anyone else. He just knew, with certainty, what had to be done, and there was no one else to do it.

Move!

Crawl near enough to the guy with the M66 for him to toss over a launcher, crawl back, fire the rocket. That got their heads down. Make the rest of the section keep firing. Crawl forward, flash a red warning torch back to the lads to stop covering fire, toss in a phosphorus grenade, reach over with the self-loading rifle, fire off a magazine to stop them picking up the grenade and tossing it back.

Phosphorus grenades are nasty things. The phosphorus, which clings to every splinter of metal, burns anything it touches. Even a fragment landing gently on your hand will burn straight through in seconds. So after one explodes in a trench, there's a hiss and smell of scorched flesh, followed by a final burst of fire, just to make sure.

The log-jam broke. It was fourteen below, and snow was beginning to gust across the slopes, but no one was aware of this, with the adrenalin flowing, the section moving as a team, pepperpotting forward, following this madman doing crazy things.

Gary was not alone in this. All three of the other section commanders were later mentioned in dispatches. He was in a world where every man in authority had to act crazy to make others do the same. All around, a dozen, a score of crazy men, acting as though they were invulnerable, ran, crept, fired, threw, ran, crept, fired . . .

Near him men were dying on both sides. At one point in the light of a flare, Gary saw a man shot, a glimpse of horror, taking a tracer in the stomach. Tracers are made luminous by phosphorus. The man saw the bullet enter. He knew the bullet would simply fry his insides. In instantaneous reaction, he plunged his whole hand into the open wound to seize the bullet. He sank to his knees, and died, kneeling, his hand still lodged inside his stomach, and a look of horror on his face.

On, taking out trench after trench, ducking from rock to rock. The trenches are still there, and so are some of the rocks. One had received a direct hit from a mortar. A soldier had been sheltering behind it. The rock had exploded, blasting the soldier with a rain of rock splinters. As Gary threw himself down beside the body, he saw there was nothing left of it. It had been riddled, turned into a sieve. Everything inside had leaked out. The body was as flat as an empty cushion.

Here was a foxhole that Gary knew for certain was one of his — a deep hole dug beneath a boulder. Around the top of the hole was a battlement of turf. It had been a great protection during the artillery barrage — it could have taken a direct hit from an M66. For an infantryman, though, it had been dead easy. A grenade in the hole, a burst of fire, and they were well cooked.

Only after an hour, two hours, perhaps more, when they had covered no more than a few hundred yards, trench by trench, did the shells start falling ahead of them again. Kiszley could reorganize the company, ready them for another push, on for a mile more, to the end of the ridge.

We reached another foxhole, this one not blasted to bits. There were toothpaste tubes, bits of poncho torn by shrapnel and the wind, old shoes, water-bottles and a bloody bandage on the ground.

'Look at this.' Gary held up a shredded glove. 'This bloke must have been holding his grenade when he was hit and it went off.' This was probably the reason for the bloody bandage. 'Looks like they were throwing in their hands already.'

Some were, poor bastards. Down there, on the lower slopes, they were mostly conscripts, utterly unprepared for the cold, some so filthy and demoralized they were covered in their own excrement. They had had dysentery. Their clothing was caked, right up their backs. Officers and better-trained troops were up above with the snipers. Many of them fled, many surrendered. Many more would have surrendered if they'd had the time, but in the heat of battle there was no time. It's a risky business to stop, disarm, and tie and hood a prisoner. Lose the momentum of battle, and you lose the battle.

On to open grass, uphill towards the end of the main ridge, falling into shell-craters every few paces, with more exploding all around as retreating Argentinians called in artillery fire behind them – impossible to see the holes in the dark and the crazy shadows of the flares, with your eyes blinded by tracers, and flares, and star-shells.

Up ahead, silhouetted in the light of the blasts and explosions and fire-fights and distant mortar-flares, Major Kiszley was flung backwards by a burst of machine-gun fire.

'Fuck's sake!'

Everyone hit the deck, thinking they were all about to get taken out. But to their astonishment, Kiszley stood up again.

He'd taken two rounds, and should have been dead. One had lodged in his compass, the other hit the bayonet-scabbard at his waist. He got away with heavy bruising on his hips, nothing more.

'Come on!' he shouted, as if aggrieved that the others were slowing things down.

Ahead, a jumble of rocks, silhouetted by a dim orange glow. The rocks – this was as far as they had to go. Into the rocks, only nine of them left out of thirty, but the momentum was still there.

They reached the rocks, and looked over. By now, the darkness was beginning to lighten. There, for the first time, Gary saw the lights of Stanley. For the last two weeks he had seen nothing but sea and moor. Stanley had been the objective, the purpose of the battle and the war, but he'd forgotten all about it. And there it was, not blacked out, but glowing like fairy lights in the twilight. He was astonished. Gob-smacked. It was so close it looked as though they could just take it.

Not yet. A hail of fire, from another rocky redout 100 metres ahead, down the far slope. Instantly, they were back under cover of the rocks. Below, Right Flank were working their way around. Gary and his section knew what they had to do: return fire, and allow Right Flank to take the enemy out. Behind, the battle was still in progress for the higher ground. It would take another hour of fierce fighting to take it.

Exhilarated by victory and the fact of their survival, they 'went firm'. Gary picked up a GPMG and began firing down on the rocks ahead. Behind him, under cover, the others were checking their kit, re-distributing ammunition picked up from the wounded, watching cowering prisoners – some of them teenagers looking like middle-aged men, haggard with hunger, and exposure and the strain of battle. Half an hour passed. At some point, Gary and one of the others, Dalgleish, went forward to drag back a couple of Guards who had been wounded in the assault on the rocks ahead.

Daylight. On the slopes below, other Guards were working their way up, with casualties, while Argentinian troops were heading out, into the valley, and towards Stanley. Many were helping wounded or carrying casualties in stretchers. No longer targets, they went untouched.

As the noise of battle began to die along the length of the mountain, twenty or twenty-five Guards started to help the newly-bandaged wounded down the hillside to a regimental aid post. They were making their way across open ground a couple of hundred yards down, when mortar rounds exploded in and around them. A single volley, no one knew where from. Eight, nine, ten men were down, the rest diving for cover.

Gary and several others ran down to help. It was like a butcher's shop. He'd seen nothing like it. Four men dead, perhaps eight others wounded. Meat everywhere. A man simply blown to pieces. Gary was about to help one of the wounded, a skinny lad, lying unconscious. Then, more mortar rounds, not so accurate this time. The boy sat up. Gary laid him down. He sat up again. Explosions, shrapnel flying. Gary forced him down, and kept him down, almost covering him with his body. The body below him reacted again, with a powerful jerk, jack-knifing Gary off his upper body on to his legs. It was a convulsion. The boy had been dead all along.

This was different. This was not simply shocking, but outside anything that anyone should ever have to see or tolerate. Casualties, harmless men, dying for nothing, when not far away Argentinian casualties were going free. You'd think that after what he'd been through, nothing more would have touched Gary. Wrong. Now there was a real anger, personal antipathy. It wouldn't last, but right then it only needed a target to find an outlet.

Back up in the rocks, focusing again on the remaining nest of Argentinians ahead, suddenly a round smacked into a rock by Gary. A sniper, somewhere behind them.

Another round. Crack-and-thump – the crack of the bullet,

the thump of the gun firing. That gave the direction. Flash-crack-thump. Now they knew where he was, and watched for him as he fired twice more, moving between shots. Not a great marksman.

'You and you, come with me,' said Kiszley to Gary and Eddie Collins. Gary picked up his GPMG, 200 rounds of ammunition and a 66 anti-tank rocket. It wasn't hard to trace the sniper. They spotted him as he was scrambling up rocks 100 metres away. It was an easy shot. Gary had the 66 prepared. The sniper was just trying to lever himself into a better position, pushing himself up backwards on to a ledge above the cliff that cuts off Tumbledown to the north, when Gary fired. The rocket hit the guy in the thighs. His lower legs, still in their boots, plopped straight down, and the rest of him vanished up and over the cliff.

'Should have apologized really, Simon,' he said, staring up at the rocks. 'You're always supposed to say "Sorry" when you hit someone with a rocket. But I was angry.'

He returned to the end of the ridge.

Below, the Argentinians were fleeing, walking off the mountain, in a slow, random stream towards Stanley.

Today, the end of Tumbledown is capped by a memorial, a cross standing at the head of a track weaving up from the moorland. The view from the ridge now was much as Gary had seen it that dawn: over to the left, the long rise of Wireless Ridge; Stanley lying at the base of a gentle slope of drought-tinged brown grass, broken by patches of open peat — here and there black peaty pools mirroring the sky.

It had taken six hours in all. What had it felt like, really?

'In some ways, Simon, they were the best six hours of my life. I was that close to the edge. It was better than any bird I've ever had, better than any car I've ever driven. Up there, I decided who lived and who died. I was God. That's how it felt.'

Now, that's a truth, and soldiers know it. But I'd never heard it said with such power and honesty.

There are other answers, longer-term ones, and he gave me these, too. He did what he had to do, but he was scarred by the experience. Like me, he had survived, while others had died. Both of us felt the wound of guilt. But unlike me in another way, he felt that perhaps his craziness that night had led others to their deaths.

I would say the opposite. I'd say that perhaps his craziness was the greatest sanity, and that by fighting well and leading well, he had saved lives.

But then, he'll never know, and the guilt will never completely heal.

13

WIRELESS RIDGE

2 December 1991

While Gary was waiting in the pool of silence and darkness in the lee of Goat Ridge for Tumbledown to begin, John was waiting to start the fight for Wireless Ridge. He described his experience of the battle as we walked together up the rough flank of the ridge from Moody Brook, the stream that separates Wireless Ridge from Tumbledown, then along the peaty, rocky crest.

He and his platoon had been lifted over by helicopter, to assemble behind Mount Kent. During the assaults on Harriet, Longdon and Two Sisters, 2 Para tabbed around Kent to the back of Longdon, while senior officers checked the next objective, Wireless Ridge.

In fact, the ridge was two ridges: one to the north, out of sight of Stanley, and one that runs along the far side of Stanley Harbour – a five-mile rise that begins opposite Tumbledown and ends beyond Stanley itself. Other companies of 2 Para were to seize the northern section; 'D' Company, including John's 12 Platoon, were to take the ridge fringeing the harbour.

The mood was very different from the build-up to Goose

Green. Then, the lads were ignorant. Now, they were veterans. They knew it would be a hard fight, knew there would be a lot of bullets coming their way. John offered no false hopes, telling his lads coldly that some of them would not be coming back, and that the best way to ensure survival was to remember what they'd been taught. Here, if anywhere, the enemy would make a stand. It was the last defence before Stanley. If Wireless Ridge went, the war was as good as over.

Because of their experience at Goose Green, some of the men were more apprehensive, and some thought it was unfair to impose on them a second time when they were meant to be a reserve battalion – 'Let someone else have a go.'

'Shut up, you lot. We were reserve before. It makes no difference.'

Besides, almost all of them had bad feet, with open sores still unhealed from the marches over the Sussex Mountains. It was a painful business squeezing on damp boots a size or more too small for their cracked and swollen feet.

They drew some strength from the knowledge that the far end of the ridge was to be taken by 'friendly forces', which they knew could only mean the SAS. For this reason the Paras were to stop advancing when they reached a line of telegraph poles across the ridge near the end of the estuary.

Waiting to start, a bitter wind froze all of them as they stood or sat, loaded down with the usual sixty pounds of ammunition. Some of them kicked rocks to work some feeling back into their numbed feet.

As soon as movement began across the start line, the cold was forgotten. The effort of carrying ammunition and weapons uphill, and the flow of adrenalin made you forget everything except the moment. This time there was no attempt to disguise the advance. Artillery shells began to blast the rocky heights, and flares – 'illum' – lit the whole area. The gunners had pre-recorded all Argentinian positions, and every company had an FOO (forward observation officer) to report the advance by radio and ensure that the supporting barrage was always landing a 'bound' – 250 metres – ahead.

Up ahead, silhouetted by artillery blasts, was the ridge, but with no real opposition yet. At one point, though, an artillery round landed nearby. John happened to be close to a young private, the medic, Jerry Godfrey. A piece of red-hot shrapnel whanged off a rock, and whizzed through the sleeve of Godfrey's windproof. Both of them dived for cover, with John on top. As they got up, Godfrey wiped his hands over his face in relief. 'That was close,' he muttered. Then his expression changed, and he sniffed. Argentinians had used the place as a latrine. His hands had been covered with excrement. So now, too, was his face.

'God!' said John. 'You'll be the death of us! Get away! Go and collect some two-inch mortar rounds!'

They climbed the ridge, and began to work their way along it. Still no opposition. A bunker off to the right, down in the valley, looked as if it was abandoned. John sent off two lads to check.

At first John's twenty men were close to two other platoons, 10 and 11, but somehow his lot were already moving faster than the others. Up ahead was a fortress of rock, silhouetted in the light of the flares. It was a natural defence, and everyone advanced warily, expecting fire.

To his surprise, nothing. The rocks were abandoned. The Argentinians had pulled out in a hurry, perhaps at the sight of the British advance, perhaps due to the artillery. They had left their radio sets behind, still switched on.

12 Platoon emerged from the rocks, and for the first time saw the full range of the darkened valley, Moody Brook below, flashes and explosions from the flanks of Tumbledown, and in the distance, a sudden brilliance.

'Sarge, look! The lights are on in Stanley!'

'Shut up, and keep moving.' John was more interested in the tail-lights of vehicles he could see down on the floor of the valley.

John turned back briefly to shepherd in the lads he'd sent off to clear the bunker, and eased forward again to rejoin the rest of the platoon. Overhead was the reassuring rush of friendly artillery shells, crashing down on the ridge ahead.

At this moment, however, hell broke loose. The noise of the shells overhead was suddenly different, not a whoosh, but an ominous whistle. They were falling short. John threw himself down, and hoped. Six rounds, a barrage from all six guns, landed together, among the group, exploding in the rocks with a fury of shrapnel and rock fragments.

As the noise died, John heard his company commander, Major Philip Neame, going mad with the FOO, telling him in the most vivid terms what he could do with his guns. Someone, somewhere, had blundered, seriously, because on the other side of the rocks a man was killed and another injured.

It took an hour to re-range the guns, while the Paras waited in the shelter of the rocks.

Once this was sorted out, they moved on over open ground towards a second mass of rocks. The artillery barrage was now steady again, but the rocks some 200 yards ahead presented a formidable obstacle. They poked up through the top of the ridge in a cluster of pinnacles, like some crazy castle with a motley collection of turrets and battlements.

Out there in the open there was no good cover. As soon as John and his men walked out of the rocks, down the soft grassy slope, flares burst overhead. They were clear as targets in a fairground.

A shout in Spanish, then a curtain of fire came at them from the rocks.

Instantly, the men hit the deck, finding whatever cover they could – low stones, clumps of earth, tiny dips in the peat.

John knew that they had to move, and yelled for them to get their heads up and return fire, force the enemy down, create a lull for a further advance. Risking himself, he ran, bent double, to the closest men, shouting at them to return fire.

It was a classic infantryman's nightmare: to return fire, they had to put themselves in view of the enemy, with flares drifting down overhead, creating a strange scene of shifting shadows, and with rounds zipping overhead and smacking into the soil.

Within a few minutes, as men realized that they had survived the onslaught, they peeked above their cover long enough to aim and fire. John led half a dozen men forward. Right by them was a pond, a pit of black. The lads ran round to either side, still in the open, heading across the flat ground to a little rise hardly visible except as a dark shadow cast by the flares.

They threw themselves down again, aimed, fired, stood, then on another fifty yards towards the base of the rocks. Once there, John knew, they would be on equal footing with the Argentinians.

He looked back. There was a body on the ground.

New orders: flares from the two-inch mortar, fire at any positions the men could see, identify the next piece of cover, and then, as soon as the flare faded into darkness, two men – Jerry Godfrey, the medic, was one of them – to run back and drag in the man who was down.

It was Fred Slough, badly hit, barely conscious. He had a bullet through the head. Godfrey began to patch him up. For some reason, Fred tried to tear the bandages off. He also had a chest wound, but they didn't see that till later.

Within minutes, the sergeant major, summoned over the radio, was up with them, organizing Godfrey and three others, one from another platoon, to act as stretcher-bearers. They headed back, doubled over, hitting the deck with each artillery burst, until they vanished in the rocks behind.

Fred survived until he reached hospital, but died later, the only casualty to die while in the expert hands of the Army medics.

Sixteen men left.

Meanwhile, John had sent Gosling and Spencer to one

175

side to clear another bunker just down from the top of the ridge.

Though reduced, the platoon was in with a good chance now. They were well protected by rock. By firing flares, they could see where the Argentinians were, and spot the next piece of cover. As the light died, eight kept firing, while the others ran forward. Then, when they were 'firm', they could do the same for their comrades.

A couple of such pepperpotting manoeuvres, and they were deep enough into the rocks to use grenades to take out individual positions. The results were still there to see — rocks shattered and scarred, exposing pink bits beneath the outer covering of grey.

Fighting forward, the Paras now found positions manned only by the dead and wounded. No one bothered with the wounded. In the heat of action, as John had told his men, it was often too dangerous to look after your own wounded — better to return for them later, when you've secured your position — so Argentinian wounded were simply disarmed, if they were lucky, and left unattended until after the battle.

The able-bodied Argentinians had retreated along the ridge, and then downhill towards Stanley, leaving the mess of two months of occupation: ponchos, toothpaste tubes, bottles, food (especially tins of bully beef), clothing, all peppered by shrapnel. It was all still there when John and I walked the ridge together, along with a pile of cow-bones marking a kitchen area and communication wires for field telephones snaking away to the company HQ further along the ridge, tucked down on the Stanley side.

John returned over the open ground to find the other two, who should have been back from clearing the bunker. He was surprised to find Major Neame standing on his own, with his radio, controlling the artillery. Neame was slight in build, but large in personality: calm, clear-thinking, quiet, dry sense of humour, always a move ahead, always visible, always accessible, and always ready to let his subordinates get on with the job. Wherever the action was thickest, that's where he would be. Good man.

'Hello, Meredith,' he said. 'What's up?'

John explained about the two he was looking for, then asked: 'Where's the rest of your headquarters, sir?' Neame should have had radio operators and the FOO with him.

'Oh, I've lost them somewhere.'

'Where's 10 Platoon, then?'

'They should be on your left, Meredith.'

'Well, there's nobody there, sir,' said John, and moved on.

He had just spotted his two lost sheep coming up the slope towards him when he heard raised voices from behind a nearby rock. Two of 10 Platoon's NCOs were arguing about whether they should be advancing or not. One was saying he'd been told to go forward by the platoon commander; the other replied: 'Well, I'm not moving until he comes and tells me.'

John stepped round the corner, and ordered them both forcefully to move up right now, and stop leaving 12 Platoon's flank exposed.

'See,' said the first as they hurried off. 'Told you.'

John collected the two privates, and returned to his own platoon, still safely in the rocky fortress.

Minutes later, they were out of the rocks, advancing over open grass, because suddenly there were no more enemy troops, and they were at the line of poles that marked their objective. Below them, the lights of Stanley glowed. They couldn't go any further without risking an encounter with the SAS, who were supposed to be advancing from the opposite direction.

It wasn't over yet. There were still bullets coming in from Tumbledown, and a few from snipers who had been bypassed in the rush forward. Bullets and glowing pieces of shrapnel zipped overhead, smacked into the grass or ricocheted off rocks.

John took shelter behind a rock. In the lull, he became aware of new sounds, shouts from over the edge of the ridge, down towards Moody Brook.

'Minnock!' John shouted across to a gunner who had a decent view. 'What can you see down there?'

A pause, then: 'I can't see anything, Sergeant.'

'Use your night-sights, dimwit.'

Another pause. 'Christ! There's hundreds of them!'

Some of the more determined Argentinians had launched a counter-attack up the hill from Moody Brook, right towards the Paras. It turned out that this counter-attack, one of the bravest actions in the war, was launched not by the regulars who had fled from the ridge, but by armoured car crewmen, from the vehicles John had seen earlier, followed by members of another company based on the lower slopes of Tumbledown, perhaps 150 men in all. There seemed to be three waves to the attack, one of which actually got within grenade range. ('Cheek!' said John, remembering.)

Fortunately, they were inexperienced, and fighting uphill, and knew the war was nearly lost. Perhaps it was to stimulate their morale that they had been shouting on the way up. That had only served to give away their position.

The 16 Paras, using four machine guns, and calling in artillery, fought off the attack in less than half an hour, without loss or injury to anyone. The only consequence was that a couple of snipers managed to sneak into the rocks through which the Paras had come earlier.

The battle died again. Still the tracers and Argentinian artillery shells were coming in. John told Gosling he could shelter behind his rock, while he himself settled into a shell-crater with Jonathan Page, company commander since Jim Barry's death, safe from the fizz and zip of snipers' bullets and shrapnel.

He had been there only a few minutes when a shadow loomed up above him. It was Neame, walking forward to check progress at first hand.

'How's it going, Meredith?' he asked in his usual casual way, as if out for a Sunday afternoon stroll.

'Fuck off, sir,' said John. 'You're attracting fire.'

'Oh, OK then, Meredith,' Neame replied mildly, and wandered away.

Perhaps it was Neame's inspiration, for not long afterwards Jonathan Page remarked: 'I'll go and check the soldiers.'

'The soldiers are all right,' John said. 'They're all in good positions. Leave them.'

'Well, I'll go and check them anyway.'

'OK, but crawl.'

'No, I'll be all right,' Page said, and stepped out of the hole. He must have been neatly silhouetted against the background, because he took three paces, and *bang*, over he went, hit by a sniper over in the rocks behind them.

Knights, the signaller, ran over, and checked Page for wounds. 'I can't feel any blood, sir. Where are you hit?'

'In the side.'

A pause. 'There's no blood. There's nothing wrong with you.'

It was true. The round had gone through his ammunition pouch, between two grenades, hit a magazine, bent all the rounds, and been deflected straight back out. Page had a massive bruise, but nothing more. Why on earth Neame wasn't picked off, John couldn't imagine.

There was nothing else to do. As dawn broke, it became clear that Tumbledown had been taken. Sniper fire from there died. The snipers in the rocks back down Wireless Ridge had been taken out or captured by other platoons. John and Jonathan Page climbed out of their shell-hole.

John walked forward to the brow of the ridge. The view looked then much as it did when we were there together. Directly below, the remains of a Marine barracks, with one of the few trees on the island. The estuary stretched away to the left, with a rough, single-track road leading along the coast to Stanley two miles away; to the right, Tumbledown, the slope punctuated by a single farmhouse.

Argentinian troops were streaming slowly off the mountain opposite, and around the head of the estuary. If the Paras had been allowed to work further forward and then cut down to the estuary, they would have trapped hundreds more on the peninsula. They could have done it, too, because the SAS never turned up – they had been driven off before they even landed.

John led me down the slope, round the edge of a rock buttress. Here was a strong position, probably the HQ. Piles of beer cans. Ammunition boxes. Some old wheels from a 120mm mortar, probably slung off the upper slopes by an eager Para. Its toolbox had a shrapnel hole torn through it.

'I wouldn't like to have assaulted this,' I said.

'Nor would I. They were well set up here. They didn't seem to be short of anything. If we'd been up here, we'd have died of old age before giving up.'

For John's sixteen remaining men, the battle was over. They had performed well: superb close-quarter fighting, with only light casualties, had led to a victory that included the defeat of the only counter-attack during the whole assault. Together with Tumbledown, Wireless Ridge had unlocked the road to Stanley – and to Argentinian surrender. Afterwards, the only sour note was – and still is – that John's commanding officer, Phil Neame, was not decorated, an omission that reflected both on the man and on those under him.

As daylight strengthened, as the noise of battle died over on Tumbledown, the Paras were ordered back along the ridge, and then down the hillside, taking a roundabout route to avoid possible mine-fields.

They were down on the road by Moody Brook when new orders came through: 'Move in fifteen minutes. They've surrendered.'

The helmets came off, the berets went on, and 2 Para tabbed on into Stanley.

14

AN END AND A NEW BEGINNING

The trip, the stresses, the dramas, were over. On the last day,
everyone else went off to look at penguins. I was happy to pack,
wander round Stanley, and think over what had happened.

Then the next morning we were off, out to MPA for the RAF
flight home. It was misty, and there was talk of the flight being
delayed. I didn't care. We would leave eventually.

As it turned out, the mist lifted, and we left on time. There
was a bit of excitement when two RAF Phantoms settled a few
feet from our wing-tips, accompanying us out of Falklands air
space, then flicking off to right and left with a roar.

I fell into a dreamy stupor. The last time I made that trip,
I had been in a haze of drugs and pain, but nothing of that
came back. The past, and its memories, were falling away
behind me.

I had been away three weeks. Only three weeks, but enough
to change my life yet again.

The burden of the past had begun to slip away from the
moment I shook Carlos's hand. Nothing else could equal the
effect of that, but everything I had experienced afterwards
removed yet another part of the burden. I had had more
than my share of stress and emotion, but Gary and John had

181

laughed me through the hard times. 'What's up with you?' Gary asked, the morning after the barmaid had a go at me. 'You look like you've combed your hair with a thunder-flash.' More than that, they had opened their past to me, and brought it alive.

As a result, there was one source of grieving I could escape from: the feeling that I had missed out, that there was another life that I had never lived – the life I had planned for myself – and the war I had never had a chance to fight. Now I came to think about it more deeply, I realized there was nothing here to grieve over after all.

For one thing, I would not have experienced much of the war even if I hadn't been burned. I would have been stuck in a trench with the other Welsh Guards until the Argentinians surrendered.

For another, I now understood better what war meant, and knew beyond doubt, more strongly than ever, that I would not have wanted to go through it. As Gary and John said, they took boys into war, and brought men out. But that maturity, that loss of innocence, was achieved at a terrible cost. There was a lot of horror there, a lot of sights and sounds that may change you but can't possibly be called *good*. I would never have wanted to kill, or risk death in action, or see mates die like that. You can see the effects on men who have been through a battle – the '1,000-yard stare', the look that has seen fearful things, the look that is always waiting to cloud the gaze of otherwise ordinary men. I had had the great good fortune to feel the fear and dreadful exhilaration of close-quarter warfare at second hand, and thanked my lucky stars I would never have to see it for myself. I never had to play God, with the power of life and death in my trigger-finger. That was a life I was glad I had not lived.

The more I thought about what the bomb meant, the stranger it all became. All anger at Carlos had disappeared. I had never thought I would blame him or hate him personally for what happened, but there had been a lot of anger stored up. I had felt it when I met him. Now it just wasn't there any more.

If he wasn't to blame, if no one was to blame, if there was no cause for anger, it seemed to me that somehow the whole thing was fated. I was fated to get injured. This thought reminded me of something that had happened on the *QE2* on the way down. We were watching a horror movie – one of the *Damien* films, I think. That was odd, because I never watched horror movies. For some reason, they bored me. Anyway, someone in the film lifted Damien's hair and found the mark of the Devil: 666, the treble six. It occurred to me then that our British Forces post office box number was 666, and I had this peculiar feeling that something terrible was going to happen.

If it was fate, then perhaps I would have got injured anyway. It's hard to imagine how, because the Welsh Guards weren't involved in the fighting. But one bloke did get killed by shell-fire on the night of 13 June, and several of the lads were injured when a Sidewinder missile malfunctioned. Perhaps, if I'd been there, I'd have been hit by a shell or blown up.

If that was a possibility that awaited me, perhaps being hit by Carlos's bomb actually saved me from something worse.

Certainly it gave me something better than I might have had. Because of the bomb, my life changed. I suffered – I'm permanently scarred – but still my future opened up in ways that would never have been possible if I had remained a Welsh Guard squaddie: the documentaries; the first book; this book; the charities; the radio; and above all Lucy and James, who were there at Brize Norton to pick me up with my Mam.

I would never have met Lucy without Carlos. Without Carlos, there would be no James.

It was great to be back, to hold Lucy, hold James, to see how much he'd grown, and know there was nothing left from the past to darken our lives together.

I have no idea yet what I'm going to do with my future, but whatever it holds, it will be for the three of us together, and I know I'm free to seize it – and enjoy it.